Fundamentals of Cost and Management Accounting

Fundamentals of Cost and Management Accounting
Second edition

PC du Plessis
M Com (PU for CHE), Senior lecturer UNISA

SJ van Vuuren
M Com (PU for CHE), HED (UP), NDC, NDO & M, Senior lecturer UNISA

Prof MA Faul
Hons B Com (PU for CHE), B Ed (PU for CHE), TED, CA (SA)
Professor in Accounting UNISA

Butterworths
Durban

South Africa	Butterworth Publishers (Pty) Ltd
	Durban 8 Walter Place, Waterval Park, Mayville 4091
	Johannesburg Grayston 66, 2 Norwich Close, Sandton 2196
	Cape Town 3 Gardens Business Village, Hope Street, Cape Town 8001
Australia	Butterworths, Sydney, Melbourne, Brisbane, Adelaide, Perth, Canberra and Hobart
Canada	Butterworths Canada Ltd, Toronto and Vancouver
Ireland	Butterworths (Ireland) Ltd, Dublin
Malaysia	Malayan Law Journal Sdn Bhd, Kuala Lumpur
New Zealand	Butterworths of New Zealand Ltd, Wellington and Auckland
Puerto Rico	Butterworth of Puerto Rico Inc, San Juan
Singapore	Butterworths Asia, Singapore
United Kingdom	Butterworths, a Division of Reed Elsevier (UK) Ltd, Halsbury House, 35 Chancery Lane, LONDON WC2A 1EL and 4 Hill Street, EDINBURGH EH2 3JZ
USA	Michie Butterworth, CHARLOTTESVILLE, Virginia

© 1992

First edition 1988
Reprinted 1989, 1990, 1992 (twice)
Second edition 1992
Reprinted 1993, 1994 (twice), 1995, 1996

ISBN 0 409 10313 6

Geset deur Adcolour Pinetown
Gedruk en gebind deur Interpak Natal, Pietermaritzburg

Preface

The authors' primary aim in writing this book was to develop a basic and comprehensive text which emphasises cost accumulation, cost analysis and cost control, while also giving attention, at an introductory level, to the use of costing information by management for planning and formulating business policy.

The content is divided into five main sections:

- Costing principles
- Costing systems
- Cost planning and control
- Management planning
- Decision-making techniques

To promote flexible use of the book by lecturers, the content of each of the main sections is divided into chapters, each of which deals with a specific subject. In turn, where appropriate the chapters are subdivided into shorter modules. Chapter 8 on Process Orientated Costing Systems, for example, is divided into eight modules. This subdivision enables lecturers to include the introductory material in their curriculum at a particular level and to deal with the more advanced aspects at a subsequent level.

The book also contains a chapter of problems covering the areas dealt with. Suggested solutions to these can be obtained by lecturers.

The book also contains a chapter of problems covering the areas dealt with. Suggested solutions to these can be obtained by lecturers from the publishers.

In writing the second edition the authors took the opportunity to make a few corrections to the text. A number of new questions have also been added.

The study of cost and management accounting is of a practical nature, very useful, interesting and challenging. We trust that this book will make a contribution to the study of the subject.

Our thanks and gratitude to our families for their forbearance and support.

Recommendations and comments concerning the text and supporting material are most welcome.

The Authors
July 1992

Contents

1

FUNDAMENTALS OF COST AND
MANAGEMENT ACCOUNTING

Function and philosophy of cost and management accounting

1 The different fields of accounting

Accounting is a specialised information system. It performs a service function, the main aim of which is to provide **relevant information** about the enterprise to a wide variety of interested parties including owners/shareholders, management of the enterprise, investors, creditors, financial advisors and government bodies.

The concept **"relevant information"** refers, in this context, to accounting information concerning the enterprise which is useful to a particular party for the making of a given decision. As is clear from the above list, "interested parties" encompasses a very wide spectrum of people and bodies who could possibly want to use accounting information and thus the accountant is faced with an extremely difficult information communication problem. In order to overcome this problem accounting has developed two mainstreams:

- ☐ Financial accounting
- ☐ Management accounting

Financial accounting

The purpose of financial accounting is to make available financial information about the enterprise by means of "general purpose" financial statements (the income statement, balance sheet and source and application of funds statement) mainly for use by interested parties who do not take part in the day-to-day management of the enterprise, in other words people and bodies who are themselves primarily **outside** the enterprise.

Such general purpose financial statements essentially provide a report of management's handling of the activities of the enterprise for a limited, already expired period, that is to say the report is a historical one. It is prepared in accordance with certain **external standards** which are widely known as "Generally accepted accounting practice" (GAAP). An important characteristic of GAAP is the emphasis placed on **objectiveness**. The personal meaning and view of those who prepare the financial statements must therefore play a very subordinate role.

Thus, one of the aims of financial accounting is the provision of **external reports** by means of general purpose financial statements.

Management accounting

Management accounting embraces the use of accounting and other information by the management of an enterprise in the planning and control of the activities of the enterprise.

Management accountants prepare **specific purpose reports** to be used by decision makers **within** the enterprise.

Because internal decision makers are chiefly concerned with the effect of their decisions on the future performance of the enterprise, most management accounting reports are **future orientated** reports. Historical data is used only in so far as it is necessary and useful in planning and decision making.

Seeing that no external criteria apply with respect to information provided for internal users, management accounting reports are often subjective in nature (in comparison with general purpose external financial reports). Thus, for example, when preparing a sales budget the management of an enterprise will be more interested in the "subjective" estimate of future sales than in an objective report of previous sales. The last-mentioned, that is to say the historical data, is always taken into consideration in future estimates.

The most important differences between financial and management accounting are summarised in Diagram D1:

Financial accounting		**Management accounting**	
1	Provides information for external users	1	Provides information for internal users
2	Generates "general purpose" financial statements	2	Generates "specific purpose statements and reports"
3	Reports on financial events in the past	3	Set up for future orientated reports
4	Must conform with standards which are extremely imposed	4	Not subject to external standards
5	Emphasises objective data	5	Uses subjective data

Diagram D1

2 The place and function of cost accounting

Thus both financial and management accountants use historical data – it is only their perspective that differs: financial accountants deal primarily with the reporting of historical costs and income. Management accountants use, *inter alia*, the same historical information as a starting point for the estimation of future costs and income.

The common ground between financial and management accountants is **cost accounting**, which embraces the collection and assimilation of current data in order to provide information for:

☐ external reporting (that is to say for **financial accountants**)

☐ internal planning and control of day-to-day (continuous) activities as well as special decisions (that is to say for **management accountants**).

Cost accounting systems were developed many years ago in such a way as to comply with the requirements of financial accounting as well. The development of bigger and more complex enterprises was also accompanied by the use of cost data in management decisions.

The **cost accounting department** of an enterprise therefore has a broad task which ranges from the routine collection of costs for financial reporting purposes to special cost studies in which the data relevant to a given problem are collected, adjusted and presented in a special format so that those who must make the decisions can interpret the special cost information fairly easily.

3 The function of management accounting

In this section management accounting will be examined more closely.

Management accounting has to do with **planning** and **control decisions**.

Planning decisions set a goal for the enterprise and design actions to attain that goal. Typical planning decisions for which management accounting information is necessary are, *inter alia*:

- ☐ How many units of a given product should be produced in the next budget period?
- ☐ How should a new product be marketed?
- ☐ Should the production facilities be expanded or reduced?
- ☐ Should the production and sale of an existing product continue or cease?
- ☐ How much should be spent on advertising, research and development?
- ☐ What are the enterprise's requirements for short-term and long-term funds going to be?
- ☐ Should a given product be manufactured by the enterprise or is it more economical to purchase it from an outside supplier?

All the above-mentioned planning decisions require estimates of future costs and, in certain cases, future income. Although the planning decisions are based on management's future expectations, historical data provide a good departure point for such future orientated estimates. Therefore financial accountants and management accountants use the same data bases.

Control decisions require the comparison of actual results with expected results and the establishment of accountability for variances from the standards originally set. This function may require further management decisions to ensure that the planned results are achieved or to amend the initial planning in the light of the prevailing conditions.

The decisions that must be taken in the control phase are mainly choices between alternative possible actions.

The place and function of financial accounting, management accounting and cost accounting can be presented diagramatically as shown in Diagram D2.

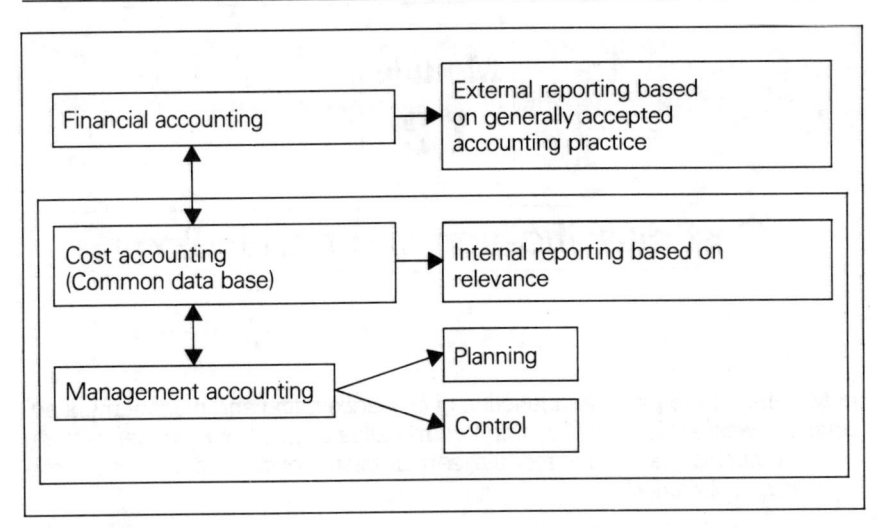

Diagram D2

4 Aim of this book

In this book only internal reporting (management accounting) and cost accounting as data bases for management accounting are covered.

In recent years the difference between cost and management accounting has become somewhat vague. It is not always possible to draw a dividing line between the two facets and in many cases where a distinction is made it is merely one of relative emphasis.

Cost accounting emphasises the **assimilation** and **evaluation** of cost data. **Management accounting** emphasises the **use** of cost data in internal planning, control and special decisions.

Because there is a close relationship between the assimilation, evaluation and use of cost data, attention is given to all these aspects. Although this book concentrates on the business enterprise, many of the concepts and techniques discussed are also applicable to non-profit orientated business enterprises. Besides, one of the most important developments in recent years has been the application of cost accounting and management accounting techniques and concepts to the management of non-profit orientated enterprises.

In modern practice most enterprises process their financial data by means of electronic computers. However, the discussion of topics in this book is presented using a non-electronic data processing system in order that the basic concepts and analysis and use of financial information may be determined.

Cost classification and terminology

In Module 1.1 the place and function of cost accounting and management accounting was explained. The first few modules of this book concentrate on cost accounting and in this module certain basic concepts and cost classifications are explained.

1 Definition of costs

Costs are an **efficacious expenditure** which is necessary for and contributes to the continuation of economic activities. A **non-efficacious expenditure** is not a cost and must be classified as an avoidable waste and written off as a loss.

2 Expired and unexpired costs

At the time that it is incurred the outlay represents an offer made in order to obtain an economic benefit. The benefit may already have been received (eg payment for the rental of a building for a period that has already expired). Until such time as the benefit is received this type of outlay is carried as a **deferred or unexpired cost** (eg prepaid insurance, raw material stock on hand and the net book value of machinery). All unexpired costs are shown as **assets** in the balance sheet of the enterprise.

If the benefit has already been received the outlay becomes an **expired cost** (an expense) and is reflected as such in the income statement. If it becomes obvious that no benefit will arise from the outlay then it also becomes an expired cost, but is reflected as a **loss** in the income statement.

Diagram D3 illustrates the above concepts:

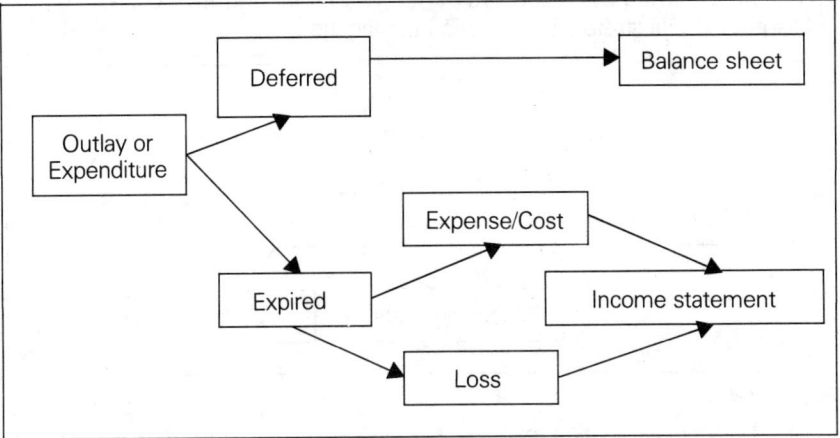

Diagram D3

3 Cost terminology and classification

It follows from the above that costs can be described briefly as the total sources "used" to achieve specified aims. Because there is a wide range of aims that can be pursued there are different ways in which costs can be **classified**. As with any other discipline, cost accounting also has its own **terminology**. Since an understanding of this terminology and classification is necessary for the study of cost and management accounting, certain basic concepts and classifications will be touched on in this section. A fuller treatment of each of the concepts and classifications will be given at the relevant places in this book and as progress is made further concepts and classifications will be introduced.

In the following discussions the manufacturing enterprise is taken as the basic point of departure.

3.1 Classification of the cost by its nature

First of all, costs can be classified by simply dividing the total operating costs of a manufacturing enterprise into two broad categories:

☐ Manufacturing costs

☐ Commercial costs

The first-mentioned is the sum of all the costs incurred in the manufacturing process. Commercial costs can be broadly divided into:

☐ marketing costs

☐ administrative costs.

Marketing costs include the costs of obtaining the order for and the delivery of manufactured products. Administrative costs include all costs relating to the day-to-day functioning of the enterprise. Often certain commercial costs are allocated to manufacturing and marketing costs (eg the salary of the managing director of the enterprise can be allocated on an equitable basis to manufacturing overheads, marketing and administrative costs).

Diagram D4 illustrates these basic classifications:

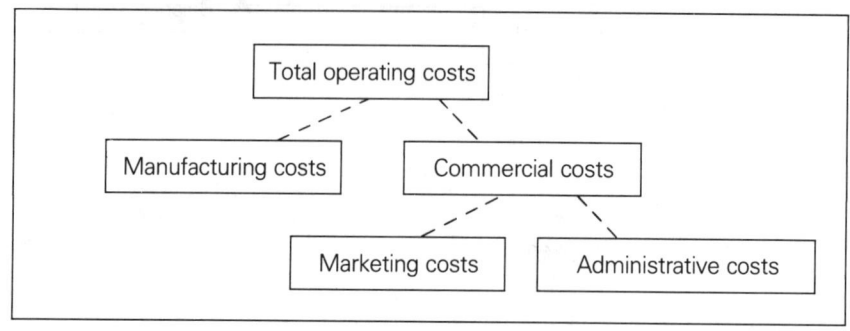

Diagram D4

This basic classification can be expanded further and subdivided into several other types of classifications, as will become evident below.

3.2 Classification as product and period costs

In a previous section the difference between expired and unexpired costs was shown. How is it determined whether a cost is expired or unexpired? For this a further cost classification between product and period costs is necessary.

Period costs are the costs associated with a given accounting period rather than a given product. For example, marketing and administrative costs are normally costs incurred to generate sales in a given period but not coupled to the sale of given units. The rentals incurred for the hire of the locations necessary for the marketing of products are also normally a fixed amount per month which is not influenced by the volume of sales. In accounting the practice is to match costs incurred during a particular accounting period against the income earned during the same period. Therefore these types of costs are classified as **period costs**.

Any unexpired period costs are classified as **deferred costs** and as already explained, are shown as assets in the balance sheet (eg prepaid advertising costs, since the benefit of the outlay has not yet been received).

Product costs, on the other hand, are associated with the products that are manufactured. Since this type of cost is coupled with the products it is sometimes treated as an **expired** cost and sometimes as an **unexpired cost**, depending on whether the product with which the cost is associated has already been sold. If still on hand it will be an **unexpired cost** (eg cost of finished goods on hand) and will thus be shown as an asset at the accounting date* in the balance sheet. Once the product is sold the cost becomes an **expired cost** and is transferred to the cost of goods sold and brought into account against the income generated by the sale of the product.

---

* The day on which the financial year ends.

Example 1

XY Enterprise Limited was incorporated on 1 January 19.2 with an initial capital of R10 000 cash. During January the enterprise purchased 2 000 units of the only product in which it trades at a cost price of R3 per unit. No units were sold in January, but in February 1 200 units were sold for cash at R5 each. Assuming that no other transactions took place, the enterprise's balance sheet and income statement are as follows on 1 January 19.2, 31 January 19.2 and 28 February 19.2:

Balance sheets	1 Jan 19.2	31 Jan 19.2	28 Feb 19.2
	R	R	R
Interest			
Capital	10 000	10 000	10 000
Plus Net income	–	–	2 400
	10 000	10 000	12 400
Assets			
Cash	10 000	4 000	10 000*
Stock	–	6 000	2 400**
	10 000	10 000	12 400

* (4 000 + 6 000)
** (800 @ R3)

Income statement for the month ending	31 Jan 19.2	28 Feb 19.2
	R	R
Sales	–	6 000*
Less Cost of goods sold	–	(3 600)**
Net income	–	2 400

* (1 200 @ R5)
** (1 200 @ R3)

Seeing that no sales took place in January, it would be incorrect to bring into account as an expired cost the amount expended during the month on the acquisition of the stock. Therefore it is shown as an unexpired cost (asset) in the balance sheet on 31 January. In February the cost of 1 200 units which were sold during that month is brought into account as an expired product cost against income derived from the sale of the same products to determine the net income for the month. The costs associated with the remaining 800 units are still shown as an unexpired cost (asset).

This process, whereby product costs are associated with the income earned from the sale of the same products and period costs are associated with the period in which they expire, is the well-known matching concept found in financial accounting.

Diagram D5 illustrates the above:

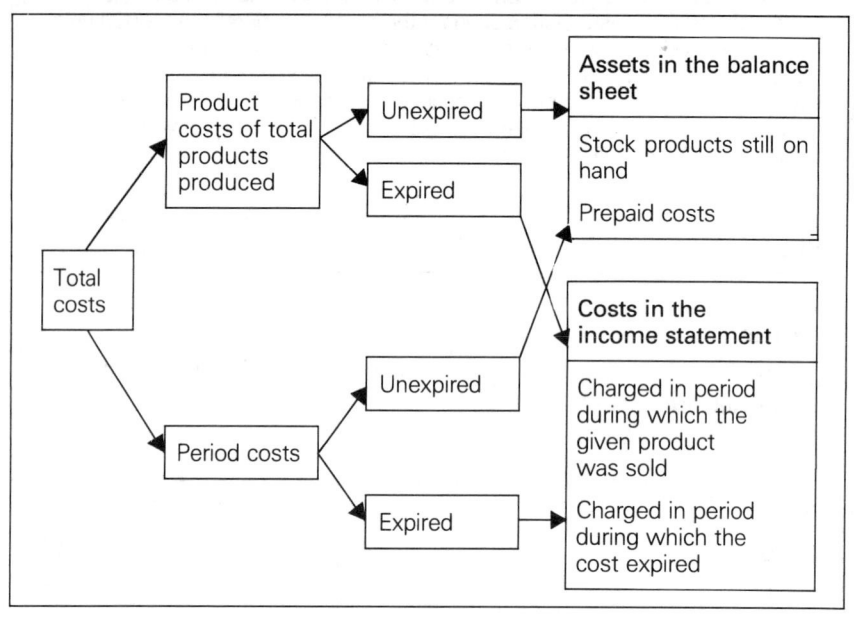

Diagram D5

3.3 Cost classification in relation to the product

How are the cost of goods manufactured in a manufacturing concern determined? Basically by:

☐ knowing which costs are **product costs** in such an enterprise

☐ having an understanding of the **flow of costs** through the accounts of a manufacturing enterprise.

In this section **product costs** in a **manufacturing enterprise** are discussed. **Cost flows** are given attention in a later module.

Product costs can also be classified in different ways. As will be seen the various classifications are not mutually exclusive, but actually overlap to an extent.

Product manufacturing costs consist of the following three elements:

☐ Direct material

☐ Direct labour

☐ Manufacturing overheads

Direct material consists mainly of primary material. It usually forms an integral part of the end product and is usually in predetermined measurable quantities proportional to the volume of the production usage. Direct material forms a cost element on its own.

Indirect material consists mainly of secondary material. It does not form part of the end product and the quantity used is not directly related to the volume of production. Indirect material does not form a cost element on its own and is normally grouped under **manufacturing overheads**.

To illustrate the difference between direct and indirect material the use of wood and sandpaper in a furniture factory can be taken as an example. The quantity of wood required for the manufacture of a specific piece of furniture can be determined accurately beforehand. However, the quantity of sandpaper used depends on the quality of the wood and can vary from piece to piece. Further, the sandpaper does not form part of the final product and consequently it is classified as indirect material.

Similarly, the concept **direct labour** refers to the cost of all essential labour physically expended on the manufacture of a product. In this case, too, it will not be possible to attribute certain labour costs incurred during the manufacturing process directly to a particular unit (or group of units). For example, the wages of welders who work in the manufacturing process would be classified as direct labour. On the other hand, the wages of machine maintenance personnel would not be classified as such but rather as **indirect labour costs**, which are classified under manufacturing overheads.

Manufacturing overheads refer to all the other costs necessary for the continuation of the manufacturing process, excluding direct material and direct labour. Examples of manufacturing overheads are indirect material and indirect labour (to which reference has already been made), the depreciation and insurance costs of production machinery and equipment, and so on. The primary characteristic of manufacturing overheads is that they cannot be attributed directly to a particular unit, but they are, in fact, incurred during the course of the production process.

3.4 Primary product costs and conversion costs

Two further subclassifications of production costs are:

☐ primary costs
☐ conversion costs.

The concept **primary costs** refers to the total of the direct material and direct labour costs. Initially in the development of costing the emphasis was on these two relatively easy physical reducible costs only, while manufacturing overheads were (wrongly) treated as mere period costs.

The concept **conversion costs** is still commonly used today and has a bearing on the total of the direct labour costs and manufacturing overheads. In this context the concept "conversion" refers to the costs that must be employed to convert raw materials to a finished product.

Bear in mind that the classification of costs into primary and conversion costs is not wholly exclusive. Total primary costs cannot, for example, be included in total conversion costs, because then the direct labour costs would be included twice.

Diagram D6 is a comprehensive illustration of the classification of the total costs of a manufacturing enterprise as developed in this module.

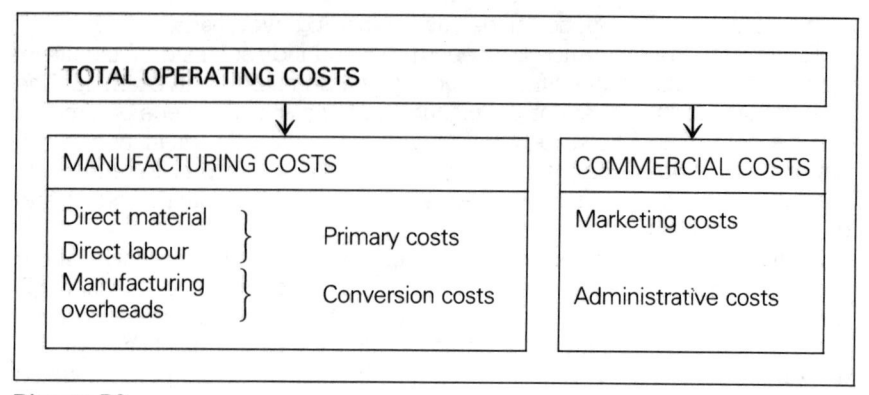

Diagram D6

Some basic cost classifications and terminology concepts were discussed in this module. Further classifications are dealt with in the relevant places.

2

MATERIAL

1 Introduction

As has already been explained, **material, labour** and **overheads,** also known as **cost elements,** are the basic divisions used for the grouping of all costs. Each cost element can be subdivided further to obtain a very refined and precise grouping of costs.

Material forms the major grouping of all costs relating to the physical raw materials used in the manufacturing process and transformed into a more refined product, as well as all costs and activities associated therewith. It is a very broad and at times confusing concept, but should be better understood after the following discussion.

2 Terminology

- ☐ **Primary material** is the basic raw material that is converted to a more refined product by the manufacturing process. Examples of primary material are the wood converted into completed pieces of furniture in a furniture factory and the flour used in a bakery for making bread. Primary material is also referred to as **direct material.**

- ☐ **Secondary material** is the material used in the manufacturing process which contributes to the conversion of the primary material, for example the sandpaper used to give a piece of furniture the finishing touches before it leaves the factory. Secondary material does not usually form part of the end product produced and is also referred to as **indirect material.**

- ☐ **Incomplete work** is primary material which has already entered the manufacturing process but is not yet complete and cannot be classified as a finished product. Normally a portion of labour and overheads is already employed so that the incomplete work comprises all three cost elements.

  Different names are given to this type of material, *inter alia* incomplete work, work in progress and half-finished work. However, in this book preference is given to the term "work in process".

- ☐ **Finished goods** are the finished products produced from the raw material in the manufacturing process.

- ☐ The term **stock** includes all the material (primary and secondary), work in process and finished goods in the enterprise's possession at a given moment. It is thus a relatively broad concept.

3 Stock piling

The main reason why stock piling takes place is that usually, in practice, there is a time difference between the acquisition of the material and the use or employment thereof. For example, material may be purchased now but used in a week or two's time. In the meantime it is held as stock.

It is very important that material is available when it is required, otherwise unnecessary costs and losses may occur. Think what would happen if a furniture manufacturer did not have any wood or a bakery any flour – the entire manufacturing process would come to a standstill.

The same situation can occur in a commercial enterprise. A traveller who cannot purchase petrol at a garage because there is no stock will simply go to another garage. The garage that did not have a stock of petrol consequently loses the transaction and the income that would have flowed therefrom.

Stock piling also takes place for various other reasons, and the following terminology is important in this regard:

☐ **Normal stock** is the material which is in stock of necessity because it is in the process of production, is about to enter production, or has just been completed.

☐ **Buffer stock** as the name indicates, is a type of stock piling used to form a buffer between production and usage in situations where there is constant production but usage is erratic. The supply of water to a city is a good example. There is a fixed quantity of water that can be delivered per hour and the usage thereof fluctuates, depending on the time of day. Water is stored temporarily whenever usage is low to make provision for peak periods when usage is higher than supply.

☐ **Safety stock** is a broader concept than buffer stock and is specifically aimed at ensuring that the enterprise can continue with production as usual if it should happen that a specific type of material is not delivered within the normal delivery period or is temporarily not available.

☐ **Strategic stock** is stock that is held for economic reasons – a large price increase may be expected and therefore more than the usual quantity is purchased before the increase.

☐ **Speculative stock** is stock that is held for economic reasons – a large price increase may be expected and therefore more than the usual quantity is purchased before the increase.

☐ **Stock-in-transit** is stock that has already been purchased but has not yet been received, in other words it is still in the process of delivery.

☐ **Economic and technical stock** Technical stock is stock that is physically in the enterprise's possession, while **economic stock** represents the amount of stock after all adjustments have been taken into account, for example stock already paid for but not yet received, stock already sold but not yet delivered, etc.

☐ **Overstocking and understocking** Overstocking occurs whenever the amount of stock held is not justified by the volume of production. **Understocking** is the opposite situation.

☐ **Average stock** The average stock is a figure often used in calculations. Naturally it is possible to determine the average stock precisely, but it is so cumbersome that usually the following formulae are sufficient for calculating it:

Average stock = (Opening stock + Closing stock) ÷ 2

or, alternatively:

Average stock = (Order size ÷ 2) + Safety stock

☐ **Maximum stock** This is the greatest possible stock of a particular item that can be carried in the interests of the enterprise. It is more than the order size plus the safety stock, and usually occurs when a new order is delivered earlier than the normal delivery period.

4 Stock activities

The different **activities** associated with stock piling can be categorised as follows:

Acquisition
Storage
Distribution and consumption
Stock valuation

4.1 Acquisition function

In larger enterprises this function is normaly fulfilled by a purchasing department. It is more comprehensive than it first appears and includes, *inter alia*, the following activities:

4.1.1 Determination of the requirements

This function can be summarised by the question: "**How much** of **what** is required **when?**"

If too little is purchased the enterprise runs out of stock. If too much is purchased capital is invested in stock unnecessarily and storage space is wasted. If the wrong material is purchased unnecessary losses may result. The same applies if the material is not received timeously.

First, it is obvious that **specifications** must be prepared before purchasing can proceed. These specifications must indicate clearly the quality, the dimensions and the combination of the material required.

> The factory foreman might know that he requires a specific 10mm stainless steel bolt for the manufacture of gearboxes, but what about the order clerk? The factory foreman must describe clearly what must be purchased on the **purchase requisition** so that the order clerk can order the correct product, or he might receive 5mm bolts of ordinary steel which he cannot use.

Second, the exact **quantity** to be purchased must be determined. Naturally usage remains the basic guideline, but should not an additional quantity be purchased as safety stock? Or perhaps speculative stock should be considered as a means of counteracting a possible price rise. Or perhaps the material is so important, indispensable and difficult to obtain that a strategic stock should be maintained.

Third, **when?** How much time elapses between the date of the placing of the order and the date of delivery? When must the order be placed so that the stock will be delivered timeously?

As has already been mentioned, it is essential that the material is available to the enterprise when required. Thus it goes without saying that the order size and date of the order are very important. Delivery time, also called **order period,** and the reliability of the supplier play an important role here.

The graphic presentation in Diagram D7 shows the cycle of the stock levels of a particular type of material with constant usage:

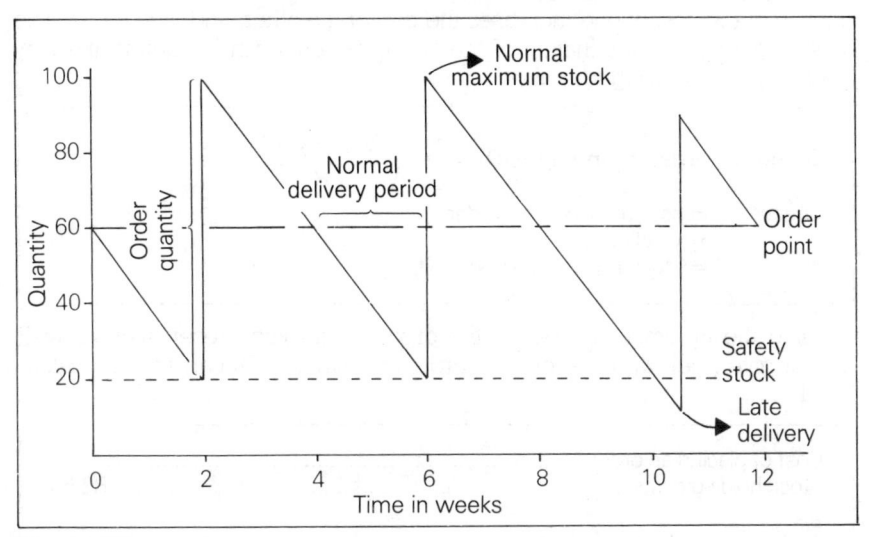

Diagram D7

The following assumptions were made in respect of the above presentation:

(i)　Average weekly usage .... 20 units
(ii)　Order period .... 2 weeks
(iii)　Order size .... 80 units
(iv)　Maximum order period .... 3 weeks

In this specific case a safety stock of 20 units is maintained The normal order period is two weeks but it can be a maximum of three weeks. Therefore provision is made for a safety stock of an extra week's usage (20 units).

The order period is usually two weeks. This means that a new order must be placed two weeks prior to the date on which the material is required, or, put differently, once the stock level falls to the level where only two week's consumption requirements plus the safety stock are on hand a new order must be placed – in this case for 60 units. This is based on a normal usage of 20 units per week for the two weeks that it takes to execute the order plus the safety stock of 20 units. The stock level at which a new order must be placed is called the **order point.** The following formula is used for the calculation of the order point:

> Order point = (Order period × normal usage) +
> **Safety stock**
> = (2 × 20) + 20
> = 60 units

The **order size** is of great importance, especially in the light of capital which might be tied up in stock. Two divergent cost items influence the decision regarding the quantity to be ordered at any one time, namely:
- [ ] the cost of placing the order
- [ ] the cost of holding stock.

A balance between the two cost items must be maintained, since the reduction of the cost of one increases the cost of the other, and vice versa. The most economical combination of the two cost items can be determined by applying the following formula:

Economic order quantity (EOQ) = $\sqrt{\dfrac{2 \times C \times U}{H}}$

where   C = cost of placing an order
                 U = yearly usage
                 H = stock holding cost per unit

Using the information given in the previous graphic presentation as well as that given below, the economic order quantity (EOQ) can now be calculated:

Cost of placing an order R10,00
Stock holding costs per unit R2,50

$$EOQ = \sqrt{\frac{2 \times C \times U}{H}}$$

$$= \sqrt{\frac{2 \times 10 \times (52 \times 20)}{2,50}}$$

$$= \sqrt{\frac{20\ 800}{2,50}}$$

$$= \sqrt{8\ 320}$$

$$= 91 \text{ units per order}$$

Thus it will be more economical to purchase 91 units rather than 80 units per order. The validity of this hypothesis can be verified as follows:

Order size (units)	80	91	100
Order costs	R130	R114	R104
Number of orders *	13	11,4	10,4
Cost per order	R10	R10	R10
Stock holding costs	R100	R113,75	R125
Average stock †	40	45,5	50
Storage costs per unit	R2,50	R2,50	R2,50
TOTAL COSTS	R230,00	R227,75	R229,00

(continued)

* 1 040 ÷ 80 = 13   † 80 ÷ 2 = 40
  1 040 ÷ 91 = 11,4   91 ÷ 2 = 45,5
  1 040 ÷ 100 = 10,4   100 ÷ 2 = 50

The safety stock has not been taken into consideration and the figures for the number of orders have not been rounded off to whole numbers to illustrate the effect of different order sizes more clearly.

However, it is important to bear in mind the size of the investment in stock, since this usually represents a material amount on which interest must be paid if the money is borrowed or interest is forgone if the stock is financed internally.

The formula can be expanded to make provision for the **effect of interest** on the investment tied up in stock:

$$EOQ = \sqrt{\frac{2 \times C \times U}{(P \times i) + H}}$$

where P = the cost per unit
$\quad i$ = the interest rate.

The effect of a high interest rate on the previous calculation is evident in the following example:

Supposing that the cost per unit is R10 and the interest rate (cost of capital) is 25% per year, then:

$$EOQ = \sqrt{\frac{2 \times C \times U}{(P \times i) + H}}$$

$$= \sqrt{\frac{2 \times 10 \times (52 \times 20)}{(R10 \times 25\%) + 2,50}}$$

$$= \sqrt{\frac{20\ 800}{5,00}}$$

$$= 64 \text{ units}$$

Due to the high interest rate and the cost of capital, smaller orders should be placed more often to reduce the investment in stock.

4.1.2 Ordering

Once the order quantity and the order point are known the next step is to place the order. Prices and conditions of payment, as well as delivery date and the reliability of the different suppliers, must be compared. The credit terms and discount policy of the different suppliers plays an important role and quantity discounts may influence the order quantity. Naturally the order is given to the supplier who offers the most favourable transaction, the above factors being taken into consideration.

Written orders should be placed. The pre-printed order form must make provision for all the relevant information to be given thereon, including product specifications, quantity, price, discount, delivery date, conditions of payment, etc.

Effective control must be exercised over the purchase function at all times and authorised persons must approve and sign all orders.

A record must be kept of all orders placed and this must be checked frequently to ensure that the goods will be delivered within the agreed period of time, that they comply with the given specifications, and so on.

4.2 Storage

When the order is executed by the supplier it is important that it is controlled to see whether it complies with the specifications laid down in the order, that the quantity is correct and that the supporting documents have been supplied. Then a **goods received voucher** is issued and the goods are stored in a safe place, usually the **warehouse.**

The **layout** of the warehouse must be such that it does not hinder the efficient flow of stock. The following factors should be taken into account when the layout of a warehouse is planned:

☐ The allocation of storage space must be done in an orderly way according to a predetermined classification policy.

☐ Safety aspects must be considered when storage space is allocated to a product series.

☐ The unique characteristics of each product must be taken into account. For example, perishable goods will be handled and stored differently from say, petrol.

☐ Stocks that move quickly and are issued regularly must be easily accessible and should be near the entrance.

☐ Entrances to the warehouse must be kept to the minimum. Also, only authorised personnel should be allowed access to the warehouse.

An additional very important aspect is whether one **centralised warehouse** or more smaller, **decentralised warehouses** should be used. The nature of the enterprise and the products stored will play a major role in this decision. With the increasing use of computers and terminals these days as aids for the supervision and administration of stock control, these aspects do not play such an important role in the decision between centralisation or decentralisation. Rather, practical implications enjoy greater consideration.

Due to the increasing use of computers the classification and codification of stock has become more important. Various methods of **codification** are used, the most important being the numerical method. The numerical code can be divided into different fields, each field being linked to a certain characteristic of the product being stored. Thus, for example, a six figure code divided into three fields can comprise the following:

2.02.008

Field 1: Basic classification
                Figure 1: Liquid products
                Figure 2: Steel products
                Figure 3:

Field 2:   Subclassification
                  Figure 01: Gears
                  Figure 02: Bolts
                  Figure 03:
Field 3:   Various types of subclassifications

Thus code 202008 can refer to a 10mm bolt of a certain length and type, for which a product specification is drawn up to eliminate any uncertainty.

The codes can be extended to make provision for more sophisticated techniques and basically have unlimited usage.

Computers are being used more and more for stock control and are replacing the old manual systems of bin cards and what goes with them. However, the principle remains the same and the computer is employed only to do the same work faster and more efficiently.

A **bin card,** so called because it is normaly kept in the bin or on the shelf on which the stock is stored, is used to obtain (on a continuous basis) a record of the quantity of each type of material in the warehouse. All receipts and issues are shown on it and it forms a valuable aid for the efficient control of the physical stock, although it does not form part of the accounting records. Other relevant information such as the order point, order quantity and safety stock is also shown on the bin card. The bin card forms the basis of a continuous stock system to exercise control over the stock quantities on a daily basis.

As has already been mentioned, bin cards do not form part of the accounting records. They also do not show the value of the relevant stock items, but only the physical quantity. A **stock ledger card** is used to calculate the value of each stock item.

However, a **physical stock count** must be done from time to time, usually at the end of the financial year, to determine the correct value and quantity of each stock item separately and of the stock in total. The bin cards and the stock ledger cards must be compared with the physical stock count and any differences should be investigated thoroughly. Differences can usually be ascribed to theft, incorrect calculations and/or transactions which do not appear on the continuous stock system.

4.3 Issuing of stock

Efficient controls over the issue of material by the warehouse must be maintained at all times. If the issuing of stock is not properly controlled the enterprise may sustain large losses.

A **requisition** is used as the basic document for the issuing of stock from the warehouse and has the dual purpose of:

☐ providing **authorisation** for the storekeeper or person in charge of the stock to issue the material

☐ serving as a **source document** for the accounting entries in the books of the enterprise and must therefore also show the reason for the issue.

4.4 Stock valuation

There are various methods for the valuation of stock:

☐ FIFO method (first-in-first-out)

- ☐ LIFO method (last-in-first-out)
- ☐ Weighted average method
- ☐ Standard price method
- ☐ Market price method

With the FIFO method of stock valuation, stock is issued in the oder in which it is received. Thus the material that is received first is issued first. With the LIFO method the material that is received last is issued first. The weighted average method uses the actual average purchase prices (weighted by the applicable quantities) to calculate the issue price. Its disadvantage is that after every receipt a new weighted average issue price must be determined.

The standard price method values stock by means of a predetermined standard unit price. Differences between the actual price paid and the predetermined standard cost are identified as price variances.

The market price method, on the other hand, uses the ruling market price as a basis for determining the issue price of stock. The first three methods of stock valuation are the most important and are discussed and explained in detail. The easiest way to explain the methods is by means of a simple example of a stock ledger card.

Example 2

Transactions concluded in respect of a particular stock item:

1 Jan : Stock on hand	50 units @ R5 per unit
3 Jan : Issued	20 units
4 Jan : Received	80 units @ R6 per unit
5 Jan : Issued	20 units
6 Jan : Issued	30 units
7 Jan : Returned to supplier	10 units (received on 4 Jan)

Solution
Stock ledger card using the FIFO method

Date	Receipts			Issues			Balance		
	Quant	Price	Amount	Quant	Price	Amount	Quant	Price	Amount
1 Jan							50	5,00	250,00
3 Jan				20	5,00	100,00	30	5,00	150,00
4 Jan	80	6,00	480,00				30	5,00	150,00
							80	6,00	480,00
5 Jan				20	5,00	100,00	10	5,00	50,00
							80	6,00	480,00
6 Jan				10	5,00	50,00			
				20	6,00	120,00	60	6,00	360,00
7 Jan	(10)	6,00	(60,00)				50	6,00	300,00

(continued)

Stock ledger card using the LIFO method

Date	Receipts			Issues			Balance		
	Quant	Price	Amount	Quant	Price	Amount	Quant	Price	Amount
1 Jan							50	5,00	250,00
3 Jan				20	5,00	100,00	30	5,00	150,00
4 Jan	80	6,00	480,00				30	5,00	150,00
							80	6,00	480,00
5 Jan				20	6,00	120,00	30	5,00	150,00
							60	6,00	360,00
6 Jan				30	6,00	180,00	30	5,00	150,00
							30	6,00	180,00
7 Jan	(10)	6,00	(60,00)				30	5,00	150,00
							20	6,00	120,00
							50		270,00

Stock ledger card using the weighted average cost method

Date	Receipts			Issues			Balance		
	Quant	Price	Amount	Quant	Price	Amount	Quant	Price	Amount
1 Jan							50	5,00	250,00
3 Jan				20	5,00	100,00	30	5,00	150,00
4 Jan	80	6,00	480,00				110*	5,73	630,00
5 Jan				20	5,73	114,54	90	5,73	515,46
6 Jan				30	5,73	171,81	60	5,73	343,65
7 Jan	(10)	6,00	(60,00)				50	5,67	283,65

* (R150 + R480) ÷ (30 + 80) = R5,73 per unit

You will notice that the value of the stock as calculated according to the three methods differs (R300 ; R270 ; R283,65).

Although the FIFO and weighted average methods are generally used more often, there is not much to choose between the various methods. What is important is that an enterprise uses the same method throughout and does not change from year to year.

5 Accounting entries

Although the accounting aspects are discussed in a separate chapter, for the sake of continuity a schematic representation of the flow of **accounting entries** in respect of material in the books of the enterprise is given:

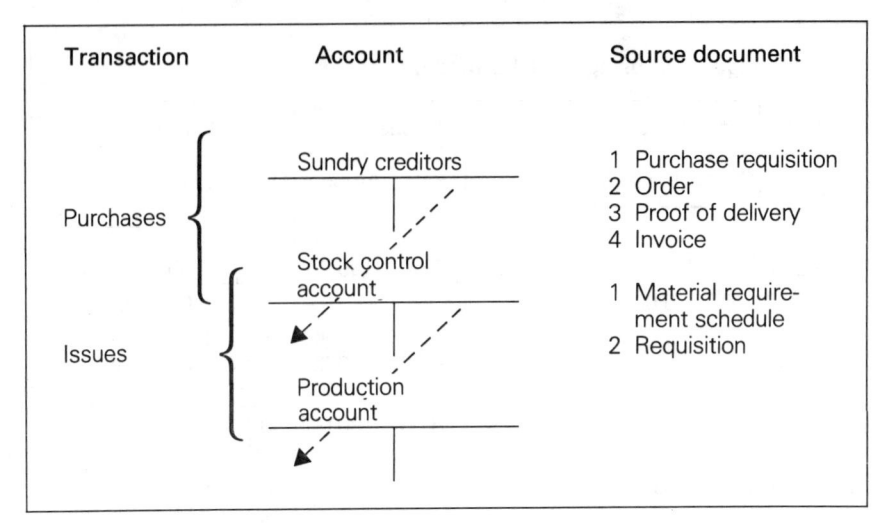

Diagram D8

6 Summary

Material is a very important cost element and material control is often seen only as a means of preventing theft. Although it forms an important aspect thereof, material control is a much broader concept and includes aspects such as investment in stock, receiving and issuing procedures, storage, efficient consumption, etc.

3

LABOUR

Module

3.1

The complexity of labour

1 Introduction

Labour, the second cost element to be discussed, is complicated and difficult to control. This is attributable to the fact that no two employees are the same – their personalities, work capacity and needs all differ. The **individuality** of each employee must always be borne in mind and the psychological aspects form just as important a component as the purely technical aspects.

Although like material it is a cost element, labour requires a much wider spectrum of involvement from management. It is not merely a case of a certain price being paid in exchange for a certain quantity of labour of a specific standard – it also embraces various other aspects such as job satisfaction and security.

First, there are certain **employee** expectations which must be satisfied, for example:

☐ the payment of a reasonable compensation to enable the employee to maintain a certain living standard within his social milieu

☐ job satisfaction

☐ security

☐ the opportunity to develop to full potential.

On the other hand, the **employer** expects more than just a labour input from the employee and lays claim to

☐ the loyalty of the employee

☐ the highest possible productivity of which the employee is capable

☐ subjective contributions such as initiative in the working environment, leadership, reliability, etc.

Therefore, enterprises which have an effective labour corps at their disposal view it as one of their most important assets and are prepared to go to great lengths to keep it and even to extend it.

A loyal and productive employee corps does not establish itself. The enterprise must give continuous attention to good employee/employer relationships and build on the factors that can give rise to further improvements and remove those that might have a negative influence.

The following aspects should be given close attention in any enterprise so as to keep potential problem areas to a minimum:

☐ The chain of command must be properly identified so that every employee knows exactly to whom he is accountable and from whom he receives his orders.

☐ People in positions of authority must be well grounded in the maintenance of good human relationships.

☐ The job and responsibility of each employee must be properly defined.

☐ A channel must be created so that employee's complaints and dissatisfactions can be brought to the attention of higher management.

☐ Discrimination, especially that which arises from personal conflicts, must be kept to a minimum.

☐ Acknowledgement must be given for a job well done.

☐ The ambitions of employees must not be unnecessarily suppressed, especially when employees have the potential to develop further.

There are many other aspects that could be mentioned here, all having the common characteristic that they build up and contribute to the achievement of a happy and contented employee corps. As a result each employee, no matter how petty his job, feels that he is part of a team that is striving towards the achievement of a common goal. The big advantage for the employer is that job satisfaction is usually associated with increased productivity from employees.

2 Productivity

Productivity is generally described as the **ratio** between a certain amount of **output** and a certain amount of **input.** By comparing the ratios of different periods and, especially, noting the trend, management is furnished with a barometer with which to evaluate productivity.

Output to **labour hours worked** is generally used to determine **labour productivity** and any change in the ratio between two periods is viewed as a change in productivity.

Determining the actual labour productivity for a given period does not present much of a problem – the output (eg units manufactured) is simply compared with the input (eg hours worked). However, **determining the standard or "ideal" productivity level is very difficult because, first, use is made of subjective data, and second, productivity varies from moment to moment and from person to person.**

However, productivity is not applicable only to labour, but also to every other facet of the enterprise. How productively are material, capital or overheads employed? By applying the following formula the productivity ratio of the enterprise as a whole can be determined for a certain period (the elements of the ratio are expressed in monetary values):

> **Output : Material + Labour + Overheads + Capital**

By comparing the productivity level, and especially the tendency that it shows, with external information supplied by production organisations, government institutions and others, the state of the enterprise as a whole and of labour in particular can be determined. If the comparison is negative then corrective action should be taken, and if it is positive then the fruits of good management and interrelationships are plucked.

One of the basic principles of good management is to strive for the highest possible productivity level, especially in view of the fact that nationally and internationally the productivity tendency has fallen sharply over the last decade, as shown in the following table*:

Productivity trends

Period	Average yearly manufacturing productivity trends in the USA
1947 – 1966	+ 3,2
1959 – 1969	+ 2,8
1969 – 1973	+ 2,5
1973 – 1978	+ 1,7
1979	+ 1,0
1980	− 0,5

2.1 Humanitarian factors which have an influence on labour productivity

When it appears that an employee cannot maintain a certain productivity level it must not merely be accepted that he is a poor employee who must be dismissed. First it must be determined why the employee is not capable of maintaining the required productivity and then attempts must be made to put whatever is right before drastic action is taken. This will allow employees to enjoy an increased feeling of security because the fear of summary dismissal will decrease.

The following are possible reasons for an employee being unable to maintain the required productivity level:

☐ The employee is physically incapable of carrying out a physically demanding job.

☐ The employee's personality and talent is such that a particular job does not allow him to develop to his full potential and the job bores him.

☐ Adequate training to enable the employee to carry out the job properly is not given.

☐ Job satisfaction is lacking and the employee is not motivated to produce a higher output.

☐ The standard or required productivity level is set too high so that employees find it too tiring to comply with in the long run.

☐ The fault might lie with the employee himself in the sense that he is lax and does not want to produce a higher output.

---

* Larry N. Kilbough & W.E. Leininger: *Cost Accounting – Concepts and Techniques for Management*, U.S.A. West Publishing Company, 1984, p. 304.

2.2 External factors which have an influence on productivity

☐ Lighting – if the lighting in the work environment is not correct it may cause the workers unnecessary stress and fatigue.

☐ Temperature – work capacity is at its highest level at normal room temperature and any deviation from this will result in a fall in productivity.

☐ Humidity – work capacity is higher in slightly moist air, subject to the moisture content remaining within limits.

☐ Noise – noise is a disturbing factor and must be limited to a minimum, especially high-pitched and intermittent noise.

☐ Time – productivity decreases in proportion to the number of hours worked. Also, productivity is generally lower during the afternoon period.

☐ Various other external factors such as political unrest, the economic stability of the country, etc also have an influence on the employees' productivity.

3 Personnel administration

Personnel administration is a field of study in its own right and hence is referred to only briefly here.

The main purpose of personnel administration is to provide an efficient labour force. Basic requirements are the accomplishment of a well-thought-out personnel policy, maintenance of sound labour relations and striving for the highest possible productivity level.

The following personnel functions are closely related to cost control:

☐ Determining labour requirements

☐ Employment procedures

☐ Job description

☐ Job evaluation

☐ Time and motion studies

☐ Resignation

The **basic requirements** for labour are established by the production planning section. The number of man hours (and usually the number of workers) and the levels of skill required to meet the expected production activities of the enterprise are determined for a future period.

The department head or foreman compares this information with the existing labour force and if there is a need for additional personnel a request is sent to the personnel department.

The personnel department then follows the normal **employment procedures** of recruiting personnel, selecting, conducting interviews, conducting aptitude tests, etc and presents a short-list to the department head/foreman for the final selection of suitable candidates who meet the requirements of the particular vacancy.

It is always important to consider people who are already employees in the service of the company for promotion if a higher post becomes vacant.

A detailed **job description** must be prepared for each employee to indicate precisely what is expected of him and for what functions and/or jobs he is responsible. It must also be placed at the disposal of the employee.

Eventually, both job and employee are **evaluated** on the basis of the job description. It is important that the evaluation is carried out as objectively as possible, because it forms the basis for upgrading or downgrading the particular job and expanding or curtailing it and also for reviewing the employee's job capabilities and standard.

It is very important that the effective execution of the job is always strived after and that methods to improve it and even develop it are investigated. **Time and motion studies** are used in the attempt to find the most efficient way of doing a specific job and to ensure the efficient employment of labour.

If it is found that a worker does not meet the requirements set for him and after all alternative actions have been considered to no avail, then he may be dismissed. However, the dismissal of an employee should be handled with caution because it can give rise to personnel unrest.

Voluntary resignations should be investigated thoroughly and the reasons behind them established. A high labour turnover indicates that everything is not in order and that corrective action should be implemented.

Labour turnover is calculated by means of the following elementary formula:

$$\frac{\text{Employees appointed during the period}}{\text{Total number of employees}} \times \frac{100}{1}$$

or a more complicated one:

$$\frac{(\text{Employees appointed} + \text{dismissed}) \div 2}{\text{Average number of employees}} \times \frac{100}{1}$$

By comparing the turnover figure with that of the rest of the industry a measure of the job satisfaction within the enterprise can be obtained.

Labour costs and control

1 Introduction

For the efficient control of labour costs some or other **norm** or **standard** must be set against which the efficiency of labour can be measured and which can serve as a basis for quantifying the difference between the expected norm (standard) and the actual output.

Basically labour is controlled mainly by a comparison of:

☐ **what must be done and the labour time allowed for it**
   with
☐ **what is done and the labour time taken to do it.**

This aspect is dealt with in more detail in Chapter 12.

This gives rise to the important requirement for any labour control system, namely the gathering and recording of data for the calculation of the actual labour costs and time, which is used partially as a basis for the calculation of the standard labour costs and time.

As has already been mentioned in Chapter 1, financial accounting and management accounting use a common data base. While financial accounting is directed more at external reporting according to generally accepted accounting practice and management accounting more at planning and control, there will also be a different emphasis with regard to the information required in respect of labour. This becomes evident in the table in Diagram D9:

Financial accounting	Management accounting
Total hours available	Time actually spent on each task, product, process or section
Total earnings of each employee on a daily, weekly or monthly basis	Labour costs in respect of each task, product, process or section

Control:
    Comparison with budget
	Control:
	    Comparison with standards

Book entries:
In the financial ledger –
    Labour control account   xxx
        Salaries payable   xxx
        PAYE*   xxx
        Pension**   xxx
        Etc   xxx
	Book entries:
	In the cost ledger –
	    Production account xxx
	    Overheads control
	    account (indirect
	    labour) xxx
	        Labour control account xxx

Diagram D9

2 Labour records

2.1 Personnel records

Naturally the personnel records, which contain the following information, are very important:

☐ The history of each employee – date of appointment, salary, promotions, increases, leave and sick leave, evaluation reports, etc.

☐ Legally required information to comply with deductions, unemployment insurance, trade unions, medical and pension funds, etc.

The keeping of these records is usually a centralised function carried out by the personnel department.

2.2 Clock cards

The first step towards labour control is the accurate determination of the labour time "purchased" from the employee. The **clock card** supplies indisputable evidence of the employee's attendance and serves as a basis for the calculation of his gross wages.

Important technological developments have taken place in this area over the past decade and different types of mechanised and computerised clocks are now in use. Most of these clocks are designed so that it is almost impossible to tamper with the clock cards – something that often happened in the past in that one employee could, for example, clock in for another person.

2.3 Job cards

While the clock card can be compared to the invoice from the supplier in material purchases, the job card can be compared to the requisition for the issue of the material.

---

* Being tax on employee's earnings deducted according to the PAYE system.
** Being the employee's contribution to his pension fund.

The job card forms the source document for the calculation of the time actually spent (or how the time 'purchased' is spent) and also indicates which task or product the time was spent on.

The clock card is of more importance to the financial accountant while the job card forms the basis for the apportionment of labour costs to the various branches and/or products by the management accountant.

The job cards must be reconciled with the clock cards on a regular basis and any material differences must be shown as idle time.

A certain amount of idle time is acceptable because time is lost due to rest periods, tea and mealtimes, but it must be monitored to ensure that unproductive time does not take on too great a dimension.

2.4 Production reports

Production reports are prepared on a regular basis and contain the following information which is used for control purposes:

☐ Total hours available
☐ Total hours worked
☐ What was worked on
☐ How much was produced

3 Assimilation of information

Although the format and layout of personnel records, clock cards and job cards may differ from enterprise to enterprise, depending on the equipment in use, the aim is to initiate the flow of data through the various phases of manufacture, as illustrated in Diagram D10:

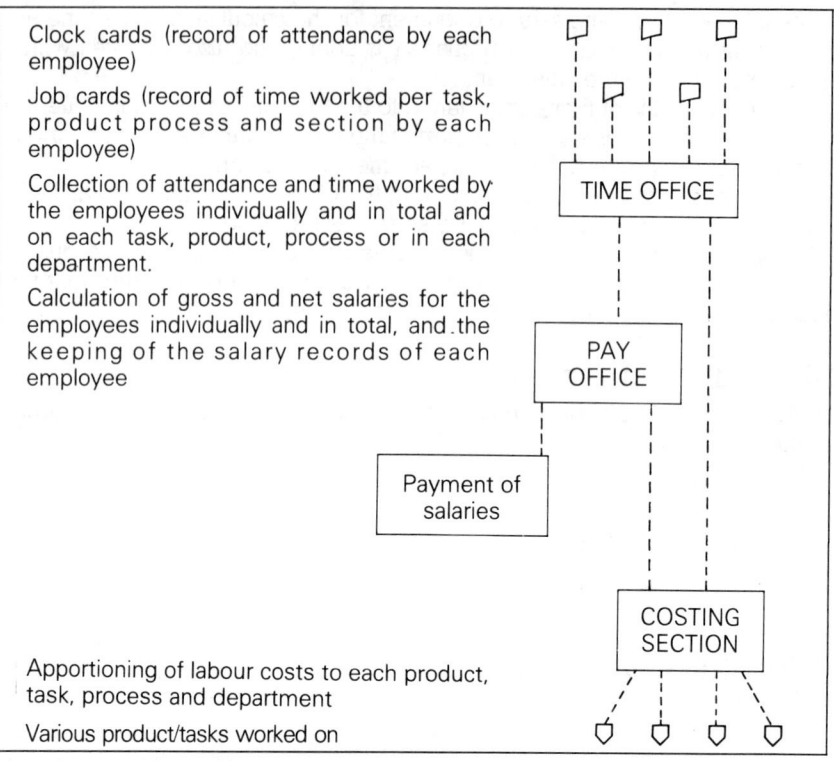

Clock cards (record of attendance by each employee)

Job cards (record of time worked per task, product process and section by each employee)

Collection of attendance and time worked by the employees individually and in total and on each task, product, process or in each department.

Calculation of gross and net salaries for the employees individually and in total, and the keeping of the salary records of each employee

Apportioning of labour costs to each product, task, process and department

Various product/tasks worked on

Diagram D10

The basic function of the **time office** is the collection of the attendance of the employees individually and in total and the tasks and/or products on which the time was spent. Seen from a costing point of view, the total time spent on each task and/or product is very important for the determination of the labour costs of the specific task and/or product.

The **pay office** calculates the gross salaries of the employees according to the hours of attendance (as supplied by the time office). All deductions from the gross salaries are brought to account and the net salaries are paid to the employees. Salary records for each employee are kept up to date on a weekly or monthly basis.

The **costing section** then uses the information collected by the time office and the pay office to apportion the labour costs to the various tasks, products, processes and/or sections.

Remuneration

1 Introduction

As has already been mentioned, a fair wage is one of the requirements laid down by the employee. The emoluments that an employee receives depend on the type of work that he performs, the degree of skill that is required for the specific work, the quality of the work that he does and, as with so many other facets of economic life, supply and demand.

The following are the methods of remuneration used:

☐ **Fixed salary method** According to this method the employee receives a fixed salary irrespective of the quantity of work that he does or the time that it takes. This form of compensation is found in administrative and supervisory functions especially, and has the disadvantage that it bears no relation to the employee's output or the number of hours worked.

☐ **Hourly wages** Here the worker is remunerated in accordance with the number of hours that he works. The disadvantage of this method is that it also does not keep pace with the employee's output, but it is advantageous in that it pays only for the number of hours that the employee is present.

Calculation:

> Hours worked × Rate per hour = Gross remuneration

☐ **Piecework** The employee is paid for the work that he does and not according to the time it takes him. This method can be used only where each employee's output can be determined precisely. It is advantageous to the employer in that he pays only for what is done.

Calculation:

> Units manufactured × Rate per unit = Gross remuneration

Various methods of combining hourly wages, piecework and fixed salaries have already been developed with the aim of utilising the advantages of each system and eliminating the disadvantages. Thus the employee receives a minimum hourly wage which increases as his output increases in accordance with piecework, with a minimum guaranteed fixed salary.

2 Calculation of labour remuneration

The calculation of the normal gross salary/wage is done in accordance with one of the above-mentioned remuneration methods. In addition, any additional earnings (overtime, incentive bonus, holiday bonus, etc) are added to compute the total gross remuneration for the period.

Ordinary overtime, that is the hours over and above the normal weekday hours worked, is **usually** remunerated at normal tariff plus 50%.† Hours worked on Sundays and public holidays are **usually** remunerated at double the normal tariff.†

Employer contributions in respect of medical and pension funds are usually not brought into account in the calculation of individual salaries, nor are they shown on the salary advice. They are calculated in total and are journalised separately. However, it has become compulsory to show fringe benefits such as housing, transport and entertainment subsidies or allowances on the salary advice, together with the corresponding deduction.

Certain deductions are made from the gross remuneration to determine the net remuneration of the employee. Some deductions are legally required, ie taxation per the pay as you earn system (PAYE) and unemployment insurance contributions (UIF), but most enterprises allow non-compulsory deductions (for example housing payments, recreational club contributions, etc) which are paid over to the relevant authority on behalf of the employee.

For the calculation of the PAYE deduction (income tax according to the pay-as-you-earn system), the taxable amount on which it is based must be determined first. The taxable amount represents the employee's total gross remuneration plus taxable fringe benefits less pension fund contributions. The calculation of the net salary is illustrated in Example 3.

Example 3

The following information is applicable to a weekly-paid employee*:

Normal working week (6 days)	45 hours
Number of hours worked	50 hours

Monday	8
Tuesday	8
Wednesday	10
Thursday	8
Friday	8
Saturday	5
Sunday	3

Normal hourly wage	R5,00
Pension fund (based on normal remuneration):	
Employer's contribution	5%
Employee's contribution	7,5%

---

† For detail, see Basic Conditions of Employment Act, 1983 (Act 3 of 1983).   (continued)
* Assume that no fringe benefits are applicable.

Medical fund:
    Employer's contribution   R13,00
    Employee's contribution   R13,00
    PAYE deduction   13%   on taxable income

    UIF deduction   R1,00

Required:

Calculate the employee's net salary for the week.

Solution

	R
Normal pay	
45 hours @ R5 per hour	225,00
Overtime pay	
2 hours × 1,5 × R5	15,00
3 hours × 2 × R5	30,00
Total gross remuneration	270,00
Less: Pension fund contributions	
(7,5% × R225)	16,88
Taxable income	253,12
Less: Sundry deductions	46,91
PAYE (13% × R253,12)	32,91
Medical fund	13,00
UIF	1,00
Net salary, payable in cash	206,21

Salaries are recorded and calculated in the salary or wage register and only the totals are journalised, but in this case, for the sake of clarity, the book entry for the above salary calculation is shown:

	Dr	Cr
Salary account	270,00	
Salaries payable		206,21
Pension fund		16,88
PAYE		32,91
Medical fund		13,00
UIF		1,00

The employer's contributions are journalised as follows:

	Dr	Cr
Employer's contribution/Salary account	24,25	
Pension fund (5% x R225)		11,25
Medical fund		13,00

Depending on the nature and management of an enterprise, further analysis can be made in the books, for example by keeping a separate account for overtime pay against which overtime wages are debited.

When the salaries are paid out and the deductions are paid over the book entries are as follows:

	Dr	Cr
Pension fund (R16,88 + R11,25)	28,13	
PAYE	32,91	
Medical fund (R13,00 + R13,00)	26,00	
UIF	1,00	
Salaries payable	206,21	
Bank (per the Payments cash book)		294,25

3 Wage incentive systems

Wage incentive schemes are aimed at promoting higher productivity and output by means of additional or increased remuneration if the employee/s perform well and maintain or produce a higher productivity.

Some of the incentive schemes are named after the people who originally developed them – Taylor, Halsey, Bedaux, Gantt and others. Few of the systems are still used in their original form today, but they are important because the principles laid down in them still form the basis for modern incentive systems.

☐ **Straight piecework**

This is an elementary incentive scheme that pays an incentive wage over and above the basic wage for production exceeding the standard. If the standard time to make one unit is 12 minutes, an employee can manufacture five units in an hour. If a particular employee earns R2,50 per hour, the labour cost is R0,50 per unit manufactured. If the employee manufactures six units per hour (1 unit better than standard) he receives an incentive bonus equal to the labour cost of one unit, that is to say R0,50. Employees are usually not penalised if actual output is lower than the standard – thus a minimum wage is guaranteed.

☐ **Taylor's differential piecework system**

Taylor used a differential rate whereby employees who achieved an output lower than the standard received compensation at a lower rate per unit and employees who managed an output higher than the standard were compensated at a higher rate per unit. This system was developed to discourage employees who could not maintain the standard, since no minimum wage is guaranteed.

☐ The standard time system

In this variation of the straight piecework system standards are always based on the time per unit manufactured. Instead of a fixed rate per unit manufactured, the standard time per unit manufactured is used in determining the remuneration. If an employee manufactures 20 units in an eight-hour shift and the standard is 16 units (or 2 units per hour), he is paid his normal hourly rate for ten hours (the standard time allowed for 20 units).

☐ Halsey bonus scheme

In this scheme the employee receives an incentive for the time he saves. If an employee manufactures 20 units in an eight-hour shift for which the standard has been set at 16, then two hours per day (or 15 minutes per unit) have been saved, for which he is compensated at his normal rate.

☐ Emerson's effiency scheme

A minimum daily wage is guaranteed and a standard time is determined for each product or task. Records are kept of the actual and standard time and when the remuneration is calculated the actual time is expressed as a percentage of the standard time. If the percentage is lower than 67% the employee receives only his minimum wage, but if it is between 67% and 100% a small bonus is paid. If the percentage is greater than 100% an additional bonus equivalent to the amount greater than 100% is added to his normal hourly rate and the employee is remunerated according to the higher rate.

☐ Bonus points

Bedaux and others allocated points on completion of each task or product, based on a standard of one point per minute. For the first 60 points per hour obtained the employee receives his normal wage. If more than 60 points per hour are obtained then a bonus is paid on these points. Sometimes this bonus is divided between the employee and the supervisor so as to motivate the supervisor as well.

☐ Measured daywork

This was an effort to combine the best characteristics of fixed remuneration and incentive systems. An employee received an increase if he performed constantly better than the standard for a certain period (say quarterly).

☐ Group bonus systems, share incentive schemes and profit-sharing schemes

These were also developed especially to involve employees at the higher levels of management in incentive schemes.

The question that must be asked now is: Is it advantageous to the enterprise if the largest portion of the savings obtained from higher productivity are paid over to the employees in the form of an incentive scheme? The answer is "yes", because the enterprise still has the advantage of better utilisation of the production facilities and consequently savings in manufacturing overheads.

4 Direct and indirect labour

As has already been stated, **direct labour** forms a separate cost element and consists of labour that is directly involved in the manufacturing process and contributes to the physical transformation of the product. Machine operators and employees who perform the physical transformation of the product fall into this category.

Indirect labour is labour that is not directly involved in the manufacturing process and falls under manufacturing overheads. Supervisors and cleaners, for example, fall into this category.

It is logical, although in practice it is not always the case, that **all the costs associated with direct labour** should fall under **direct labour costs**. Thus, for example, the employer's contribution to pension funds for direct labour should be allocated to direct labour costs, while the normal wage for a person who does indirect work is allocated to manufacturing overheads.

As has already been mentioned, this principle is not always followed in practice and the tendency is to show only the variable portion of direct labour costs as such (for example normal wages) while the fixed component (for example employer's contribution to medical funds) is allocated to manufacturing overheads.

5 Recovery of direct labour costs

Direct labour costs are usually calculated on an hourly basis and then allocated to the various products according to the number of hours worked.

It is very important that the hourly recovery tariff is calculated as accurately as possible to minimise the possibility of over or under recovery. This means that the expected number of hours for a certain future period as well as the corresponding direct labour costs for the relevant period must be determined as accurately as possible. Provision for holiday leave as well as idle time must be made and brought into account. Usually only one tariff is calculated per department or cost centre rather than one for each employee, as shown in Example 4.

Example 4

Number of weeks per year	52
Less: Holiday leave	3
Available weeks	49
Hours per week (5 working days, 8 hours each)	×40
Available hours	1 960
Less: Public holidays (10 × 8 hours each)	80
	1 880
Less: Idle time (estimated as 10%)	188
Expected productive hours	1 692

	R
Normal yearly gross salary (including leave)	4 800
Holiday bonus	480
Employer contributions	305
Total salary cost	5 585

$$\text{Hourly recovery tariff} \;=\; \frac{\text{R5 585}}{\text{1 692 hours}}$$

$$=\; \text{R3,30 per hour}$$

6 Conclusion

Labour makes great demands on management and requires particular attention at all times because of its specific nature. What complicates the situation further is the fact that labour is not always as adaptable as it is made out to be. When material is not required it is stored for later use. Because of legislation, trade unions and other external factors, as well as internal factors such as job security and a satisfied labour force, labour cannot be dismissed immediately if it is not necessary – it remains unused but is still a cost to the enterprise. This has resulted in labour costs as a whole, moving away from a variable tendency to a more fixed character – from a controllable item to an uncontrollable item. In South Africa there is a remuneration philosophy that employees should be remunerated according to a fixed wage structure and not according to contributions to profits. Thus an employee is on a wage scale with fixed increments, irrespective of contributions to profit or productivity.

Labour presents a particular challenge to management and demands careful planning and cautious control of the management accountant.

4

OVERHEADS

Classification of manufacturing overheads

1 Introduction

Overheads, the third cost element to be discussed, can be subdivided as follows:

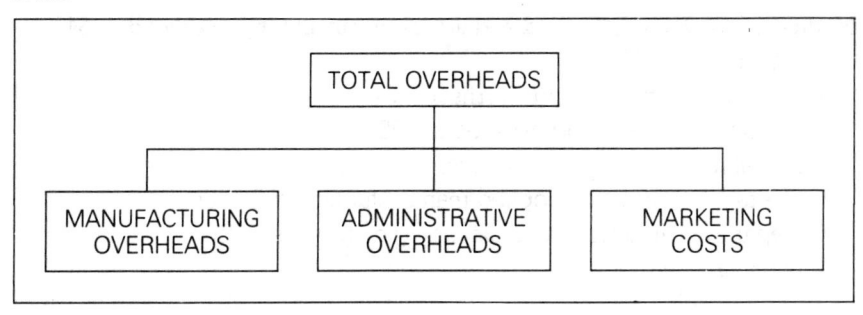

Diagram D11

Overheads include all the costs which are necessary for the enterprise's activities but which cannot be allocated to the two cost elements already discussed, namely material and labour.

In this module and the next manufacturing overheads are discussed.

Manufacturing overheads, sometimes called factory overheads, can be summarised as all the manufacturing costs necessary for the efficient continuation of the manufacturing process, excluding direct material and direct labour which are shown as separate cost elements, and thus constitutes the third element of total manufacturing costs.

Direct material	XXX
Direct labour	XXX
Manufacturing overheads	XXX
Total manufacturing costs	XXX

In the years prior to the Industrial Revolution manufacturing overheads were largely ignored as a cost element. The small industries of that time mainly revolved around the labourer who did the handiwork and overheads did not exist or were so trifling that they were not separately accounted for.

They were merely shown as an expense in the income statement. Material and labour costs were shown as the total of the manufacturing costs.

Only after the Industrial Revolution, when the emphasis changed from labour-intensive to capital-intensive manufacturing processes and the machine to a large extent replaced the worker, did overheads come into their own right. Today overheads are of such a size that no manufacturing concern can neglect to control them properly.

It will be noticeable from the following examples of cost items that are classified as manufacturing overheads that the importance and volume thereof have increased in proportion to mechanisation and automation, which have become the centre of the modern manufacturing set-up:

Hire of factory premises
Maintenance of machinery and equipment
Depreciation
Supervision
Quality control, etc

In the small cottage industries of the past the above cost items would not have had much influence on the cost structure and on the determination of the price.

2 Cost price calculation and manufacturing overheads

2.1 Problems associated with overheads

The apportionment of manufacturing overheads to the various products manufactured is the single largest problem with regards to cost calculation.

The cost of direct material used in the manufacture of a product can easily be calculated from the material requisitions. Labour costs can be determined reasonably accurately from the clock cards. Manufacturing overheads, however, are not so easily determined.

In earlier times manufacturing overheads were calculated on a historical basis. The sum total of the manufacturing overheads for a certain period, usually a day or week, was divided by the number of units manufactured during that period to give the overheads per unit.

However, due to the administrative workload and the greater extent of modern production facilities it is no longer practical to prepare statements on a daily or weekly basis in order to determine the figure. To aggravate the complexity of the problem the information is also no longer so easily collectable. Think of the cost of power, where electricity usage is calculated on a monthly basis and the enterprise is informed of the cost a few weeks after the end of the month. Also, diversification has ensured that an enterprise seldom manufactures only one product, as was the case in the past, but usually manufactures a series of products simultaneously. All these factors have contributed to the calculation of unit costs and cost prices on a historical cost basis becoming obsolete and falling into disuse.

A new method had to be found to bring manufacturing overheads into account in determining the cost. **These days the cost is allocated on the basis of the causal relationship between the products.** Here the cause (cost) is linked to the effect (the product), and vice versa. But this division is also very difficult, especially in enterprises which manufacture heterogeneous products in different departments.

2.2 Classification and analysis of overheads

In order to divide the manufacturing overheads by means of the causal relationship which exists between costs and products, an analysis and classification of the overheads is necessary.

The most important **classification** of manufacturing overheads is according to their fixed and variable characteristics:

☐ Fixed manufacturing overheads
☐ Variable manufacturing overheads
☐ Semi-fixed manufacturing overheads
☐ Semi-variable manufacturing overheads

☐ **Fixed manufacturing overheads,** sometimes also called period costs, are costs that are constant in total for a certain period and are not linked to the number of units manufactured during that period. They can also be viewed as the costs that are incurred to establish the **capacity** (manufacturing facility), that is to say the **costs of being in business.** An example is the hire of a factory location, a fixed amount per annum irrespective of the number of units manufactured during the year.

A very important fact is that the cost is fixed in total, but if it is calculated per unit it decreases as long as the number of units increases.

Example 5

	100 units	500 units
Total hire per annum	R6 000	R6 000
Hire per unit per annum	R60	R12

Graphic representation

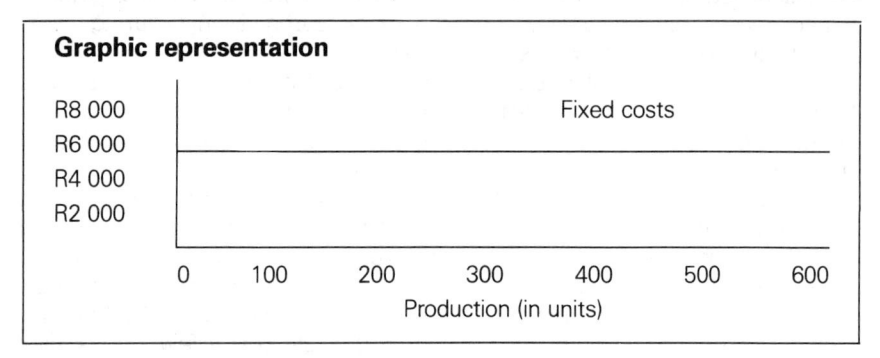

The hire remains **constant in total** at R6 000 per annum and does not vary with the volume of production. The cost per unit produced decreases as the volume of the production increases.

Fixed costs are fixed for a **given capacity level** and **period** only. This capacity level, usually indicated by minimum and maximum limits, is known as the **relevant range** within which the fixed costs will not change. If, however, the manufacturing capacity is expanded to a level outside the relevant range, the total amount of fixed costs will also increase.

☐ **Variable manufacturing overheads,** sometimes also called direct overheads, have characteristics opposite to those of fixed manufacturing overheads. These are incurred in the utilisation of the available capacity, that is to say they are the costs of **doing business.**

Variable costs have a direct bond with and vary directly in relation to the volume of production, because the cost per unit produced is constant.

Example 6

	100 units	500 units
Variable manufacturing overheads per unit	R5	R5
Total variable manufacturing overheads	R500	R2 500

Graphic representation

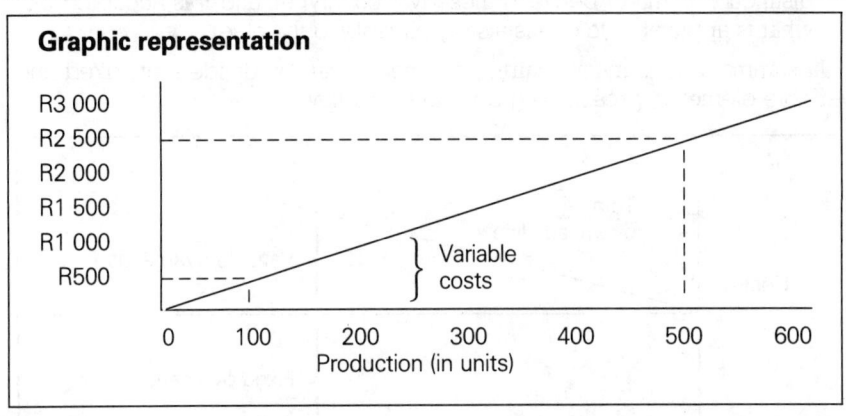

☐ **Semi-fixed and semi-variable manufacturing overheads** have both a variable and a fixed element. Transport can be taken as an example of semi-fixed costs. A truck with a capacity of 2 tonnes can transport a certain number of units. Increase the load to more than 2 tonnes and either a bigger truck must be acquired or two journeys must be made. The costs thus increase by degrees in proportion to the production volume increase.

Example 7

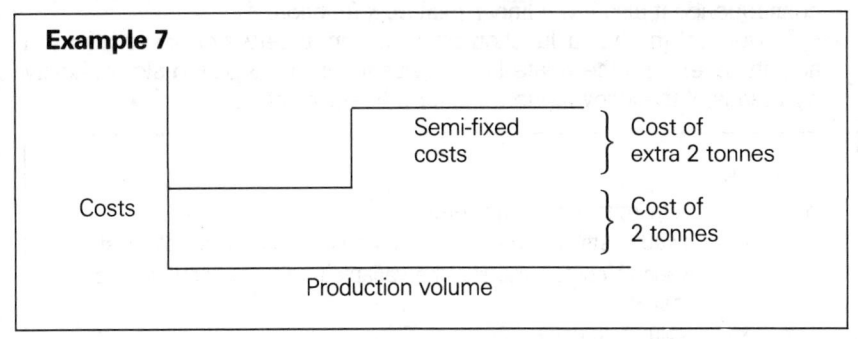

The cost of an emergency generator is a good example of **semi-variable manufacturing overheads.** Fixed monthly maintenance is a certain amount, but whenever it is used provision must also be made for petrol costs.

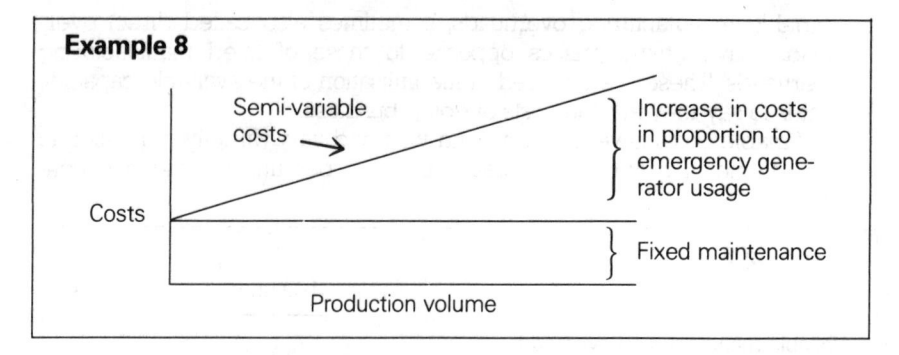

Since there is little difference in the handling and controlling of semi-fixed and semi-variable manufacturing overheads, in this book no further distinction is made between these two cost types and it is accepted that what is applicable to one is also applicable to the other.

In summary, total manufacturing overheads can be divided into fixed and variable elements, presented graphically as follows:

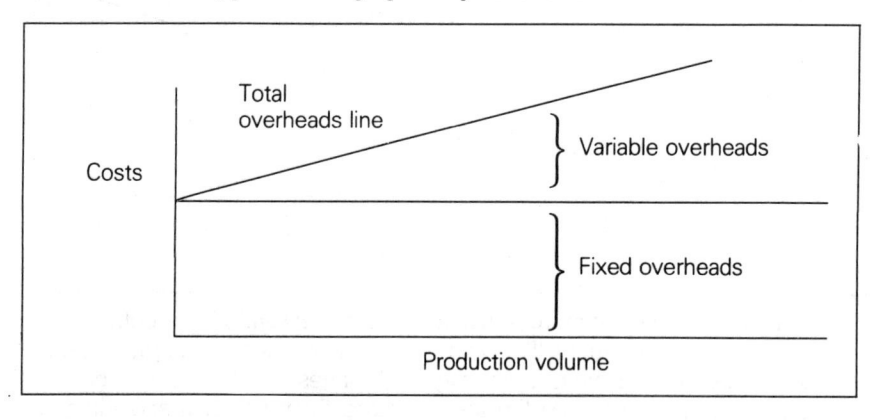

☐ Total manufacturing overheads and the linear function

Because a constant variable cost per unit is accepted in costing, as a consequence it also has a **linear total cost function.**

In general the linear function evolves from a series of observations of activity levels and the related cost. Thus it can be depicted algebraically by means of the following formula for a linear function:

$$T = a + bx$$

where $T =$ total manufacturing overheads
       $a =$ fixed costs (including the fixed portion of semi-variable costs)
       $b =$ variable costs (including the variable portion of semi-variable costs)
       $x =$ volume in units

3 Techniques for dividing manufacturing overheads

The division of manufacturing overheads into its fixed and variable elements has great advantages for control purposes.

The amount of fixed manufacturing overheads is relatively easily **controllable because the total amount is constant**. If the amount is exceeded there is wastage or ineffective employment of funds and the cause can be determined.

The amount of variable manufacturing overheads is also easily **controllable because the cost per unit is constant**. The costs per unit multiplied by the number of units manufactured gives the total variable manufacturing overheads, which can be used to determine whether there is any wastage or whether ineffective usage has taken place.

Some types of manufacturing overheads can easily be divided into their fixed and variable elements, but with others this is impossible unless one of the following **techniques** is used:

Regression analysis
High-low method
Simple regression
Multiple regression

☐ Regression analysis

Regression analysis can be applied by preparing a scatter diagram of different observations of volume on one side with the associated costs in respect of the various volumes on the other side. (Graphically the volume is shown on the X axis and the cost on the Y axis.)

Thus, by drawing a comparison between the volume of production on the one hand and the manufacturing overheads on the other, the tendency between the fixed and variable elements can be traced as illustrated in Example 9:

Example 9		
Month	Number of units manufactured	Total manufacturing overheads
		R
January	450	8 600
February	600	10 200
March	700	11 000
April	650	10 300
May	600	10 100
June	550	9 600
July	550	9 300
August	500	8 800
September	500	9 100
October	450	8 600
November	450	8 400
December	400	8 000

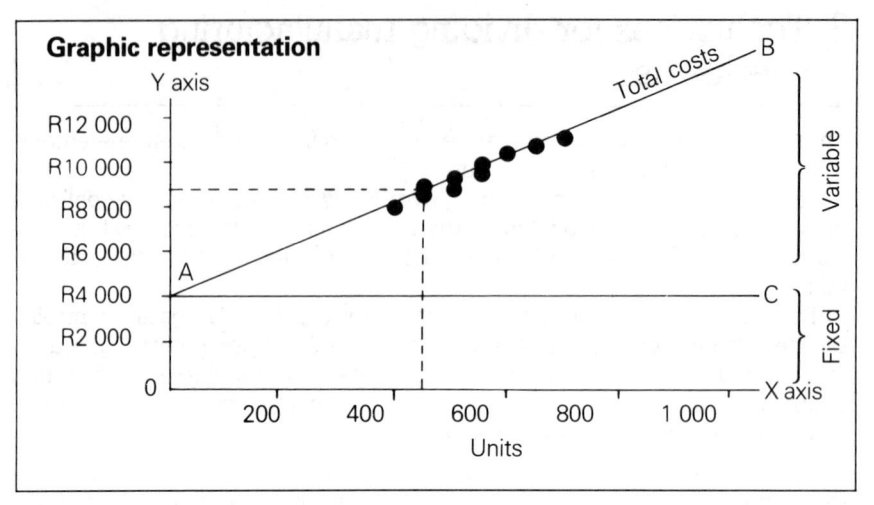

Graphic representation

By drawing a straight line (AB) through the various points, as indicated, and by connecting it to the Y axis (A) and then drawing a straight line parallel to the X axis from the intersection (A), we get a graphic representation of the fixed and variable elements of the total manufacturing overheads.

In this case line AC represents the fixed overheads (R4 000) and AB the total manufacturing overheads. The variable overheads are represented by the area between lines AB and AC. By dividing the variable costs by the number of units the variable cost per unit (R10) is obtained.

However, this method is not very accurate, since everyone will draw the line AB with a different gradient through the various points. The division between fixed and variable will therefore differ, but should provide adequate information for control purposes.

☐ High-low method

This method is basically the same as regression analysis except that it takes only the highest and lowest volumes into consideration. The advantage of this method, although it is not as accurate as the others, is that it is quick and easy to make the distinction.

Example 10

(Use the same information as in Example 9.)

	Volume	Manufacturing overheads
		R
Highest	700	11 000
Lowest	400	8 000
Difference	300	3 000

As a starting point the principle that fixed costs are constant in total and do not vary with the production volume is used. Thus the increase in manufacturing overheads (R3 000) is attributable to the variable element and the manufacture of the 300 extra units. Variable manufacturing overheads thus amount to R10 per unit, or R3 000 divided by 300 units. The fixed costs can now be calculated as follows:

	Total overheads	Variable	Fixed
	R	R	R
Highest	11 000	7 000*	4 000
Lowest	8 000	4 000	4 000
* 700 × R10 = R7 000			

If the costs of the highest and lowest volumes show abnormality, for example exceptionally low costs compared with the highest volume, the high-low method cannot be used for the division as it will show an unrealistic amount for the fixed costs.

☐ Simple regression

As has already been stated, regression analysis is a technique for drawing a straight line through a given quantity of observations.

In contrast with the scatter profile, where the line is drawn according to the judgement of the person who prepares it, it can also be determined with mathematical precision by means of a technique known as **simple regression** (the least squared method). Simple regression is the development of an equation which indicates the relationship between one fixed and one variable factor.

In Example 11 the application of **simple regression** and the solving of the equations is illustrated. (The symbols X and Y are used to indicate the production volume and the total overheads respectively.)

Example 11
(Using the same information as previously.)

Month	Production volume X	Overheads Y	XY	X^2
		R		
Jan	450	8 600	3 870 000	202 500
Feb	600	10 200	6 120 000	360 000
March	700	11 000	7 700 000	490 000
April	650	10 300	6 695 000	422 500
May	600	10 100	6 060 000	360 000
June	550	9 600	5 280 000	302 500
July	550	9 300	5 115 000	302 500
Aug	500	8 800	4 400 000	250 000
Sept	500	9 100	4 550 000	250 000
Oct	450	8 600	3 870 000	202 500
Nov	450	8 400	3 780 000	202 500
Dec	400	8 000	3 200 000	160 000
	6 400	112 000	60 640 000	3 505 000

(continued)

Σ	=	the sum of
ΣX	=	6 400
ΣY	=	112 000
ΣXY	=	60 640 000
ΣX^2	=	3 505 000

Simple regression is a mathematical technique whereby the following two equations must be solved:

(i) $\Sigma xy = a\Sigma x + b\Sigma x^2$
(ii) $\Sigma y = na + \cdot b\Sigma x$

x = number of units produced
y = total overheads for the relevant production volume
n = number of observations
a = fixed overheads for the period
b = variable overheads for the period

Solution
(i) $\Sigma XY = a\Sigma x + b\Sigma x^2$
(ii) $\Sigma Y = na + b\Sigma x$

By replacing x and y with values:

(i) (a)   60 640 000 = (a × 6 400) + (b × 3 505 000)
(ii) (a)   112 000 = (12 × a) + (b × 6 400)

By substitution:

(i) (b) 6 400 a = 60 640 000 − 3 505 000 b
(ii) (b)   12 a = 112 000 − 6 400 b

If equation (ii) (b) is multiplied by 533,333 (obtained by dividing 6 400 a by 12 a), the two equations will have the same value iro 6 400 a.

Deduct equation (ii) (c) from (i) (c):

(i) (c) 6 400 a = 60 640 000 − 3 505 000 b
(ii) (c) 6 400 a = 59 733 332 − 3 413 333 b

———————————————————————

0   =   906 668 −   91 667 b

By substitution:

91 667 b =   906 668

$$b = \frac{906\ 668}{91\ 667}$$

b =   R9,89   (variable cost per unit)

Replace b with R9,89 in equation (ii) (b):

12 a =   112 000 − (6 400 × 9,89)
   =   112 000 − 63 296
   =   48 704
a =   R4 058,66   (fixed cost per month)

For the sake of completeness attention can also be given to **multiple regression** which shows the influence of one fixed component and two or more variable components. The application takes place by means of the following simple formula:

$$Y = a + bx + b^1x^1 + \ldots\ldots + b^nx^n$$

where Y = total costs
$\qquad a$ = fixed costs
$\qquad x \ldots x^n$ = the variables that have an influence on Y
$\qquad b \ldots b^n$ = the values of the variables

For example, x can be represented by man hours, machine hours or any other variable, while b represents the tariff per man hour/machine hour or such variable.

Just as the total manufacturing overheads in the previous three methods can be divided between the fixed and variable elements, each individual cost element can also be divided into its fixed and variable components.

As has already been mentioned, for control purposes it is necessary that overheads are divided. It is also an important aid for pre-planning and for the preparation of budgets.

Budgeted, applied and actual manufacturing overheads

1 Introduction

It is very important that a clear distinction is made between the concepts **budgeted, applied** and **actual manufacturing overheads** now to eliminate confusion later.

2 Budgeted manufacturing overheads

Actual manufacturing overheads are available only after the last transaction for a given period has been entered in the books. Naturally the information is already outdated and of little value for price determination and pre-planning.

As has already been mentioned, the allocation of manufacturing overheads to the various products or jobs manufactured presents a big problem for cost determination. Since actual overheads are only of historical importance in cost determination and price determination, a scientific forecast of the manufacturing overheads for the future period must be prepared to serve as a basis for the calculation of allocation tariffs.

The **budgeted manufacturing overheads** must be calculated with caution so as to get it as close as possible to the actual situation, but it must also be prepared in such a way that it can serve as a guideline for expenditure without concealing any wastage and spillage.

Budgeted manufacturing overheads must not be confused with applied manufacturing overheads.

While **budgeted manufacturing overheads** is a scientific forecast of the overheads for a future period, **applied manufacturing overheads** is the amount of overheads **applied to the production process** during the period according to a **predetermined rate,** based on the budgeted overheads. Briefly, applied overheads represents the amount of overheads recovered during the year and brought into account in determining the cost and the total production costs.

Seeing that budgets and the preparation of the manufacturing overheads budget are discussed in Chapter 11, no further attention is given to the subject in this chapter.

Direct material	XXX
Direct labour	XXX
Applied manufacturing overheads	XXX
Total manufacturing costs	XXX

By dividing each overhead item into its fixed and variable elements, determining the expected production volume accurately and paying attention to economic tendencies, a reasonably reliable estimate of the overheads in a future period can be made. By comparing estimate with the previous year's actual overheads it can be ascertained whether or not it is realistic.

The projection of the expected production volume, or capacity utilisation, is of particular importance, especially in the calculation of the allocation tariffs, which is discussed later, and in the calculation of budgeted fixed and variable overheads. (The various capacity levels are discussed in Chapter 12.)

3 Applied manufacturing overheads

Applied manufacturing overheads is the amount of overheads allocated to the production process and/or products manufactured during the manufacturing period according to a predetermined rate (tariff), based on the budgeted overheads and expected capacity utilisation.

When calculating the predetermined overhead allocation rate it is necessary to find a suitable basis upon which this rate can be based. The following bases may be considered:

- ☐ Product unit basis
- ☐ Labour hour basis
- ☐ Labour cost basis
- ☐ Machine hour basis
- ☐ Material cost basis
- ☐ Primary cost basis
- ☐ Combinations of the bases mentioned

The **formula** for the calculation of the predetermined rate is as follows:

$$\text{Allocation rate} = \frac{\text{Budgeted manufacturing overheads}}{\text{Suitable basis}}$$

The calculation of predetermined overhead rates is illustrated in Example 12:

Example 12

The following is the budget of a manufacturing enterprise that produces only one type of product:

	Total	Per unit
Budgeted production (units)	1 000	
Budgeted direct material cost	R15 000	R15
Budgeted direct labour cost	R20 000	R20
Budgeted manufacturing overheads:	R12 000	
– fixed	R8 000	
– variable	R4 000	
Budgeted direct labour hours	4 000	4
Budgeted machine hours	3 000	3

Required

Calculate the predetermined overhead rate according to each of the bases mentioned.

☐ Product unit basis

$$\text{Allocation rate} = \frac{\text{Budgeted manufacturing overheads}}{\text{Budgeted number of units produced}}$$

$$= \frac{\text{R12 000}}{\text{1 000}}$$

$$= \text{R12,00 per unit}$$

For each unit that is produced during the year R12,00 of overheads is allocated to the manufacturing process. As soon as 1 000 units are produced during the year the budgeted overheads will have been recovered in total.

Calculation of the manufacturing cost per unit:

	R
Direct material	15,00
Direct labour	20,00
Applied overheads	12,00
Total manufacturing cost	47,00

This basis for the allocation of overheads can be used fruitfully in enterprises which produce only a single type of product. It is a simple and synoptic method which can be applied without much administration.

☐ Labour hour basis

$$\text{Allocation rate} = \frac{\text{Budgeted manufacturing overheads}}{\text{Budgeted labour hours}}$$

$$= \frac{\text{R12 000}}{\text{4 000}}$$

$$= \text{R3 per labour hour}$$

Manufacturing overheads are allocated at a rate of R3 per labour hour. Four labour hours are expended on one product, thus R12 per unit is re-covered.

This basis of allocation is perhaps, along with the machine hour basis, used most generally. Administratively the rates and the allocated amount are easily calculated, since the total available hours and the time expended on each product or task are usually already available. It can also be used fruitfully in enterprises which are very labour intensive and/or produce a wide range of products.

☐ Labour cost basis

$$\text{Allocation rate} = \frac{\text{Budgeted manufacturing overheads}}{\text{Budgeted labour cost}} \times \frac{100}{1}$$

$$= \frac{\text{R12 000}}{\text{R20 000}} \times \frac{100}{1}$$

$$= 60\% \text{ of labour cost}$$

The rate is usually expressed as a percentage of direct labour cost. This is a simple method of allocating overheads.

Manufacturing cost per unit	
	R
Direct material	15,00
Direct labour	20,00
Applied overheads (60% of R20)	12,00
Total manufacturing cost	47,00

One limitation of this method of allocation is that a labour-intensive or highly remunerated section might have a higher labour cost, yet use little or no machinery. The overheads (which comprise principally depreciation and the maintenance of machinery and equipment) which are allocated to this department on the basis of labour costs will then be relatively higher than they rightly should be.

☐ Machine hour basis

$$\text{Allocation rate} = \frac{\text{Budgeted manufacturing overheads}}{\text{Budgeted machine hours}}$$

$$= \frac{\text{R12 000}}{\text{3 000}}$$

$$= \text{R4,00 per machine hour}$$

This is a relatively easy method to use in enterprises which are mechanised to a large extent. An additional advantage is that management's attention is drawn to the output of the machine.

Provision must be made for the maintenance, repair and adjustment of machinery and idle time and under-utilisation must be eliminated.

☐ Material cost basis

$$\text{Allocation rate} = \frac{\text{Budgeted manufacturing overheads}}{\text{Budgeted material cost}} \times \frac{100}{1}$$

$$= \frac{\text{R12 000}}{\text{R15 000}} \times \frac{100}{1}$$

$$= 80\% \text{ of material cost}$$

This is not an accurate method, because usually there is no direct connection between material costs and overheads. A product that is made from expensive material and without much processing will carry a greater portion of overheads than, for example, a product that is made from cheap material but requires a lot more processing.

☐ Primary cost basis

$$\text{Allocation rate} = \frac{\text{Budgeted manufacturing overheads} \times 100}{\text{Budgeted material cost} + \text{budgeted labour cost}}$$

$$= \frac{\text{R12 000} \times 100}{\text{R15 000} + \text{R20 000}}$$

$$= 34,3 \% \text{ of primary cost}$$

The same limitations as for the material cost basis are also applicable here, although to a smaller degree.

The composition of the products and the way in which they are manufactured will, to a great extent, determine which basis is used for the calculation of the predetermined overhead rate. It is necessary that the most logical and accurate method with the greatest causal connection between costs and product is used as the basis for the allocation.

As has already been mentioned, the total actual manufacturing overheads is known only after the product is finished and sold and it has little or no influence on the allocation rate.

4 Actual manufacturing overheads

Actual manufacturing overheads are the amounts actually spent during a given period as shown by the financial statements and records of the enterprise at the end of the period.

The various overhead items are usually aggregated in the Manufacturing overheads control account, and are obtained from several subsidiary books which include, *inter alia*, the cash book, purchases journal, fixed assets register, etc.

The most important types of cost items found under manufacturing overheads are the following:

- ☐ Depreciation of machinery and equipment
- ☐ Interest on capital
- ☐ Indirect material usage
- ☐ Indirect labour
- ☐ Rental and maintenance of factory buildings

☐ Depreciation of machinery and equipment

Depreciation is an important overhead item, especially in capital-intensive enterprises which are mechanised to a large extent.

Two methods used generally in South Africa to calculate depreciation are the reducing balance method and the straight-line method.

In the first-mentioned method the depreciation is calculated annually on the book value, while in the second method a fixed amount, calculated on the cost price, is written off. The two methods are illustrated in Example 13:

Example 13

Cost of machinery	R10 000
Date purchased	1 Sept. 19.4
Depreciation	20% per annum
Financial year end	28 February

Solution

		Reducing balance method	Straight-line method
1/9/19.4	Cost	R10 000	R10 000
28/2/19.5	Depreciation @ 20% for six months	1 000	1 000
1/3/19.5	Book value	9 000	9 000
28/2/19.6	Depreciation for one year @ 20%		
	$\dfrac{20}{100} \times \dfrac{9\ 000}{1}$	1 800	
	$\dfrac{20}{100} \times \dfrac{10\ 000}{1}$		2 000
1/3/19.6	Book value	7 200	7 000

A third method, **the fixed instalment method,** is used especially in contracts when the value of the machinery is written off over its economic useful life.

Cost	R10 000
Economic life	4 years
Depreciation per annum	R2 500

The scrap value at the end of the economic life can also be taken into account, which means that the annual depreciation charge will decrease accordingly.

Economic life means the period for which an asset can be profitably employed. When a new development can do the same task more economically the old machine is deemed to be **economically obsolete,** although technically it may still be in good condition.

Technical life means the period for which an asset is capable of performing a specified task, after which it is usually written off as scrap or sold.

☐ Interest on capital/investment

This is an aspect which is largely ignored in South Africa, especially when a machine is purchased for cash and interest is apparently not paid. However, when a machine is purchased on credit the interest that is paid is usually capitalised and recovered in the form of depreciation.

Whether the machine is purchased for cash or on credit, interest is a sacrifice made to obtain the machine and should, as such, be classified as an overhead. This aspect is also discussed in Chapter 14 (Long-term planning).

☐ Indirect material and indirect labour

Although direct material and direct labour form separate cost elements, indirect material and indirect labour are classified as manufacturing overheads.

☐ Rental and maintenance of factory buildings

Over the past few years this cost increased in importance because of the high interest rates which were applicable. It usually forms a fixed manufacturing overhead.

5 Over or underapplied manufacturing overheads

Over or **underapplied manufacturing overheads** represent the **difference** between **applied** and **actual manufacturing overheads.**

Overapplied overheads arise whenever the applied manufacturing overheads exceed the actual manufacturing overheads, and under applied overheads occur in the converse situation.

The following are possible causes for the existence of over or underapplied overheads:

☐ Incorrect predetermined overhead rates

☐ Actual overheads which are more/less than budgeted

☐ More/less activity in the base according to which overheads are applied

In a situation where insufficient overheads are applied during the year (underapplied) all the overheads are not recovered and at the end of the year there is a balance remaining. This balance (underapplied overheads) must be applied at the end of the year. This is done by debiting **cost of sales** and consequently increasing the cost of sales by the amount that was underapplied during the year.

A portion of the underapplied overheads should, rightly, also be debited to finished goods and incomplete work which is in stock at that date, but because it is difficult to implement it is not usually done in practice.

When overheads are overapplied during the period the same procedures are followed, except that the cost of sales is credited.

The accounting entries for over or underapplied overheads are explained in Example 14:

Example 14

	R
Applied overheads	10 000
Actual overheads	8 000
Cost of sales	100 000
Overapplied overheads	2 000
Material used	70 000
Labour employed	20 000

Solution

Applied overheads

Overhead control acc	10 000	Production account	10 000

①

Production account

Applied overheads	10 000	Finished goods/	
Material	70 000	Cost of sales	100 000
Labour	20 000		

②

Manufacturing overheads control account

| Actual costs | 8 000 | Applied overheads | 10 000 |
| Cost of sales | 2 000 | | |

③

Cost of sales

| Finished goods | 100 000 | Overheads control acc | 2 000 |

In the above example too large an amount of overheads was applied (R10 000) in comparison with the actual amount incurred (R8 000). The manufacturing overheads control account thus has a credit balance of R2 000 as an overapplication of overheads to production. To close the manufacturing overheads account off the balance of R2 000 is credited to cost of sales.

Underapplied overheads are treated in the same manner, except that the cost of sales is eventually debited with the amount.

6 Departmentalisation of manufacturing overheads

It is usually not feasible to use only one overhead recovery rate for all the branches of a factory. Some divisions generate more overheads than others and if only one tariff is used the result will be an unfair and inaccurate recovery.

Briefly, **departmentalisation of overheads** means the division of overheads among the various sections of the factory so that eventually an accurate allocation rate can be estalished for **each department** separately.

Departmentalisation implies, first, that the factory must be divided into **cost centres.** The various departments can usually be viewed as separate cost centres because of the grouping together of related activities in departments. Two or more departments can, however, be combined into one cost centre, or one department can be divided into two or more cost centres.

The requirement laid down for a cost centre is that all the activities performed in the particular cost centre must have more or less the same degree of exposure to overheads. In short, the activities must show a degree of uniformity, they must use more or less the same machinery and share proportionately in the overheads of the cost centre. A small manufacturer can be taken as an example – in one department the parts are cut out of metal and in the next department they are assembled. As a result of the diversity of activities a separate allocation rate must be determined for each department (or cost centre).

A **cost carrier** is a product or job which is in the process of being manufactured, which accumulates costs as it nears completion and against which overheads can be allocated according to a predetermined tariff.

The departmentalisation of overheads can be divided into two actions, namely:

☐ **primary departmentalisation,** also called primary allocation or apportionment, where the manufacturing overheads are divided among **all** the departments/cost centres (including service departments)

☐ **secondary allocation,** where the costs of the service departments are allocated to the production departments.

A department/cost centre is classified as a service department if it does not make a direct contribution to the transformation process of the cost carrier, but provides a service to the other departments/cost centres involved in the transformation of the cost carrier, for example quality control, which only monitors whether the cost carrier complies with certain standards and does not actually do any transformation itself.

Diagram D12 is a diagrammatic representation of the primary and secondary allocation of manufacturing overheads:

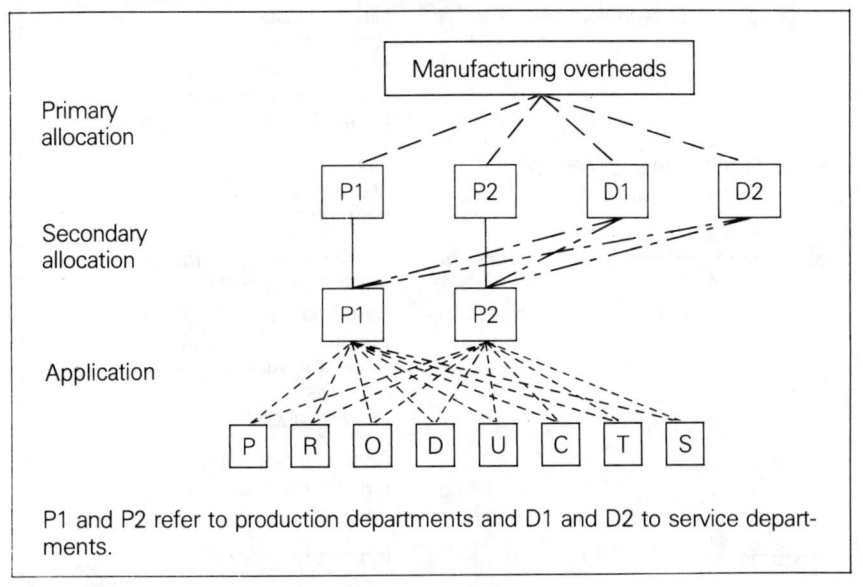

P1 and P2 refer to production departments and D1 and D2 to service departments.

Diagram D12

6.1 Primary allocation of manufacturing overheads

Primary allocation of overheads, as the name indicates, is the first and perhaps the most important allocation of overheads, where every overhead item is apportioned to all the production and service departments of the enterprise.

For this primary allocation it is necessary that a **suitable basis** is found for the division of the individual cost items among the various departments according to the causal relationship which exists between the cost and the ultimate product. Thus, for example, it could be found that the number of employees employed by each department is the fairest basis for the division of the cost of protective overalls among the various departments.

It is necessary that an in-depth study is made of all aspects of the enterprise in its entirety to find various bases for the allocation of overheads. Diagram D13 gives some examples of the bases that can be used and what they can be used for.

Basis	Cost
Area utilised by each cost centre	Hire of location Property tax Maintenance of buildings Insurance on buildings Heating/cooling of buildings
Value of machinery and equipment	Depreciation Maintenance Insurance
Number of workers in each cost centre	Personnel administration Protective overalls Cafeteria Security Transport subsidy Supervision Indirect labour
Material usage	Cost of stock piling Indirect material Insurance
Requisitions	Indirect material
Time sheets	Indirect labour
Kilowatt hours	Electricity
Machine hours	Maintenance of machines Power usage Indirect labour

Diagram D13

Each cost item must be analysed separately to determine which basis will provide the greatest causal relationship between the cost and the department for that specific cost item. As soon as an appropriate basis is found the costs are divided and allocated to all the separate departments/cost centres.

6.2 Secondary allocation of manufacturing overheads

There is no way that the costs of service departments can be allocated directly to the final product and/or job. The only method is first to divide the costs of the service departments among the production departments and from there to divide them among the final products and/or tasks.

This second phase of allocation, where the costs of the service departments are divided among the production departments, also known as **secondary allocation,** also requires a fair basis for allocation based on the causal relationship between the service rendered and the department that makes use of the service. The table in Diagram D14 shows a few of the bases that can be used.

Service department	Allocation basis
Purchases	Number of orders Material cost
Stock piling	Material cost Number of issues Number of units
Personnel	Number of employees Man hours Labour costs
Repairs and maintenance	Machine hours Services rendered Value of machines
Quality control	Number of units Man hours Services rendered

Diagram D14

Some service departments render an independent service, for example repair work or maintenance, and the cost can be divided between the various production departments exactly, according to time sheets or work sheets.

The nature of the enterprise, the type of products manufactured and the composition of the production process will ultimately determine which basis is the fairest for the allotment of a specific service department's costs.

When there is more than one service department in an enterprise the costs of the smallest service department are usually allocated first, including the other service departments so that each department receives its rightful portion. In the process the smallest department is totally closed off. Thereafter the second smallest service department is apportioned and closed off, then the next, and so on. Eventually, after all the service departments have been allocated and closed off, costs will be showing against the production departments only.

6.3 Application to the products and/or jobs

At this stage the tariff or rate at which the overheads of the production departments are applied to the various products and/or jobs that are manufactured are calculated. The different bases according to which it can be calculated were discussed in Section 3 'Applied manufacturing overheads'. Generally, labour hours and machine hours are used most.

It is important to note that the budgeted overheads must be departmentalised first so that the predetermined overhead rates can be calculated. At the end of the period the actual manufacturing overheads must also be departmentalised to determine whether the overheads recovered during the period by means of the predetermined overhead rates were sufficient to cover the actual overheads.

If the applied or recovered overheads are more than the actual overheads an over-recovery exists, and vice versa.

Example 15 illustrates the primary and secondary allocation of overheads (departmentalisation of overheads), as well as the determination of the allocation rate whereby the overheads are allocated to the various products that are manufactured.

Example 15

An enterprise has gathered the following information with the aim of departmentalising its manufacturing overheads:

	Departments		
	Production A	Production B	Service C
Direct labour hours	6 500	7 100	1 875
Machine hours	950	850	465
Number of employees	21	27	6
Value of machinery	R31 000	R28 000	R19 000
Floor area	1 300 m^2	1 100 m^2	300 m^2
Material usage	R74 000	R29 000	R13 000

The following amounts represent the budgeted manufacturing overheads for 19.1:

	R
Insurance	
Buildings	10 800
Machinery	3 120
Cafeteria	4 698
Depreciation on machinery	11 700
Maintenance of buildings	9 450
Cost of stock piling	4 640
Protective overalls	1 458
Heating of factory building	2 025
Indirect material	
Production A	731
Production B	1 966
Service C	811

Machine hours are used as a basis for the secondary allocation of the service department.

Required:

Calculate the allocation rate for each of the production departments based on direct labour hours.

Solution

Overhead allocation statement

Cost item	Basis	Total	Departments		
			Production A	Production B	Service C
		R	R	R	R
Primary allocation:					
Building insurance (Note 1)	Area	10 800	5 200	4 400	1 200
Machinery insurance	Value	3 120	1 240	1 120	760
Cafeteria	Employees	4 698	1 827	2 349	522
Depreciation	Value	11 700	4 650	4 200	2 850
Building maintenance	Area	9 450	4 550	3 850	1 050
Stock piling	Material	4 640	2 960	1 160	520
Protective overalls	Employees	1 458	567	729	162
Heating – building	Area	2 025	975	825	225
Indirect material	Given	3 508	731	1 966	811
		51 399	22 700	20 599	8 100
Secondary allocation:	Machine hours	–	4 275	3 825	(8 100)
Total allocated overheads		51 399	26 975	24 424	–

Calculation of application rate

$$\text{Production A} : \frac{\text{Allocated overheads}}{\text{Labour hours}}$$

$$= \frac{\text{R26 975}}{6\ 500}$$

$$= \text{R4,15 per labour hour}$$

$$\text{Production B} : \frac{\text{Allocated overheads}}{\text{Labour hours}}$$

$$= \frac{\text{R24 424}}{7\ 100}$$

$$= \text{R3,44 per labour hour}$$

Note 1: Division of insurance costs in respect of buildings

Basis:　Floor area

Ratio:　$1\ 300\ m^2\ :\ 1\ 100\ m^2\ :\ 300\ m^2$

Production A:
$$\frac{1\ 300}{1\ 300\ +\ 1\ 100\ +\ 300} \times R10\ 800$$
$$=\ \frac{1\ 300}{2\ 700} \times R10\ 800$$
$$=\ R5\ 200$$

Production B:
$$\frac{1\ 100}{1\ 300\ +\ 1\ 100\ +\ 300} \times R10\ 800$$
$$=\ \frac{1\ 100}{2\ 700} \times R10\ 800$$
$$=\ R4\ 400$$

Service C:
$$\frac{300}{1\ 300\ +\ 1\ 100\ +\ 300} \times R10\ 800$$
$$=\ \frac{300}{2\ 700} \times R10\ 800$$
$$=\ R1\ 200$$

An alternative method for the secondary allocation of the costs of the service departments, called the **repeated allocation method**, is still acknowledged by some European writers but seldom applied in practice in South Africa.

The method implies that the costs of each service department are also allocated to all the other service departments. The service departments are thus not immediately closed off in this method of allocation because the costs of the other sevice departments are again divided among the relevant service departments. Because a large portion of the costs is also allocated to the production departments each time, the costs of the service departments reduce with each allocation until eventually a paltry amount which can be ignored remains. Example 16 illustrates the application of the secondary allocation method.

Example 16

Primary allocation of overheads:

	R
Production departments	
P1	6 408
P2	7 125
P3	4 895
Service departments	
D1	4 405
D2	4 690

Secondary allocation basis:

P1	35%
P2	30%
P3	20%
D1	10%
D2	5%

Solution

	P1	P2	P3	D1	D2
Allocation basis	35%	30%	20%	10%	5%
Primary allocation	6 408	7 125	4 895	4 405	4 690
Secondary allocation					
First allocation	1 728	1 481	987	494	(4 690)
	1 905	1 633	1 089	(4 899)	272
First repetition	100	86	57	29	(272)
	11	10	6	(29)	2
Second repetition	1	1			(2)
	10 153	10 336	7 034	–	–

7 Summary

A clear distinction between the concepts budgeted overheads, applied overheads and actual overheads is necessary because if it is not made a great deal of confusion may arise. The accurate establishment of the predetermined allocation rate for overheads can mean the difference between success and failure for the enterprise. Too often in times of high inflation it happens that the predetermined overhead rates do not keep pace with increases in costs and the selling price which is based thereon does not provide sufficient income to cover all the costs. Nothing is more burdensome for management than to find out at the end of an expected successful year that there is a substantial under-recovery of overheads which must be indirectly written off against the profits and which turns the potentially good results into a fiasco.

5

MARKETING COSTS

1 Introduction

Marketing costs, as a component of commercial costs, include all the costs arising from the acquisition of orders up to the delivery of the finished goods.

In contrast to manufacturing costs, marketing costs are neglected in most business enterprises. The classification, division, planning and control of costs is actually just as important for marketing as for manufacturing overheads.

2 Classification of marketing costs

Diagram D15 illustrates the basic classifications of marketing costs.

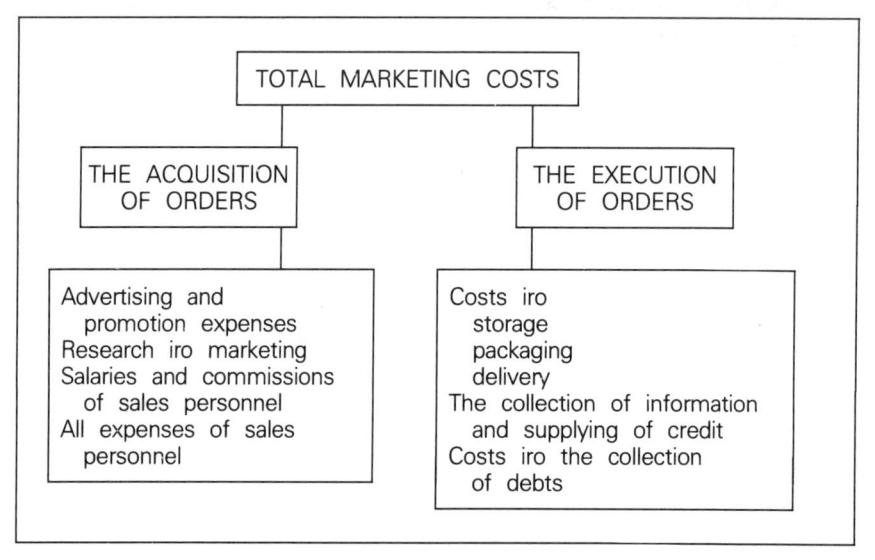

Diagram D15

It is important to divide each of the items given into its fixed and variable elements so that management may have effective control over them.

3 Bases for apportionment

The sort of product, the type of marketing costs and the nature of the enterprise will determine the basis for apportionment of each type of marketing cost. A number of typical apportionment bases are illustrated in Diagram D16.

Type of cost	Basis of apportionment
Direct selling expenses Salaries of sales personnel Commissions of sales personnel Bonuses of sales personnel Sales management expenses	Selling value of product

Administrative expenses
Salaries and office expenses
Expenses iro accounts section
Other expenses
	Number of sales invoices
	Number of sales invoices
	Sales value of each product or
	  number of orders received
	  for each product

Advertising expenses Salaries and office expenses General advertising expenses Product advertising Samples	Sales value of product Sales value of product Directly to product Specific costs of each product sample

Storage
Salaries of personnel
Depreciation
Material supplied
Insurance
 	
Packaging costs
	Number of units sold or ratio
	  of weight of product to
	  total handled
	Average value of each product
	  on hand
	Number of units sold

Transport costs
Freight-out
Salaries of sales department
Delivery costs
	Sales value of product or
	  weight of product or ratio of
	  size of product weighted to
	  quantity sold

Expenses iro credit provision and collection of debt Salaries Indirect material Hire Legal costs Uncollectable debts	Sales value of product Number of accounts and products sold to each

Diagram D16

4 Planning and control

Like manufacturing overheads, marketing costs require an effective system of planning and control. The aim in manufacturing is to keep the manufacturing costs as low as possible so that maximum profits can be achieved. This principle must be applied very carefully with regard to marketing costs, since a cut in certain marketing costs can give rise to lower sales in the long term.

In order to plan and control marketing costs effectively three methods of analysis, which are illustrated briefly below, may be used:

☐ Per product
☐ Per area
☐ Per size of order

☐ Products

In this method marketing costs are allocated to the various products that are marketed. An example of this is storage costs, which are allocated to the various products according to the space utilised by each product.

Example 17

The following information relates to Masters Limited, which manufactures and markets product M and L:

	R
Sales: M 600 000 units @ R2 each	
L 400 000 units @ R3 each	
Cost of sales: M	900 000
L	800 000
Advertising expenditure (M 60%; L 40%)	50 000
Selling costs	60 000
Storage costs	18 000
Delivery costs	15 000
Packaging costs	30 000
Sales office expenses	60 000
Direct selling expenses	15 000

Additional information:

(i) Storage space: m^2 per R100 of sales:

      M 4

      L 5

(ii) Number of orders executed:

      M 30 000

      L 10 000

(iii) Delivery costs:

      M 45%

      L 55%

Required

Calculate the net income of products M and L separately.

Solution

Income statement

	Basis	Total	M	L
		R	R	R
Sales:		2 400 000		
600 000 × R2			1 200 000	
400 000 × R3				1 200 000
Less: Cost of sales		1 700 000	900 000	800 000
Gross profit		700 000	300 000	400 000
Less: Marketing costs		248 000	145 250	102 750
Advertising	60%/40%	50 000	30 000	20 000
Selling costs	Value [1]	60 000	30 000	30 000
Storage costs*	4 : 5	18 000	8 000	10 000
Delivery costs	45%/55%	15 000	6 750	8 250
Packaging costs	Units [2]	30 000	18 000	12 000
Sales office	Orders [3]	60 000	45 000	15 000
Selling expenses	Value [1]	15 000	7 500	7 500
Net income		452 000	154 750	297 250

*Calculation of basis
    Product M (R1 200 000 ÷ R100) × 4 = 48 000
    Product L (R1 200 000 ÷ R100) × 5 = 60 000
Because the turnover of M and L is the same, the ratio remains 4 : 5

□ Areas

This method apportions marketing costs according to areas to enable management to identify the non-profitable areas.

[1] In proportion to total sales value
[2] In proportion to number of units sold
[3] In proportion to number of orders

Example 18

Spreaders Limited manufactures and markets one type of product in three different areas. The following information, taken from the previous accounting period, is available:

Area	Sales	Cost of sales
	R	R
Brits	400 000	210 000
Ceres	300 000	160 000
Parys	110 000	60 000

Marketing costs:
Sales personnel	
– Salaries	40 000
– Commissions	40 500
Advertising	61 200
Storage and transport	32 400
Sales office expenses	15 000
Administrative	60 750
Packaging	10 000

Additional information:

(i) Direct advertising costs are allocated as follows: R

Brits	20 000
Ceres	10 000
Parys	15 000

(ii) Number of orders handled

Brits	400
Ceres	300
Parys	500

(iii) Number of units sold

Brits	200 000
Ceres	150 000
Parys	50 000

(iv) Four commercial travellers, each of whom receive the same salary plus 5% commission on all sales, are employed and grouped as follows:

Brits	2
Ceres	1
Parys	1

Required

Calculate the net income for each area separately.

Solution

Income statement

	Basis	Total	Brits	Ceres	Parys
		R	R	R	R
Sales		810 000	400 000	300 000	110 000
Less: Cost of sales		430 000	210 000	160 000	60 000
Gross profit		380 000	190 000	140 000	50 000
Less: Marketing costs		259 850	124 000	83 000	52 850
Personnel					
– Salaries	2:1:1	40 000	20 000	10 000	10 000
– Commissions	5%	40 500	20 000	15 000	5 500
Advertising					
– Direct	Given	45 000	20 000	10 000	15 000
– General	Value	16 200	8 000	6 000	2 200
Storage	Value	32 400	16 000	12 000	4 400
Sales office	*	15 000	5 000	3 750	6 250
Admin.	Value	60 750	30 000	22 500	8 250
Packaging	Units	10 000	5 000	3 750	1 250
Net income		120 150	66 000	57 000	(2 850)

(*Number of orders)

☐ Size of orders

An analysis of marketing costs according to the size of orders will show, as a rule, that small orders generally contribute a negative amount to net income.

Example 19

The cost accountant of an enterprise which makes frozen food allocated the enterprise's marketing costs on the following basis and also made an analysis of the size of the orders:

Allocation of marketing costs

Marketing costs	Total	Number of orders	Number of items	Mass kg
	R	R	R	R
Sales costs	5 000	2 500	1 500	1 000
Packaging	2 200	700	500	1 000
Administrative	4 600	2 500	1 600	500
Sundries	1 100	300	600	200
	12 900	6 000	4 200	2 700

Size of orders

	Number of orders	Number of items	Mass kg
Under 50 kg	4 000	4 000	20 000
50 – 199 kg	3 000	8 000	70 000
200 – 499 kg	500	2 000	15 000
	7 500	14 000	105 000

Required

An allocation of marketing costs per kg of frozen food for each group of order.

Calculations

ALLOCATION OF MARKETING COSTS

SIZE	ORDERS			NUMBER OF ITEMS			MASS – KG		
	NUMBER	COST PER ORDER	TOTAL	NUMBER	COST PER ITEM	TOTAL	KG	COST PER KG	TOTAL
Under 50 kg	4 000	R 0,80	R 3 200	4 000	R 0,30	R 1 200	20 000	R 0,0257	R 514
50–199 kg	3 000	0,80	2 400	8 000	0,30	2 400	70 000	0,0257	1 800
200–499 kg	500	0,80	400	2 000	0,30	600	15 000	0,0257	386
	7 500	0,80[1]	6 000	14 000	0,30[2]	4 200	105 000	0,0257[3]	2 700

[1] Cost per order $= \dfrac{R6\ 000}{7\ 500}$

$= R0,80$

[2] Cost per item $= \dfrac{R4\ 200}{14\ 000}$

$= R0,30$

[3] Cost per kg $= \dfrac{R2\ 700}{105\ 000}$

$= R0,0257$

Solution

ALLOCATION OF MARKETING COSTS STATEMENT

	TOTAL KG	ORDERS		ITEMS		MASS – KG		TOTAL	
		Amount	Cost per kg	Amount	Cost per kg	Amount	Cost per kg	Amount	Cost per kg
		R	R	R	R	R	R	R	R
Under 50 kg	20 000	3 200	0,160	1 200	0,060	514	0,0257	4 914	0,2457
50–199 kg	70 000	2 400	0,343	2 400	0,034	1 800	0,0257	6 600	0,0943
200–499 kg	15 000	400	0,267	600	0,040	386	0,0257	1 386	0,0924
	105 000	6 000		4 200		2 700		12 900	

5 Summary

The increasing importance of marketing costs gave rise to the marketing management concept. The marketing manager must manage his department in an effective manner so as to contribute to the increased efficiency of the concern. Control over marketing costs must be handled carefully so that savings and curtailments do not take place at the cost of effectiveness.

6

THE MANUFACTURING FACILITY
AND COST FLOWS

The manufacturing facility

1 Introduction

Now that the various cost elements to be found in a manufacturing situation have been introduced, it is time to pay attention to the manufacturing process itself.

Before manufacturing can be discussed it is necessary that the four **production factors,** namely capital, labour, raw materials and entrepreneurship, are yoked together to form a harmonious whole which aims at carrying out an economic actitivy.

Raw materials and labour have already been discussed. By **entrepreneur** is meant the person or organisation who takes the initiative to plan and bring about the manufacturing facilities and to set them in motion. In short, we can view entrepreneurship as the driving force behind the creation of manufacturing facilities.

Capital refers to the funds required first, to bring about the manufacturing facilities and second, to set these facilities in motion. It includes, *inter alia,* the following:

☐ Initiating capital: Research
Patents
Manufacturing rights
Set-up costs, etc

☐ Investment of capital: Land and buildings
Machinery and equipment

☐ Working capital: Stock
Cash resources

Only when all four of these production factors are present and yoked together to form a harmonious whole can the manufacturing process begin.

2 Planning

However, to combine these production factors into an economically viable unit requires considerable research and planning including, *inter alia,* the following:

2.1 Establishment

The very important decision as to where the facility is to be established must be taken right at the beginning of the planning phase, and should take the following factors into consideration:

☐ The existing infrastructure of the area (transport network, roads, post of-fice, telephones, etc)

☐ The availability of raw materials, the distance the raw materials have to be transported to the premises, the method of transport, the cost thereof, etc

☐ The availability of manpower, especially if the enterprise is to be labour intensive

☐ The market – how far the finished product has to be transported to the market, etc

☐ Logistics (here the maintenance of the machinery and equipment is especially important)

Seen from the management accountant's point of view, the cost aspects of the decision regarding the location of the manufacturing facility are very important. Already at this early stage thought must be given to the cost effectiveness of the enterprise and an attempt must be made to create an atmosphere in which this can be maximised.

2.2 Factory layout

The initial planning of the layout of the factory is very important, especially since later changes are usually associated with higher costs and inefficient planning gives rise to unnecessary working costs. In particular, the unnecessary transporting to and fro of material and products, the time wasted if employees have to move around too much, and the time taken whenever there is a delay between processes must be kept to a minimum.

Diagram D17 shows a schematic representation of a properly planned factory layout:

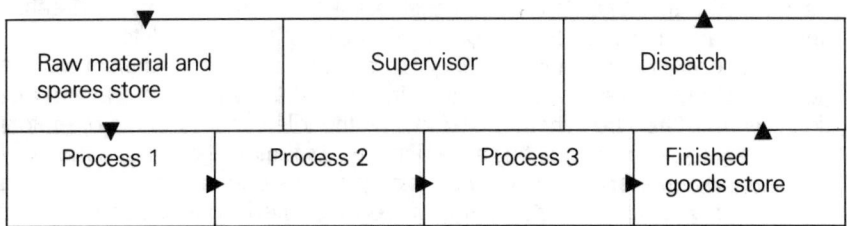

Diagram D17

2.3 The production line

Proper research must be done to determine which machines are suited to the purpose for which the enterprise requires them. Especially important are the capacity and the working costs of each machine, as well as the quality of work that can be done by the machines. Further attention is given to these aspects in Chapter 14.

The production line must be designed so that the capacities of the machines in successive processes are synchronised so that no idle capacity exists or it is kept to a minimum.

The schematic explanation in Diagram D18 gives an indication of how machines can be arranged to give a synchronised production line capable of manufacturing up to 200 units per hour. Four processes are assumed and the figures in the blocks, which represent the machines, indicate the capacity of each machine.

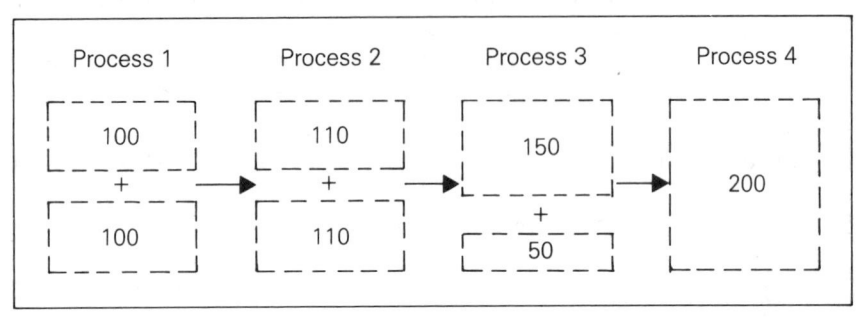

Diagram D18

The required capacity that must be maintained is 200 units per hour, of which each process is capable. Process 2 has a capacity of 220 units per hour, which means that an idle capacity of 20 units per hour exists. If the costs in respect of this idle capacity are unavoidable, for example because there is no machine on the market that can produce exactly 200 units more economically, it must be accepted and not shown as a waste.

2.4 Labour

While still in the planning phase attention must be given to the labour factor. Important questions for which answers must be obtained are the number of employees required, the degree of skill required of the employees, the training of employees, etc. It is very important that in planning the labour force management always takes into consideration the fact that it is dealing with the human factor and that it cannot be treated in the same manner as, for example, machines. Therefore rest breaks, change of work, recreation amenities and human needs, amongst others, must be looked into.

But, just as the machines on the production line are synchronised, the number of employees (or rather machine operators who serve the production line) must also be synchronised to limit the idle capacity of the operators to a minimum. The possibilities are unlimited, but once again the human factor must be taken into account. For example, one operator could be given the task of serving two machines provided that the fatigue factor is not too high. Or, as an alternative, the operator could carry out another less fatiguing task, for example a quality control check, at the same time. However, the question remains whether a better-trained operator could not take care of both machines simultaneously.

Seen from a management accountant's point of view, the efficient employment of labour is of great importance. Is every employee employed to his fullest potential and does every employee work to the best of his ability?

It must also be remembered that, to a large extent, the output of the employee is dependent on the machinery and equipment with which he is working and the raw materials being used. If something goes wrong with the machine it usually means that the employee is also not able to function. Poor quality raw materials could mean that the employee is delayed in doing his job. Thus, management must ensure that the machinery and equipment are properly maintained and that good controls are exercised over the quality of raw materials.

2.5 Material (raw material)

The availability of materials is important, but attention must also be given to the types of materials that are going to be used. Especially important are the quality of the material, the stage of processing, the choice between alternative raw materials, and so on. The quality of the end product produced depends to a large extent on the type of raw material used.

3 The manufacturing process

If proper planning is done with regard to the foregoing aspects a production facility capable of the effective manufacturing of a product or products should exist.

One of the important management functions is the **scheduling** of the production process. In summary this can be described as the bringing together of the raw material, the employee and the machine, in sufficient quantities and at the required stage, with the necessary controls, so that each one of the factors is utilised to its fullest potential and a full-fledged final product is manufactured.

A further important aspect is that no manufacturing process is static. There is constant development, either internally in an effort to make the process more economical or externally in the form of new developments in machinery or other production aids, or techniques. Management must guard against stagnating when a workable combination is found and try to keep at the forefront of new developments and techniques.

There are various techniques that management can use in its endeavour not to stagnate. Time and motion studies can be carried out to ensure the effective employment of labour, research into raw materials can be done to determine whether alternative raw materials which can lead to better products and/or production methods are available, etc.

4 Control

Notwithstanding the planning and scheduling functions of management, control forms an important facet of the overall management function. In the previous and also in the following chapters this aspect is discussed at length. Here it is merely emphasised that it is a very important management function.

From the management accountant's point of view it is especially important that all costs incurred are incurred for a purpose. Any expense or waste that is avoidable and not necessary for the continuation of the manufacturing process must be classified as a waste and should be shown directly in the income statement as a loss rather than being classified as a cost and appearing in the cost statement as such.

Therefore it is also important that the management accountant exercises continuous control over the manufacturing process to ensure that any waste, whether material, man hours or any other item, is kept to a minimum if it cannot be eliminated completely.

One form of control that management can hardly neglect to carry out properly is over the quality of the products that are manufactured. It is preferable that an independent person or a division not directly concerned with manufacturing performs quality control.

Quality control is especially important for two reasons; first, to prevent production factors being wasted in the manufacturing of an inferior product, and second, to prevent an inferior product being marketed and damaging the enterprise's reputation.

Quality control should be carried out on a continuous basis and findings should be made known to all levels of management, as well as to the employees themselves where the findings affect them. Preventative action must be instituted as quickly as possible to avoid the repetition of poor results.

To sum up, it can be said that the manufacturing process is the pivot around which any manufacturing enterprise turns. Further, it spreads to all sectors such as the trading enterprises which market the product and the users who ultimately purchase the product. Thus the importance thereof cannot be overemphasised and must not be neglected by any enterprise.

Cost flows in a manufacturing enterprise

1 The flow of activities in a manufacturing enterprise

To determine the cost of goods manufacturing (finished goods) you must:
- [ ] have a knowledge of what product costs in a manufacturing enterprise consist of
- [ ] gain some understanding of the flow of costs through such an enterprise.

The elements of product costs, namely direct material, direct labour and manufacturing overheads, have already been dealt with in chapters 2, 3 and 4. In this module the basic accounting procedures necessary for recording the costs are explained.

A manufacturing enterprise's cost calculation system and product cost accounting should be logical and run parallel to the sequence of the activities in the enterprise. The following activities are typical of any manufacturing enterprise:

- [ ] **Procurement** Raw materials (direct material) and consumable stocks (indirect material) necessary for the manufacturing process are ordered, received and stored.
- [ ] **Direct** and **indirect labour** is obtained.
- [ ] **Production** (assimilation or manufacturing) Raw materials are transferred from the storage room to the production process and are transformed by means of the employment of labour, machinery and equipment.
- [ ] **Storage** Finished goods are transferred from the production floor to storage areas in the expectation of the sale thereof.
- [ ] **Sales** The finishing goods are sold to clients and dispatched to them. In the accounting section the client is invoiced for the goods at the selling price.

2 Accounting procedures in a manufacturing enterprise

As costs are incurred in each of the above activities in a manufacturing enterprise the costs of the particular activities are recorded and transferred to the next section in accordance with the progression of the manufacturing activities. Therefore provision must be made for recording the costs in appropriate accounts.

☐ **Procurement**

Accounts aim to place on record the purchasing and costs of material, labour and overheads. The relevant costs are accumulated in these accounts until they are transferred to the production or assimilation process.

Accounts typically employed for this purpose are raw material (material) control accounts, direct labour and manufacturing overheads control accounts.

☐ **Production**

A production account is used to accumulate the manufacturing costs as they enter the manufacturing process.

☐ **Storage**

A finished goods account is used to collect the costs of the goods that have been completed.

☐ **Sales**

A cost of goods sold account (cost of sales account) is used to place on record the **costs** of the goods that are sold. The usual accounts, debtors and sales, are used in the last instance to place on record the **selling price** of the same goods.

3 Cost flows

The establishment of the above cost accounts makes it possible to place on record the costs corresponding to the successive activities of procurement, production, storage and sales. In this regard there is reference to the flow of costs through the system.

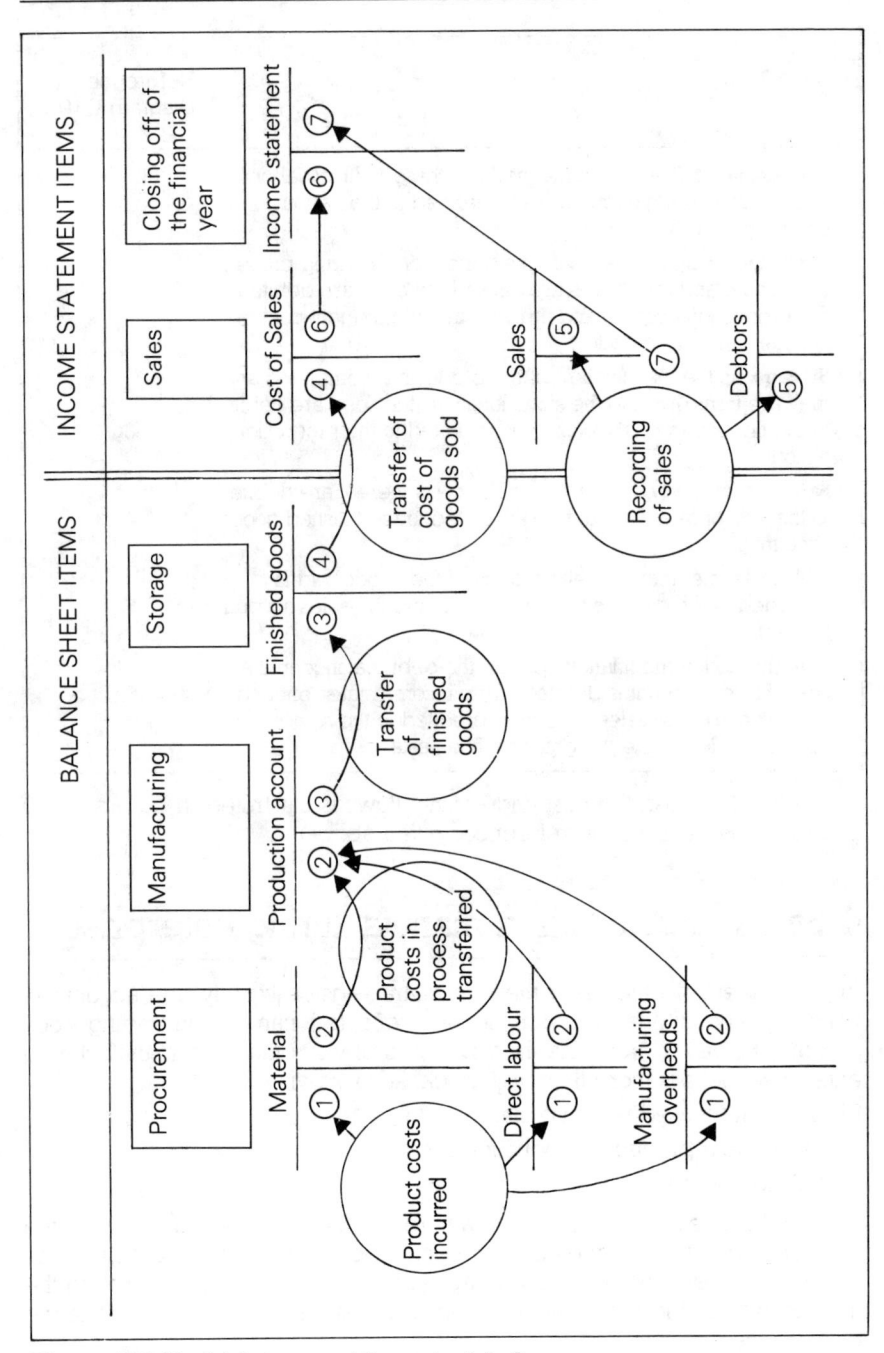

Diagram D19 The link between cost flow and activity flow

	Reference to Diagram D19
Procurement The cost of material purchased, direct labour and manufacturing overheads are debited to the various control accounts.	1
Manufacturing As material enters the manufacturing process and labour and overheads are utilised the costs are debited to the production account and the various procurement control accounts in 1 are credited.	2
Storage As the manufacture of the products is completed and they are transferred to the stock locations the costs are debited to the finished goods account and credited to the production account.	3
Sales As finished goods are sold the costs thereof are debited to the cost of sales account and credited to the finished goods account.	4
At the same time the selling price of the goods sold is recorded in the debtors account (debit) and the sales account (credit).	5
At the end of the financial period the debit balance in the cost of sales account is debited to the income statement and the balance of the sales account is credited to the same account to determine the gross profit on sales.	6
	7

The link between the cost and activity flows is illustrated in Diagram D19 (in this connection use the references given above).

4 Stock accounts in a manufacturing enterprise

In a commercial enterprise there is characteristically only one account in which the cost of unsold merchandise is reflected, namely the trading stock account. However, from Diagram D19 it is obvious that in a manufacturing enterprise there is more than one "stock" account, viz

☐ material (unused raw material)
☐ incomplete products (production account)
☐ finished goods.

Thus the relevant cost accounts are really also stock accounts, or, in the case of labour and overheads, cost control accounts. To the extent that the amounts in these various accounts are debited and not yet transferred to the next account in the cost flow, they represent **assets** which are shown in the balance sheet at cost.

The balance sheet and the income statement items are also identified in Diagram D19.

The elements that were identified in the previous paragraphs are clearly illustrated in Example 20.

Example 20

On 1 January 19.3 ZAL Manufacturers Limited had opening stock valued at R40 000, R20 000 and R60 000 in their material control, production and finished goods accounts respectively. There were no debtors or creditors on that date.

The following is a summary of the transactions and activities of the firm during January 19.3.

1 Direct material costing R100 000 was purchased on credit
2 Direct material costing R120 000 was issued to the production division
3 The salaries and wages of the factory personnel amounted to R50 000 for the month and consisted of the following:

Direct labour	R30 000
Indirect labour	R20 000

4 Depreciation of machinery and equipment for January 19.3 was R20 000
5 Other indirect manufacturing expenses amounted to R30 000 and were settled in cash
6 The total manufacturing overheads and direct labour costs incurred were absorbed in the production process
7 Products with a manufacturing cost of R200 000 were transferred to finished goods
8 Products with a cost of sales which amounted to R130 000 were sold during the month on credit for R280 000 (journal entries 8 and 9)

Journalisation of the above transactions	R	R
1 Direct material control account	100 000	
Creditors		100 000
2 Production account	120 000	
Direct material control account		120 000
3 Direct labour	30 000	
Overheads control account (indirect labour)	20 000	
Pay statement		50 000
Pay statement	50 000	
Bank		50 000
4 Overheads control account (depreciation)	20 000	
Accumulated depreciation		20 000
5 Overheads control account (indirect production costs)	30 000	
Bank		30 000
6 Production account	100 000	
Direct labour		30 000
Overheads control account		70 000
7 Finished goods account	200 000	
Production account		200 000
8 Cost of sales	130 000	
Finished goods		130 000
9 Debtors	280 000	
Sales		280 000

Ledger accounts

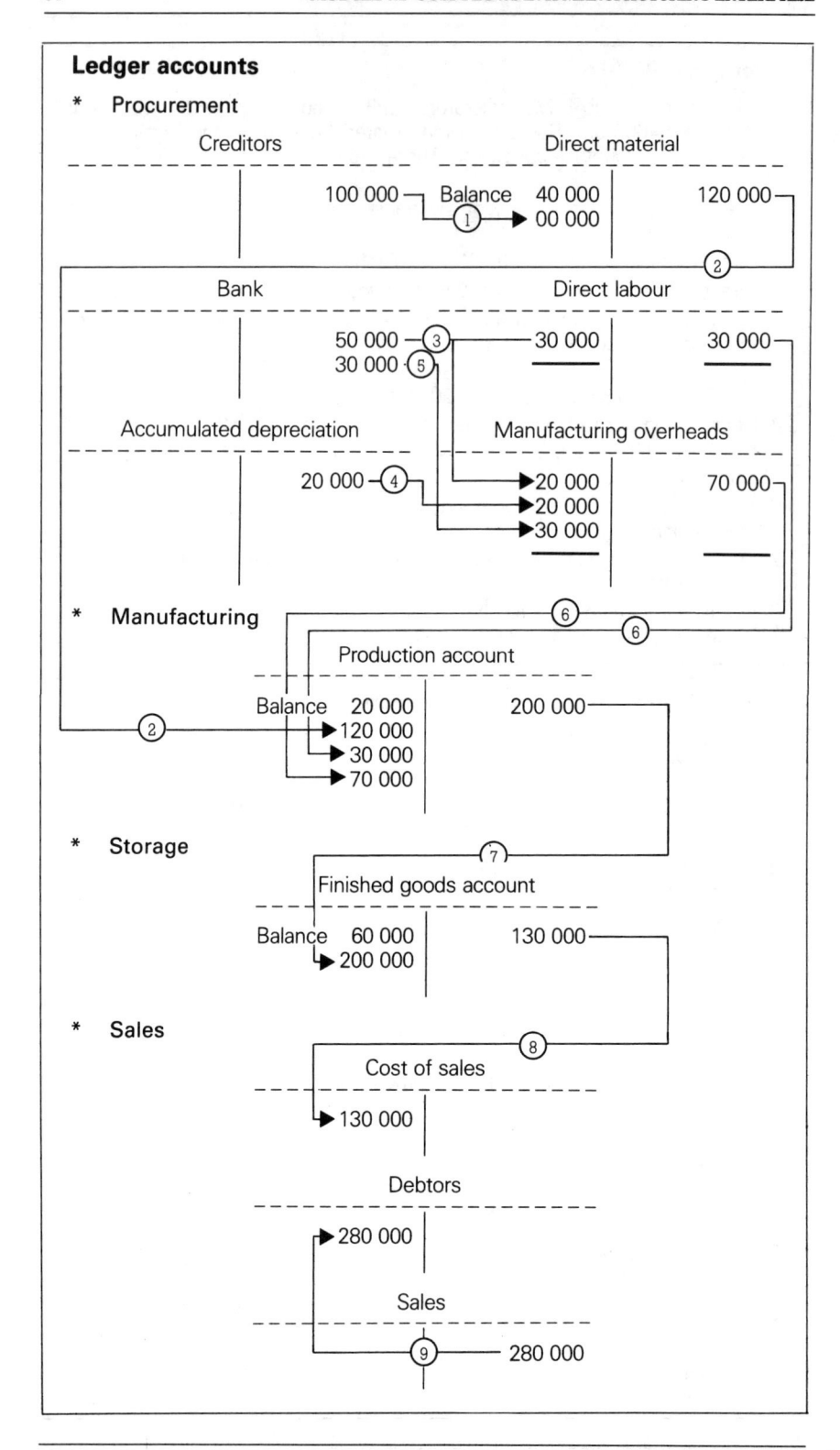

* Procurement
* Manufacturing
* Storage
* Sales

From the above it is evident that the balances on the various stock accounts will be as follows:

			R
Direct material	(40 000 + 100 000 − 120 000)	=	20 000
Incomplete work	(20 000 + 120 000 + 30 000 + 70 000 − 200 000)	=	40 000
Finished goods	(60 000 + 200 000 − 130 000)	=	130 000

This stock will be shown on the balance sheet of the enterprise on 31 January 19.3 as closing stock on hand.

5 The income statement of a manufacturing enterprise

Whereas a trading enterprise purchases completed goods for resale, in a manufacturing concern material and other sources are used to convert raw materials to complete goods. Therefore the income statement of the manufacturing enterprise must, as a matter of course, contain all the details of the manufacturing costs and the stock accounts. With reference to Example 20, the income statement of ZAL Manufacturers can be compiled as shown.

ZAL MANUFACTURERS LIMITED
Income statement for the month ended 31 January 19.3

	R
Sales	280 000
Less: Cost of sales	130 000
Stock of incomplete work (beginning)	20 000
Cost of material used	120 000
Material on hand (beginning)	40 000
Purchases	100 000
Cost of material available	140 000
Less: Material on hand (closing)	20 000
Direct labour	30 000
Manufacturing overheads	70 000
Indirect labour	20 000
Depreciation	20 000
Indirect production costs	30 000
Total manufacturing costs	240 000
Less: Stock of incomplete work (closing)	40 000
Cost of goods transferred to finished goods	200 000
Add: Stock of finished goods (beginning)	60 000
Finished goods available for sale	260 000
Less: Stock of finished goods (ending)	130 000
Gross profit	150 000
Less: Administrative and sales expenses	?
Net income before taxation	?

Care must be taken in the presentation of the information, which should be such that it is easy to read and analyse. Unnecessary information must be kept to the minimum, but no essential data must be left out.

The information given must be **logical** and **understandable,** prepared with the needs of the users thereof in mind. Information that can be given to one user might not be suitable for the next user.

Seeing that cost statements are often prepared for interim periods – especially for control purposes – it will inevitably happen that the manufacturing overheads allocated must sometimes be used because the actual manufacturing overheads for the period are not yet known. The use of the term "... at normal" for example "**manufacturing costs at normal**", indicates that allocated manufacturing overheads and not the actual manufacturing costs are used for the calculation of the total manufacturing costs. Whenever **actual manufacturing overheads** are used this is indicated by coupling the terms "... **at actual**" with the cost.

Marketing and administrative overheads are still shown directly in the income statement.

6 Columnar form of cost and income statement

Example 21 illustrates the use of applied and actual manufacturing overheads on a columnar form cost worksheet.

Example 21

The following information is available:

	1 July 19.2	31 Dec. 19.2
	R	R
Stock levels		
Material	28 000	34 000
Incomplete work	21 000	27 000
Finished goods	35 000	43 000
Costs for the period		R
Material purchased (including indirect material)		120 000
Direct labour		150 000
Indirect labour		15 000
Indirect material used		6 000
Administrative costs		40 000
Marketing costs		30 000
Supervisory wages		12 000
Hire of factory premises		24 000
Depreciation of machinery		38 000
Turnover for the period		469 000

Manufacturing overheads are applied at 60% of direct labour.

Required

Prepare a cost and income statement for the period.

Solution

Cost statement for the six months ended 31 December 19.2

	Calculation	Cost	Incomplete work	Finished goods
	R	R	R	R
Opening stock				
Finished goods				35 000
Incomplete work			21 000	
Direct material		108 000		
Opening stock	28 000			
Add: Purchases	120 000			
Available	148 000			
Less: Closing stock	34 000			
Total usage	114 000			
Indirect material	6 000			
Direct labour		150 000		
Applied overheads		90 000		
Manufacturing overheads @ normal			348 000	
			369 000	
Less: Closing stock of incomplete work			27 000	
Cost of units completed during the period @ normal				342 000
Available for sale @ normal				377 000
Less: Closing stock of finished goods				43 000
Cost of sales @ normal				334 000
Add: Underapplied overheads				5 000
Cost of sales @ actual				339 000

(continued)

Calculation 1

	R
Actual manufacturing overheads:	
Indirect labour	15 000
Indirect material	6 000
Supervisory wages	12 000
Hire of factory premises	24 000
Depreciation of machines	38 000
Actual manufacturing overheads	95 000
Less: Applied manufacturing overheads	90 000
Underapplied manufacturing overheads	5 000

Income statement for the six months ended 31 December 19.2

		R
Sales		469 000
Less: Cost of sales		339 000
Gross profit		130 000
Less: Sundry expenses		70 000
Administrative costs	40 000	
Marketing costs	30 000	
Net profit		60 000

The recovery of fixed costs:
direct and absorption costing

1 Introduction

The recovery of fixed costs creates a problem for management in the sense that it must decide which method of recovery to use. The decision is a very important one because it can have an influence on the net income of the enterprise, especially in the short term.

It must be emphasised that the manner in which fixed costs are recovered does not influence the amount of the fixed costs, but only the way in which and when it is reflected in the financial statements. It does have an influence, in the short term, on net income, but because all fixed costs must be recovered in the long term this effect will eventually be neutralised.

Direct costing (marginal costing) and absorption costing are the two methods used most generally. They differ in that:

☐ with **direct costing** fixed costs are recovered on the basis of the **number of units sold** during the period

☐ and with **absorption costing** fixed costs are recovered on the basis of the **number of units manufactured** during the period.

2 The application of direct and absorption costing

It is obvious that the net income for a certain period can differ for the two methods because there is usually a time difference between the manufacturing action and the selling action of the product or production. A logical conclusion is that if the full production is manufactured and sold in the same period there will be no difference in the net income obtained by the two methods. Only if the full production is not sold during the same reporting period will there be a difference, but the difference between the two methods is still reconcilable if closing stock is brought into account.

This aspect is illustrated in the following simple example:

Example 22

Units manufactured during 19.1	1 000
Units sold during 19.1	900
Variable costs per unit	R5
Fixed costs for the year	R6 000
Selling price per unit	R15

When the direct costing method is used the fixed costs are recovered by the 900 units sold.

Income statement using direct costing

	Calculation	R
Sales	900 × R15	13 500
Less: Variable costs	900 × R5	4 500
Marginal income		9 000
Less: Fixed cost		6 000
Net income		3 000

The closing stock of 100 units is valued at the variable cost of R5 per unit, and thus is R500 in total.

When absorption costing is used the fixed costs are recovered by the 1 000 units manufactured.

Income statement using absorption costing

	Calculation	R
Sales	900 × R15	13 500
Less: Manufacturing costs		9 900
– Variable	900 × R5	4 500
– Fixed	900 × R6*	5 400
Net income for the year		3 600

* Calculation of fixed costs: R6 000 ÷ 1 000 units
= R6 unit manufactured

When this method is used the closing stock has a higher value because it includes fixed costs.

		R
Variable costs	100 × R5	500
Fixed costs	100 × R6	600
Closing stock		1 100

The differences between the two methods can be explained as follows:

	Direct costs	Absorption costs	Difference
	R	R	R
Net income	3 000	3 600	(600)
Closing stock	500	1 100	600

When direct costing is used the fixed costs of R6 000 are borne by the 900 units sold, while when absorption costing is used they are borne by the 1 000 units manufactured.

When direct costing is used the fixed costs are written off against sales in full during the period in which they occurred, while when absorption costing is used they are partially "carried over" to the next period because an amount of fixed costs is, by implication, in the closing stock.

As has already been mentioned, these differences are largely neutralised in the long term, since what is in closing stock at the end of the year is usually sold during the following year. Compare the following example with the previous one:

Units manufactured during 19.2	900
Units sold during 19.2	1 000
Selling prices and costs remain the same.	

Income statement using direct costing

		R
Sales	1 000 × R15	15 000
Less: Variable costs		5 000
– Opening stock	100 × R5	500
– Production	900 × R5	4 500
Marginal income		10 000
Less: Fixed costs		6 000
Net income		4 000

Income statement using absorption costing		
		R
Sales	1 000 × R15	15 000
Less: Cost of sales		11 600
– Opening stock	100 × R11	1 100
– Variable costs	900 × R5	4 500
– Fixed costs		6 000
Net income for the year		3 400

The difference between the two methods is neutralised as follows:

	Direct costs R	Absorption costs R
Net income 19.1	3 000	3 600
Net income 19.2	4 000	3 400
Total for the two years	7 000	7 000

Thus, if more units are produced than sold the net income will be higher for absorption costing than for direct costing, and vice versa. The cost statement is further complicated by the use of standard recovery tariffs, but this aspect is explained in chapter 12 on standard costs.

For management purposes it is necessary that total costs are analysed further. Where possible, selling and administrative costs must be divided into their fixed and variable elements.

Diagram D20 shows how the cost elements that are divided into fixed and variable elements are handled by both methods:

Direct costing	Absorption costing

Sales
Less: Variable costs
 	
    Direct material
    Direct labour
    Variable costs
       Manufacturing overheads
       Selling costs
       Administrative costs
 	
  = Marginal income
 	
Less: Fixed costs
 	
    Manufacturing overheads
    Selling costs
    Administrative costs
 	
  = Net income
	Sales
	Less: Manufacturing costs
	
	    Direct material
	    Direct labour
	    Manufacturing overheads
	       Variable
	       Fixed
	
	  = Gross profit
	
	Less: Sundry costs
	
	    Selling costs (total)
	    Administrative costs
	    (total)
	
	  = Net income

Diagram D20

7

PRODUCT ORIENTATED
COST SYSTEMS

Job costing system (piecework system)

1 Introduction

This module is the first in a number of successive modules on the systems of product cost determination. The most important aim of product cost determination is the establishment of **unit manufacturing costs.** The unit cost is indispensable to a manufacturing enterprise for financial reporting, especially for the valuation of stock and the determination of the cost of goods sold.

In this and the following few modules product cost determination is discussed from an **absorption** approach. This approach is described because it makes provision for the absorption of all the manufacturing costs (whether fixed or variable) by the units produced. This system is also described as the "total cost" approach.

Basically there are two types of product costing systems:
- [ ] Job costing systems
- [ ] Process costing systems

Process costing systems are used where large ranges of homogeneous products are manufactured using the same production facilities. Oil refineries, sawmills and canning factories are some examples. In process costing systems the total costs incurred in the production process during a particular period are determind first and then the cost per product is calculated by dividing the total costs of the process by the quantity of units manufactured during the period.

Job costing systems are used in cases where heterogeneous products, that is products which differ from each other, are manufactured using the same manufacturing facilities. Construction enterprises, shipbuilding and general engineering repair shops are examples of enterprises that will use job costing systems.

Each of these costing systems furnishes a product cost according to a physical standard, for example units, kilograms, litres, etc.

Job costing is discussed in this module and process costing in the next chapter. Contract costing, which is a special application of job costing, is discussed in Module 7.2.

The discussion which follows is based on certain aspects that have already been covered in previous modules:
- [ ] Cost elements
    - Direct material (Chapter 2)
    - Direct labour (Chapter 3)
    - Manufacturing overheads (Chapter 4)

☐ Flow of costs (Chapter 6, Module 2)
☐ Predetermined overheads tariffs (Chapter 4, Module 2)

In the study of job costing systems each one of these aspects is examined again, as is the manner in which they are involved in the determination of unit costs.

2 The job description

Before a job is begun a job description is prepared by the production planning department. The job description initiates the execution of a job, either on special order or for restocking items for which repeat orders are received.

Copies of the job description, together with engineering specifications, where applicable, are sent to all the sections involved in the manufacturing process to ensure that the required material, labour, tools and machinery are available timeously in order that the job may be completed on time.

3 Cost determination of a job

As the name "job costing system" indicates, the costs of each different product or job are accumulated and determined. The cost of direct material and direct labour that can be ascribed to a specific job (piecework), which can consist of a single unit or batch of units, is a portion of the cost of that particular job. Normal overheads are allocated to the job according to a predetermined overheads tariff.

4 Stock ledgers

The stock records in a job costing system include control accounts as well as **subsidiary ledgers.** The control accounts include the following:
☐ Raw material stock account
☐ Production account (incomplete work)
☐ Finished goods account (completed goods)

For each of these accounts there is a supporting ledger containing detailed accounts which support the balances in the control accounts, namely:
☐ a **material ledger,** in which the quantities and unit costs of each type of material are recorded on a separate ledger card (see Diagram D21)

STOCK NUMBER: KP3-3047 DESCRIPTION: Copper pipe LOCATION: Roof 2/102			RE-ORDER QUANTITY: 2000 MAX/MIN QUANTITY: 6 000/1 000			
Date	Document reference	Unit cost	Received	Issued	Balance	
					Units	Price
19.8 Feb. 2	Inv D770 Zed Ltd	R 0,50	6 000		6 000	R 3 000
7	Req 302	0,50		1 000	5 000	2 500

Diagram D21

☐ a **cost ledger** in which a **job cost card** is kept for each job on which the enterprise works. The job card serves as a supporting record for work in progress. As Diagram D22 indicates, each of these cards shows the cost of direct material and direct labour and the applied overheads relevant to the job. When a job is completed the total costs are divided by the number of units in the job in order to obtain the unit cost.

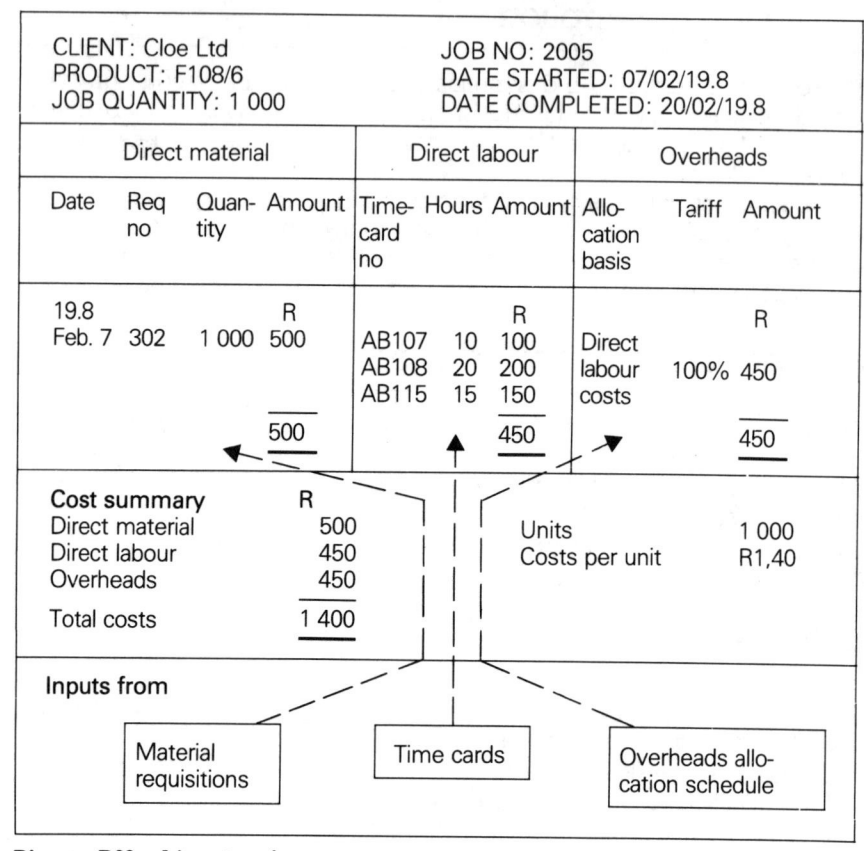

Diagram D22   Job cost card

☐ a **finished goods ledger** in which every card is identified by the stock number and description of the product and shows quantities, unit costs and total costs.

FINISHED GOODS STOCK CARD

STOCK NO.: F108/6   MINIMUM QUANTITY: 500

Date	Acquisitions			Sales		Balance		
	Job cost card	Quan-tity	Unit price	Invoice no	Quan-tity	Quan-tity	Unit price	Total cost
19.8 Feb 20	2005	1 000	R 1,40	–	–	1 000	R 1,40	R 1 400

Diagram D23

Diagram D24 shows the relationship between the various control accounts and supporting ledgers (in "T"-format).

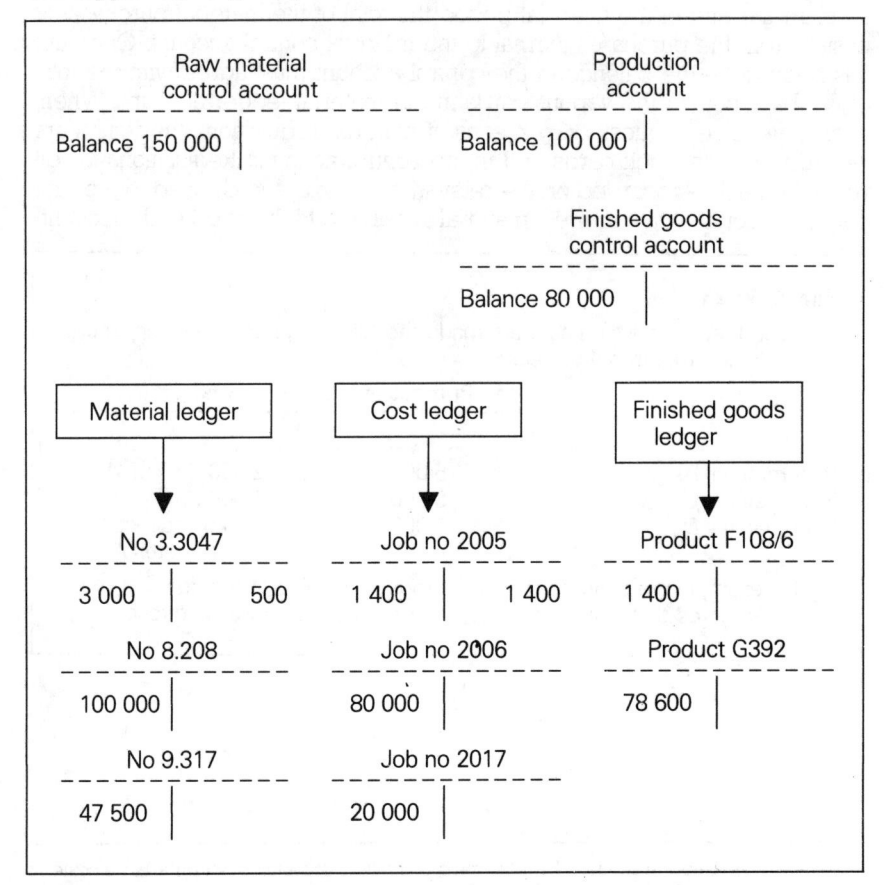

Diagram D24 Stock control accounts and supporting ledgers of a manufacturing enterprise

The relationship between the control accounts and supporting ledgers and the purpose of these accounts in a manufacturing enterprise thus corresponds with the relationship and purpose of these accounts in a retailing enterprise. In both cases the supporting ledger is kept up to date on a continuous basis while the control accounts are brought up to date periodically.*

5 Comprehensive example of a job costing system

The following example illustrates a job costing system. Ayed Manufacturers manufactures two products, A and Z, for its own stock purposes. Two raw materials (B and C) are part of the products, while material D is used in the factory but is not incorporated in the products as such. (The necessary book entries are illustrated diagrammatically and in journal entry form.)

☐ The recording of material costs

Upon receipt the material purchased is shown on the relevant material stock card. At the end of the financial period the total of the material purchases is posted from the purchases journal to the material control account. Once this has been done the balance in the control account must agree with the total of the balances on the various cards in the material ledger account. Whenever material is requested by means of material requisitions the issues are recorded on the stock cards and in the control account. Requisitions for direct material are recorded on the relevant job cards and debited to the production account, while indirect material is debited to the overheads account.

Example 23

Suppose that Ayed Manufacturers made the following purchases and issues during its first month of business:

	Purchases	Issues
	R	R
Raw material B	5 000	2 000 (for job 1)
Raw material C	3 000	1 000 (for job 2)
Raw material D	1 000	400 (indirect material)

(In this example we concentrate on the monetary value of the items. It must be remembered that units, where applicable, must also always be recorded.)

---

*As already indicated in Module 1.1, electronic computers are employed on a large scale in modern businesses. Stock and control records comprise an area which is well-suited to the employment of computers. In such a system the physical ledger is replaced by the computer software.

(1) Journal entry for purchases of material

	R	R
Material stock account	9 000	
Creditors		9 000
Purchases of the following:*		
Raw material B R5 000		
Raw material C R3 000		
Raw material D R1 000		

*Details from supporting records.

(2) Journal entry for the issue of material

	R	R
Production account (incomplete work)	3 000	
Manufacturing overheads	400	
Material stock account		3 400
Issue of the following:*	R	
Raw material B (Job 1)	2 000	
Raw material C (Job 2)	1 000	
Raw material D	400	

*Details to supporting records.

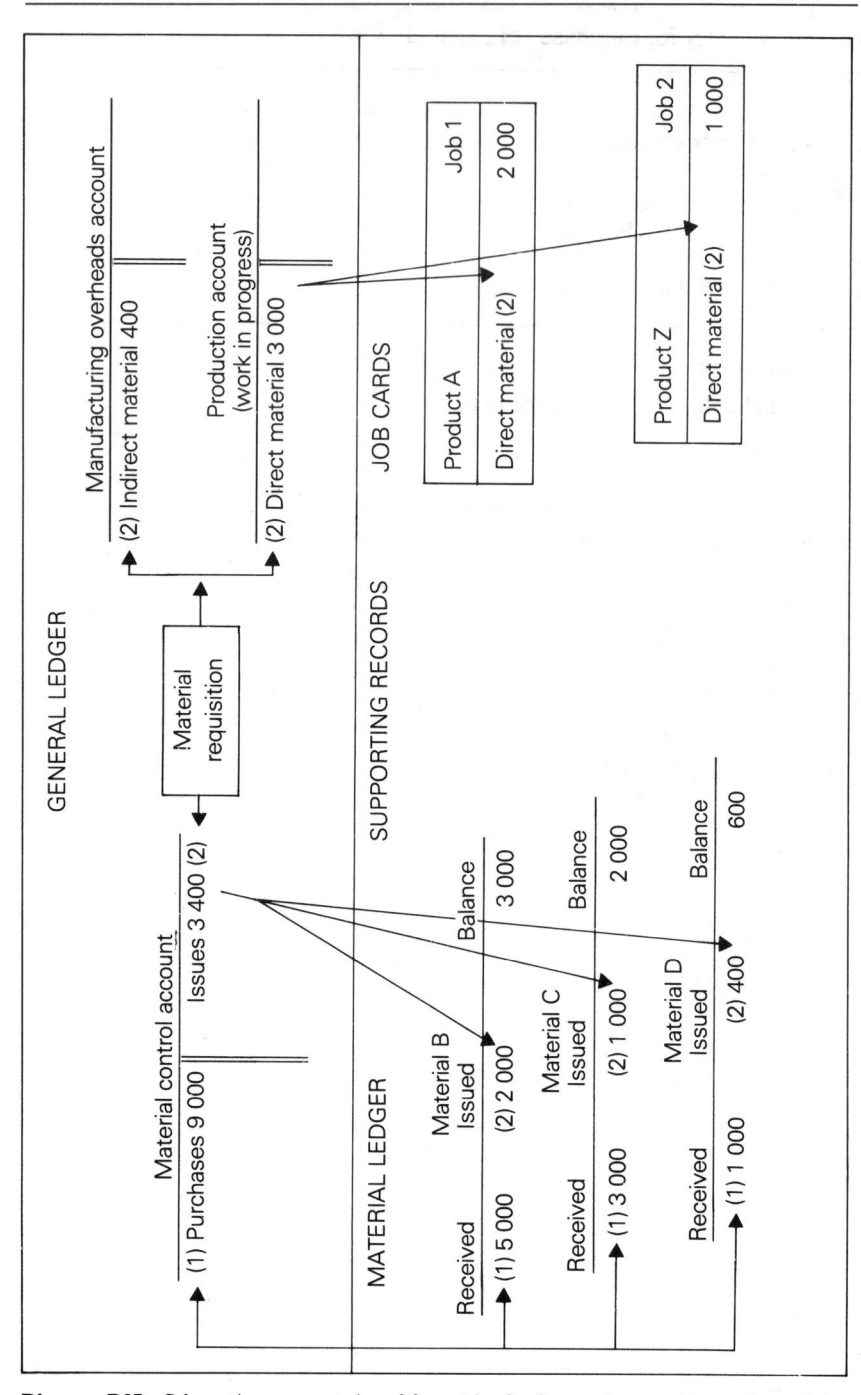

Diagram D25   Schematic representation of the entries for the purchase and issue of materials

☐ The recording of labour costs

In order that the labour costs associated with specific jobs may be identified time cards are used to determine the time spent by employees on various jobs. The hourly wage tariffs can be used to determine the labour costs of the various jobs. The details are transferred periodically from the time cards to the job cards.

Example 24

Suppose that Ayed Manufacturers incurred the following labour costs:

	Hours	Cost
		R
Direct labour – Job 1	400	1 600
– Job 2	200	800
Indirect labour for the period		1 000

A time card provides an hour-by-hour summary of the activities of an employee. When an employee works on a particular job (direct labour) he indicates the job number and the time spent on it on his daily time card. He also indicates the time spent on, for example, the maintenance of machinery (indirect labour).

The daily time cards of all the employees on the production floor are aggregated on the labour summary sheet and analysed in order that the appropriate apportionment may be made.

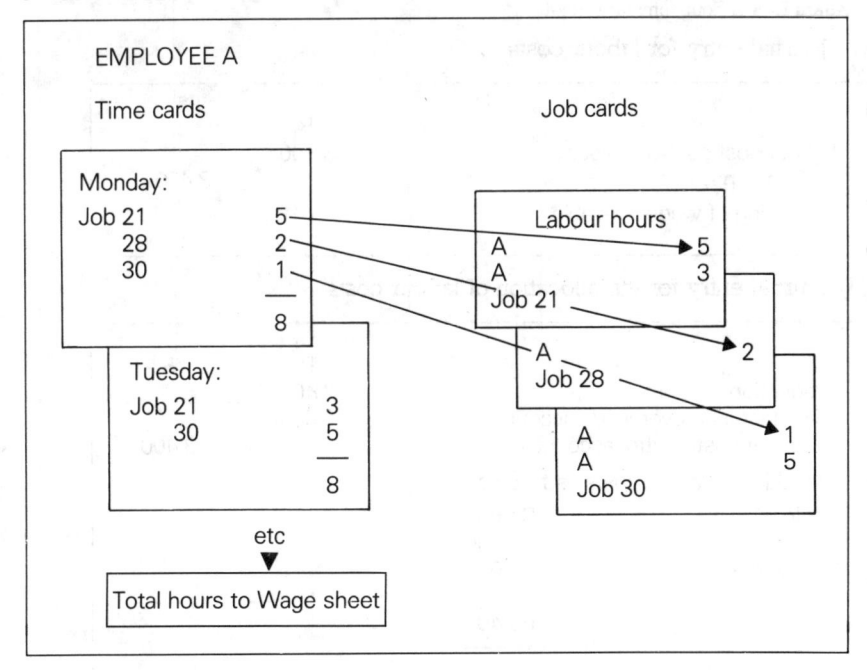

Diagram D26 Schematic representation of the apportionment procedures using time cards

```
                              TIME CARD
                            - - - - - - - - - - -
EMPLOYEE:                   PERSONNEL NO:. . . . HOURLY RATE: . . . .
CLOCK CARD
NUMBER:
DEPARTMENT:
JOB/PIECEWORK:
TIME STARTED:
TIME ENDED:
                            _____

TIME SPENT:
                            _____

SIGNED:
  EMPLOYEE:
  SUPERVISOR:
```

Diagram D27 Typical time card

Date	Time card number	Job number	Depart-ment	Hours	Rate	Cost

Diagam D28 Labour summary sheet

(3) Journal entry for labour costs

	R	R
Labour cost control account	3 400	
Wages payable		3 400
Recording of wages payable		

(4) Journal entry for the allocation of labour costs

	R	R
Production account	2 400	
Manufacturing overheads account	1 000	
Labour cost control account		3 400

Allocation of labour costs as follows:

Job 1	R1 600
Job 2	800
Overheads	1 000
	R3 400

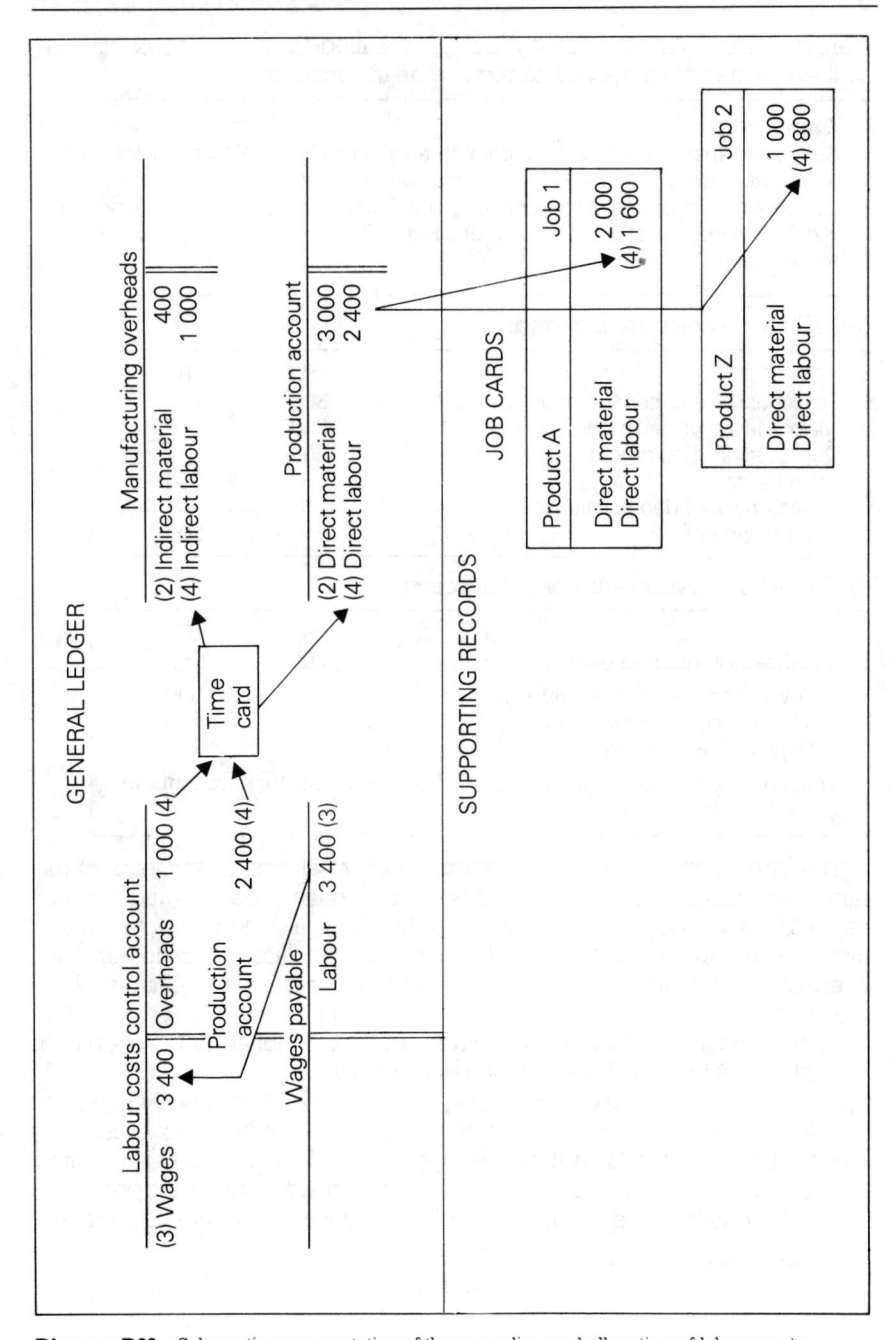

Diagram D29   Schematic representation of the recording and allocating of labour costs

☐ The recording of manufacturing overheads

When the recording of material and labour was dealt with it was shown that indirect material and indirect labour are recorded in the production overheads account. Periodically other overhead items are transferred to this account from the accounts in which they were recorded when the costs were incurred. As has already been explained, this account is also described as the **actual manufacturing overheads account.**

Example 25

Supposing that Ayed Manufacturers, in addition to indirect material and indirect labour costs, incurred the following overheads during the relevant financial period: power and water consumption R300; maintenance of equipment R200; and depreciation of equipment R200. These entries are recorded as follows (in journal form):

---

(5) When the costs are incurred:

	R	R
Power and water consumption	300	
Maintenance of equipment	200	
Depreciation: Equipment	200	
Creditors		500
Accumulated depreciation:		
Equipment		200

(6) Transfer to overheads control account:

	R	R
Overheads control account	700	
Power and water consumption		300
Maintenance of equipment		200
Depreciation: Equipment		200
Transfer of production overhead costs from individual cost accounts to control account		

The direct material and direct labour costs are allocated by means of material requisition forms and time cards directly to the products (and the relevant job cards). However, it is not possible to allocate the indirect manufacturing costs **directly** to the cost of a particular product and **predetermined overheads tariffs** are used (as has already been explained in Chapter 4) for the allocation of indirect manufacturing overheads.

As the **actual manufacturing costs** arise they are **debited** to the overheads control account (as explained in journal 6 above).

Overheads that are allocated to the products during the period in question are **debited** to the production account (and to the applicable job card) by means of the **overheads tariff** and the applied overheads account is **credited.** Suppose that Ayed Manufacturers uses an overheads tariff of R3 per direct labour hour, then in the example the following allocation would take place:

(7) Allocation of overheads

	R	R
Production account	1 800	
Applied overheads account		1 800
Allocation of overheads @ R3 per direct labour hour:		
Job 1 (400 hours × R3)	R1 200	
Job 2 (200 hours × R3)	600	

Once the overheads have been entered on the job card it contains all the cost elements incurred in respect of each job to date.

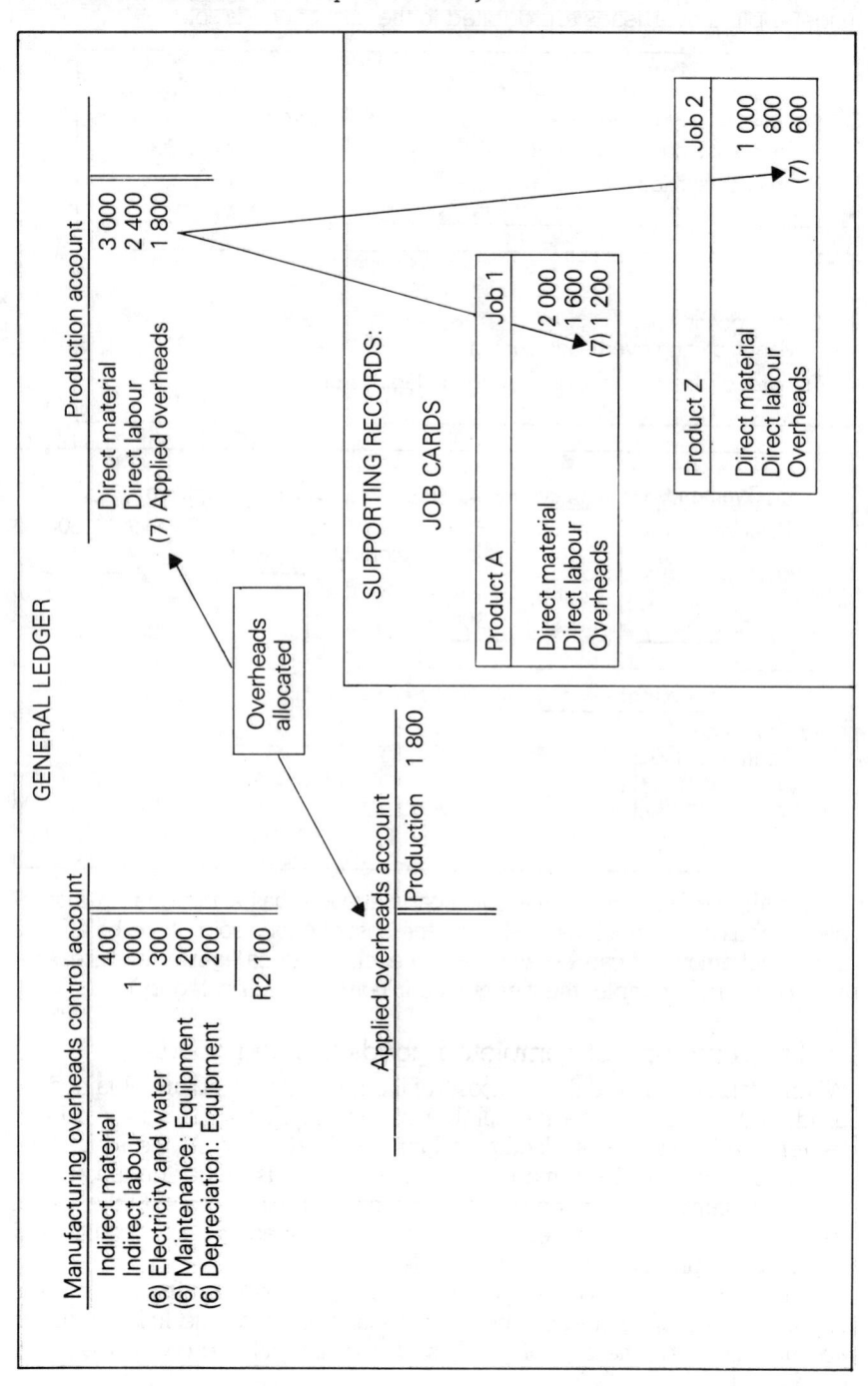

Diagram D30 Schematic representation of the transfer of indirect costs to the overheads control account

It is noticeable that the overheads applied (R1 800) are R300 less than the actual costs incurred. As has already been explained in chapter 4, the underapplied overheads are debited to the cost of goods sold.

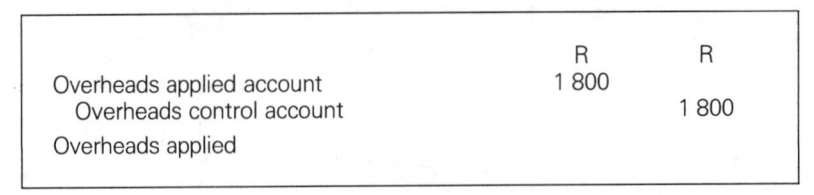

	R	R
Overheads applied account	1 800	
Overheads control account		1 800
Overheads applied		

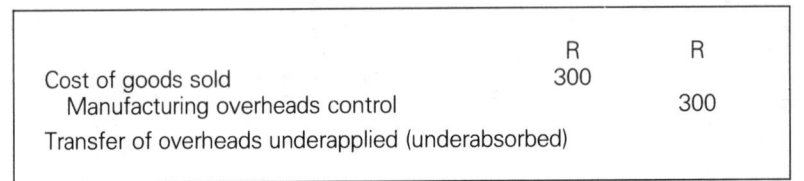

	R	R
Cost of goods sold	300	
Manufacturing overheads control		300
Transfer of overheads underapplied (underabsorbed)		

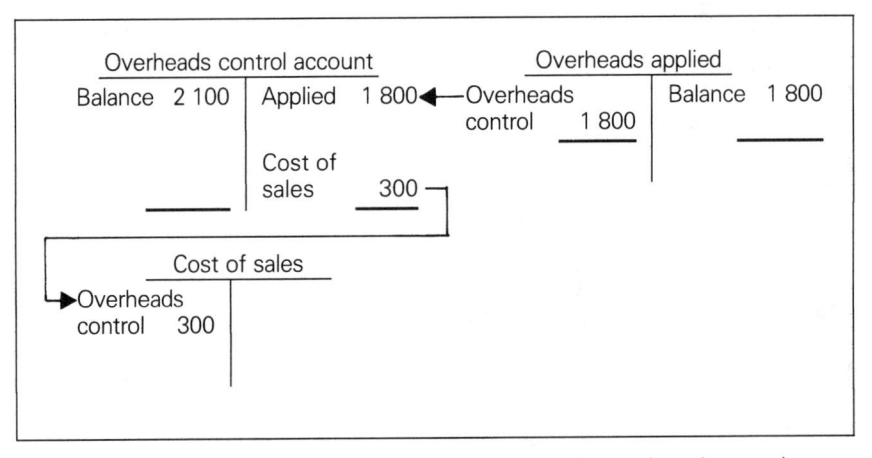

In truth, the balance on the overheads account has a bearing on incomplete goods still in stock as well as on the cost of goods sold. If the balance is a material amount it can be allocated to each of the categories on a reasonable basis (for example, the direct labour hours of each category).

☐ The recording of completed goods/finished goods

When a job is complete the unit costs of the items in that job are obtained by dividing the total costs by the number of units produced. The job card can be removed from the production ledger and filed away. At the same time the necessary entries are made in the finished goods ledger on the applicable stock cards to show the quantity, unit costs and total costs. At the end of the period an accounting entry debiting the finished goods accounts and crediting the production account is made.

When goods are sold the appropriate entry is made on the stock cards and at the end of the period an entry is made to credit the finished goods account and debit the cost of goods sold account with the cost price of the goods sold.

Example 26

Suppose that Job 1 is completed by Ayed Manufacturers during the first month, that 1 000 units are produced and that 600 of these units are sold during the month. Job 2 is still in progress. The book entries are as follows:

		R	R
(8)	Finished goods	4 800	
	Production account		4 800
	Job 1 (1 000 units of Product A completed at a cost of R4,80 per unit)		
(9)	Cost of goods sold	2 880	
	Finished goods		2 880
	Cost of 600 units of Product A sold (cost: R4,80 per unit)		
(10)	Debtors	3 200	
	Sales		3 200
	Sale of 600 units of Product A		

Once transactions (8) to (10) have been recorded the entries in the relevant accounts and subsidiary records will be as in Diagram D31. Special attention must be paid to the following:

☐ There is an obvious relationship between the physical flow of the goods and the associated book entries.

☐ The various supporting records contain a detailed analysis of the total amounts and balances which appear in the associated control accounts in the general ledger.

(c) The cost of finished goods results in the entries being made for the cost price as well as the selling price of the goods.

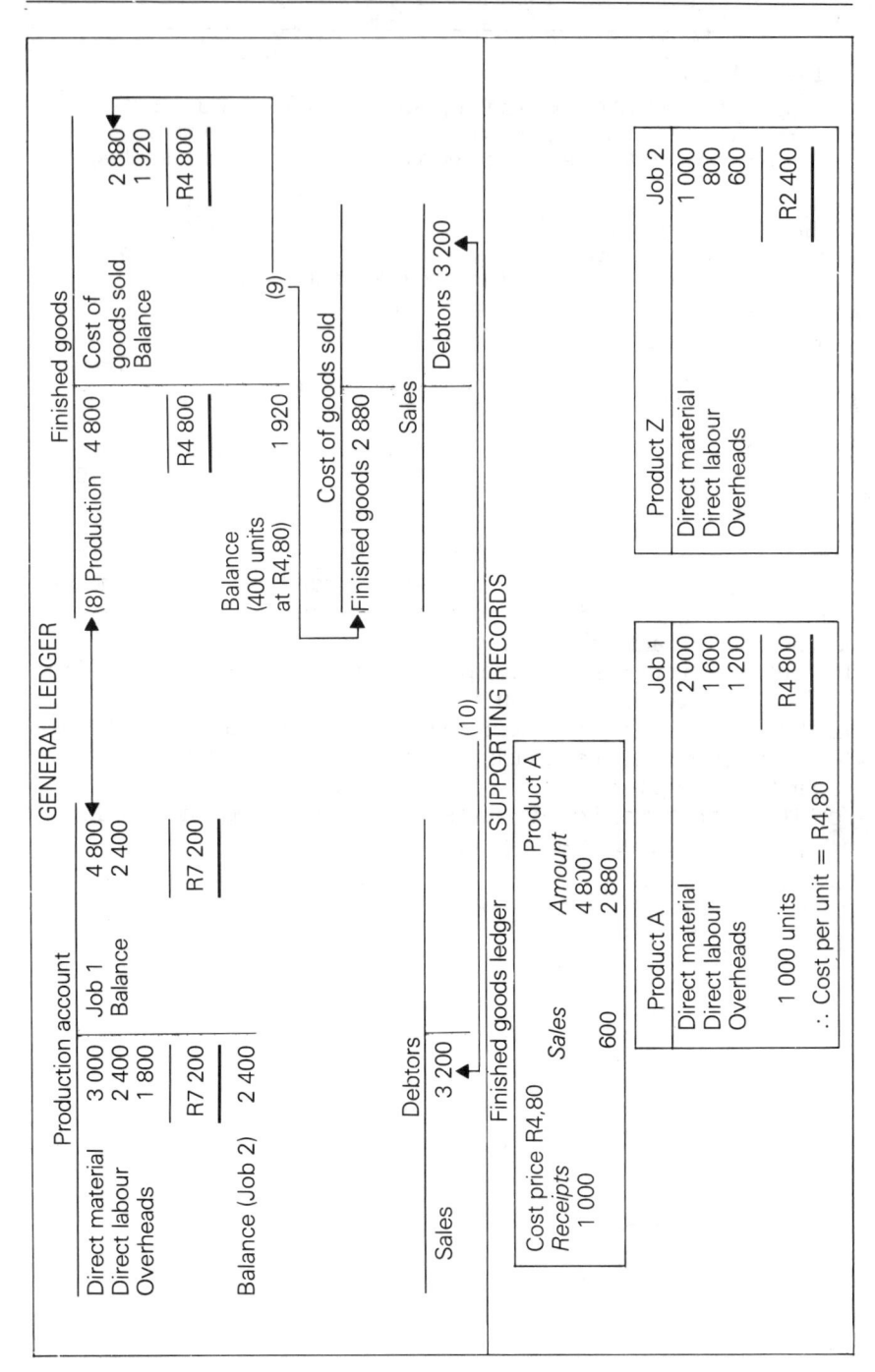

Diagram D31   Schematic representation of the book entries of finished goods and sales

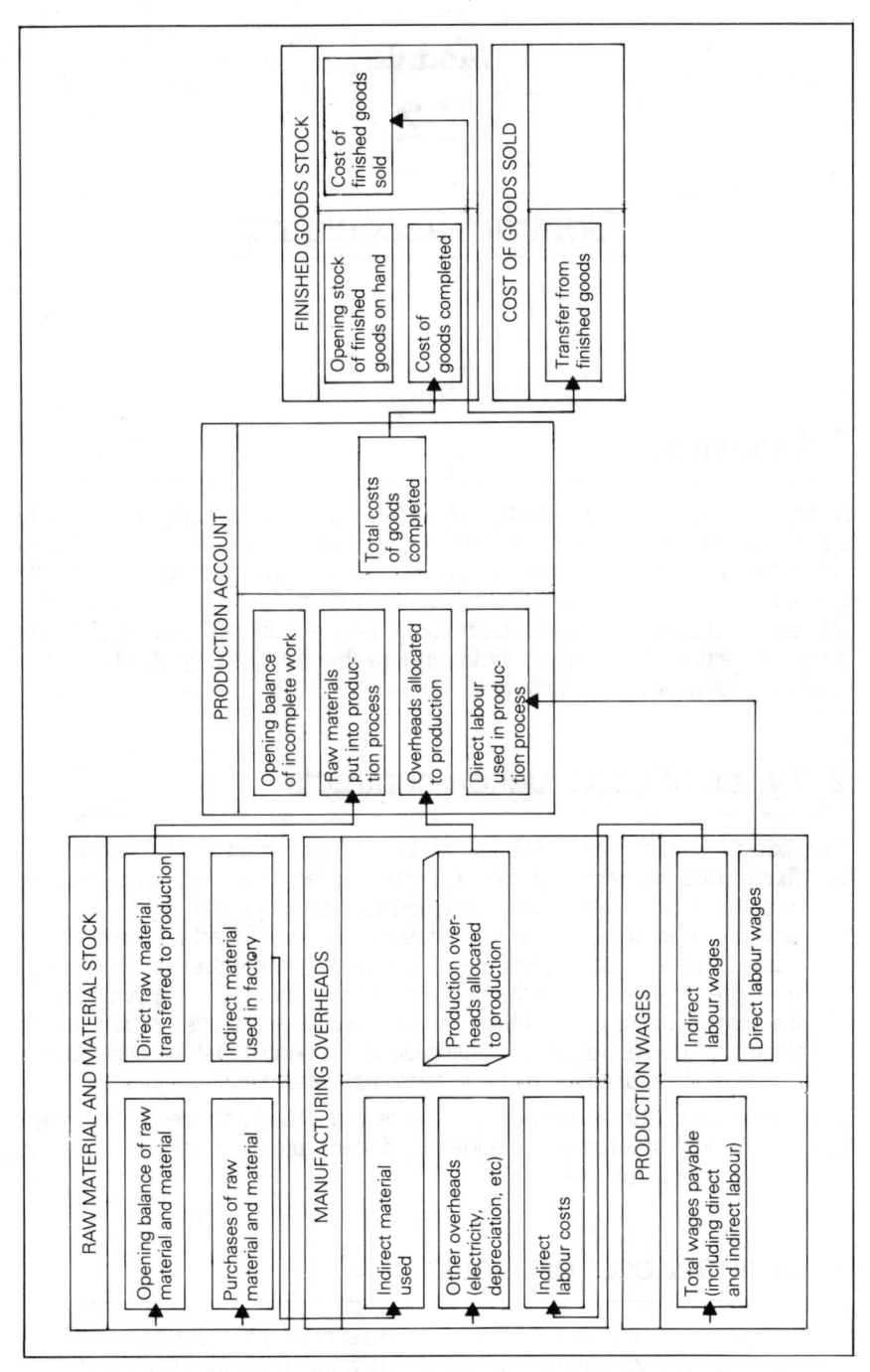

Diagram D32   Summary of the book entries (in "T" account block format) in a job costing system

Contract accounting

1 Definition

Contract costing is the application of the principles of job costing systems to substantial projects, in particular units which take a relatively long time to complete. The last-mentioned are known as long-term construction projects and examples are the construction of bridges, dams, ships and buildings and the manufacturing of complex equipment. Basically these types of activities have the nature of job costing and therefore the principles applicable to job costing systems are also applicable here.

2 Types of construction contracts

Two basic types of construction contracts can be distinguished, namely:
- [ ] **fixed-price contracts,** where the parties agree to a fixed contract price which is usually subject to a provision for cost escalation
- [ ] **cost-plus contracts,** where the contractor is reimbursed for the costs incurred plus a fixed percentage of the costs as an entrepreneur's wage or a predetermined fixed amount. The main problem with such a contract is the description of the type and nature of the costs incurred and what is to be reimbursed. In this case it is essential that the cost clauses are carefully worded in order to avoid any later disputes.

If a contract covers a number of projects and if they and the costs and receipts connected thereto can be identified, each project must be viewed as a separate accounting unit.

3 Contract cost elements

For the purposes of cost identification and recording the duration of a project is considered to run from the date the contract is signed until the project is substantially complete and handed over to the client.

Costs incurred by an enterprise before a contract is signed are usually viewed as period costs and are written off as such. If, however, the costs can be directly identified with a future project and there is reasonable certainty that the contract will proceed, then the pre-contract costs can be accumulated and viewed as project costs. The costs normally incurred by a construction enterprise can be classified into two groups, namely **contract costs** and **general costs.**

☐ Contract costs

Contract costs can be classified into two categories:

☐ **Direct contract costs** are incurred for a specific project. Examples are material purchased directly for a project, material charged out from a central store to a specific project, site or project wages (including supervision), subcontract work and depreciation of machinery and equipment used by the project (the cost of moving equipment to a site must also be considered a direct cost of the project).

☐ **Indirect contract costs** in connection with general project activities are allocated to individual projects. Examples are general insurance, warehouse costs, and transport.

☐ General costs

General costs are those incurred in order that the enterprise may function and include general administrative and selling costs, financing costs and research and development. (Financing costs are usually viewed as a general cost, but where funds are borrowed specifically for a particular project the interest must be viewed as a direct cost of the project.)

General costs are usually viewed as a period cost and not as a project cost. However, in exceptional circumstances where general costs have a direct connection with a particular project, they can be applied as a project cost. When determining a contract or tender price allowance must be made for general costs which cannot be allocated.

4 Characteristics of contract costing systems

In a single module of this nature it is not possible to establish a basic costing and recording system for a construction contract, since there is such a variety of contracts. Further, the sophistication of the accounting system of an enterprise determines to a large extent in what way information can be made available to management. However, it is a basic requirement that each project's costs and receipts are identified, recorded individually and accumulated. Irrespective of whether the system is manual or electronic it will entail keeping general control accounts with an analysis of costs per cost item in a supporting account, book or record. A further accounting complication with regard to construction projects is that in many cases the work is done on the project site. This necessitates a proper, planned site recording system and communication channels between the head office and the site.

The basic procedure is to open a separate account for each contract in a supporting ledger, the contracts ledger. In fact, this account is debited with all the contract costs and credited with the contract price. Each contract account is thus a separate profit and loss account in which the profit or loss of the specific contract is determined.

The following are characteristic of contract costing:

☐ A **contract number** is assigned to every separate contract.

☐ Most of the **material** is ordered specifically for the contract. It will thus be debited directly to the contract from the supplier's invoice.

Material drawn from a central warehouse which serves numerous contracts will, as in job costing systems, be requested by means of material requisitions.

☐ Most of the **other costs** are also direct costs, for example labour and subcontractors employed on a specific contract only.

☐ **Head office costs** must be allocated to the contracts on a suitable basis. Head office expenses will originate in respect of the preparation of tenders for contracts, material procurement and labour administration. Thus they will tend to keep in relation with the primary cost of contracts and a **primary cost** recovery tariff can be used quite effectively for the apportionment of head office costs to contracts.

☐ **Machinery and equipment costs** can be charged to a contract in two ways:

    (i) If the equipment is going to be used for a particular contract for a long time the entire cost is charged to the contract. Upon completion of the contract the contract costs are credited with any machinery and equipment costs recovered, for example from the proceeds of equipment sold or the value at which it is transferred to another contract.

    (ii) A hire basis may be used. The hire for each piece of equipment is charged to a contract, usually on the basis of a machine hour tariff.

If the contract extends beyond one financial period and the first method is used the machinery and equipment debited to the contract must be revalued at the end of each financial period. The difference in value at the beginning and the end of a financial period is the depreciation cost for that period. In such a case the depreciated value is credited to the contract and carried down as an opening debit balance for the next period in the contract account.

An alternative method of charging depreciation to a contract is a usage basis, for example using a machine hour tariff.

5 Specific contract terminology

☐ Certified work

It is general practice in the construction industry to make **progress payments** during the course of the contract. This is done according to certificates which are issued by the client's supervising architect. A certificate specifies the contract value of the approved work completed up to the date of the certificate. The contractor requests progress payments from his client on the grounds of the certified work.

It is important to note that the work is specified in terms of the contract price and not in terms of the contractor's costs.

☐ Retention money

In order to protect themselves against defective work by contractors it is usual for entrepreneurs to withhold a certain percentage of each progress payment. The money withheld is known as **retention money** and usually provision is made for it in the agreement between an entrepreneur and a contractor.

Retention money is usually held for a specified period after the completion of the contract or until all retention work has been carried out to the satisfaction of the supervising architect.

☐ Uncertified work

The determination of the work done for which the architect issues his certificate is done at times to which the parties agree. Since it need not necessarily happen on the last day of the contractor's financial period there will usually be a portion of the contract that has progressed since the issuing of the last certificate. The **costs** of such uncertified work must be determined at the end of the financial period as this is the work-in-progress amount.

☐ Material on site

With incomplete contracts there is usually unused material that has been ordered specifically for the contract on hand at the end of the financial period. Such material is valued at cost price and carried over to the next period.

6 Profit determination for contracts

6.1 Short-term contracts

Short-term contracts are deemed to be those contracts that are begun and completed during a single accounting period. Profit determination is not a problem in such contracts, since costs and income for short-term contracts are incurred and earned during the same accounting period.

Profit determination for short-term contracts will always take place according to the completed contract method (see 6.3).

6.2 Long-term contracts

Long-term contracts are contracts which stretch over more than one accounting period. As a result the question whether the profit must be calculated on completion of the contract or periodically (at least annually) arises. If the calculation of the profit is deferred until a long-term contract is completed, to a certain extent the financial statements will not be a proper reflection of the different years' activities but rather merely the results of projects completed during that particular year and there will be unnecessary and material fluctuations in the profit figures from year to year.

6.3 The two methods of profit determination for long-term contracts

There are two methods of profit determination for long-term construction projects, namely the **completion contract method** and the **percentage of completion method.**

☐ The completed contract method

When the completed contract method is used no profit is brought into account until the project is complete, irrespective of how long the work on the project lasts. It is a conservative method of profit determination and leaves no doubt about the profitability or otherwise of the project, since all costs and income are realised and brought into account.

The main advantage of this method is that the eventual result is beyond all doubt and there is no reliance on estimates which might result in adjustments because of unforeseen costs and losses. The risk of taking profits which are possibly not realisable or are not realisable is thus eliminated.

The greatest disadvantage of the completed contract method is that reported profits refer only to the results of projects completed during a particular year and are not necessarily a reflection of the activities of a particular year. Thus work can be done on a fairly large project for a number of years with no results being reported, but if such a project is completed within a single year all the profits are calculated in that particular year, which gives rise to fluctuating profit reporting. Basically the problem centres around the time that elapses between the incurring of the costs (the supplying of the service) and the realisation of the income which results. Costs are incurred to earn income, but the income is not brought into account during the accounting period in which the costs are incurred.

Example 27

Profit determination in accordance with the completed contract method

Lomax Construction was busy on two contracts during the past year, namely Project 2, with a contract price of R300 000 and Project 3, with a contract price of R1 000 000.

At the end of the financial year ended 31 December 19.8 Project 2 was completed and handed over, while Project 3 was still at an initial stage. The enterprise calculates profits only when projects are complete and the contract price has been received or is receivable.

Further details in respect of the two projects for the past year are as follows:

	Project 2	Project 3
	R	R
Material used	80 000	20 000
Apportionment of depreciation on machinery in use	13 000	12 000
Labour costs	130 000	15 000
Overheads allocated	40 000	20 000
Work certified by architects	300 000	–
Cash received	300 000	–
No retention money is outstanding		

Required:
Show how the details will be recorded in the ledger.

Solution

Construction account: Project 2

	R		R
Material	80 000	Debtors: Project 2	300 000
Depreciation	13 000	(work certified)	
Labour	130 000		
Overheads	40 000		
Profit: Project 2	37 000		
	R300 000		R300 000

Construction account: Project 3

	R		R
Material	20 000	Incomplete work:	
Depreciation	12 000	Project 3 in progress	67 000
Labour	15 000		
Overheads	20 000		
	R67 000		R67 000
Incomplete work:			
Project 3 in progress	67 000		

The amount of R67 000 is shown in the balance sheet under current assets as construction work in progress at cost, while the profit of R37 000 on Project 2 is shown in the income statement as profits.

☐ The percentage of completion method

This method recognises profits on the basis of work executed and divides the total profit on a long-term contract over the relevant accounting periods in relation to the work completed during each of the periods. The advantage of this method is that income and profits are brought into account as and when they are earned and during the period in which the costs are incurred and the activities to earn the income were carried out. Thus it is a genuine application of the matching principle.

It is necessary that such periodic profit determination is done with caution and that in each case prior consideration is given to each of the following:

☐ Indications of factors which could cause increased costs in the future
☐ The costs relating to the project must be known and be identifiable so that the results to date can be compared with predetermined parameters
☐ The reliability of the results, estimates and forecasts
☐ The progress of the work must be determined so that losses as a result of delays and slow progress can be taken into consideration
☐ If a loss is anticipated over the total project provision must be made, in full, for the loss now

The **stage of completion** of the project can be measured by means of any of the following methods:

☐ **The relationship between costs incurred to date and the estimated total**

costs of the project In such a case costs incurred but not used must not be included in the costs for the purposes of profit determination. Examples of this are the cost of unused material, advances to subcontractors for services which still have to be supplied and the undepreciated value of machinery and equipment if the cost of the machinery and equipment is debited to the project.

☐ **The relationship of the value of the work certified to the total contract price** The success of the application of the percentage of completion method rests, to a large extent, on the reasonableness with which future costs and risks can be estimated and identified. **Unless the final result of the project can be estimated with a reasonable degree of accuracy no interim profits should be calculated.** In such a case the completed contract method must be used.

In the calculation of the total costs to date and the total estimated additional costs to complete the project it is necessary that possible costs arising after completion of the project, such as services and repairs as a result of a guarantee clause, are taken into consideration. Further, when a project stretches over a number of years it must be remembered that circumstances and risks vary from year to year and that profits already reported must be reviewed in order to report the profits to date as rationally as possible. Adjustments to prior years' profits might indicate the necessity for further provisions for expected losses. The reported profit for a particular year can thus be a combination of the calculated profit for that particular year and adjustments for previous and future years.

In some enterprises it is customary for a project to be contracted for in stages. In other words, the project is completed, delivered and invoiced in stages. In such a case the stages can be viewed as separate 'projects' without provision being made for expected losses in the next stages.

Example 28

Application of the percentage of completion method

	Year 1	Year 2	Year 3
	R	R	R
Contract price	1 000 000	1 000 000	1 000 000
Incomplete work @ cost	80 000	595 000	860 000
Estimated future costs	720 000	255 000	–
Estimated total costs	800 000	850 000	860 000

Percentage completion
(according to the cost basis):

Year 1 $\dfrac{80\ 000}{800\ 000} \times \dfrac{100}{1}$

Year 2 $\dfrac{595\ 000}{850\ 000} \times \dfrac{100}{1}$

Year 3 $\dfrac{860\ 000}{860\ 000} \times \dfrac{100}{1}$

     = 10%   = 70%   = 100%

The percentage so established can be applied in two ways to ascertain the periodic profit figure. (Because the total expected loss must be provided for in the year in which it occurs, Method 1 can only be used successfully if the company continuously runs at a profit).

Method 1

Percentage completion applied to total contract price

	Year 1	Year 2	Year 3
	R	R	R
Total contract price	1 000 000	1 000 000	1 000 000
Percentage applicable in each separate year	10%	70%	100%
Less: Already accounted for in previous years	–	10%	70%
Progress during the year	10%	60%	30%

Calculation of profit for each year:

	R	R	R
Contract price of work completed in each year (% × contract price)	100 000	600 000	300 000
Cost of work completed during the year	80 000	515 000	265 000
Incomplete work	80 000	595 000	860 000
Less: Accounted for in previous years	–	80 000	595 000
Profit for the year	20 000	85 000	335 000

Method 2

Percentage completion applied to estimated profit

	Year 1	Year 2	Year 3
	R	R	R
Contract price	1 000 000	1 000 000	1 000 000
Less: Estimated total cost	800 000	850 000	860 000
Estimated profit on contract as determined at the end of each year	200 000	150 000	140 000
Percentage completion	10%	70%	100%
∴ Estimated profit recognised	10% × 200 000	70% × 150 000	100% × 140 000

	R	R	R
Profit to date	= 20 000	= 105 000	= 140 000
Less: Already earned in previous years	–	20 000	105 000
Profit applicable for each year	20 000	85 000	35 000

Since the underlying principle is the same in both cases they give the same results.

Because there is still an element of risk in the calculation of interim profits some people want to **present a conservative picture by showing only a portion of the calculated profits as realised.** In this connection the figure two thirds of the calculated profit has already found favour in some circles, but this is purely a question of policy and therefore a general rule cannot be based on it.

In order to bring **only realised profits** into account, **cash received to date** is also sometimes taken into consideration. The formula for the calculation of the interim profit then has the following components:

- ☐ Total contract price minus total estimated costs = estimated profit
- ☐ Costs to date in relation to total estimated costs gives a theoretical stage of completion
- ☐ Cash received in relation to cash receivable indicates the extent of absolute realisation of interim profits

---

Thus the formula is:

$$\frac{\text{Cash received}}{\text{Cash receivable}} \times \frac{\text{Costs to date}}{\text{Total estimated costs}} \times \frac{\text{Estimated total profit}}{1}$$

Example 29

Conservatism in profit determination

LX Construction Limited signed a contract on 2 January 19.4 for the erection of an office building at a total contract price of R2,5 million.

The company has estimated that it will cost R1,5 million to complete the project.

At 31 December 19.4, the close of the company's financial year, costs of R1,1 million have already been incurred. On the same date the value of the certified work amounted to R1,75 million. The client has paid this amount, less 5% retention which, under the agreement, is payable three months after the completion of the contract. It is the policy of LX Construction Limited to account for profits using the percentage of completion method and taking into consideration the cash received.

Required:

(a) Determine the profit/loss on the contract for 19.4
(b) Show the information applicable to the contract in the balance sheet of the company on 31 December 19.4.

Solution

(a) 1 Determination of percentage completion in accordance with estimated costs

	R (millions)
Contract price	2,50
Total cost	1,50
Costs incurred to 31/12/19.4	1,11
Estimated future costs	0,39
Estimated total profit	1,00

$$\therefore \text{Percentage completion} \quad \frac{1,11}{1,50} \times \frac{100}{1}$$

$$= \quad 74\%$$

2 Calculation of profit with total contract price as a basis

	R (millions)
Total contract price	2,5
% completion applied (74% × R2,5m)	1,85
Cost of work completed during the year	1,11
Profit for the year	0,74

Profit earned in relation to cash received only:

$$\frac{95}{100} \times \text{R0,74 m} = \text{R703 000}$$

Or by applying the following formula:

$$\frac{\text{Cash received}}{\text{Cash receivable}} \times \frac{\text{Costs to date}}{\text{Estimated total costs}} \times \frac{\text{Estimated total profit}}{1}$$

$$= \frac{95\% \times \text{R1,75m}}{\text{R1,75m}} \times \frac{\text{R1,11m}}{\text{R1,50m}} \times \frac{\text{R1,0m}}{1}$$

$$= \text{R703 000}$$

The difference between the calculated profit of R740 000 and the "realised" profit of R703 000 amounts to R37 000.

(b) Balance sheet

	R	R
Construction work in progress:		100 000
Costs to date	1 110 000	
Profit to date	703 000	
Reserve for contingencies	37 000	
	1 850 000	
Less: Contract money receivable	1 750 000	
Received	1 662 500	
Retention	87 500	
Debtors		87 500

In the above solution the profit is calculated on the basis of 74% completion, since it is representative of the actual activities to date. An **alternative approach** sometimes found in practice is to reduce the profit calculation to the value of the **certified work.**

With reference to the information in the previous example:

Value of work certified

$$= \text{R1,75 million or}$$
$$\frac{\text{R1,75m}}{\text{R2,5m}} \times \frac{100}{1}$$
$$= 70\% \text{ of contract price}$$

The cost of the certified work is thus R1 050 000

(calculated as $\frac{70}{74} \times$ R1,11 million)

The cost of uncertified work thus amounts to R60 000

(calculated as $\frac{4}{74} \times$ R1,11 million).

The last-mentioned is now shown as the stock of incompleted work.

The estimated profit on the contract as a whole is R1 000 000. If the profit calculation is reduced to the value of the certified work, R700 000 (70% of R1 million) can be taken as profit for the year and the summarised contract account will be as follows if the profit (as above) is further adjusted in relation to the cash received:

Contract account

Costs incurred	1 110 000	Debtors (certified	
Profit credited to		work)	1 750 000
income statement	665 000	Stock (incomplete	
(95% × R700 000)		work not certified	
Reserve for		@ cost)	60 000
contingencies	35 000		
(5% × R700 000)			
	1 810 000		1 810 000
Balance b/f	60 000		

☐ The choice of method

The risks and uncertainties peculiar to a particular project will substantially determine which method of profit determination is used. The enterprise can make use of both methods, depending on the particular circumstances. Further, certain periods can be set, for example projects that are short to medium term can be handled using the completed contract method, while projects that are long term can be handled using the percentage completion method.

Thus the method or methods selected are, in the last instance, a question of accounting policy. Care must be taken that this is applied consistently and if changes occur in this connection they must be properly disclosed. It is natural to recommend that as far as possible there is standardisation and a policy is established so that the reported results are at all times a reasonable reflection of the actual situation and comparable with previous years.

The method of profit determination will be stated in the statement of accounting policy. The fact that the amount of the contract debtors is not immediately wholly realisable can be stated by way of a note. The details concerning the construction projects can also be summarised by way of a note.

7 Provision for losses

If at any time during the project period it appears that a **loss** is going to be made, provision must be made for such a loss in accordance with the prudence policy. If such a provision for estimated losses appears to be necessary it must be made irrespective of whether the work has already begun and of the stage of completeness of the project and the expected profit on other projects. It is conceded that the size of such a provision requires judgement, but it should be made as accurately as possible in the light of prevailing and expected circumstances. In the same way provision should be made for possible claims against the entrepreneur or penalties for late completion of the project.

Claims instituted by the entrepreneur or compensation for **additional work** done can only be included in the records as such if there is proper agreement between the parties involved.

8 The valuation of incomplete work

The valuation of incomplete work for the purposes of accounting disclosure is closely related to the method of profit determination being used. Because incomplete construction work represents "stock" and the general principles of stock valuation are thus applicable, the incomplete work must be valued at cost or realisable value, whichever is the lower.

☐ The completed contract method

If the completed contract method of profit determination is used all the incomplete work will be valued at the cost to date less provisions for anticipated losses (the debit of the provision is written off to the income account), less cash received or receivable in respect of the project with separate sub-totals for costs and receipts.

In the case of cash received/receivable, an alternative method of crediting the amounts to a separate account and showing it as a liability in the balance sheet can be used.

☐ The percentage of completion method

In this method the profit element is added and the value of the project to date is the costs already incurred less provisions for losses plus the attributable profit (the credit goes to the income account). If the cash received or receivable is deducted from this the balance will represent the value of uncertified or "incomplete" work.

8

PROCESS ORIENTATED
COSTING SYSTEMS

Basic characteristics of process
costing systems

1 Introduction

In job costing systems the manufacturing usually takes place according to the particular specifications of the client, which means that manufacturing does not begin before the client has placed an order. In job costing the jobs are usually not identical, although naturally repeat orders do occur. The costs are collected **per job** and are **finalised after completion of the job.**

A **process costing system** is different in every respect. In the first place, products are manufactured on a continuous basis according to standard specifications. The products are thus identical and are manufactured in large quantities. Because the units are identical each unit manufactured requires just about the same quantity of material, labour and manufacturing overheads. In addition costs are not collected per job, but for a fixed **period**.

Thus process costing is suited to enterprises which manufacture homogeneous products on a continuous basis. Therefore it is used in the petrol, chemical, food and electronic industries, where standardised products are produced on a continuous basis.

In a process costing system production departments or processes* are thus cost collection points (centres). The proper classification of the production activities of a factory into departments or processes is one of the first and most important steps in the business of a process costing system. The factory can be divided according to the nature of the enterprise into processes with relatively large spheres of activity or into smaller cost centres (or places) limited to a single activity.

2 Departmentalisation and unit costs

In a **job costing system** a **job card** is the collection point for all the manufacturing costs incurred for each job. The final cost of the job is determined only after it is completely finished. The manufacturing process may stretch over more than one accounting period, in which case the costs at the end of the first period are merely classified as "incomplete work" and the accumulated costs are transferred to the next period.

---

*The terms "departments" and "processes" are used interchangeably in this book when process costing is discussed.

In the process costing the manufacturing costs are collected by **department or process** for **fixed periods**. The **number of units** manufactured is also determined by department or process. Since each process manufactures a standard product, the **average cost per unit** of a specific department for an accounting period can easily be calculated as follows:

$$\frac{\text{Total manufacturing costs (for the period)}}{\text{Number of units manufactured (in the period)}}$$

Responsibility for process costs thus implies two especially important aspects:

☐ The responsibility for **costs** (the numerator in the above formula)
☐ The responsibility for **quantities** (the denominator in the above formula)

3 Product and cost flows

After processing, the initial input into the first process in a multiple processing system is transferred to the next process where it is one of the inputs for that process. Here further material can be added and further conversion costs are incurred.

Unit costs are calculated periodically for each department and will increase by department as the output of a previous department forms one of the inputs into the next department.

The ability to understand and visualise the transfer of partly completed products from one department to the next (the product flow) and the associated cost flow is a key factor in the solution of process costing problems. The basic product and cost flow in a multiple process costing system is illustrated in Diagram D33.

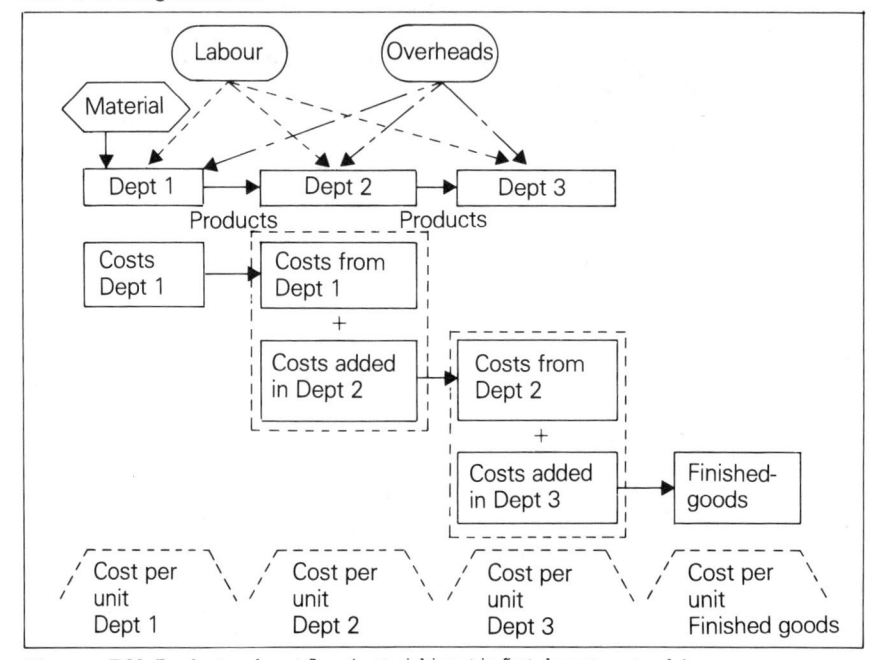

Diagram D33 Product and cost flow (material input in first department only)

The product and cost flows in process costing systems can take different forms. Study Diagram D34.

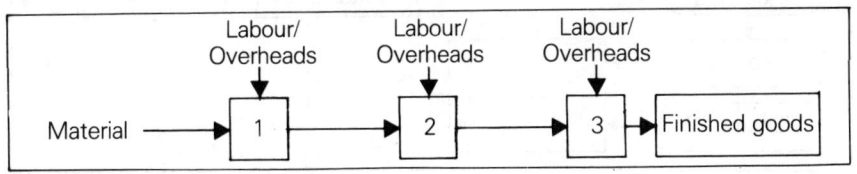

Diagram D34

In Diagram D34 the complete production system stretches over three departments. The completed product from Department 1 becomes the input for the next department, and so on. Raw materials are added at the start of the process in Department 1 only. In all three of the processes conversion costs are incurred.

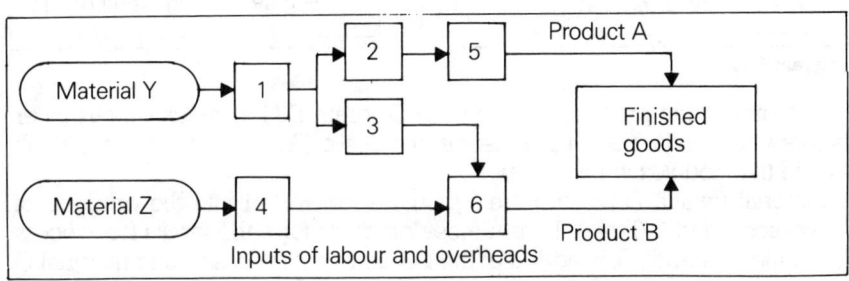

Diagram D35

In Diagram D35 materials Y and Z enter the process at the start of the processing in Departments 1 and 4. The output of Department 1 becomes the input for Departments 2 and 3. The output of Department 2 is transferred to Department 5, from which the final output, Product A, emerges. The outputs of Departments 3 and 4 form the input for Department 6, in which Product B is completed. Thus Departments 1, 2 and 5 form a production line in which Product A is produced and Departments 1, 3, 6 and 4 form a production line in which Product B is produced. Material is inserted only at the commencement in Departments 1 and 4 respectively. Labour and overheads are added in all departments.

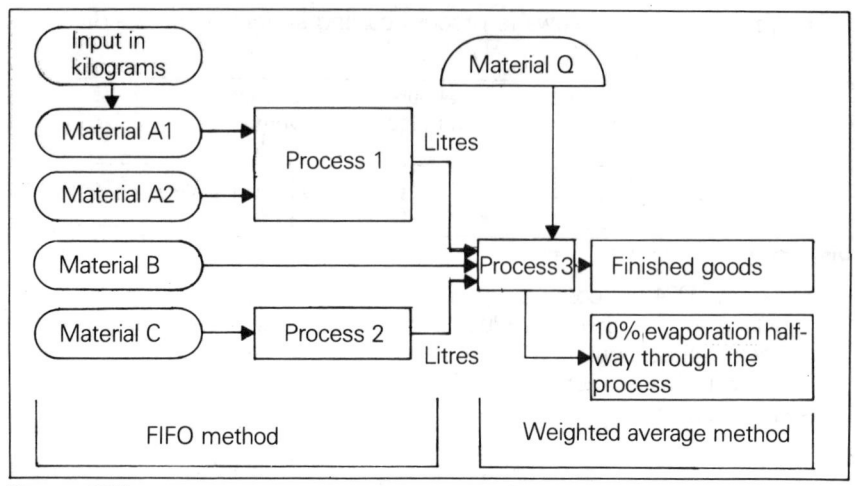

Diagram D36

The production programme shown in Diagram D36 includes various other factors which influence departmental unit costs. (All these factors are dealt with in the modules which follow.)

Material (which is put in in kilograms) is converted into the products of Processes 1 and 2 (litres). In turn these products form the inputs for Process 3. Another material, B, is added at the beginning of Process 3 and material Q is added at the end of the process. In Process 3 evaporation (10%) takes place at the halfway stage.

The output of Process 3 forms the final finished product. Stock valuation is by the first-in-first-out method in Process 1 and Process 2, but by the weighted average method in Process 3.

Production diagrams are thus useful for analysing and organising data for process costing.

Module

8.2

Production cost reports

1 Introduction

Specific process costing methods are determined by the type of manufacturing of each enterprise, but the following methods are representative of the various manufacturing industries:

☐ Single product, single process
☐ Single product, multiple processes
☐ Multiple products, single or multiple processes

These methods will be discussed in the following modules. The instrument used to record the costs and production flow of a process, the **production cost report** is dealt with first.

2 Process cost reports

Total and unit costs for each department or process are summarised and determined on a **production cost report.** Production cost reports can be prepared using different formats, but for the sake of consistency only one format is used in this book. The following steps are necessary every time a process cost report is prepared.

Step 1	Quantity or production statement

The quantity statement shows how many units are received in the department or process and how these are disposed of, in other words whether they are transferred to the next process or to finished goods or whether they are still being processed in the department (incomplete work).

The quantity statement deals with the **physical flow** of the units as well as the stage of completion reached by the units in the process.

The units shown in the quantity statement are expressed in terms of the department's finished product (for example litres, kilograms, etc). All the units manufactured in the department must be expressed in one and the same standard.

Suppose that ladies' dresses are made in a particular department and that two metres of material are required for each dress. If 2 000 metres of material enter the process then the quantity statement will show 1 000 **dresses** (2 000 metres material @ 2 metres per dress), since dresses is the unit in which the department's production is measured.

| Step 2 | Establishment of production costs |

The total production costs incurred by a department in an accounting period are determined in the cost statement of the report. The costs for any period can arise from various sources:

☐ They can, for example, be connected with the incomplete units that were in the process at the beginning of the period (ie the units and their associated costs transferred from the previous period).

☐ If the department or process is not the first cost centre (place) in the production process the costs from the previous departments or processes will be received when the units are transferred from there to this department.

☐ Each process will incur labour and manufacturing overheads and possibly further material costs.

| Step 3 | Calculation of equivalent units and unit costs |

The unit costs are determined not only for the product as a whole, but also for each of the cost elements – costs from previous departments and costs added in this department (material, labour and overheads).

If all the units in the department are not completed in the period covered by the report the **equivalent production** must also be calculated. (This is discussed in Module 8.3.)

| Step 4 | Allocation of costs |

Once the total costs for which a department is responsible have been determined by Step 2, account must be given thereof: a portion of the costs will be attributable to units which were transferred to other departments or finished goods. The rest of the costs will be attributable to units which are still being processed in the department and, if applicable, to lost units.

| Step 5 | Proof that all costs are accounted for |

Eventually it must be seen to that the sections of the report dealing with costs (step 2 and 4) agree.

3 Single product, single process (no beginning or ending stock)

Enterprises which manufacture a single product in a single process will prepare a single process cost statement for each accounting period for which a report must be made.

The costs of the material which enters the process are obtained from the material requisitions and the labour costs are attained from the relevant wage analysis statements. Overheads are allocated to the department by application of the appropriate tariff.

In Example 30 it is assumed that 50 000 units enter the process in the period concerned and are completed in the same period. The production costs are shown on the statement.

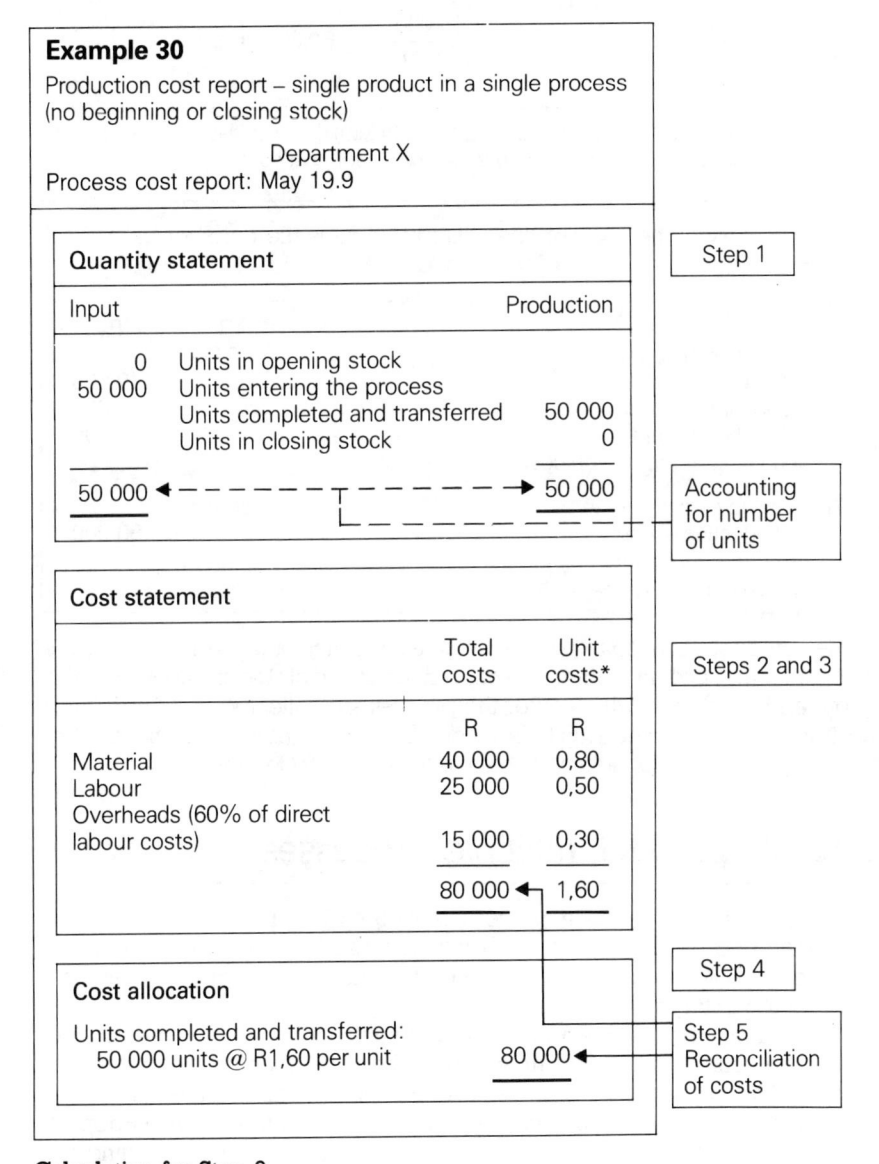

Example 30
Production cost report – single product in a single process (no beginning or closing stock)

Department X
Process cost report: May 19.9

Quantity statement — Step 1

Input		Production
0	Units in opening stock	
50 000	Units entering the process	
	Units completed and transferred	50 000
	Units in closing stock	0
50 000		50 000

Accounting for number of units

Cost statement — Steps 2 and 3

	Total costs	Unit costs*
	R	R
Material	40 000	0,80
Labour	25 000	0,50
Overheads (60% of direct labour costs)	15 000	0,30
	80 000	1,60

Cost allocation — Step 4

Units completed and transferred:
50 000 units @ R1,60 per unit   80 000

Step 5 Reconciliation of costs

Calculation for Step 3
All the units which entered the process (50 000), is complete. Thus there are no incomplete units.

Material costs per unit	=	$\dfrac{R40\ 000}{50\ 000}$	=	R0,80 per unit
Labour costs per unit	=	$\dfrac{R25\ 000}{50\ 000}$	=	R0,50 per unit
Overheads per unit	=	$\dfrac{R15\ 000}{50\ 000}$	=	R0,30 per unit

* Comment: Note how not only the total unit cost (R1,60), but also the unit cost of each element is calculated. These are important figures for cost control.

The summary of the costs on the cost statement is the basis for the following journal entries at the end of the period:

		R	R
(1)	Production account	80 000	
	Material control		40 000
	Labour control		25 000
	Overheads control		15 000
	Recording of production costs for the month		
(2)	Finished goods	80 000	
	Production account		80 000
	Transfer of completed units:		
	50 000 units @ R1,60 each		

The production account, sometimes also called the work-in-progress account, is an account in the general ledger in which the costs of material, labour and overheads which enter the process are collected and from which the transfer of completed units is made. If there is more than one department or process a production account will be opened for each.

4 Single product, multiple processes

In most enterprises where a process costing system is employed there is more than one department through which a product must move consecutively in order to be converted into the finished product which is manufactured by the enterprise.

The costs incurred in **each** of the departments through which the product moves are collected and accounted for in the same manner as for a single process. The total costs of each department (which will include in the second and further departments the costs transferred from a previous department) are divided by the production of that department to determine the unit cost for the department. To illustrate this an enterprise which manufactures steel bumpers for motor vehicles is used as an example.

Example 31

Single product, multiple processes – no incomplete work at the beginning or end of the accountable period.

The only raw material is sheet metal.

In Department 1 the sheet metal is cut to specifications. The cut metal pieces are then transferred to Department 2, where special equipment is used to bend and form them into mudguard shapes. The shaped mudguards are then transferred to Department 3, where they are completed and polished, and then they are transferred to the finished goods storage area. Thus there is a continuous physical flow of the products being processed through various departments which are simultaneously involved in the various facets of the manufacturing action.

The production diagram for this enterprise thus corresponds with that given in Diagram D33: material enters the manufacturing process in Department 1 only, while conversion costs (that is to say labour and overheads) are incurred in each of the departments. These costs must be collected by department and allocated to the units processed in each department.

In the following example it is assumed that all the units which enter the process in each department during a fixed period are completed in the same period:

Asterk Manufacturers started manufacturing steel bumpers for motor vehicles on 1 June 19.6. The following data relates to its activities for June:

1 Plate metal from which 10 000 units can be manufactured is cut in Department 1.
2 The units were completed during the month.
3 Costs incurred:

	Department		
	1	2	3
	R	R	R
Material	30 000	–	–
Labour	4 000	8 000	2 000
Overheads	2 000	4 000	1 000

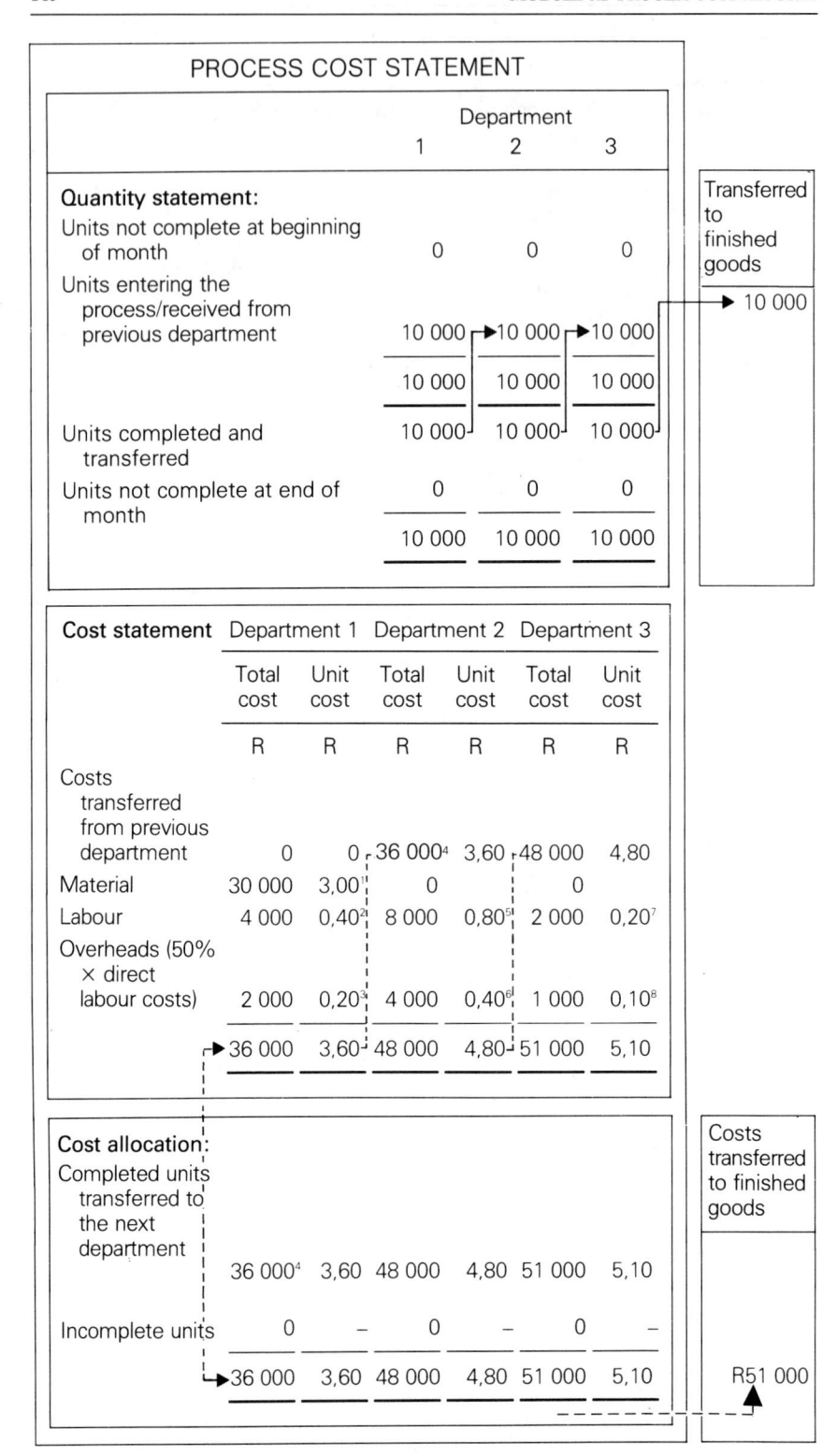

PROCESS COST STATEMENT

	Department 1	Department 2	Department 3	
Quantity statement:				Transferred to finished goods
Units not complete at beginning of month	0	0	0	
Units entering the process/received from previous department	10 000 →10 000 →10 000			→ 10 000
	10 000	10 000	10 000	
Units completed and transferred	10 000┘	10 000┘	10 000┘	
Units not complete at end of month	0	0	0	
	10 000	10 000	10 000	

Cost statement	Department 1		Department 2		Department 3	
	Total cost	Unit cost	Total cost	Unit cost	Total cost	Unit cost
	R	R	R	R	R	R
Costs transferred from previous department	0	0	36 000[4]	3,60	48 000	4,80
Material	30 000	3,00[1]	0		0	
Labour	4 000	0,40[2]	8 000	0,80[5]	2 000	0,20[7]
Overheads (50% × direct labour costs)	2 000	0,20[3]	4 000	0,40[6]	1 000	0,10[8]
	36 000	3,60	48 000	4,80	51 000	5,10

Cost allocation:							Costs transferred to finished goods
Completed units transferred to the next department	36 000[4]	3,60	48 000	4,80	51 000	5,10	
Incomplete units	0	–	0	–	0	–	
	36 000	3,60	48 000	4,80	51 000	5,10	R51 000

Calculations

[1] R30 000 ÷ 10 000
[2] R4 000 ÷ 10 000
[3] R2 000 ÷ 10 000
[4] 10 000 units × R3,60 per unit

[5] R8 000 ÷ 10 000
[6] R4 000 ÷ 10 000
[7] R2 000 ÷ 10 000
[8] R1 000 ÷ 10 000

Note in the example how (because there are no incomplete units at the end of the period in any of the departments) the total costs are transferred from one department to the next in proportion to the units that have physically moved to the next department until they are eventually transferred to completed goods. Note, also, how the unit costs gradually increase:

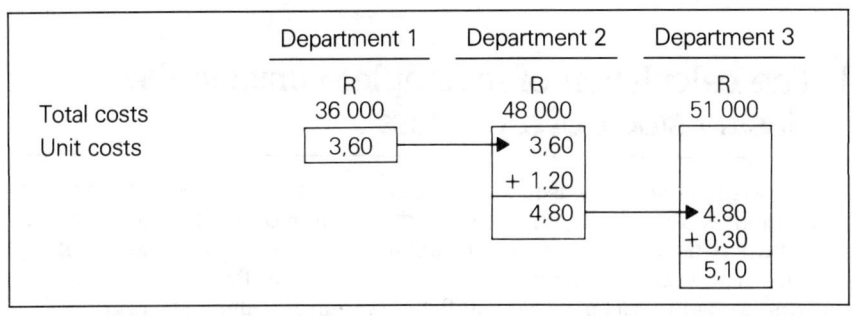

	Department 1	Department 2	Department 3
	R	R	R
Total costs	36 000	48 000	51 000
Unit costs	3,60	3,60	
		+ 1,20	
		4,80	4,80
			+ 0,30
			5,10

Diagram D37

The following journal entries can now be prepared from the process cost report:

	R	R
Production account (Dept 1)	30 000	
Material control		30 000
Recording of material costs		
Production account (Dept 1)	4 000	
Production account (Dept 2)	8 000	
Production account (Dept 3)	2 000	
Wages control		14 000
Recording of labour costs		
Production account (Dept 1)	2 000	
Production account (Dept 2)	4 000	
Production account (Dept 3)	1 000	
Overheads control		7 000
Recording of overheads allocated		
Production (Dept 2)	36 000	
Production account (Dept 1)		36 000
Transfer of units from Dept 1 to Dept 2		
Production account (Dept 3)	48 000	
Production account (Dept 2)		48 000
Transfer of units from Dept 2 to Dept 3		
Finished products	51 000	
Production account (Dept 3)		51 000
Transfer of 10 000 completed units @ R5,10 per unit to finished goods		

Incomplete units and equivalent production

1 The calculation of incomplete units in the closing stock of a process

As was seen in the previous module, the calculation of the "cost per unit" in a department where all the units enter production and are completed in the same period does not present a problem. However, in a process costing system which is continuous in nature it is unlikely that there will be no partially processed products present at the end of an accounting period.

The presence of partially processed products creates a new problem: the total manufacturing costs for a period must be allocated to both completed and incomplete units. The situation can be presented as shown in Diagram D38.

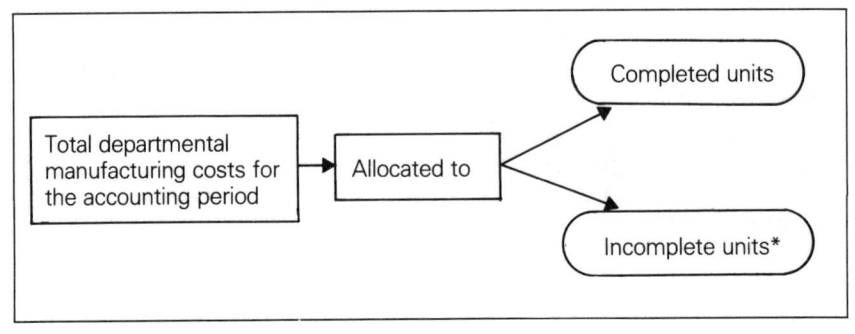

Diagram D38

It would be nonsensical merely to add the number of completed units to the number of incomplete units and use the total to calculate the average unit cost, because then a meaningless mixture of units is used and the resulting cost per unit is not acceptable.

2 Equivalent completed units

In such cases it is necessary to express the completed and incompleted units in terms of **equivalent completed** units **of the product. Using the con-**

---

* Often referred to as work in process.

cept equivalent completed units (ECU) the number of units of a department that must be used in the calculation of the cost per unit can be determined. Example 32 explains the concept ECU.

Example 32

Department: X 03
Period: June 19.6

Units entering the process	20 000
Units completed and transferred	14 000
Units still in process at the end of the period	6 000

The last-mentioned are thus the partially processed or incomplete units.

Although only 14 000 units were completed and transferred during the period this does not represent the complete production activity of the department for the period, because work was also done on the 6 000 incomplete units. The **amount of work** done on the **incomplete units** must thus be determined and added to the production effort of the completed units to determine the department's total production for the period.

This is done by determining the **equivalent completed production** of the incomplete units by inspecting the units and establishing what **percentage of the total resources** necessary to **complete the units has been expended on the incomplete units.** ("Total resources" include all the production resources, viz material, labour and overheads.)

Assume that an inspection of the incomplete units shows that they are 70% complete, then the ECU is calculated as follows:

$$ECU = 6\,000 \times 70\%$$
$$= 4\,200$$

The department's output in terms of ECU is determined as follows:

Completed units	14 000	
Equivalent completed units in closing stock	4 200	(6 000 × 70%)
ECU	18 200	

The latter figure is now used to calculate the unit cost.

3 Ways of using manufacturing resources

Next the "use of resources" in the production process and how this influences the calculation of equivalent production must be investigated.

Actually it boils down to the calculation of the cost per equivalent production of each cost element.

Resources are used in two ways in the production process, namely:

☐ continuously during the process (in this case it is also assumed that the use occurs evenly)

☐ in lots at specified stages in the process.

Although this is not always valid, it is generally accepted that labour and overheads are used continuously and evenly during the production process. On the other hand, material usually enters the process in lots at specified stages.

The **costs** of labour and overheads are thus accounted for on a regular basis and the costs of material at the stages when it enters the process.

The way in which the manufacturing resources are used has an important effect on the calculation of unit costs:

☐ For resources which are used continuously and evenly, the equivalent production is deemed to be directly in proportion to the extent of completeness of the product (eg 70%).

☐ For resources which are added to the production process in lots at certain stages the equivalent completed units are the units which have already passed the stage at which the resource is used.

Example 33

Suppose that 20 000 units are added to the process and that all the material is added at the beginning of the process while labour and overheads are used continuously and evenly.

No units are completed during the accounting period. All the units are physically 70% complete at the end of the period.

Calculation of equivalent production:

	Equivalent completed units	
	Direct material	Conversion costs
Closing stock of incomplete work:		
20 000 units		
20 000 × 100%	20 000	
20 000 × 70%		14 000

All the units have already moved past the point at which the material is added (at the start of the process), therefore they are 100% complete in respect of material.

Because it is assumed that both labour costs and overheads are incurred on a regular basis, the two cost resources are combined as **conversion costs**. This makes no difference to the allocation calculations, provided that both labour costs and the overheads are expended to the same degree (70% in this example).

Incomplete units and unit

cost calculations

1 Incomplete units in closing stock

This aspect has already been touched on in the previous module. It is now developed further by considering the production information of a department which receives products from a previous department as its input and then processes them further.

Example 34

Assume the following information:

Department 2: Production information August 19.3

☐ Units:

Opening stock of incomplete units	0
Units received from Dept 1	30 000
Units completed	25 000
Closing stock of incomplete units:	
100% complete in respect of material	
60% complete in respect of conversion costs	

☐ Costs: R

Transferred from Dept 1	60 000
Direct material	30 000
Direct labour	14 000
Overheads employed (50% of direct labour)	7 000

☐ Material is added at the beginning of the process when the input is received from the previous department. Conversion costs are incurred continuously and evenly in the process.

Thus the flow of the units in Department 2 can be presented schematically as follows:

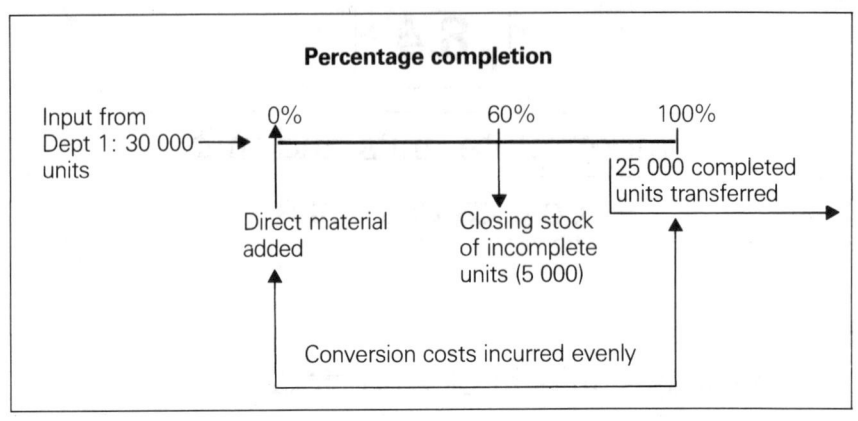

Diagram D39

In the department there are thus three groups of costs that must be taken into consideration:

☐ Costs from the previous department
☐ Direct material added in this department
☐ Conversion costs incurred in this department

It is not necessary to analyse the costs received from the previous department into its elements (material, labour and overheads). In Department 2 it is merely (in total) treated as a cost element of the department.

The calculation of the equivalent completed units of Department 2 is as follows:

	Total	Group 1 Previous dept		Group 2 Material		Group 3 Conversion costs	
			ECU*		ECU*		ECU*
Incomplete units (opening)	0		0		0		0
Units completed	25 000	100%	25 000	100%	25 000	100%	25 000
Incomplete units (closing)	5 000	100%	5 000	100%	5 000	60%	3 000
			30 000		30 000		28 000

* ECU = Equivalent completed units, also called equivalent production

Therefore the cost per unit for the various cost groups is:

Group 1:	$\dfrac{R60\ 000}{30\ 000}$	= R2,00 per unit
Group 2:	$\dfrac{R30\ 000}{30\ 000}$	= R1,00 per unit
Group 3:	$\dfrac{(R14\ 000 + R7\ 000)}{28\ 000}$	= R0,75 per unit

The complete process cost report of this department can be prepared as follows:

Department 2

Process cost report: August 19.3

Quantity statement

Input	Production	Previous dept	Equivalent production Material %		Conversion costs %	
0 Incomplete units (opening)	–	–		–		–
30 000 Units received from Dept 1						
Units completed and transferred	25 000	25 000	100	25 000	100	25 000
Incomplete units (closing)	5 000	5 000	100	5 000	60	3 000
30 000	30 000	30 000		30 000		28 000

Cost statement

	Total costs R	Unit costs R
Costs transferred from previous dept	60 000	2,00
Material	30 000	1,00
Conversion costs	21 000	0,75
	111 000	3,75

(continued)

Cost allocation:		R
Completed units transferred to the next department		93 750
(25 000 units @ R3,75 per unit)		
Incomplete units at end of month *		17 250
Transferred from previous department	5 000 × 2,00	10 000
Material	5 000 × 1,00	5 000
Conversion costs	3 000 × 0,75	2 250
		111 000

* **Important:** Note that as far as the incomplete units are concerned in the cost allocation section **all three** of the cost groups are brought into account at their equivalent unit costs, otherwise the cost statement and cost allocation sections will not reconcile.

2 Incomplete units in opening stock

The next factor in a process costing system is the opening stock of incomplete goods in the different processes. In the examples dealt with thus far it has been assumed that there was no opening stock of partially completed goods present in the departments. In practice it seldom happens that there is no opening stock of incomplete goods present in a department or process because of the continuous nature of the process costing system. The closing incomplete work in Department 2 in the previous example automatically becomes the opening stock present in the system at the beginning of the next period.

Two methods in particular are used to account for the cost of the opening stock in the calculation of unit costs.

☐ Weighted average method

The cost of the opening stock is added to the costs of the current period so that all units which are completed have the same unit cost.

Thus the units in the opening stock are treated in the same way as the units which are started and completed in the current period.

This method will be referred to throughout as the **weighted average method**.

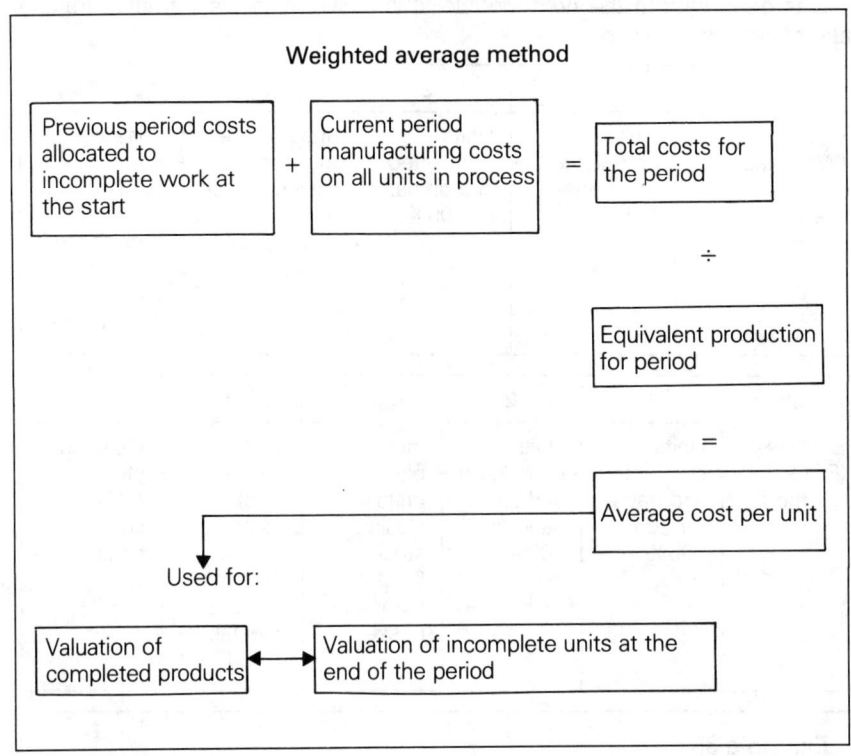

Diagram D40
(Note: In the above diagram "lost units" which are covered later are not taken into account.)

☐ First-in-first-out method (FIFO)

In the FIFO method the costs of the units in the opening stock which are subsequently completed are kept **separate** from the costs of the units which are begun and completed in the current period.

The costs of the goods which are completed and transferred are made up of:

☐ the cost of the units completed which were in the opening stock
☐ the cost of the units which were started and completed in the current period.

The closing stock of incomplete work is valued at the unit cost of the current production. The unit cost of the current production is determined by dividing the production costs incurred in the current period (only) by the equivalent units.

☐ Difference in equivalent units

The equivalent units calculated by means of the FIFO method differ from those calculated by means of the weighted average method due to the different ways in which the opening stock is treated in the two methods.

The formulae for the determination of the equivalent completed units (ECU) by the two methods is as follows (Note: Although the treatment of lost units is dealt with in the next module, it is included in the formulae for the sake of completeness.):

	1	2	3	4
ECU (Weighted average method)	Units = completed and transferred	Units + completed and on hand @ 100%	Incomplete + units in closing stock @ % of completeness	Units + lost @ % of completeness at the time the loss is ascertained

	1	2	3	4	5
ECU (FIFO-method)	Units = completed and transferred @ 100%	Units + completed and on hand @ 100%	Incomplete + units in closing stock @ % of completeness	Units + lost @ % of completeness at the time the loss is established	Opening − stock @ % of completeness

---

Example 35

Quantity statement:

Opening stock (40% complete for all cost elements)	2 400
Put in process	3 600
	6 000
Units completed and transferred	5 400
Closing stock (20% complete for all cost elements)	600
	6 000

Equivalent completed units according to the weighted average method:

(1*)   (2)   (3)   (4)

5 400   +   0   +   120   +   0   =   5 520
                        (20% × 600)

Equivalent completed units according to the FIFO method:

(1)   (2)   (3)   (4)   (5)

5 400 +   0   +   120   +   0   −   960   =   4 560
                  (20% × 600)   (2 400 × 40%)

---

* These figures refer to the steps in the previous formulae.

Example 36

Weighted average method (opening and closing stock)

Assume that the following details refer to Process X during March 19.7:

Production details

Units of incomplete work (opening) (100% complete iro material, 40% complete iro conversion costs)	12 000
Units received from previous department	21 000
	33 000
Units completed and transferred	24 000
Units of incomplete work (closing) (100% complete iro material, 70% complete iro conversion costs)	9 000

Details in connection with costs	R
– Opening incomplete work:	80 175
Costs of previous department	63 150
Direct material	11 340
Conversion costs	5 685
– Costs incurred during March:	172 650
Transferred from previous department	113 400
Direct material	21 000
Conversion costs	38 250
	252 825

Solution

Department X

Process cost report: March 19.7 (Weighted average method)

Quantity statement: Calculation of equivalent completed units

Input		Produc-tion	Previous dept	Material %		Conversion costs %	
				Equivalent production			
12 000	Incomplete units (begin-ning of the month)						
21 000	Received from previous dept						
	Completed and transferred	24 000	24 000	100	24 000	100	24 000
	Incomplete units at end of month	9 000	9 000	100	9 000	70	6 300
33 000		33 000	33 000		33 000		30 300

Cost statement

	Opening stock	Current period	Total	Average cost per unit
	R	R	R	R
Previous dept costs	63 150	113 400	176 550	5,35
Material	11 340	21 000	32 340	0,98
Conversion costs	5 685	38 250	43 935	1,45
	80 175	172 650	252 825	7,78

Cost allocation:

		R
Completed units transferred		
24 000 × R7,78		186 720
Incomplete work at end of month		66 105
Previous dept costs	9 000 × R5,35	48 150
Material	9 000 × R0,98	8 820
Conversion costs	6 300 × R1,45	9 135
		252 825

Calculations:

Average cost per unit per cost element:

Previous department costs	$\dfrac{\text{R176 550}}{\text{33 000}}$	= R5,35
Material	$\dfrac{\text{R32 340}}{\text{33 000}}$	= R0,98
Conversion costs	$\dfrac{\text{R43 935}}{\text{30 300}}$	= R1,45
Completed unit cost		R7,78

Note (in the quantity statement) how the opening stock and the units added during the month are **combined** (refer to the formula) to calculate the equivalent production and the average cost per unit.

Note (in the calculations) that since the total costs comprise three cost groups (previous department's costs, material and conversion costs), it is necessary to calculate the average unit cost of each of the three components using the equivalent completed units (as determined in the quantity statement) in order to be able to calculate the value of the incomplete units at the end of the period.

Example 37

First-in-first-out method (opening and closing stock)

Refer to Example 36. To make the comparison of the weighted average and the FIFO methods easier, exactly the same information is used.

From the previous discussion it is obvious that in contrast with the weighted average method, where the total costs are eventually attributed to **two** production groups (completed units and incomplete units at the end of the period), in the FIFO method there is also a third group to which costs must be attributed. The three groups are:

☐ Group 1: The 12 000 units which were present in the opening stock.
☐ Group 2: A further 12 000 units which were started and completed during the period (Groups 1 and 2 are thus the 24 000 units completed during the period).
☐ Group 3: The 9 000 units which were still incomplete at the end of the period.

It also seems obvious that the costs that are attributable to the first group consist of the costs from the previous period (R80 175) plus the costs incurred in the current period to complete the units. Moreover, it is obvious that the rest of the costs incurred in the period (Note: This includes the cost input of units received during the month from the previous department) are divided among the second and third cost groups (complete and incomplete units).

The FIFO procedures can be presented as shown in Diagram D41.

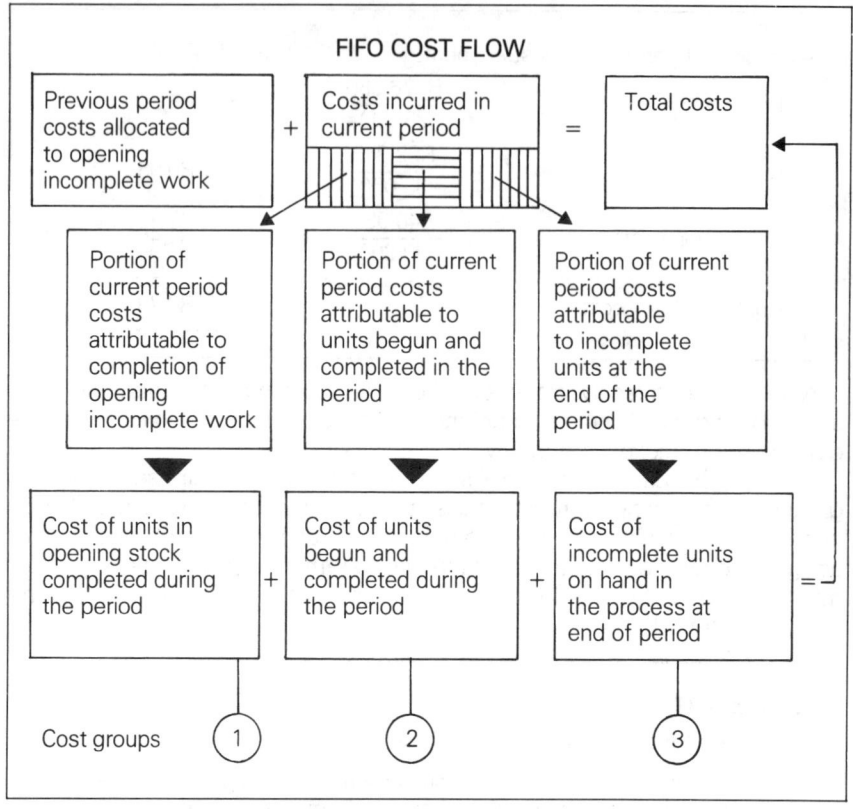

Diagram D41

Note: In the above diagram "lost units" have been ignored for the sake of clarity.

Solution

Department X

Process cost report: March 19.7 (FIFO method)

Quantity statement

Input		Produc-tion	Previous dept		Material		Conversion costs	
					%		%	
12 000	Incomplete units (opening) 100% complete iro material, 40% complete iro conversion costs							
21 000	Received from previous dept Completed and transferred from opening stock	12 000	0	0	0	60*	7 200	
	Begun and completed during the month	12 000	12 000	100	12 000	100	12 000	
	Completed units transferred	24 000						
	Incomplete units (closing)	9 000	9 000	100	9 000	70	6 300	
33 000		33 000	21 000		21 000		25 500	

Cost statement

	Costs R	Current period costs per unit R
Opening stock	80 175	
Received from previous dept	113 400	5,40
Direct material	21 000	1,00
Conversion costs	38 250	1,50
	252 825	7,90

* The units were 40% complete at the beginning of the month. The remaining 60% was completed during the month.

Cost allocation

	R
Units from opening stock completed	90 975
Previous period costs (12 000 units)	80 175
Costs incurred in current period to complete these units (7 200 units × current period conversion costs R1,50)	10 800
Units begun and finished in current period (12 000 × R7,90)	94 800
Total cost of units completed and transferred (24 000 units)	185 775
Incomplete units (end of the month)	67 050
Cost from previous dept (9 000 × R5,40)	48 600
Material (9 000 × R1)	9 000
Conversion costs (6 300 × R1,50)	9 450
	252 825

Calculations:

FIFO unit cost per equivalent completed units: R

Previous department	$\dfrac{\text{R}113\ 400}{21\ 000}$	=	5,40
Direct material	$\dfrac{\text{R}21\ 000}{21\ 000}$	=	1,00
Conversion costs	$\dfrac{\text{R}38\ 250}{25\ 500}$	=	1,50
			7,90

Note (in the quantity statement) that equivalent production is calculated for the three groups, viz opening stock of incomplete work, units begun and completed during the period and incomplete work at the end of the period. Since the opening stock of incomplete units is already 100% complete in respect of material, it is necessary only to calculate the equivalent units in respect of conversion costs for this component.

Note that the equivalent unit costs are calculated for costs incurred in the current period only.

Note (in the cost allocation section of the production cost report) how the total costs of the 24 000 units (12 000 from the opening stock and 12 000 from units that were begun and completed in the period) is determined. It is completely different from the method used in the weighted average cost method (compare the production cost report in Example 36 with the above example.)

The cost of the incomplete work (closing) is determined in the same way as in the weighted average method, but differs in total due to the difference in the costs per unit calculation of the three components contained in the calculation.

3 Alternative setting out of the combined production cost report

It is also possible to use an alternative layout of the production cost report in the form of a combined quantity and production cost statement. The advantage of this layout is clarity and the fact that it is self-balancing. With reference to Example 37:

Example 38

Department X

Combined quantity and production cost statement for March 19.7

	Quantity	Value	Unit price
		R	R
Incomplete work (opening)	12 000	80 175	6,68*
Received from previous dept	21 000	113 400	5,40
Production during the month:			
Material		21 000	1,00
Conversion costs		38 250	1,50
Total input	33 000	252 825	7,90

(continued)

Completed and transferred			
From opening stock	12 000	90 975	7,58*
Previous period costs		80 175	6,68
Costs in current period to complete these units (7 200 × R1,50)		10 800	0,90
Units begun and completed in current period (12 000 × R7,90)	12 000	94 800	7,90
Completed and transferred	24 000	185 775	7,90
Incomplete work (closing)	9 000	67 050	
Costs from previous dept (9 000 × R5,40)		48 600	
Material (9 000 × R1)		9 000	
Conversion costs (9 000 × 70% × R1,50)		9 450	
Total proceeds	33 000	252 825	7,90

* Unit price opening stock of incomplete work (alternative method):

Costs already incurred	R80 175
÷ number of units	12 000
Cost per unit	R6,68
Plus: Conversion costs added (60% × R1,50)	0,90
	R7,58
Completed and transferred:	
Number of units	12 000
Cost per unit	× R7,58
	R90 975†

† Difference is due to rounding: $\dfrac{R80\ 175}{12\ 000} = R6,68125$

               Rounded to   R6,68

Increase in units and unit costs

1 Increase in units as a result of the addition of material

The addition of material to a process usually means that the unit cost will increase. If material is added evenly during the course of a process, the degree of completeness to determine the equivalent production in respect of material will be the same as for conversion costs.

In certain manufacturing processes the addition of material means, however, that the number of units in the process **increases,** for example if 1 000 litres of chemical mixture is received from the previous department and a further 500 litres of liquid is added to the mixture in the process the physical volume increases to 1 500 litres. Since the liquids are mixed and thus can no longer be distinguished, the total cost must be spread over the 1 500 litres.

Example 39

Increase in units as a result of the addition of material (weighted average method)

Assume the following information:

ZAR Manufacturers: Department 2, October 19.8

Units:

Work in process (opening)	
(20% complete iro material, 10% iro conversion costs)	1 000
Received from Department 1	13 000
Increase in units as a result of material added	
(at the beginning of the process)	2 000
	16 000
Completed and transferred	14 800
Closing stock of work in process	
(33⅓% complete iro material, 75% iro conversion costs)	1 200

(continued)

Costs: R

  Opening stock of incomplete work   4 246

     Costs of previous department   4 000
     Material   160
     Conversion costs   86

  Costs incurred during the month   91 490

     Transferred from Dept 1   65 000
     Material   12 760
     Conversion costs   13 730

                                     95 736

Solution

ZAR MANUFACTURERS

Process cost report: October 19.8

Quantity statement

Input		Produc-tion	Previous dept	Equivalent production Material		Conversion-costs	
				%		%	
1 000	Incomplete units (opening)						
13 000	Received from previous dept						
2 000	Increase in units						
	Completed and transferred	14 800	14 800	100	14 800	100	14 800
	Incomplete units (closing)	1 200	1 200	33⅓	400	75	900
16 000		16 000	16 000		15 200		15 700

(continued)

Cost statement

	Opening stock	Current period	Total	Average cost per unit
	R	R	R	R
Previous department's cost	4 000	65 000	69 000	4,3125
Material	160	12 760	12 920	0,8500
Conversion costs	86	13 730	13 816	0,8800
	4 246	91 490	95 736	6,0425

Cost allocation

Completed units transferred

(14 800 × R6,0425) R89 429

Work in process (closing): 6 307

Previous department costs	(1 200 × R4,3125)	=	5 175
Material	(400 × R0,85)	=	340
Conversion costs	(900 × R0,88)	=	792

R95 736

Calculations:

Average cost per unit:

Previous department	$\dfrac{R69\ 000}{16\ 000}$	=	R4,3125
Material	$\dfrac{R12\ 920}{15\ 200}$	=	R0,85
Conversion costs	$\dfrac{R13\ 816}{15\ 700}$	=	R0,88

After 13 000 units were received from Department 1 during the month material costing R12 760 was added in Department 2. As a result the number of units increased by 2 000. In the weighted average cost method (on an equivalent production basis) the cost of these units is simply carried by all the units which were processed during the period (16 000). In the cost allocation it is divided between the completed goods (14 800) and work in process in the closing stock (1 200).

It must be borne in mind that the unit cost of units received from Department 1 (R5, calculated by R65 000 ÷ 13 000) fell (to R4,3125) as a result of the increase in the number of units in Department 2.

Example 40:

Increase in units as a result of the addition of material: FIFO method
(The information is the same as for the previous example.)

Solution

ZAR MANUFACTURERS

Process cost report

Quantity statement

Input		Produc-tion	Previous dept	Equivalent production Material		Conversion-costs	
				%		%	
1 000	Incomplete units (opening)						
13 000	Received from Dept 1						
2 000	Increase in units						
	Completed and transferred from:						
	Opening stock	1 000		80	800	90	900
	Begun and completed during the month	13 800	13 800	100	13 800	100	13 800
	Completed units transferred	14 800					
	Incomplete units (closing)	1 200	1 200	33⅓	400	75	900
16 000		16 000	15 000		15 000		15 600

(continued)

Cost statement

	Costs R	Current period cost per unit* R
Work in process (opening)	4 246	–
Received from Dept 1	65 000	4,3334
Direct material	12 760	0,8507
Conversion costs	13 730	0,8801
	95 736	6,0642

Cost allocation:

	R
Units completed ex-opening stock (1 000)	5 719
Previous department costs	4 246
Costs incurred in current period to complete Material (800 × R0,8507)	681
Conversion costs (900 × R0,8801)	792
Units begun and completed in the current period (13 800 × R6,0642)	83 686
Total cost of units completed and transferred	89 405
Work-in-process closing stock:	6 332
Costs from previous department (1 200 × R4,3334)	5 200
Material (400 × R0,8507)	340
Conversion costs (900 × R0,8801)	792
	95 737

*Calculations:

FIFO equivalent unit cost			
Previous department	$\dfrac{\text{R65 000}}{\text{15 000}}$	=	R4,3334
Direct material	$\dfrac{\text{R12 760}}{\text{15 000}}$	=	R0,8507
Conversion costs	$\dfrac{\text{R13 730}}{\text{15 600}}$	=	R0,8801

Remember that in the FIFO method the work in process of opening stock is not brought into account in the calculation of the current period's equivalent unit costs. As in the weighted average method, the addition of material also results in the number of units increasing. Since it is assumed that it happens at the beginning of the department's process, the increase in the number of units in any period has a bearing on the **new products** only. If the increase in units takes place because the material is added continuously throughout the process the increase in the number of units will have a bearing on both the new production and the opening stock.

Since the FIFO method is used the equivalent units in the opening stock are deducted to determine the **unit costs** for material and conversion costs.

The value of the opening work in process is not added to the current period's costs as in the weighted average method.

In the cost allocation section of the process cost report the following must be borne in mind:

☐ Since the opening stock was only partially processed (material 20% and conversion costs 10%), further costs in respect of the two cost elements are assigned to the opening work in process in order to complete it. (Refer to the quantity statement.).

☐ In the FIFO method the completed goods which are transferred consist of two groups of costs: the opening stock of work in process (1 000 units) now completely processed at a total cost of R5 719 and 13 800 units from current production at a cost of R83 686.

☐ The closing stock of work in process comprises three cost elements, each of which is allocated to the work in process according to the equivalent production and at the applicable unit cost.

Joint and by-products

1 Introduction

From previous modules it is obvious that the collection and allocation of costs occur so that manufacturing costs can be allocated to products, as is evident from Diagram D42.

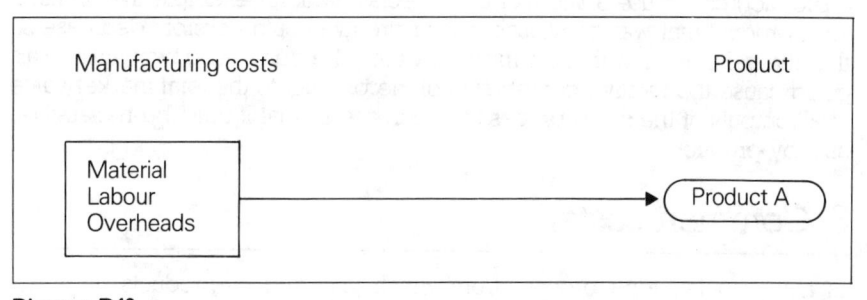

Diagram D42

In this module attention is given to the manufacturing processes in which more than one product results from the same inputs and process, as illustrated in Diagram D43.

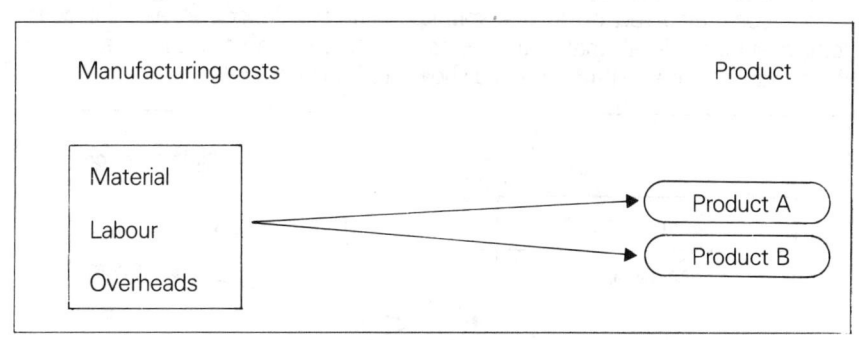

Diagram D43

The petroleum industry is a good example of an industry in which such **common products** occur. The processing of raw oil gives rise to various products such as petrol, power-paraffin, oil, etc.

2 Classification into joint and by-products

Common products which arise from the same manufacturing process can be either **joint or by-products.**

☐ **Joint products** are common products which are produced in large quantities and make a material contribution to the market value of all the outputs of a manufacturing process.

☐ **By-products** are products which are incidental to the production of the joint products and contribute a relatively small amount to the total market value of all the outputs of a process.

The classification is not determined by a precise ratio (or percentage) of the value of a product to the total value. It is a question of sound judgement. For example, when a log is processed in a sawmill the various grades of planks which result therefrom are joint products, while the bark and sawdust which inevitably result from the same process are by-products.

Changing circumstances (such as a change in the relative market value of a product) can cause a product to be reclassified, for example the demand for a product that was previously a joint product could possibly decrease so that the selling price thereof must inevitably be adjusted downwards. This could cause the relative contribution of the product to the total market value of all outputs of the same process to decrease so that it must be reclassified as a by-product.

3 Common costs

In any manufacturing process from which joint and by-products originate there is a point up to which it is not possible to identify the individual products. After this point they are clearly identifiable. The point in the process where the individual products are clearly identifiable is known as the **split-up point** (or separation point).

The costs incurred up to the split-up point are described as **joint costs.** Joint costs include all material, labour and overheads costs incurred to get the product to the split-up point as shown in Diagram D44.

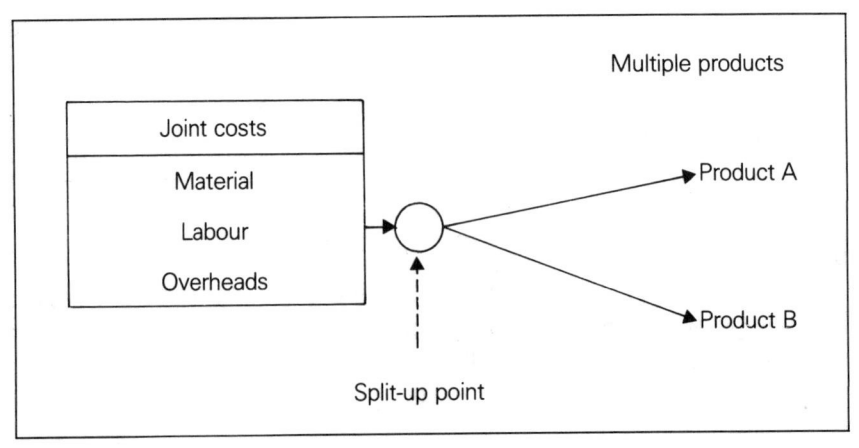

Diagram D44

4 Costing methods for joint products

The underlying costing problem that arises is: How are the joint costs allocated to the multiple products? Two basic methods are used for this purpose.

☐ The physical standard method uses a physical standard to make the allocation. The physical standard can be a quantity (units, litres, metres) or a weight (kilograms).

☐ The relative market value method uses the market value of the joint products at the split-up point.

Example 41 explains the two methods.

Example 41:

X Manufacturers processes a single material into two separate products, A-ONE and A-TWO. Both products can be sold immediately after their separation at the split-up point, product A-ONE at R20 per litre and product A-TWO at R10 per litre. During March 19.3 9 000 litres of the material input was used at a joint cost of R21 000. The manufacturing process produced 6 000 litres of A-ONE and 3 000 litres of A-TWO.
  The total production for March was sold during the month.
  Diagram D45 presents the basic information of the example.

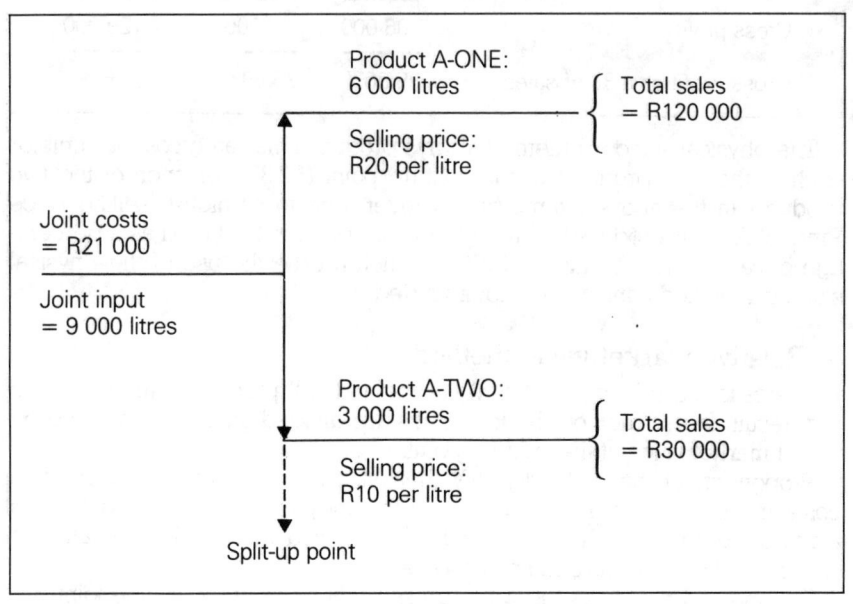

Diagram D45

☐ The physical standard method

In this method the joint costs are allocated to each product in relation to the physical quantity of each product produced.

The facts necessary for the application of the method emerge quite clearly from the diagram:

☐ 9 000 litres were placed in the joint process.

☐ From this 6 000 litres of product A-ONE and 3 000 litres of A-TWO were produced.

Product	Quantity produced (litres)	Ratio	Total joint costs	Allocation of joint costs	Costs per liter
A-ONE	6 000	6 000÷9 000	× R21 000	R14 000	R2,334
A-TWO	3 000	3 000÷9 000		R7 000	R2,334
	9 000			R21 000	

INCOME STATEMENT			
	Products		Total
	A-ONE	A-TWO	
	R	R	R
Sales	120 000	30 000	150 000
Joint costs	14 000	7 000	21 000
Gross profit	106 000	23 000	129 000
Gross profit as a % of sales	88,33%	76,69%	86%

The physical standard method always produces the same cost per unit for each of the joint products at the split-up point (R2,334 for each of the two products in the above example). However, due to its higher selling price Product A-ONE produces a far higher gross profit in total (and as a percentage of sales) than Product A-TWO. In such a case the use of the physical standard method cannot be recommended.

☐ Relative market value method

In this case the relative market value method will produce a more satisfactory result. In this method the joint costs are divided on the basis of the potential **market value** at the split-up point.

Proponents of the method justify their standpoint by reasoning that joint costs are incurred with the expectation that they will be recovered and that a reasonable profit will be made. In this method there is thus a ratio between production costs and selling value.

The method produces the same gross profit percentage for the joint products.

Product	Pro-duction (litres)	Selling price at split-up price	Market value	Ratio	Total joint costs	Portion of joint costs	Cost per litre
			R		R	R	R
A-ONE	6 000	× R20 =	120 000	120÷150		16 800	2,80
					× 21 000		
A-TWO	3 000	× R10 =	30 000	30÷150		4 200	1,40
	9 000		150 000			21 000	

INCOME STATEMENT

	Products A-ONE	A-TWO	Total
	R	R	R
Sales	120 000	30 000	150 000
Joint costs	16 800	4 200	21 000
Gross profit	103 200	25 800	129 000
Gross profit as a % of sales	86,0%	86,0%	86,0%

5 Additional processing costs

Often joint products are not sold directly after the split-up point but are processed further in separate processes. The additional processing costs incurred by each product are known as **separable costs** because they can be allocated to the distinguishable products by means of either job or process costing systems. Diagram D46 illustrates such a situation.

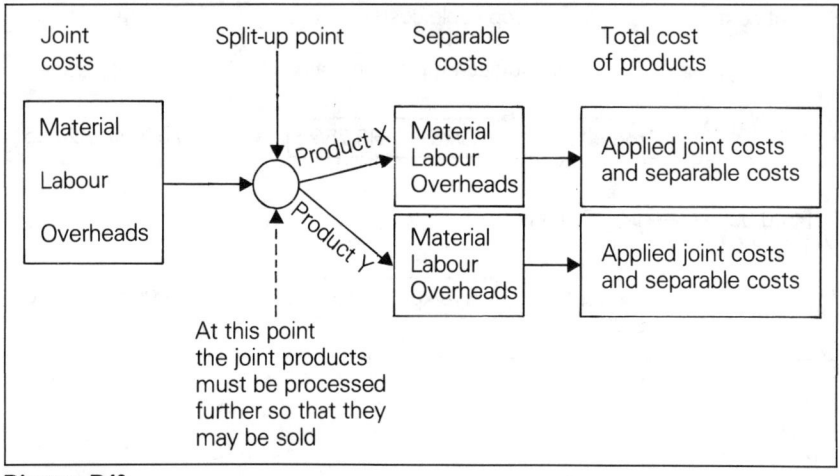

Diagram D46

6 Approximate market value at the division point

If the market value of the joint products is not known at the split-up point it can be estimated using the separable costs and the maket value after the processing of the various products.

This is done by taking the eventual selling price of a product and deducting the separable processing costs incurred after the split-up point from the selling price. The result is the **estimated market value** at the split-up point. This estimated value can be used to allocate the joint costs according to the relative market value method.

Example 42

LS Manufacturers produces two products, X and Y, using a single raw material as input into the manufacturing process. The products cannot be sold after the split-up point unless they undergo further processing.

During October 19.7 150 000 kilograms of the raw material was processed at a joint cost of R300 000. All the units were complete at the end of the month. The following information is relevant to the two products:

	Product X	Product Y
Production (kilograms)	75 000	75 000
Sales (kilograms)	60 000	45 000
Closing stock (kilograms)	15 000	30 000
Selling price	R24/kilogram	R42/kilogram
Separable costs:		
Manufacturing	R9/kilogram	R18/kilogram
Marketing	R3,75/kilogram	R10/kilogram

The facts can be presented schematically as follows:

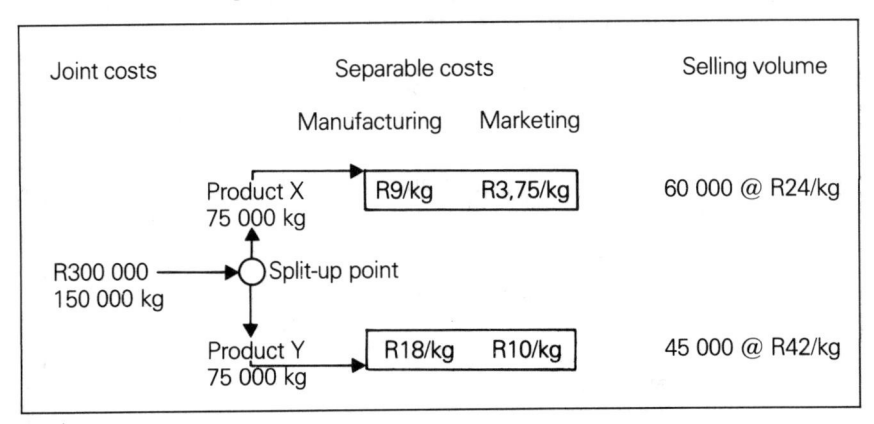

Since no market value is known at the split-up point, it can be estimated as follows:

| | Product | | |
	X	Y	Total
Production volume (kg)	75 000	75 000	150 000
	R	R	R
Selling price per kg	24	42	–
Total sales	1 800 000	3 150 000	4 950 000
Deduct separable costs	900 000	1 800 000	2 700 000
Manufacturing	675 000[1]	1 350 000[2]	2 025 000
Marketing	225 000[3]	450 000[4]	675 000
Estimated market value at split-up point	900 000	1 350 000	2 250 000
Ratio	$\frac{900}{2\,250} = 40\%$	$\frac{1\,350}{2\,250} = 60\%$	= 100%
Portion of joint costs			
40% × R300 000	120 000		
60% × R300 000		180 000	R300 000

[1] 75 000 × R 9   = R 675 000
[2] 75 000 × R18   = R1 350 000
[3] 60 000 × R 3,75 = R 225 000
[4] 45 000 × R10   = R 450 000

7 Costing methods for by-products

By-products have already been identified as the incidental output of a manufacturing process. Although there are a number of methods of accounting for by-products, all are actually variations of the following two methods:

☐ A value that corresponds to the **net market value of the by-products at the split-up point** is allocated to the products. This amount is then used as a **reduction of the joint production costs.** The **net market value** of by-products is: market value less further processing costs (if applicable) less administrative costs. This concept is also referred to as net realisable value.

☐ No value is allocated to the by-products at the split-up point. The proceeds from the sale of the by-products can be treated in various ways:
- as a reduction of the joint production costs
- as a separate item in the income statement: proceeds of sales of by-products
- as a reduction of the cost of goods sold

Example 43

Suppose that a manufacturer produces two joint products and a by-product from a process and that a typical production run results in the following:

Product	Quantity	Market value at split-up point
X	1 400 units	R40 per unit
Y	600 units	R30 per unit
By-product Z	80 units	R4 per unit

All products are sold after the split up. The joint costs up to that point are R148 320.

In this case the joint costs will be allocated according to the net market value method as follows:

		R
Total joint costs		148 320
Deduct: Net realisable value of By-product Z (80 × R4)*		320
Net joint costs		148 000

Product	Units	Market value at split-up point	Total market value	Ratio	Joint costs	Portion of joint costs
			R			R
X	1 400	R40 p.u.	56 000	56÷74	× 148 000	112 000
Y	600	R30 p.u.	18 000	18÷74		36 000
			74 000			148 000

---

* **If no portion of the joint costs is allocated to the by-products** the total joint costs (R148 320 in the previous example) will be allocated to the joint products as if the by-product did not exist.

By-products can be divided into two categories, namely:

☐ those that require further processing
☐ those that can be sold without further processing after separation at the split up point.

Where no joint costs are allocated to by-products the proceeds from the sale of the by-products are disclosed directly in the income statement by means of one of the methods mentioned above. This is illustrated in Example 44.

Example 44

No joint costs allocated to by-products

The following information is used to show the various ways of dealing with by-products when no joint costs are allocated to them:

	Joint products kg	By-products kg
Production	100 000	40 000
Sale	96 000	38 000
Closing stock	4 000	2 000
Selling price	R2 per kg	R0,35 per kg
Cost of further processing (by-product only)		R0,05 per kg
Joint production costs		R90 000
Marketing and administration costs		R50 000

Solution

Calculations

1 Income (net market value) from by-products

= Total units sold × (Selling price − Separable costs)

= 38 000 × (R0,35 − R0,05)

= R11 400

2 Value of closing stock of joint products

$$= \frac{4\ 000}{100\ 000} \times R90\ 000$$

= R3 600

Income statement:

No value allocated to by-products; proceeds from sale treated as:			
	1 Reduction of cost of sales	2 Reduction of joint production costs	3 A separate income statement item
	R	R	R
Sales			
Joint products (96 000 × R2)	192 000	192 000	192 000
By-products (Calculation 1)	–	–	11 400
Total sales	192 000	192 000	203 400
Cost of sales	75 000	75 000	86 400
Joint production costs	90 000	78 600*	90 000
Less net proceeds By-products	11 400	–	–
	78 600	78 600	90 000
Less closing stock: Joint products	3 600	3 600	3 600
Gross profit	117 000	117 000	117 000
Marketing and administrative costs	50 000	50 000	50 000
Net income	67 000	67 000	67 000

* R90 000 – R11 400 = R78 600

8 Reversal cost method

This is an alternative method whereby the joint costs are divided between the various joint products. Although an inaccurate method, it is sometimes found in practice because it is easy to use.

As the name indicates, the reversal cost method is based on the assumption that the expected profit percentage for some products is known. The percentage can be obtained by drawing a comparison with similar products manufactured by other organisations in the same industry, or by a projected yield rate set as a minimum by management.

If the expected profit percentage is known the projected net profit for each product can be calculated. With this figure as a basis the income and costs after separation can be reversed to determine what portion of the joint costs can be absorbed by each product. Thus it is concerned with what amount each product can absorb, rather than the correct principle of what amount should be allocated to each product. This is illustrated in Example 45.

Example 45

LM Manufacturers produces products A, B and C using a single raw material as input into the manufacturing process. The following information is available:

| | Products | | |
	A	B	C
	R	R	R
Sales	500 000	30 000	20 000
Costs after split up	80 000	3 000	2 000
Selling and marketing expenses	30 000	2 000	1 000
Opening and closing stock	–	–	–
Expected profit percentage on sales		20%	15%
The production costs prior to separation amounted to R200 000			

Required

Prepare an income statement using the reversal cost method.

Solution

Cost and income statement

| | A | B | C | Total |
	R	R	R	R
Sales	500 000	30 000	20 000	550 000
Less: Attributable items	110 000	11 000	6 000	127 000
Marketing costs	30 000	2 000	1 000	33 000
Costs after split up	80 000	3 000	2 000	85 000
Expected profit		6 000	3 000	9 000
(% of sales)				
Available income	390 000	19 000	14 000	423 000
Joint costs	167 000	19 000	14 000	200 000
Expected profit (Product A)	223 000	–	–	223 000

Total expected profit:

	R
Product A	223 000
Product B	6 000
Product C	3 000
	232 000

9 By-products and waste material

By-products and waste material are not always easy to distinguish since both arise from the manufacturing process. If shirts for example, are cut at a clothes factory, there are always pieces of waste material that might have a minimum market value. However, this is usually so little that there is some doubt as to whether waste material can be referred to as a "product". Any proceeds from the sale of waste material are treated as a reduction of the cost of the main product.

Module

8.7

Accounting for spoilt units

1 Introduction

In the preceding discussion of piecework and process costing systems it was accepted that **all** units which enter the manufacturing process are eventually converted into saleable finished products.

☐ Spoilt products

This assumption is not valid in practice, however, because in most manufacturing processes **spoilt products**, that is products which do not meet the quality specifications laid down occur.

Management must consider the degree of defectiveness of such products to decide whether the products should be shown as **wasted units** or whether it is possible to re-process them to get an approved product.

☐ Wastage

Suppose that an enterprise receives an order for the manufacture of 50 000 units of Product X and that after completion of the manufacturing process it is found that 600 of the units do not comply with the client's specifications. The 600 must be evaluated to decide:

☐ whether the spoilt units must be classified wholly or partially as **wasted units** and sold as junk

☐ whether the spoilt units, or some of them, can possibly be **re-processed** so that they comply with the quality specifications and can be sold as normal products.

☐ Shrinkage and evaporation

Besides wastage, units can be lost during a manufacturing process as a result of shrinkage and evaporation. This arises when the quantity of material necessary to complete a given job or process is more than the quantity that is necessary theoretically. In contrast to wastage, with shrinkage and evaporation there are no spoilt products to speak of.

Changes in the temperature during a chemical process can cause higher than normal or expected evaporation, with the result that a lower number of units than projected is produced.

Since accounting for wastage and for shrinkage and evaporation is done in the same manner, from here on reference is made to wastage only.

Wastage can be classified into two categories, namely normal wastage and abnormal wastage.

2 Normal wastage

Normal wastage is wastage that is inherent in the product or the manufacturing process. It is thus wastage that is anticipated (in other words it usually occurs) and occurs repeatedly. Therefore provision is made for it in the planning of the production. Suppose, for example, that 1 000 units must be manufactured and the normal wastage in the relevant process is 100 units, then 1 100 units will be put into production.

Since normal wastage is expected, it is accounted for by treating the cost of the normal wastage as part of the cost of the "good" products.

> The cost of the normal wastage is thus deemed to be a product cost and is allocated to the acceptable units manufactured.

3 Abnormal wastage

This is wastage which is not anticipated and could be avoided, in other words it is wastage which is deemed to be **controllable**. Suppose, for example, that the normal wastage rate in a process is 5%. If the actual wastage rate is 8% the abnormal wastage is the difference between the actual wastage rate and the normal wastage, being 3%.

> Since abnormal wastage is not anticipated, the cost thereof is written off as a loss in the income statement in the period in which it occurred.

4 Scrap

In most manufacturing processes there are shavings or splinters which arise from the manufacturing process. This is known as **scrap**. It usually has little value and is therefore not shown in the stock account as an asset.

If scrap is sold the proceeds are credited to the actual overheads account as follows:

Cash (or debtors)	XXX	
Actual overheads		XXX
Recording of the sale of scrap		

Since the amount of the proceeds of the scrap reduces the actual overheads, this will be taken into account in the determination of the overheads recovery rate.

5 Accounting for spoilt work in job costing systems

☐ As a general manufacturing cost

In job costing systems various jobs are carried out on orders from clients and according to their specifications. A certain amount of normal wastage is to be expected seeing that (particularly with piecework) substantially the same machinery and labour is used on all the jobs in a particular enterprise although the jobs are not similar.

The costs of this normal wastage are associated with **all** the tasks carried out during a given period and are consequently attributed to them rather than to a specific task.

The most general way in which the allocation of the costs of normal wastage to the total production for a period is carried out is by including an allowance for normal wastage in the predetermined overheads tariff. This is done by estimating the cost of the normal wastage at the beginning of the period for the entire period and including the estimate as part of the total estimated overheads used to calculate the overheads tariff.

Example 46

Accounting for normal and abnormal wastage in a job costing system.

Suppose AX Manufacturers estimates that normal wastage for all jobs amounts to 5% of the units which enter production and that the enterprise makes provision for the cost thereof in the determination of the overheads tariff.

The following information refers to completed Job no AX 573:

Cost of direct material used	R2 000
Direct labour costs	R2 500
Overheads employed	R2 500
Total costs	R7 000

The required material to complete 1 000 units for the job was put into production.

The total wastage was 90 units.

The expected wastage for the particular task is 5% × 1 000 units = 50 units. In this case the abnormal wastage is thus 90 − 50 = 40 units.

The unit cost for Job no AX 573 = $\dfrac{\text{R7 000}}{1\,000}$ = R7,00 per unit.

The unit cost includes a provision for normal wastage which is built into the overheads tariff used for the allocation of overheads to the job.

In this case the costs of the approved (not spoilt) units and the normal and abnormal wastage are calculated as follows:

					R
Approved units completed	=	910 × R7 pu	=		6 370
Normal wastage	=	50 × R7 pu	=		350
Abnormal wastage	=	40 × R7 pu	=		280
		1 000			7 000

The journal entry for the recording of the completion of Job no AX 573 is as follows:

	R	R
Finished goods	6 370	
Actual manufacturing overheads	350	
Loss iro abnormal wastage	280	
Production (Job no AX 573)		7 000

Bear in mind that the cost of normal wastage is debited to the actual manufacturing overheads account since the estimated normal wastage has already been credited to it and has been allocated to the production account by means of the overheads tariff.

☐ Job-related normal wastage

In contrast with the forgoing procedure, where normal wastage is associated with the total production, an alternative procedure in which a special job wastage tariff is employed may also be used.

Example 47

Job associated wastage

Suppose that as in the previous example, AX Manufacturers, estimates that the expected normal wastage tariff for all jobs is 5% and that provision is made for this in the overheads tariff. However, the enterprise carries out an order which has particular manufacturing problems associated with it.

A wastage tariff of 15% is expected for the job (no AX 920). (As a result of the high wastage tariff the enterprise will require a higher price for the special job.)

The following information refers to the job:

	R
Cost of material used	29 600
Direct labour	50 000
Overheads employed	50 000
Total costs of the job	129 600

The material required to make 600 units was put into production. After completion of the task the completed units were inspected and it was found that 475 units complied with the client's specifications.

In this example there are three possible types of wastage:

General process-related wastage	5%
Job-related wastage	10%
Total expected wastage	15%
Abnormal wastage – everything above	15%

The general process-related wastage is thus	5% × 600 =	30	units
The job-related wastage is thus	10% × 600 =	60	units
Expected wastage is thus		90	units

However, the actual wastage was $600 - 475 = 125$, therefore the abnormal wastage is $125 - 90 = 35$ units.

The cost per unit is $\dfrac{R129\ 600}{600} = R216,00$ per unit.

The allocation of the total costs of R129 600 is as follows:

Approved units (475 × R216,00)	=	R102 600
Job-related normal wastage (60 × R216,00)	=	12 960
Costs allocated to 475 approved units	=	R115 560
Process-related normal wastage (30 × R216,00)	=	6 480
Abnormal wastage (35 × R216,00)	=	7 560
		R129 600

The job-related normal wastage is thus allocated to the cost of the approved units. It increases the average unit cost of these units from R216 to R243,28 calculated as follows: $\dfrac{R115\ 560}{475}$. It reflects the additional costs of completing this particular job.

The journal entry for the recording of the completed job is:

Finished goods (475 × R243,28)	115 560*	
Actual manufacturing overheads (30 × R216)	6 480	
Abnormal wastage loss (35 × R216)	7 560	
Production (Job no AX 920)		129 600

☐ Re-processing costs

By incurring additional costs in respect of material, labour and overheads, it is sometimes possible to re-process some of the spoilt units so that they com-

---

* 475 × R243,28 = R115 558: The difference is due to rounding to two decimals.

ply with the manufacturing specifications and can be reclassified as approved units. These additional costs can be treated in two ways:

☐ If they are **process-related** they may be debited to **actual manufacturing overheads** and allocated to the total production for the year by means of the overheads tariff.

Suppose, for example, that the following re-processing costs are incurred in respect of Job no 1059:

	R
Direct material	700
Direct labour	500
Overheads employed	500
	1 700

The additional costs will be recorded as follows:

	R	R
Actual manufacturing overheads	1 700	
Material control account		700
Wages control account		500
Overheads employed account		500

☐ If the re-processing costs are **job-related** (in other words, caused by the special requirements of the job), the costs of R1 700 will be debited to the production account for the specific job.

Module
8.8

Accounting for spoilt units:
treatment in process costing systems

1 Introduction

Seeing that enterprises in which process costing systems are used undertake mass production of standardised products, there will be no job-related wastage in these systems. Thus in process costing systems all wastage is either normal wastage associated with the process or abnormal wastage.

In job costing systems the expected cost of normal wastage is included in the overheads recovery tariff. **In contrast with this, in process costing systems the cost of normal wastage is calculated at the end of the accounting period and, depending on the stage reached in the manufacturing process when the wastage is detected, is allocated to work in process and completed units.**

Wastage is usually detected at fixed inspection points in the process. **The cost of normal wastage is allocated only to the approved units that have already passed an inspection point or wastage point.**

Losses or wastage can occur at any of the following stages in the production process:

☐ At the beginning of the process

☐ At any stage during the process

☐ At the end of the process

In the first two cases where the work in process has reached the wastage point, the cost of **normal wastage** is absorbed by:

☐ units manufactured and transferred to the next process or to finished goods

☐ work in process (closing)

☐ abnormal losses.

However, if the wastage occurs during or at the **end** of the process and there is incomplete work in process which has **not yet reached the wastage point,** no cost of normal wastage is allocated to such incomplete work. In this situation the cost of normal wastage will be absorbed only by:

☐ complete units

☐ abnormal losses.

Study Diagram D47 and the information given.

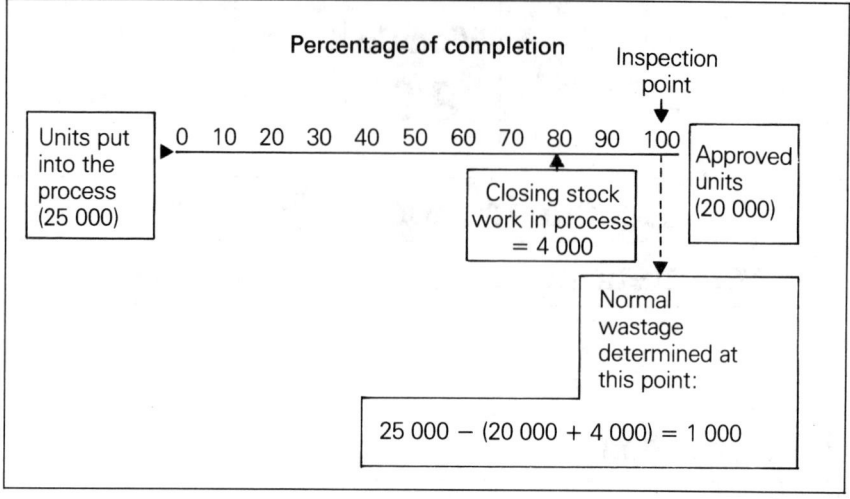

Diagram D47

In the above example there is no opening stock. The diagram shows that 25 000 units were put into the process and that normal wastage amounts to 1 000 units. The only wastage point in this example is on completion of the units. In this case the cost of the normal wastage (since there is no abnormal wastage) will be allocated to the 20 000 completed units. The work in process (4 000) has not yet reached the wastage point and therefore no cost of normal wastage is allocated to it.

The various possibilities are illustrated in the examples which follow.

2 Accounting for wastage where the weighted average method is applied

Example 48

Normal wastage at the **beginning** of process
No opening or closing stock of work in process

The following information relates to Process 1 of Fox Manufacturers for May 19.7:

Work in process	0
Input of material	100 000 kg
Completed and transferred to Process 2	95 000 kg
Material cost (added at the start of the process)	R190 000
Conversion costs (incurred evenly during the process)	R47 500

Normal wastage (inherent in the manufacturing process) is estimated at 5% of the input and occurs at the start of the process.

<table>
<tr><td colspan="7" align="center">Fox Manufacturers
Process cost report: May 19.7</td></tr>
</table>

Quantity statement

Input	Production	Equivalent units			
		Material		Conversion costs	
		%	Units	%	Units
– Work in process (opening)					
100 000 Put into process					
Completed and transferred	95 000	100	95 000	100	95 000
Normal wastage (5% × 100 000 input)	5 000		–		–
100 000	100 000		95 000		95 000

Cost statement

	R	Equivalent units	Cost per unit
Costs from previous month	0	–	–
Costs for current month			
Material	190 000	95 000	R2,00
Conversion costs	47 500	95 000	0,50
	237 500		R2,50

Cost allocation

	R
Units completed and transferred to Process 2 (95 000 × R2,50)	237 500
Work in process (closing)	0
	237 500

From the above example it is obvious that:
- □ normal wastage has no influence on the total production cost
- □ normal wastage does have an influence on the unit cost, because the cost of normal wastage is absorbed by the "approved" units
- □ because normal wastage is inherent in the manufacturing process the number of wasted units is left out of the calculation of the equivalent units.

As has already been seen in Module 8.7, for various reasons the actual wastage is seldom equal to the estimated normal wastage. This gives rise to abnormal wastage. The treatment of abnormal wastage becomes evident in the examples which follow.

Example 49

Normal and abnormal wastage at the start of the process
No opening or closing stock of work-in-process

The same information as given in Example 48 is valid for this example, with the exception that only 93 000 approved units are transferred to Process 2.

Fox Manufacturers
Process cost report Process 1: May 19.7

Quantity statement

Input		Production	Equivalent units Material Units	Conversion costs Units
0	Work in process (opening)			
100 000	Introduced into process			
	Completed and transferred	93 000	93 000	93 000
	Normal wastage (5% × 100 000 input)	5 000	–	–
		98 000		
	Abnormal wastage	2 000[1]	2 000	
100 000		100 000	95 000	93 000

(continued)

Cost statement

	R	Equivalent units	Cost per kg
Cost from previous month			
Work in process (opening)	0	–	
Cost for current month			
Material	190 000	95 000	R2,0000
Conversion costs	47 500	93 000	0,5108
	237 500		R2,5108

Cost allocation

	R
Units transferred to Process 2 (93 000 × R2,5108)	233 504,40
Cost of abnormal wastage	4 000,00[2]
Material (2 000 × R2,00)	4 000,00
Conversion costs	0
	237 504,40*

* The difference of R4,40 is due to the rounding of the unit costs to the fourth decimal place.

1 Seeing that (in this example) abnormal wastage takes place at the beginning of the process, that is to say with the input of the material into the process but before any conversion costs are incurred, it is added for the calculation of equivalent unit costs of material but not for conversion costs.

2 The cost of the abnormal wastage is transferred to an abnormal wastage account (refer to the relevant journal entries in the previous module) and eventually appears as a separate item in the costing and profit and loss account.

3 It is also obvious that the completed units and the abnormal wastage absorb the cost of the normal wastage by means of the use of the equivalent units.

Example 50
No incomplete work at the start of the process
Wastage at the beginning of the process
Incomplete work at the end of the process

Kalke Limited manufactures a single product in two processes. The following information is relevant to Process 1 for March 19.6:

Work in process (opening)	0
Material put into process	
(50 000 kg)	R135 000
Direct labour	R82 000
Overheads applied	R20 200
Work in process (closing)	6 000 kg
Percentage completion	
Material	100 %
Labour	50 %
Overheads	40 %
Units transferred to Process 2	38 000

Normal wastage is estimated at 10% of inputs.
Wastage takes place at the start of the process.

Kalke Limited

Process cost report: Process 1 March 19.6

Quantity statement:

Input (kg)	Production	Material %	Material Units	Labour %	Labour Units	Overheads %	Overheads Units
0 Work in process (opening)	0						
50 000 Input during the month							
Completed and transferred	38 000	100	38 000	100	38 000	100	38 000
Work in process (closing)	6 000	100	6 000	50	3 000	40	2 400
Normal wastage (10% × 50 000)	5 000						
	49 000						
Abnormal wastage	1 000	100	1 000				
50 000	50 000		45 000		41 000		40 400

(continued)

Cost statement

	Total cost	Equivalent production	Cost per unit
	R		R
Material	135 000	45 000	3,00
Labour	82 000	41 000	2,00
Overheads	20 200	40 400	0,50
	237 200		5,50

Cost allocation statement

Work in process (opening)	0
Units completed and transferred (38 000 × R5,50)	209 000
Work in process (closing)	25 200
Material (6 000 × R3,00)	18 000
Labour (3 000 × R2,00)	6 000
Overheads (2 400 × R0,50)	1 200
Abnormal wastage	
Material (1 000 × R3,00)*	3 000
Labour	0
Overheads	0
	237 200

Wastage takes place at the beginning of the process. Thus, as in the previous example, only material costs are involved in the abnormal wastage. Therefore, nothing in the allocation statement added to the cost of the abnormal wastage in respect of labour and overheads.

Note again that in this example the cost of the normal wastage is absorbed by the three elements, namely units completed and transferred, work in process (closing) and abnormal wastage.

Example 51

No opening stock of work in process
Closing stock on hand
Wastage occurs **during** the process

Zoulda Limited manufactures a single product in two processes. The following information is applicable to Process 1 for June 19.8:

	R
Work in process (opening)	0
Input of material (100 000 kg)	360 000
Conversion costs incurred	173 600
Units completed and transferred to Process 2	80 000
Work in process (closing)	8 000 units
Percentage completion	
Material	100%
Conversion costs	75%

All material is issued at the beginning of the process. Conversion costs are incurred evenly during the process.
Normal wastage is estimated at 10% of inputs and takes place when production is 40% complete.

Zoulda Limited
Process cost report: Process 1 June 19.8

Quantity statement

Input (kg)	Production	Production	Equivalent units Material %	Equivalent units Material Units	Equivalent units Conversion costs %	Equivalent units Conversion costs Units
0	Work in process (opening)					
100 000	Input					
	Completed and transferred	80 000	100	80 000	100	80 000
	Work in process (closing)	8 000	100	8 000	75	6 000
	Normal wastage (10% × 100 000)	10 000				
		98 000				
	Abnormal wastage	2 000[1]	100	2 000[2]	40	800[3]
100 000		100 000		90 000		86 800

(continued)

Cost statement

	R	Equivalent production	Cost per kilogram
Material	360 000	90 000	R4,00
Conversion costs	173 600	86 800	2,00
	533 600		R6,00

Cost allocation	R
Units completed and transferred (80 000 × R6,00)	480 000
Work in process (closing)	44 000
Material (8 000 × R4,00)	32 000
Conversion costs (6 000 × R2,00)	12 000
Abnormal losses	9 600
Material (2 000 × R4,00)	8 000
Conversion costs (800 × R2,00)	1 600
	R533 600

1 Losses take place after the units are 40% converted. The closing work in process is already 75% complete. Consequently the total input of 100 000 units is already past the wastage point.

2 Material is issued at the start of the process. Thus the equivalent units in respect of material are 2 000 x 100%.

3 Conversion costs are incurred evenly during the process. Wastage takes place whenever the units are 40% complete. The units which are lost as a result of abnormal losses were thus 40% complete in respect of conversion costs when the wastage took place, that is to say the equivalent of 2 000 × 40% = 800 units.

Example 52

Normal and abnormal wastage
Wastage takes place at the **end** of the process
Both opening and closing stock of incomplete work is present

GS Company Limited: June 19.9

Units:

Work in process (opening)	
(100% complete iro direct material, 50% complete iro conversion costs)	24 000
Units put into the process	48 000
Total	72 000
Approved units completed	36 000
Spoilt units	
(Normal wastage is 10% of completed units, wastage is determined at the end of the process)	6 000
Work in process (closing):	
(100% complete iro material, 60% complete iro conversion costs)	30 000
	72 000

Costs	R
Work in process (opening)	108 000
Direct material	80 000
Conversion costs	28 000
Costs for June 19.9	280 000
Direct material	160 000
Conversion costs	120 000
Total costs	R388 000

The relevant process cost report is as follows:

GS Company Limited

Process cost report: June 19.9

Quantity statement

Input	Production	Material %	Material Units	Conversion costs %	Conversion costs Units
24 000 Work in process (opening)					
48 000 Put into the process					
Approved units completed	36 000	100	36 000	100	36 000
Work in process (closing)	30 000	100	30 000	60	18 000
Normal wastage (10% × 36 000)	3 600	100	3 600	100	3 600
Abnormal wastage (6 000 − 3 600)	2 400	100	2 400	100	2 400
72 000	72 000		72 000		60 000

Cost statement

	Work in process (opening)	Current month	Total	Cost per unit
	R	R	R	R
Direct material	80 000	160 000	240 000	3,334[1]
Conversion costs	28 000	120 000	148 000	2,466
Total	108 000	280 000	338 000	5,80

(continued)

Cost allocation:

	R
Abnormal wastage	15 225
2 400 × R5,80	13 920
Part of normal wastage	
(2 400/38 400 × R20 880)	1 305
Finished goods	228 375
36 000 × R5,80	208 800
Part of normal wastage	
(36 000/38 400 × R20 880)	19 575
Work in process (closing)	144 408
Direct material (30 000 × R3,334)	100 020
Conversion costs (18 000 × R2,466)	44 388
Total	388 008[2]

The cost of the normal wastage is in this case allocated only to the "abnormal wastage" and the "finished goods" as the closing work in process had not yet reached the point of wastage.

1 Wastage occurs at the end of the process. The units lost are thus fully completed.
2 The difference of R8 is due to rounding the unit costs to the third decimal place.

Calculations: Cost per unit

Direct material	=	$\dfrac{R240\ 000}{72\ 000}$	=	R3,334
Conversion costs	=	$\dfrac{R148\ 000}{60\ 000}$	=	R2,466

The calculation of equivalent completed units for spoilt units is, as previously explained, based on the stage of completeness that the products have reached when the wastage occurs. In this example it is at the **end** of the process. Therefore the **full** applicable amount of material and conversion costs is allocated to the spoilt units.

Because the weighted average costing method is used, the cost (in the cost statement) of the opening stock of work in process is added to the costs incurred in the current period and is divided by the equivalent units of the relevant cost components to obtain an average cost (R5,80) per unit.

The journal entry to record the job upon completion is thus:

	R	R
Losses in respect of abnormal wastage		
(2 400 × R5,80) + R1 305	15 225	
Finished goods		
(36 000 × R5,80) + R19 575	228 375	
Production		243 600

3 Accounting for wastage where the FIFO method is applied

Example 53

Refer to Example 52. Exactly the same information holds, but in this case the FIFO method of calculating the equivalent production is used.

GS-Company Limited
Process cost statement: June 19.9

Quantity statement

Input		Production	Material		Conversion costs	
			Equivalent units			
			%		%	
24 000[4]	Incomplete units (opening)					
48 000	Put into process					
	Completed:	36 000				
	Ex opening stock	21 819[1]			50	10 910
	From current production	14 181	100	14 181	100	14 181
	Incomplete units (end)	30 000	100	30 000	60	18 000
	Wastage	6 000				
	Normal	3 600		1 419[2]		2 509[3]
	Abnormal	2 400	100	2 400	100	2 400
72 000		72 000		48 000		48 000

1 24 000 × 100/110, or the wastage is 10% of the completed units
2 3 600 − 2 181 already completed in opening stock, 10% of 21 819 = 2 181
3 3 600 − (2 181 × 50%) already completed in opening stock
4 The opening stock work in process had in the previous period not yet reached the point where wastage occurs. It is therefore still subject to wastage.

(continued)

Cost statement	Amount R	Cost per unit R
Work in process (opening)	108 000	–
Direct material	160 000	3,334[1]
Conversion costs	120 000	2,500[2]
	388 000	5,834

Cost allocation:	R
Normal wastage: (3 600)	20 820
Cost previous period (2 181 × R4,50)	9 815
Cost current period	
1 091 × R2,500 i.r.o. opening stock	2 727
1 419 × R5,834 i.r.o. current month	8 278
Less: Division	20 820
Abnormal wastage (2 400/38 400 × R20 820)	1 301
Completed units:	
Opening stock (21 819/38 400 – R20 820)	11 830
Current production (14 181/38 400 × R20 820)	7 689
Abnormal wastage:	15 303
2 400 × R5,834	14 002
Part normal wastage	1 301
Completed units: (36 000)	
Ex opening stock[1]	137 291
21 819 × R4,50	98 186
Added (10 910 × R2,500)	27 275
Part normal wastage	11 380
Ex current production[2]	90 421
14 181 × R5,834	82 732
Part normal wastage	7 689
Uncompleted work (end):[3]	145 020
Direct material (30 000 × R3,334)	100 020
Conversion (18 000 × R2,500)	45 000
	388 035[4]

1 Total cost per unit (R137 291/21 819) R6,292
2 Total cost per unit (R90 421/14 181) R6,376
3 The uncompleted work has not yet reached the point of wastage and is therefore not charged with the cost of normal wastage
4 Difference due to rounding off to three decimals.

The above report shows all the characteristics of a FIFO system which have already been explained: when the method is used it is assumed that the units completed during the month (36 000) arise from two sources, namely open work in process (21 819) and units put into the process during the month (14 181). Further, it is assumed that the closing work in process and spoilt units all arise from activities during the current month.

In the cost allocation section all five of these elements are accounted for. The cost per unit (R5,834) is calculated by taking into account only the current month's costs (direct material and conversion costs). (There is, as has already been explained, no aggregation of the costs of the previous period as with the weighted average method.)

As in the previous weighted average method example, the cost of the normal and abnormal wastage is accounted for at the full unit cost for the month (R5,834) because the wastage is determined at the end of the process. The journal entries to record the wastage is as follows:

	R	R
Normal wastage	20 820	
Production		20 820
Abnormal wastage	1 301	
Completed goods	19 519	
Normal wastage		20 820

In practice it often happens that the normal wastage is only charged against the approved production started and completed in the current month. (Opening stock work in process and abnormal wastage not being charged.) In this case the calculations would be as follows:

	R
Abnormal wastage (2 400 × R5,834)	14 002
Completed units:	
Ex opening stock	138 000
Prior period (24 000)	108 000
Added (24 000 × 50% × R2,500)	30 000
Ex current production	91 010
12 000 × R5,834	70 008
Normal wastage (3 600 × R5,834)	21 002
Work in process	145 020
	388 032

Although this method is theoretically not correct, it is often used in practice because of the ease of application. Students should, however, not follow this method.

THE RELATIONSHIP BETWEEN THE FINANCIAL AND COST LEDGERS

Costing double-entry systems:
the cost ledger system

1 Introduction

In this module the ways in which cost recording fits into the double entry framework are examined.

There are basically two types of recording systems:[1]

☐ Linked accounting systems (also known as cost ledger systems)
☐ Integrated accounting systems

The size of the enterprise will have a strong influence on the type of system used by the enterprise. Smaller manufacturing enterprises will probably keep only basic costing records which are not linked with the financial records in any way. Larger enterprises will keep more complete costing records which are independent of the financial records, but linked to them. In such cases periodic reconciliations of the cost and financial records will be necessary.

2 The cost ledger system

2.1 Characteristics

In a cost ledger system a **separate** ledger is kept for all transactions which affect the costing data of the enterprise. The **cost ledger** functions independently of the **financial ledger,** but is also written up according to the **double-entry system.** Both the cost and financial system use the same basic data and therefore the two separate ledgers should agree with each other in essence.

In order that the cost and financial ledgers may be linked, a memorandum account known as the **cost ledger contra account**[2] is opened in the cost ledger. The account is used to complete the debit or credit portion of the double entry for all transactions which are recorded in the cost ledger and have their origin in the financial accounts. (The opposite portions of the double entry are **recorded** in the relevant cost control accounts in the cost

---

1 In practice different variations of these two basic methods are found.
2 The account is also known as the cost ledger control account or the plant control account for short.

ledger, as will become evident later.) There is thus no double entry which spans the cost and financial ledger. The financial ledger is the ordinary "general ledger" found in the financial accounting system. It is by no means affected or influenced by the existence of the cost ledger.

2.2 Typical accounts and transaction accounting in a cost ledger

The acounts which usually appear in a cost ledger, the recording of transactions in the cost ledger and the relationship of the cost ledger to the financial ledger are explained by means of Diagram D48 and Example 54.

☐ Cost ledger contra account

This account is used to complete the double entries in the cost ledger and thus to make the ledger "self-balancing". Various income and expense items which originate in the financial records are accounted for in this account, for example debtors, creditors and cash. In addition, any transfers from the cost records to the financial records, for example equipment manufactured by the enterprise for its own use, are recorded in this account. It is important to bear in mind that no entries are recorded in the cost ledger from the financial records: **All such entries must go through the cost ledger contra account.**

The balance in the account represents the balance of all the other accounts in the cost ledger (thus the use of the alternative name cost ledger control account).

The entries in the account are evident from the journal entries which follow:

Example 54

X Manufacturers Limited commenced operations on 1 January 19.7. The enterprise decided to use separate financial and cost ledgers. During January 19.7 the following transactions were concluded:

Cost and financial ledger transactions:

1 Equipment costing R60 000 was purchased on credit
2 R30 000 of material was purchased on credit
3 Wages of R9 000 were paid
4 Operating expenses (manufacturing as well as marketing and administrative – R4 200) of which R7 000 were paid
5 Credit sales of R50 000 were made
6 Depreciation of equipment for the month was R1 000

Cost ledger transactions:

	Total	Direct	Indirect	Marketing/ Admin costs
	R	R	R	R
7 Material issued per material requisitions	25 000	23 000	2 000	
8 Wages allocated from time sheets	9 000	8 500	500	
9 Overheads apportioned	10 200	6 000		4 200

(continued)

10	Completed goods transferred to finished products	28 000
11	Cost of finished products sold	24 000
12	Overheads under-applied written off	
13	Closing entries (both ledgers)	

☐ Material control account

The purchase of equipment is recorded only in the financial ledger as follows:

(1) Purchase of equipment

(F1) | Equipment | 60 000 |
|---|---|
| Creditors | 60 000 |

		Cost ledger	Financial ledger
(2) Purchase of material	(C2) Material control 30 000 Cost contra account 30 000		(F2) Purchases 30 000 Creditors 30 000
(7) Issuing of material	(C7) Production 23 000 Overheads control 2 000 Material control 25 000		

The balance in the material control account at the end of the period represents the cost of the material on hand.

The material control account is supported by a subsidiary ledger, the **material ledger**, in which individual accounts for each type of raw material appear. All receipts and issues are shown in these individual accounts and therefore the balance of the material control account should agree with the total of the balances of all the individual accounts in the material ledger.

☐ Labour control account

		Cost ledger	Financial ledger
(3) Labour costs incurred	(C3) Labour control 9 000 Cost contra acc 9 000		(F3) Wages 9 000 Bank 9 000
(8) Allocation of labour costs	(C8) Production 8 500 Overheads control 500 Labour control 9 000		

☐ Overheads control account

Although reference is made mainly to manufacturing overheads here, separate accounts can also be opened for marketing and administrative overheads in the cost ledger. This will mean that all operating expenses in the financial accounts are also in the cost ledger.

In this example, for the same of conciseness, no separate accounts are opened and only a single overheads control account is kept. Non-manufacturing overheads are described as "other overheads" and are allocated directly to the costing profit and loss account.

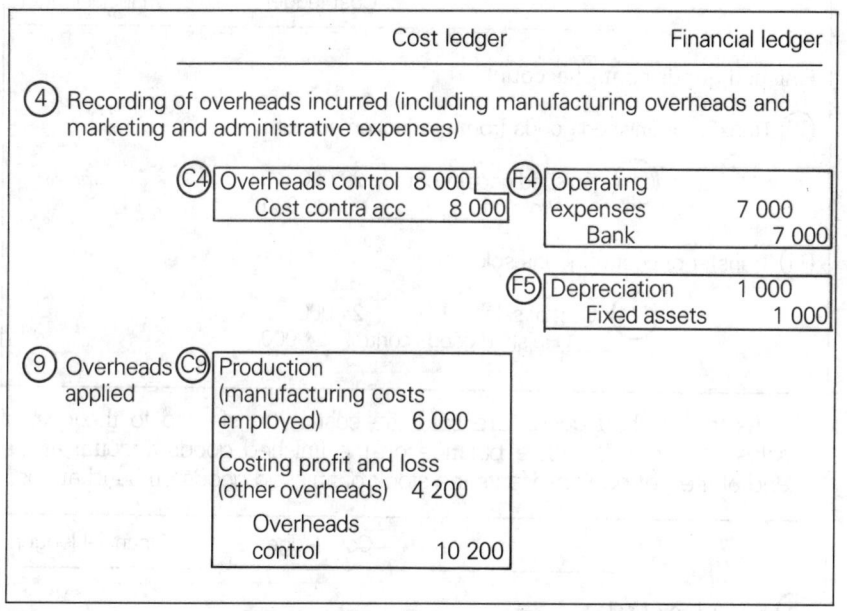

	Cost ledger	Financial ledger

④ Recording of overheads incurred (including manufacturing overheads and marketing and administrative expenses)

C4 | Overheads control 8 000 | F4 | Operating expenses 7 000
Cost contra acc 8 000 | Bank 7 000

F5 | Depreciation 1 000
Fixed assets 1 000

⑨ Overheads applied | C9 | Production (manufacturing costs employed) 6 000
Costing profit and loss (other overheads) 4 200
Overheads control 10 200

Manufacturing overheads are allocated to the production account by means of the already well-known procedures (predetermined overheads tariffs). Marketing and administrative overheads are period costs and are written off directly against profits.

Remember that any remaining balance (overheads underapplied or overapplied) on the overheads control account must be analysed and eventually written off in a suitable manner against incomplete work, finished products and cost of sales. In this example (see the ledger accounts that follow) the balance of R300 is written off against cost of sales for the sake of simplicity only.

	Cost ledger	Financial ledger

⑫ Overheads underapplied written off

C12 | Cost of sales 300
Overheads control 300*

---

* Actual overheads [Indirect material R2 000 + Indirect labour R500 + Operating expenses (R7 000 − R4 200) + Depreciation R1 000] less Overheads applied R6 000 = R300 underapplied overheads.

☐ Production account

This account represents work in process and is supported by a production ledger (or work-in-process ledger) in which production costs are debited to the various individual jobs.

The debit entries in this account arise from transactions C7, C8 and C9 above. The balance on the account at the end of the period represents the stock of incomplete work at production cost.

	Cost ledger	Financial ledger

Finished goods control account

⑩ Transfer of finished goods from production account

Ⓒ10 Finished goods control 28 000
　　　　Production　　　　　　　28 000

⑪ Transfer of cost of goods sold

Ⓒ11 Cost of sales　　　　24 000
　　　Finished goods control　24 000

As the finished goods are sold the cost is transferred to the cost of sales account (C11). The balance on the finished goods account at the end of the period represents the stock of finished goods on hand at cost.

	Cost ledger	Financial ledger

⑤ Recording of sales

Ⓒ5 Cost contra acc 50 000　Ⓕ5 Debtors　50 000
　　　Sales　　　　　50 000　　　　Sales　50 000

	Cost ledger	Financial ledger

⑬ Closing entries

Ⓒ13 Costing profit and loss 24 000　Ⓕ13 Income account　47 000
　　　Cost of sales　　　　24 000　　　Purchases　　　30 000
　　　　　　　　　　　　　　　　　　　　Wages　　　　　9 000
　　Sales　　　　　50 000　　　　　Operating expenses 7 000
　　　Costing profit and loss 50 000　　Depreciation　　1 000

　　Costing profit and loss 21 500　　Sales　　　　　50 000
　　　Cost control account 21 500　　　Income account　50 000

　　　　　　　　　　　　　　　　　Stock　　　　　18 500*
　　　　　　　　　　　　　　　　　　Income account　18 500

* See page 211

Income account	21 500	
Appropriation account		21 500

Transaction The net profit according to the costing profit and loss account is R50 000 – R28 500 = R21 500, which is credited to the cost ledger contra account.

After the preceding transfer of the net profit and loss account the cost ledger contra account shows a credit balance of R18 500.

If a post closing trial balance of the cost ledger were to be extracted at this stage, it would appear as follows:

	Dr	Cr
Cost ledger contra account		18 500
Material control account	5 000 (a)	
Production account (incomplete work)	9 500 (b)	
Finished goods account	4 000 (c)	
	18 500	18 500

Thus it is the plant ledger contra account that makes the plant ledger self-balancing.

Items (a), (b) and (c) in the above trial balance represent the total stock at the end of the month, that is to say raw material and material (R5 000), incomplete products (R9 500) and finished goods (R4 000). This stock is now accounted for in the financial ledger in the usual manner.

*Item (13)

Stock on hand	18 500	
Trading profit and loss account		18 500

Once the preceding journal entry has been posted the two ledgers appear as follows:

COST LEDGER

Cost contra account

⑤	Sales	50 000	②	Material	30 000
	Balance c/d	18 500	③	Labour	9 000
			④	Overheads	8 000
			⑬	Net profit	21 500
				Balance b/d	18 500

Material control account

②	Cost contra acc.	30 000	⑦	Production account	23 000
			⑦	Overheads control	2 000
				Balance c/d	5 000
	Balance b/d	5 000			

Labour control account

③	Cost contra acc.	9 000	⑧	Production account	8 500
			⑧	Overheads control	500

Overheads control account

④	Plant contra acc	8 000	⑨	Production account	6 000
⑦	Indirect material	2 000	⑨	Costing profit & loss (other overheads)	4 200
⑧	Indirect labour	500	⑫	Cost of sales (overheads under-applied)	300

Production account

⑦	Material control	23 000	⑩	Finished goods	28 000
⑧	Labour control	8 500		Balance c/d	9 500
⑨	Overheads control	6 000			
	Balance b/d	9 500			

Finished goods control account

⑩	Production account	28 000	⑪	Cost of sales	24 000
				Balance c/d	4 000
	Balance b/d	4 000			

Cost of sales

⑪	Finished goods	24 000	⑬	Costing profit & loss	24 300
⑫	Overheads under-applied	300			

Sales

⑬	Costing profit & loss	50 000	⑤	Cost contra acc.	50 000

Costing profit and loss account

⑨	Other overheads	4 200	⑬	Sales	50 000
⑬	Cost of sales	24 000			
⑫	Overheads under-applied	300			
		28 500			
⑬	Cost contra (net profit)	21 500			
		50 000			50 000

FINANCIAL LEDGER

Creditors

			①	Equipment	60 000
			②	Purchases	30 000

Purchases

②	Creditors	30 000	⑬	Income account	30 000

Stock

⑬	Income account	18 500	

Wages

③	Bank	9 000	⑬	Income account	9 000

Operating expenses

④	Bank	7 000	⑬	Income account	8 000
⑥	Depreciation	1 000			

Bank

			③	Wages	9 000
			④	Expenses	7 000

Equipment

①	Creditors	60 000	⑥	Depreciation	1 000

Sales

⑬	Income account	50 000	⑤	Debtors	50 000

Debtors

⑤	Sales	50 000	

Income account

⑬	Purchases	30 000	⑬	Sales	50 000
⑬	Wages	9 000	⑬	Closing stock	18 500
⑬	Expenses	8 000			
		47 000			
	Net income	21 500			
		68 500			68 500

The transactions in the preceding example are explained schematically in the following diagram:

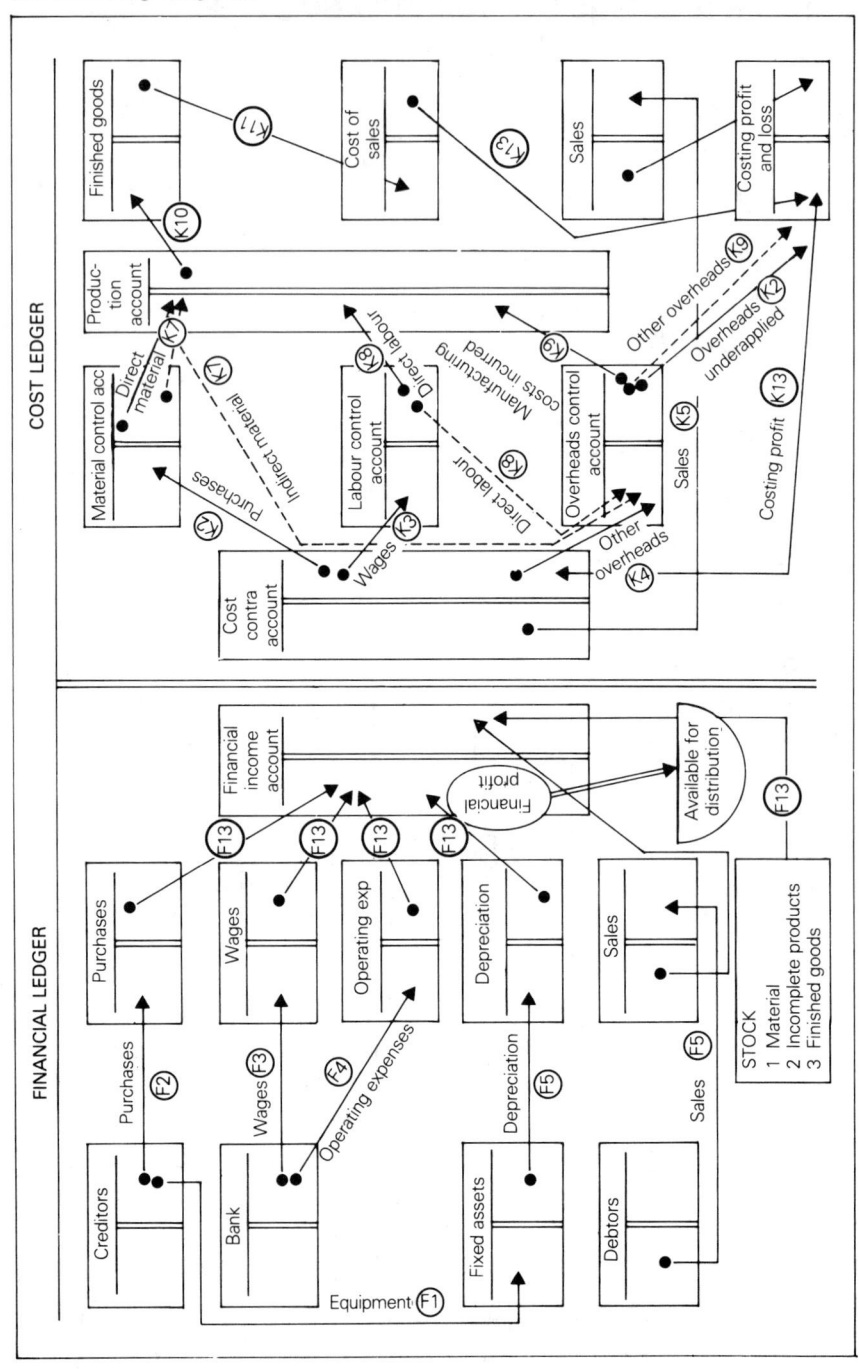

Diagram D48

3 Reconciliation of the differences in costing profit and financial net income

Once the closing entries have been recorded the net profit per the costing profit and loss account and the net income per the financial books are the same amount. This is (theoretically) inevitable, since the transactions which determine the costing profit and the financial income in both ledgers are in essence, the same. However, the two amounts will often differ and it is then necessary to establish the reasons for the difference in order to **reconcile** the two profit figures.

☐ Reasons for differences

Differences between the two figures can arise from the following sources, amongst others:

☐ Items which appear in the financial accounts only:

Writing off of bad debts
Interest payable on loans and overdrafts
Profits and losses upon realisation of investments
Interest and dividends received
Other sundry items such as damages paid or received, fines paid, etc
Company taxation
Dividends paid out
Transfers to reserves and provisions

☐ Items which appear in the cost accounts only:

There are few such items, but two examples are the following:

☐ Interest on capital

It might be a policy of the enterprise to charge interest on capital employed in manufacturing in order to show the nominal cost of the employment of the capital in the enterprise rather than the investment thereof outside the enterprise.

☐ Internal charges in lieu of rent

It might also be the enterprise's policy to charge a nominal amount for the "hire" of the enterprise's own production premises in order that the production costs may be compared with those of other enterprises which must hire premises.

The charging of such items will increase the production costs and consequently reduce the profit per the costing ledger.

☐ Items for which the method of accounting differs in the plant and financial records:

The following items are examples of such accounting differences:

☐ Abnormal losses in production and storage

In the financial records such losses will be "absorbed" in the ordinary course of business in the applicable nominal accounts. For example, in the financial accounts abnormal losses in respect of material will simply be included in the cost of material. In the cost accounts abnormal material losses may be considered to fall outside the scope of the production costs.

☐ Differences in the valuation of stock

Incomplete and finished products can be valued at total production costs in the cost accounts (ie including manufacturing overheads), while in the financial accounts they are valued at direct cost only (ie excluding overheads).

☐ Differences in depreciation

Depreciation can be brought into account in the cost accounts on the basis of production units or hours, while in the financial accounts it is provided for on the basis of time elapsed.

☐ Reconciliation procedures

The reconciliation of the profit figures of the two ledgers can be carried out according to either of the following two methods:

☐ Preparation of a **reconciliation** statement
☐ Preparation of an **adjustment account** (sometimes also called a memorandum adjustments account)

The two methods are illustrated in Example 55:

Example 55

An enterprise's financial income statement is as follows:

	R		R
Material purchases	75 630	Sales: 150 000 units	
Less: Closing stock	12 240	@ R1,50 per unit	225 000
	63 390	Discounts received	780
Direct wages	31 500	Profit on sale of	
Manufacturing overheads	36 390	fixed assets	7 020
Marketing costs	21 300		
Administrative costs	16 020		
Depreciation	3 300		
Net income	60 900		
	R232 800		R232 800

The costing net profit amounted to R59 310. In the costing records:

☐ closing stock is valued at R12 840
☐ manufacturing overheads are applied at 100% of direct labour
☐ marketing costs are charged at 10% of sales and administrative costs at R0,10 per unit
☐ depreciation is charged at R2 400.

The items discount received and profit on sale of fixed assets appear in the financial records only.

☐ Reconciliation according to the adjustments account method

Adjustments account				
	R			**R**
Lower stock value in financial ledger	600	Costing profit		59 310
Items debited at a higher amount in the financial records:		Items not credited in cost ledger:		
Overheads	4 890	Discount received	780	
Administrative costs	1 020	Profit on fixed assets	7 020	7 800
Depreciation	900			
	7 410	Items debited at a higher amount in cost records		
		Marketing costs		1 200
Net income per financial statements	60 900			
	68 310			68 310

☐ Reconciliation according to the reconciliation statement method

1 Start with the costing profit.
2 Determine and adjust each of the differences as follows:

Ask the question: "If the costing figures were the same as the financial figures, would the **costing profit** have been **more or less?**" If **more:** add the difference in respect of the specific item to the costing profit, and **if less:** deduct the difference.

	Cost ledger	Financial ledger	Difference	Total
				R
Costing profit				59 310
Add:				
Difference in marketing				
costs 10% × R225 000	22 500	21 300	1 200	
Discount received	–	780	780	
Profit on fixed assets	–	7 020	7 020	9 000
				68 310
Deduct:				
Difference in valuation of closing stock	12 840	12 240	600	
Difference in overheads	31 500	36 390	4 890	
Administration costs (R0,10 × 150 000 units)	15 000	16 020	1 020	
Difference in depreciation	2 400	3 300	900	7 410
Net income per financial accounts				60 900

Module

9.2

Double-entry systems:
integrated bookkeeping

1 Definition

The term **integrated accounting** refers to a single accounting system which comprises both the financial and cost accounts. Theoretically speaking, all the accounts are in a single ledger.

2 Illustration of an integrated system

The basic characteristics of an integrated accounting system are explained in Diagram D49 (which is an oversimplified presentation of the relevant accounts in the ledger.

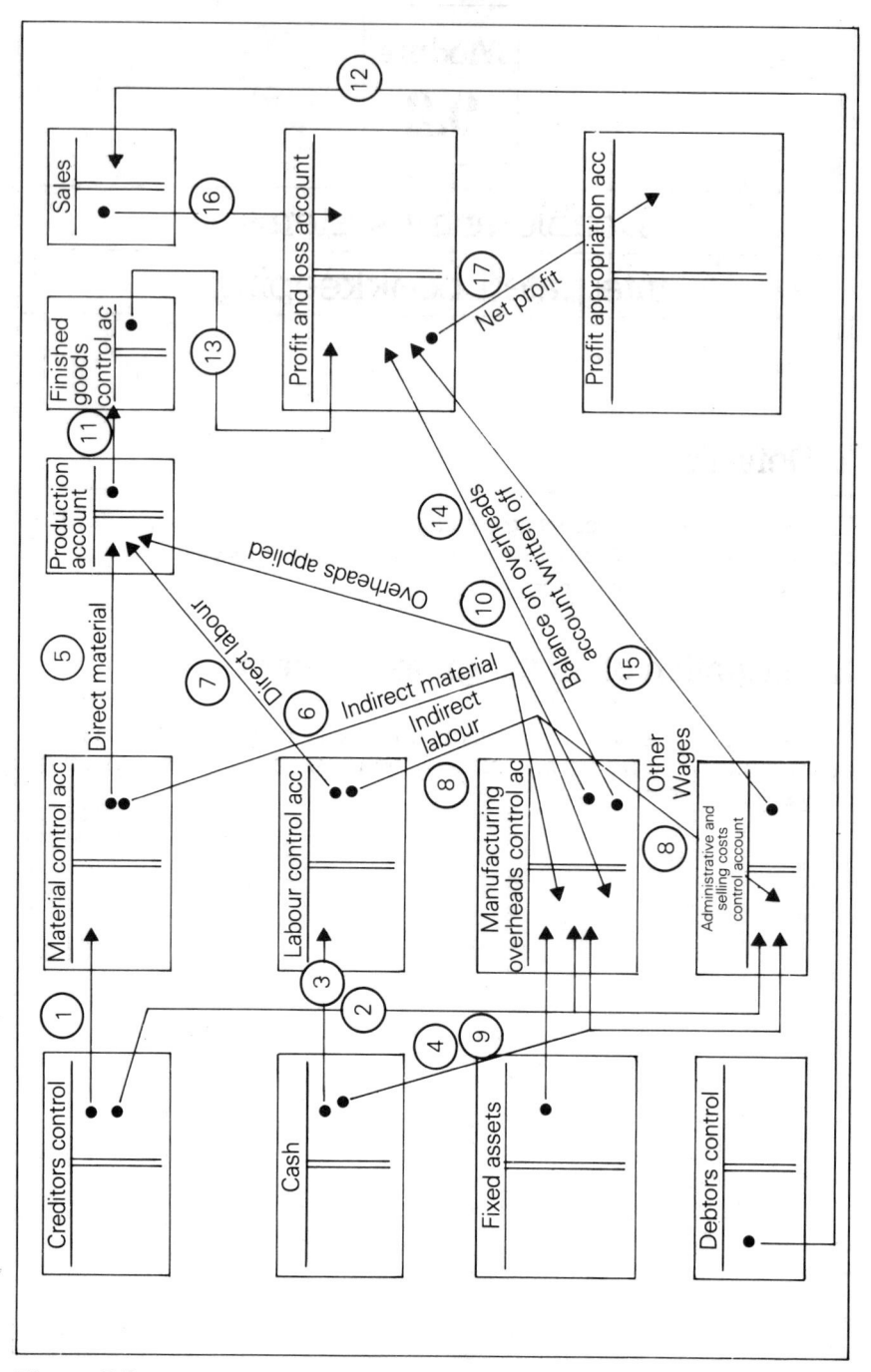

Diagram D49

The system makes extensive use of control accounts. Each of these control accounts is supported by a subsidiary ledger.

The flow of transactions in the integrated system is dealt with briefly:

1 and 2 Material purchases (1) and cost and expense items (2) resulting from transactions with the enterprise's suppliers are posted to the applicable control accounts and the individual accounts.

Material control account	Dr X
Manufacturing overheads control account	Dr X
Admin and selling costs control account	Dr X
Creditors control account	Cr X

3 and 4 Payment of the wages (3) and purchases (4) give rise to debits to the labour control and applicable overheads control account from wage statements and cash purchase invoices.

Labour control account	Dr X
Manufacturing overheads control account	Dr X
Admin and selling costs control account	Dr X
Cash	Cr X

5 and 6 The issue of direct material (5) against production and of indirect material (6) against manufacturing overheads control are recorded from material requisitions.

Production account	Dr X
Manufacturing overheads control account	Dr X
Material control account	Cr X

7 and 8 Direct labour (7) and indirect labour (8) are recorded from the wage statement to the production account and various overheads control accounts.

Production account (direct labour)	Dr X
Manufacturing overheads (indirect labour)	Dr X
Admin and selling costs (other wages)	Dr X
Labour control account	Cr X

9 Depreciation is debited to the manufacturing overheads control account by means of the following journal entry:

Manufacturing overheads control	Dr X
Fixed assets/Accumulated depreciation	Cr X

| 10 | Using the predetermined overheads recovery tariff, overheads are allocated to production. |

| Production account | Dr X | |
| Manufacturing overheads control | | Cr X |

| 11 | Manufactured goods which are complete are transferred to the finished goods account. |

| Finished goods | Dr X | |
| Production account | | Cr X |

| 12 | Debtors are debited and the sales account credited with the selling value of the finished goods sold. |

| 13 | The cost of the goods sold is transferred from the finished goods to the profit and loss account. |

| 14 | The balance of the manufacturing overheads control account (debit balance = overheads underapplied, credit balance = overheads overapplied) is written off in the profit and loss account. |

Profit and loss	Dr X	
Manufacturing overheads control		
(If debit balance)		Cr X

| 15 | All other administrative and selling costs and the balance of the sales account (16) are transferred to the profit and loss account, where the net profit or loss is determined and transferred to the appropriation account (17). |

In each of the material, production and finished goods accounts there will be, in the ordinary course of things, closing balances. These represent the closing stock in respect of each of these accounts.

From the above it is obvious that there are no fundamental differences between ordinary financial accounting systems and integrated systems.

10

COST-VOLUME-PROFIT ANALYSIS

1 Introduction

The success of an enterprise is often measured in terms of the profit that it makes. To a large extent such success can be ascribed to efficient profit planning and control of the enterprise. In order to do thorough planning, which is the primary function of management, decisions must be made continuously at all levels of the enterprise. Further, management must make choices as to which of various alternative possibilities will be the most advantageous to the enterprise. To help management with these policy decisions **cost-volume-profit analysis** was developed as a basic technique for short-term planning. This technique is used to analyse the influence of volumes on costs, income and profits and, *inter alia*, to provide answers to the following questions:

> ☐ What profit will a given sales volume yield?
> ☐ How many units must be sold to achieve the planned profit?
> ☐ How will a change in costs affect profits?
> ☐ What effect will a change in costs have on profit?
> ☐ How will a change in the volume of business affect the profit potential of the enterprise?
> ☐ At what volume of production are costs and income equal?

2 Marginal costing

Historical figures, as reflected in the conventional income statement, are not suitable for the planning and making of decisions. Therefore the **marginal costs account** was developed for determining the marginal costs, marginal income and the influence of changes in volume, price and costs on the income figure for planning purposes. If a marginal costs account is to be used effectively all costs and expenses must be divided into their fixed and variable components.

With marginal costing the units manufactured are debited with variable costs only while the fixed costs for the given period are written off against the profits.

The advantage of marginal costing is that control is exercised over the **marginal costs** and the **marginal income** per unit.

2.1 Marginal costs

Economically speaking, **marginal costs** are the changes in total costs which arise if an additional unit is manufactured – hence the name "marginal costs". In a costing context **marginal costs** represent the total of the **variable costs** employed to manufacture and market a product or products.

2.2 Marginal income

This is the difference between the selling value and the total variable costs (marginal costs) of that sale. This amount has a greater practical value for the system of break-even analysis if it is expressed as a per unit amount. When the marginal income (in total or per unit) is expressed as a percentage of the selling value this is known as the **marginal income ratio**.

3 Break-even analysis

Break-even analysis is a system which shows management what the profit structure of the enterprise is at present and what it will be in future under various proposed alternatives. A primary requirement of break-even analysis is that all costs, whether production, selling, distribution or administrative, must be divided into their fixed and variable components.

The following techniques are used in the application of cost-volume-profit analysis:

- ☐ Marginal income per unit method
- ☐ Marginal income ratio method
- ☐ Equation method
- ☐ Algebraic method
- ☐ Graphic method

The application of the techniques of cost-volume-profit analysis are illustrated by means of the following simple example:

Example 56

The following information is available regarding Product P:

Expected sales volume	40 000 units
Expected sales price per unit	R20
Expected variable cost per unit	R15
Expected total fixed costs	R100 000

☐ Marginal income per unit method

The marginal income per unit represents the difference between the sales value and the variable costs of a unit, as illustrated by the following:

	R
Selling price	20
Marginal costs	15
Marginal income	5

Thus, if only one unit of Product P is sold it gives a marginal income of R5 which is available to pay the fixed costs of R100 000. If a second unit is sold it increases the marginal income to R10 and R10 of the fixed costs can be paid.

The question now is how many units of Product P must be sold before the marginal income is sufficient to pay the total fixed costs?

The volume (number of units that must be sold) at which the marginal income is sufficient to pay the fixed costs is known as the **break-even point.**

The break-even quantity or volume is thus the minimum quantity of products that must be sold in a given period to ensure that all the fixed costs are recovered and that the enterprise does not sustain a loss. The break-even quantity for the previous example can be calculated according to the marginal income per unit method as follows:

$$\text{Break-even quantity} = \frac{\text{Total fixed costs}}{\text{Marginal income per unit}}$$

$$= \frac{\text{R100 000}}{\text{R5}}$$

$$= 20\ 000 \text{ units}$$

The break-even value represents the sales value of the break-even quantity and is calculated as follows:

$$\text{Break-even value} = \text{Break-even quantity} \times \text{Selling price per unit}$$

$$= 20\ 000 \times \text{R20}$$

$$= \text{R400 000}$$

☐ The marginal income ratio method

The marginal income ratio represents the ratio of the marginal income to sales, calculated on a product unit basis or in total. This ratio is usually expressed as a percentage.

$$\text{Marginal income ratio} = \frac{\text{Marginal income}}{\text{Sales}} \times \frac{100}{1}$$

$$= \frac{5}{20} \times \frac{100}{1}$$

$$= 25\%$$

Any change in marginal income (as a result of changes in sales or variable costs) is reflected in the marginal income ratio, which is of great benefit to management. This ratio shows management how profits are affected by a change in the selling value or variable costs.

The break-even value can be calculated with the aid of the marginal income ratio method as follows:

$$\begin{aligned}
\text{Break-even value} \quad &= \frac{\text{Total fixed costs}}{\text{Marginal income ratio}} \\
&= \frac{\text{R100 000}}{25\%} \\
&= \frac{\text{R100 000}}{,25} \\
&= \text{R400 000}
\end{aligned}$$

As an alternative to the above method, the break-even value can be calculated without first calculating the marginal income ratio, as follows:

$$\begin{aligned}
\text{Break-even value} \quad &= \frac{\text{Fixed costs}}{1 - \dfrac{\text{Variable costs per unit}}{\text{Selling price per unit}}} \\
&= \frac{\text{100 000}}{1 - \dfrac{15}{20}} \\
&= \frac{\text{100 000}}{\dfrac{5}{20}} \\
&= \frac{\text{100 000}}{1} \times \frac{20}{5} \\
&= \text{R400 000}
\end{aligned}$$

It is advisable to explain the following concepts before the remaining methods are dealt with:

Margin of safety

This represents the amount by which the sales value exceeds the break-even value. From a management point of view it is more practical to express this value as a percentage of the sales value which is known as the margin of safety ratio.

Margin of safety :	Sales – Break-even value
Expressed in value terms :	(40 000 × R20) – R400 000 = R800 000 – R400 000 = R400 000
Expressed in units :	40 000 – 20 000 = 20 000 units

(continued)

Margin of safety ratio :

$$\frac{\text{Sales} - \text{Break-even value}}{\text{Sales}} \times \frac{100}{1}$$

$$= \frac{\text{R800 000} - \text{R400 000}}{\text{R800 000}} \times \frac{100}{1}$$

$$= \underline{50\%}$$

Alternatively :

$$\frac{40\ 000\ \text{units} - 20\ 000\ \text{units}}{40\ 000\ \text{units}} \times \frac{100}{1}$$

$$= \underline{50\%}$$

The margin of safety ratio is useful in that it gives to management an indication of the extent to which the sales volume can fall before the enterprise will start showing a loss.

Expected profit or return

With the aid of the cost-volume-profit technique the sales value that will produce a certain net profit can also be determined. Suppose that in the example given an expected profit of R20 000 is wanted from the sales of Product P. The calculation will be as follows:

Sales volume	$= \dfrac{\text{Fixed costs} + \text{Expected profit}}{\text{Marginal income per unit}}$
	$= \dfrac{\text{R100 000} + \text{R20 000}}{\text{R5}}$
	= 24 000 units
Sales value	= 24 000 units × R20
	= R480 000

Changeover point

If a decison is made to switch over from one set of cost-volume-profit ratios to another this is known as the changeover point. This concept is explained by means of Example 57:

Example 57

The following information was taken from the books of COP Manufacturing Company Limited for the year ended 30 June 19.1:

Sales	40 000 units @ R5 each
Variable costs	R3 per unit
Fixed costs in total	R30 000

(continued)

It is planned to change the equipment during the coming year so that 50 000 units can be manufactured. This will increase the fixed costs by R10 000 while the variable costs will decrease by R0,50 per unit. The selling price will remain unchanged at R5 per unit.

Required

Calculate the quantity (changeover point) at which the profit will be the same in each of the alternative situations and test the correctness of your answer.

Solution

Production quantity:

$$\frac{\text{Proposed fixed costs} - \text{Existing fixed costs}}{\text{Existing variable costs} - \text{Proposed variable costs}}$$

$$\frac{\text{R40 000} - \text{R30 000}}{\text{R3,00} - \text{R2,50}}$$

$$= \quad 20\ 000 \text{ units}$$

Alternative:

$$\frac{\text{Proposed fixed costs} - \text{Existing fixed costs}}{\text{Proposed marginal income per unit} - \text{Existing marginal income per unit}}$$

$$\frac{\text{R40 000} - \text{R30 000}}{\text{R2,50} - \text{R2,00}}$$

$$= \quad 20\ 000 \text{ units}$$

Test for correctness:

	Existing R	Proposed R
Marginal income :		
20 000 × R2,00	40 000	
20 000 × R2,50		50 000
Less: Fixed costs	30 000	40 000
Net income	10 000	10 000

☐ Equation method

The profit can also be calculated by means of the equation method as follows (assume the same details as in Example 56):

Sales volume = Variable costs + Fixed costs + Profit

Alternatively:

Profit = Sales value − Variable costs − Fixed costs
$$= (40\ 000 \times R20) - (40\ 000 \times R15) - R100\ 000$$
$$= R100\ 000$$

The break-even quantity of Product P can be calculated as follows if the sales volume is expressed as Q:

$$\begin{aligned}
\text{Sales value} &= \text{Variable costs + Fixed costs + Profit} \\
20Q &= 15Q + R100\ 000 + 0 \\
20Q - 15Q &= 100\ 000 \\
Q &= 20\ 000 \text{ units}
\end{aligned}$$

☐ Algebraic method

With the aid of algebraic symbols and formulae an elementary equation for calculating the unknowns in the break-even analysis can be developed. Basically, the elementary algebraic equation contains every concept/aspect of a condensed income statement, as follows:

Sales	S
Less: Variable costs	V
= Marginal income	MI
Less: Fixed costs	F
= Profit	P

Each symbol in the above income statement can be determined by means of a simple equation:

Sales	S	$= V + F + P$
Variable costs	V	$= S - F - P$
Marginal income	MI	$= S - V$
Fixed costs	F	$= S - V - P$
Profit	P	$= S - F - V$

The calculation of the unknowns in the break-even analysis can be expanded further with the aid of the following formulae:

Marginal income ratio :	MIR	$= \dfrac{S - V}{S}$ or $1 - \dfrac{V}{S}$ or $\dfrac{MI}{S}$
Break-even quantity :	BEQ	$= \dfrac{F}{S-V}$ or $\dfrac{F}{MI \text{ per unit}}$
Break-even value :	BEV	$= \dfrac{F}{MIR}$ or $\dfrac{F}{1 - \dfrac{V}{S}}$
Margin of safety :	MS	$= S - BEV$
Margin of safety ratio :	MSR	$= \dfrac{S - BEV}{S}$

(continued)

Required minimum turnover in value :   RV $= \dfrac{F + TP^*}{MIR}$

Required minimum turnover in quantity :   RQ $= \dfrac{F + TP^*}{MI\ per\ unit}$

* where TP = planned profit

Example 58

The following information is available :

Sales	R10 000
Variable costs	R6 000
Margin of safety ratio	50%

Required:

Calculate the following with the aid of algebraic calculations:

(i)   Marginal income
(ii) Marginal income ratio
(iii) Net income (profit)
(iv) Fixed costs
(v)   Break-even value
(vi) Safety margin

Solution:

(i)   Marginal income : $\begin{aligned} MI &= S - V \\ &= 10\ 000 - 6\ 000 \\ &= \underline{R4\ 000} \end{aligned}$

(ii) Marginal income ratio : $\begin{aligned} MIR &= \dfrac{S - V}{S} \\ &= \dfrac{10\ 000 - 6\ 000}{10\ 000} \times \dfrac{100}{1} \\ &= \underline{40\%} \end{aligned}$

(iii) Profit : $\begin{aligned} P &= S - V - F \\ &= 10\ 000 - 6\ 000 - F \\ &= 4\ 000 - F \end{aligned}$

Since there are two unknowns in the above equation another alternative must be found in order to solve it.

If the marginal income (R4 000) decreases by 50% (safety margin ratio) this represents the profit. In other words, the marginal income can decrease by 50% before any losses will occur.

$\begin{aligned} P &= MI \times MSR \\ &= 4\ 000 \times 50\% \\ &= R2\ 000 \end{aligned}$ or $\begin{aligned} MIR \times MS \\ = 40\% \times 5\ 000 \\ = \underline{R2\ 000} \end{aligned}$

(continued)

(iv)   Fixed costs : $F = S - V - P$

$$= 10\ 000 - 6\ 000 - 2\ 000$$
$$= R2\ 000$$

(v)   Break-even value : $BEV = \dfrac{F}{MIR}$

$$= \dfrac{2\ 000}{40}$$
$$= R5\ 000$$

(vi)   Margin of safety : $MS = S - BEV$

$$= 10\ 000 - 5\ 000$$
$$= R5\ 000$$

☐ Graphical method

Break-even graphs:

A break-even graph shows the connection between costs, volume and profit at various sales volumes. The value of a break-even graph lies in the simple manner in which the profit structure is conveyed to management at a glance. The preparation of the graph can best be explained by an example (see Example 59):

Example 59

Expected sales for the period	1 000 units
Selling price per unit	R10
Variable costs per unit	R6
Total fixed costs for the period	R2 000

Procedures for the preparation of the break-even graph :

(a) Choose a scale suited to the graph paper available. Use the vertical (or Y) axis for monetary values, using a scale of 1 cm = R1 000.

The horizontal (or X) axis represents the volume in units on a scale of 1 cm = 100 units. It is important that the scales are shown clearly on the graph.

(b) The fixed cost line is drawn first once all the axes have been drawn to scale on the graph paper. In the example the fixed costs are R2 000 in total and stay the same for all volumes. Therefore this line is drawn parallel to the X axis from the R2 000 point on the Y axis (line FK on the graph).

(c) From point H on the X axis measure the total costs, R8 000 (fixed R2 000 = variable 1 000 × R6). The straight line FV represents the total costs while VK represents the variable costs.

(d) Draw a straight line from the origin (0-point) of the graph to the maximum value of the proceeds (point S). This represents the total value of the proceeds of R10 000 for 1 000 units.

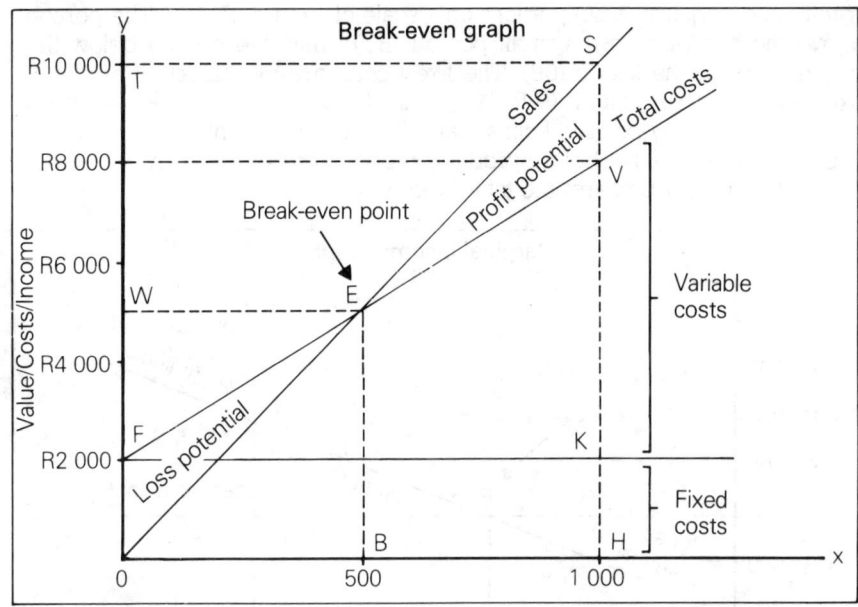

Diagram D50

Scale

X-axis : 1 cm = 100 units
Y-axis : 1 cm = R1 000

Deductions from the graph:

(a) The break-even point: This is the point at the intersection of the sales line OS and the total costs line FV. If a line EB is drawn perpendicular to the X axis and line EW is drawn perpendicular to the Y axis, they show the break-even volume (B) and the break-even value (W) respectively.

(b) Profit/loss: At a given volume the vertical distance between the sales line and the total cost line shows the profit or loss amount. In this example a profit of R2 000 is earned (distance SV).

(c) Safety margin: This is the distance between the break-even point and the units sold. The safety margin is the distance BH on the graph, which amounts to 500 units (1 000 − 500).

Marginal income graph (Profit-volume diagram):

The marginal income graph was developed in order to overcome certain deficiencies in the break-even graph. The cost line cannot always be expressed as a straight line because there are continuous changes in costs. In addition to being proportional, variable costs can also increase or decrease progressively or digressively in relation to the volume of business. The same argument is applicable to sales, because the selling price per unit can also change and then sales can no longer be expressed as a straight line.

A further disadvantage of the break-even diagram is that different income and cost lines for the purposes of comparison are not easily drawn on the same graph.

Procedures for the preparation of the graph:

Take the example that was used to illustrate the break-even graph. On the horizontal (or X) axis the sales value is measured off on a scale of 1 cm = R1 000. The break-even line divides the Y (or vertical) axis into positive (profit) and negative (loss) portions on a scale of 1 cm = R1 000. The portion above the line depicts the profit portion (BY), while the portion below the line represents the losses (OB). The fixed costs are measured off on the Y axis of the graph at point F (−R2 000), while the profit of R2 000 is measured off on the line SV at point P. Points E and P joined represent the profit line. It is important to note that before production begins there is already a total loss of R2 000, which represents the total fixed costs.

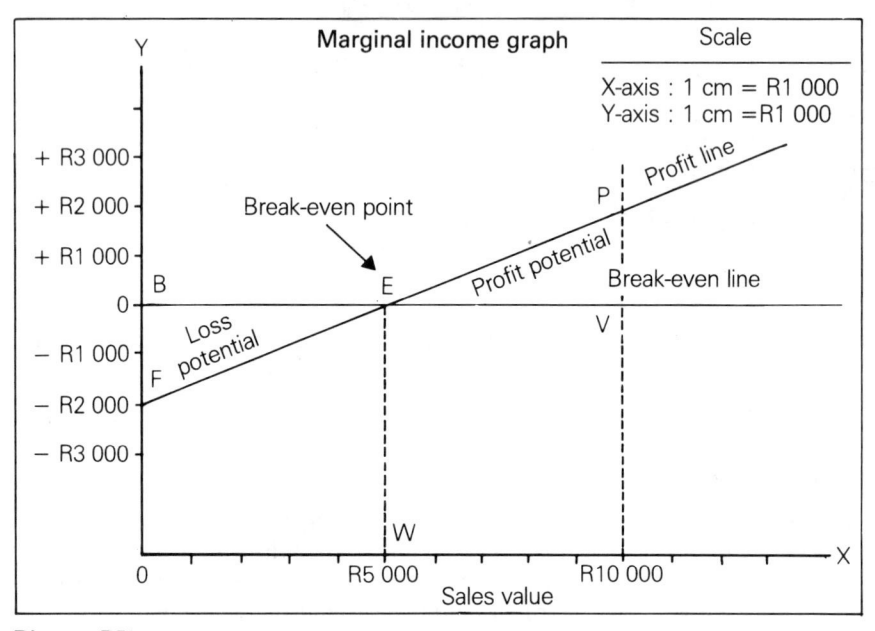

Diagram D51

From the graph it is obvious that the break-even point is point E, where the profit line cuts the break-even line. The safety margin is the distance EV.

The usefulness of the marginal income graph is highlighted in Example 60, in which there is a production mix.

Example 60

The following information refers to an enterprise which manufactured products A, B and C during the past year:

PRODUCTS

	A	B	C	TOTAL	
	R	R	R	R	%
Sales	30 000	50 000	20 000	100 000	100
Marginal costs	18 000	25 000	18 000	61 000	61
Marginal income	12 000	25 000	2 000	39 000	39
Fixed costs				20 000	
Net income				19 000	

Required:

Determine the break-even value with the aid of a marginal income graph.

Solution

First calculate the marginal income ratio of each product separately and rank them in order from the largest to the smallest.

	A	B	C
Marginal income ratio	$\dfrac{12\ 000 \times 100}{30\ 000\ \ \ \ \ \ 1}$	$\dfrac{25\ 000 \times 100}{50\ 000\ \ \ \ \ \ 1}$	$\dfrac{2\ 000 \times 100}{20\ 000\ \ \ \ \ \ 1}$
	= 40%	= 50%	= 10%
Order:	B A C		

	Y axis of graph	B	B + A	B + A + C
	R	R	R	R
Sales	Nil	50 000	80 000	100 000
Net income	(20 000)	5 000	17 000	19 000
Marginal income Brought forward	Nil (20 000)	25 000 (20 000)	12 000 5 000	2 000 17 000

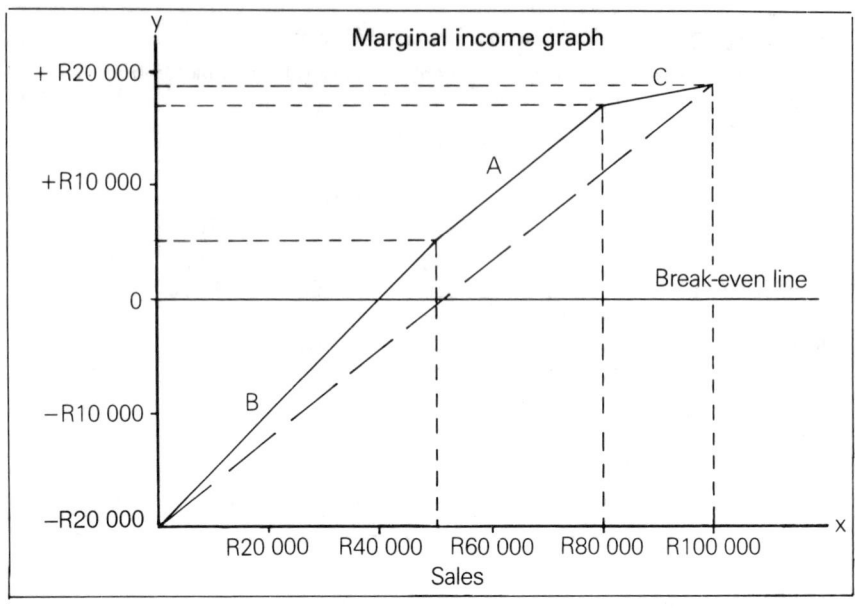

Diagram D52

4 Critical evaluation of break-even analysis

In our complex modern economy it is highly unlikely that selling prices and variable costs per unit, fixed costs in total and the sales volume will remain constant for a given period. Therefore certain assumptions are part of the break-even analysis, with its fixed ratio of cost, volume and profit which makes use of linear equations and conventional break-even graphs.

The usefulness of the break-even analysis is limited only by the degree of validity of the following assumptions:

☐ The selling price per unit remains constant, irrespective of the sales volume. Hence sales are expressed graphically as a straight line.

☐ All costs and expenses can be expressed as either fixed or variable.

☐ Fixed costs remain constant, irrespective of the volume of business, while variable costs vary in a direct ratio with volume. These assumptions ensure straight cost lines in the break-even graph.

☐ The sales mixes are constant for different types of products.

The above assumptions are also the greatest reason for criticism of this technique, as they give it a theoretical character while it should be a practical aid for management. In spite of this, break-even analysis is a handy management instrument for short-term decision making and profit planning.

5 Break-even analysis under changing circumstances

In the discusson and the illustrative examples up to now it was assumed that all the factors such as prices, costs and volumes remained constant. The question is what will happen if one or more of these factors change? Example 61 presents such a situation.

Example 61

Information relating to Decisions Ltd

Volume of trade	70%
Selling price per unit	R10
Variable cost per unit	6
Marginal income	4
Total fixed costs for the period	R40 000

(a) Change in selling price

An increase in the selling price of a product usually leads inevitably to a lower sales volume as a result of consumer resistance. Cost-volume-price analysis will show management to what level the sales volume can fall before the planned profit suffers.

Take as an example the information relating to Decisions Ltd and assume a price increase of 5% and a planned profit of R20 000.

Required:

How many units must be sold to:
- □ break even
- □ achieve the planned profit?

Solution

	Current	After price increase
	R	R
Selling price per unit	10	10,50
Variable costs	6	6,00
Marginal income	4	4,50
Marginal income ratio	40%	42,8%
Increase in marginal income		R0,50
Break-even quantity (units)	10 000	8 889
Number of units to achieve planned profit	15 000	13 334

(b) Change in variable costs:

Selling prices may also decrease as a result of more effective employment of production resources and competition, which gives rise to lower profit taking or forced curtailment of production costs.

The following analysis shows the influence of a 10% change in variable costs:

Solution

	Current	Variable costs (10% decrease)
	R	R
Selling price	10	10,00
Variable costs	6	5,40
Marginal income	4	4,60
Marginal income ratio	40%	46%
Break-even quantity	10 000	8 696
Break-even value	100 000	86 960
Number of units to achieve planned profit	15 000	13 044

(c) Change in fixed costs

A change of R10 000 in fixed costs (for example a new advertising campaign) will affect Decisions Ltd as follows:

Solution

	Current	Fixed costs increase
	R	R
Selling price	10	10
Variable costs	6	6
Marginal income	4	4
Marginal income ratio	40%	40%
Fixed costs	40 000	50 000
Break-even value	100 000	125 000
Break-even quantity	10 000	12 500
Number of units to achieve planned profit	15 000	17 500

(d) Product mix

Where more than one product is marketed the break-even analysis becomes complicated and a less accurate answer is the result. Because each product has its own marginal income ratio a sales mix must be established so that a marginal income ratio can be calculated on a weighted average basis.

Example 62 illustrates the situation:

Example 62

The following information is a forecast for a manufacturing enterprise which manufactures and sells three different products:

	Products		
	A	B	C
	R	R	R
Selling price per unit	10	15	20
Variable costs per unit	7	12	18
Fixed costs in total		R56 000	
Sales mix	(5:	3	:2)

Required:

Calculate the break-even quantity and value.

Solution

Products:	Marginal income R	Mix	Total R
A	3	5	15
B	3	3	9
C	2	2	4
Average per unit (R28 ÷ 10)	2,80	10	28

Break-even: $\dfrac{R56\ 000}{R2,80}$

$= 20\ 000$ units

Break-even quantity with a mix of 5 : 3 : 2 :

A $\dfrac{5}{10} \times 20\ 000 = 10\ 000$ units

B $\dfrac{3}{10} \times 20\ 000 = 6\ 000$ units

C $\dfrac{2}{10} \times 20\ 000 = 4\ 000$ units

Break-even value:

A	10 000 × R10 =	R100 000
B	6 000 × R15 =	R90 000
C	4 000 × R20 =	R80 000
		R270 000

6 Cost structure

Sometimes the cost structures of two enterprises in the same branch of an industry differ materially from each other. Example 63 illustrates this principle:

Example 63

	Enterprise			
	Y		Z	
	R	%	R	%
Sales	50 000	100	50 000	100
Variable costs	30 000	60	15 000	30
Marginal income	20 000	40	35 000	70
Fixed costs	15 000	——	30 000	——
Net income	5 000		5 000	

Several factors must be taken into consideration when the profitability and profit potential of the two enterprises are compared.

Enterprise Z will be in a better position if sales should increase, for example to R60 000, because its marginal income ratio is higher and its profits will usually be higher.

However, if sales should fall Enterprise Y will enjoy the advantage, because its fixed costs are considerably lower than those of Enterprise Z.

The cost structures of the two enterprises for various situations can be illustrated as follows:

	Enterprise Y			Enterprise Z		
	Current	Increase	Decrease	Current	Increase	Decrease
	R	R	R	R	R	R
Sales	50 000	60 000	40 000	50 000	60 000	40 000
Variable costs	30 000	36 000	24 000	15 000	18 000	12 000
Marginal income	20 000	24 000	16 000	35 000	42 000	28 000
Fixed costs	15 000	15 000	15 000	30 000	30 000	30 000
Net income	5 000	9 000	1 000	5 000	12 000	(2 000)

7 Operating leverage

Operating leverage reflects the difference in net income which arises as a result of a change in the sales volume. The formula for its calculation is:

$$\frac{\text{Marginal income}}{\text{Net income}}$$

Example 64

Use the same information as in Example 63:

	Enterprise	
	Y	Z
Sales = R50 000:	$\dfrac{\text{R20 000}}{\text{R5 000}}$	$\dfrac{\text{R35 000}}{\text{R5 000}}$
	= 4	= 7
Sales = R60 000:	$\dfrac{\text{R24 000}}{\text{R9 000}}$	$\dfrac{\text{R42 000}}{\text{R12 000}}$
	= 2,67	= 3,5

The operating leverage will reduce in proportion to the increase gap between the sales value and the break-even point.

The operating leverage is a management instrument which shows, relatively easily, the effect of a change in turnover on net income.

Suppose that there is an increase of 20% in sales in the above example:

	Increase in sales	Operating leverage	% increase in net income
Y	20%	4	80%
Z	20%	7	140%

Test for correctness:

$$\frac{\text{Increase in net income}}{\text{Net income}} \times \frac{100}{1}$$

$$Y: \frac{4\ 000}{5\ 000} \times \frac{100}{1} = 80\%$$

$$Z: \frac{7\ 000}{5\ 000} \times \frac{100}{1} = 140\%$$

The operating leverage is thus a management technique which indicates the effect of different sales volumes on net income without detailed statements having to be prepared.

8 Conclusion

The break-even technique is a management instrument by means of which alternative actions can be planned and tested. This technique clearly reflects the effects that changes in prices, costs and volumes have on the profit structure of the enterprise.

11

BUDGETS

1 Introduction

In modern society there is no organisation or enterprise, be it state, public or private sector, or an individual, which does not make use of some or other form of budget. The goal of most of the enterprises in the private sector is profit maximisation. Careful planning and effective cost control is essential to achieving this. Budgets and budget control are among the most important of the management instruments that enable management to fulfil these aims.

Thus budgets must be designed so that they are helpful to management in the planning, coordination and control of the various functions within the enterprise such as the sales, production and administration of the entire enterprise. Because the circumstances of an enterprise are never static it is also necessary to draw up various budgets (a variable budget) for various levels of operating capacity.

2 The concepts budget and budget control

It is necessary to describe the concepts budget and budget control more precisely, since incorrect meanings are often attached to them.

2.1 Budgets

A budget can be described briefly as a plan of action for achieving a stated goal. It is thus the **route** that must be followed from the current period and situation to a future target.

More scientifically, budgets can be defined as the careful planning of the future performance of all the activities of the enterprise that must be carried out in order to give substance to the policy of management by attaining a specific goal during a particular period. This plan, expressed in quantitative measurable terms, must be prepared in writing and should be realistic.

From the above definition it is clear that first, a specific **goal** must be set for the enterprise. Second, how management plans to achieve this goal must be clearly spelled out. A comparison between the budget and the actual results serves as a basis for evaluating the performance and taking corrective steps, if necessary.

2.2 Budget control

While the budget indicates the route that must be followed to achieve a specific goal, budget control is the watch-dog which ensures that there is no deviation from the route and that the goal is achieved in good time.

This is done mainly by measuring, on a continuous basis, the results attained against the budgeted target. It must be determined whether what was planned in the budget can be carried out in practice. Another important function of budget control is to establish the cause if there is a difference between the planned and actual results, and to take the action necessary to correct or avert it in time.

3 Functions of budgets and budget control

Briefly, budgets can be viewed as having a planning function and budget control as having a controlling and coordinating function. Since budgets and budget control are so closely allied and intertwined, in practice it is not always easy to draw a distinction between them. In many cases it is only a matter of relative emphasis. In the discussion which follows the communal attributes are discussed with emphasis on what is applicable only to one or the other.

3.1 Planning

The planning function is a very broad concept. However, it can be summarised as the proper and scientific planning of how the assets and resources that the enterprise has at its disposal will best be employed so that the greatest advantage is obtained in the short and the long term. Thus it embraces a study of what must be done, what is necessary for this, how it must be done and what the eventual outcome ought to be.

Once a realistic target has been established the first step is to determine what is necessary to achieve it. The assets and capacity at the disposal of the enterprise must be analysed critically to determine whether they are adequate and satisfactory and whether they will be fully utilised and occupied by the proposed activities.

The employment of raw material and labour must be planned, as must the administration of the enterprise. Sales strategies must be well thought out. Briefly, every facet and function of the enterprise must be analysed to determine whether it is employed to the greatest advantage of the enterprise as a whole.

The planning activities must be quantified in physical amounts and monetary values and projections of income and costs/expenses must be prepared for the budget period. Eventually the expected state of affairs as at the end of the period must be incorporated in a pro-forma balance sheet, from which the profitability of the enterprise during the budget period can be inferred. Although the planning is initially global (say only an expected profit figure), it is refined over time until each aspect is analysed and described in such minute detail that a guideline (not only in quantities but also in monetary values) for future actions, expenditure and income is produced.

3.2 Coordination

Due to the extent of the planning function and its wide involvement in each facet of the enterprise as a whole it is necessary to piece all the underlying aspects together by means of the "master plan" or **master budget.**

Coordination implies more than just the piecing together of the underlying or subsidiary budgets (for example production, sales and labour budgets); it also incorporates coordinating all of the activities and production resources of the enterprise as a whole. It is thus a bridging function which involves and unites the subdivisions in one whole. Thus the inefficiency of the individual, whether a person, division, asset or resource, is kept to a minimum by the synchronisation of all the separate facets.

3.3 Control

As has already been mentioned, control takes place mainly in the form of comparisons of the results achieved with those envisaged. It should be carried out on a continuous basis and any variation should be investigated immediately, the reasons for it established and corrective steps taken. Control leads to further planning.

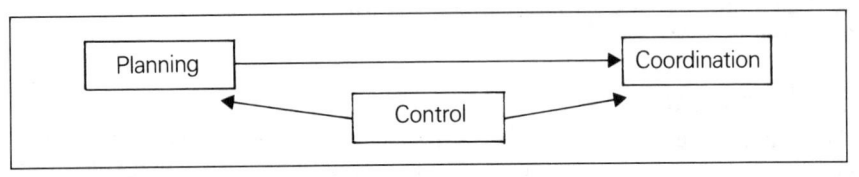

Diagram D53

4 Aims of budget control

It is absolutely necessary to demarcate the responsibility of each person who makes a contribution to the budget.

The broad aims of a system of budgets and budget control are:

- ☐ to put together the various ideas of all levels of management in the preparation of the budget
- ☐ to coordinate all the activities of the organisation efficiently
- ☐ to centralise controls in the case of decentralised activities
- ☐ to lay a basis for future policy when unforeseen situations affect the budget
- ☐ to plan costs and income in such a way as to achieve maximum profits
- ☐ to use capital expenditure in the most profitable manner
- ☐ to use production factors in the most economical way
- ☐ to serve as a standard against which actual results can be compared
- ☐ to establish the causes for variances between actual and budgeted results and to advise management to remedy unfavourable deviations or to take advantage of favourable situations.

Budgets and budget control must never be seen as an independent system — on the contrary, it is merely an aid for management in the carrying out of its duties.

5 The advantages of budgets and budget control

- ☐ They serve as an aid for achieving the objectives which management has set.
- ☐ Budgets facilitate the establishment of standards if a standard costing system is in use.
- ☐ The costs of the three cost elements in manufacturing are planned and controlled.

- [ ] Budget control leads to effective management principles; it makes the delegation of authority possible.
- [ ] The relationship between planned profit and planned employment of capital can be determined by means of budgets.
- [ ] The occurrence of cost variations exposes the weaknesses in the enterprise.

6 Disadvantages of budgets

- [ ] The uncertainty of forecasts adversely affects the system.
- [ ] Defining personnel responsibility gives rise to problems due to the overlapping of some duties.
- [ ] Forecasts can never be 100% accurate (the effectiveness of budgets depends on the accuracy of the forecasts).
- [ ] The degree of the willingness and cooperation of all the members of management involved in the system will determine its success.
- [ ] The budget programme requires additional administrative work and is thus an expensive system to implement.

It is clear that the advantages of budgets and budget control outweigh their disadvantages.

7 Important aspects of the preparation of budgets

7.1 The human factor

In a manufacturing enterprise the emphasis is on people, machines and material. Budgets and budget control, which have efficiency and greater productivity as their aim, shine the spotlight on the human factor.

If the personnel understand the purpose of the budgets and are correctly guided and motivated by management to give their wholehearted cooperation to the budget programme, it wll be successfully implemented.

7.2 Budget period

The length of the period, which depends on special circumstances, is usually a financial year. For control purposes the budget period is divided into quarterly or monthly budgets.

The following factors determine the length of the budget period:

- [ ] For enterprises which are subject to seasonal fluctuations the budget period should cover at least one cycle.
- [ ] The period should be long enough to cover the completion of all the products that are manufactured.
- [ ] As far as possible the budget period should link up with the financial period in order to facilitate the comparison of the actual results with the budgeted results.

7.3 Budget personnel

The budget committee, which usually comprises senior personnel members of the enterprise, is responsible for the preparation and administration of the budget. This committee reviews, discusses and coordinates all the budget activities. After the various budgets have been thoroughly reviewed they are combined into a final budget which is submitted to top management for approval.

7.4 Budget factor

In any enterprise there are certain factors which determine the limits of virtually all the relevant activities. These factors are not limited to the well-known production factors, but also include factors such as distribution, location and transport. If material or labour, for example, is not readily available for the manufacture of a product the production process will be hindered. The availability of capital will determine the production volume because it determines the limit of the operating capital. These scarce factors, collectively described as the **budget factor,** must be taken into account in the determination of the entire budget programme.

8 Types of budgets of a manufacturing enterprise

8.1 Introduction

The main or master budget is built up from the operating and financial budgets together with their working papers and anlyses of the enterprise's activities for the budgeted periods. It can be presented schematically as shown in Diagram D54.

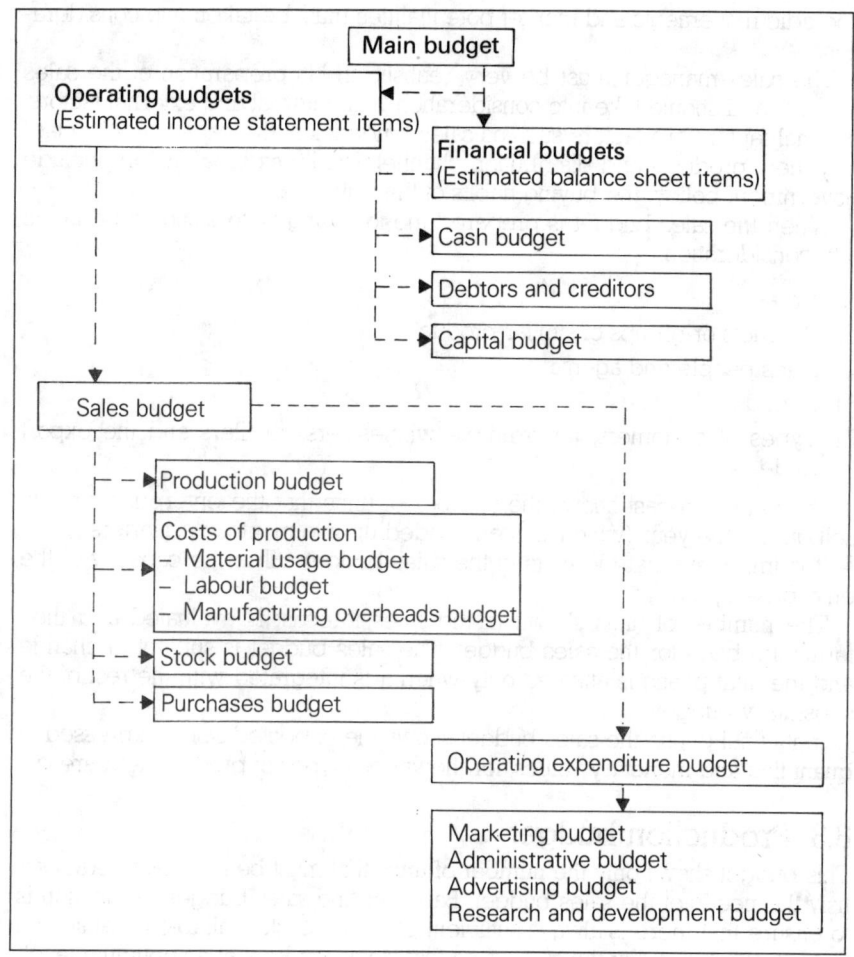

Diagram D54

The number of units that can be sold forms the basis of all the budgets and subsidiary budgets, especially if distribution cannot be influenced by management or if price control is instituted by the government. Once the number of units that can be sold is known it is possible to determine the number of units that must be manufactured. Thereafter it can be ascertained whether the available production capacity is adequate to manufacture the number of units shown in the production budget.

8.2 Sales budget

The sales budget must be reliable and very accurately forecast because it forms, in most enterprises, the basis of all the budgets.

The sales budget is based on estimated volumes and prices which in turn are based on an analysis of past sales and future market and sales tendencies and competition.

Because an enterprise makes a profit only if its products are sold, **market research** plays an important role when things such as seasonal fluctuations, sporadic movements and market potentialities must be taken into consideration.

The sales manager must be very realistic in his preparation of the sales forecast and should take into consideration both internal and external factors. **Internal** factors are factors such as sales tendencies, the capacity of the factory, new products and distribution channels, while **external factors** include government policy, the buying habits of the public, etc.

When the sales budget is prepared the following factors should be taken into consideration:

☐ Areas
☐ Products or groups of similar products
☐ Sales people and agents
☐ Periods
☐ Types of customers, for example wholesalers, retailers and the export trade

The sales forecast shows the number of units that the enterprise aims to sell during the year (which is often divided up into months or quarters).

It is important that the units in the sales budget utilise the capacity of the enterprise optimally.

The number of units shown in the sales forecast is evaluated and then forms the basis for the sales budget. The sales budget is subject to change and the final phase is attained only when it is integrated with the rest of the subsidiary budgets.

In its final phase the sales budget shows the expected sales, expressed in **quantities and monetary** values, for the various types of products and areas.

8.3 Production budget

This budget shows only **the number of units** that must be manufactured to satisfy the needs of the sales budget. Based on the sales budget, its function is to ensure that there is always sufficient physical stock available to satisfy the expected sales and at the same time that stock are kept at an optimum level.

When planning and preparing the production budget the production manager makes provision for seasonal fluctuations so that a constant production stock level and a stable labour force can be maintained. In cooperation with his personnel he prepares production schedules which show detailed product specifications of all the products that must be manufactured during the budgeted period.

The ideal is that the sales should fit in with the existing production capacity. If this is not the case and sales exceed the production capacity, additional production factors must be procured to increase the production correspondingly. If the excess sales are only temporary in nature the sales can be supplemented from existing stocks. Generally it is not possible to expand the production facilities immediately and consequently the sales budget must be based on the existing production capacity. The enterprise will be compelled, under these circumstances, to devote itself to the most advantageous production items which provide the greatest contribution per production hour.

The holding of stocks cannot be dispensed with in most enterprises and the estimated production units to satisfy the sales budget is calculated as follows:

Opening stock + Production = Sales + Closing stock

∴ Production = Closing stock + Sales − Opening stock

8.4 Plant utilisation budget

This budget shows how the plant available in the factory will be utilised. All the manufacturing sections complete separate production budgets which show what each department or cost centre is capable of producing at a normal or expected capacity.

The plant utilisation budget is based on the total of all these production budgets. It shows the work-load required of each section or machine group in order to accomplish the total production budget.

This budget is an important aid since it shows the available and utilised plant hours of each cost centre which, for control purposes, can be expressed as a utilisation percentage. Further, it will show whether work must be transferred from one section to another, or machinery must be expanded, or some of the work must be given to subcontractors.

The plant utilisation budget is valuable since it shows any over or under-capacity.

8.5 Direct material or raw material budget

The direct material budget shows the estimated quantity and cost of the raw materials required to manufacture the expected quantity of completed or finished goods. There must be adequate raw materials on hand in order to ensure a constant flow of these to the production process.

It is important that the right sort of material is available at the right place when needed. However, the enterprise must guard against overinvesting in stock, as this will affect its solvency and liquidity.

Some enterprises use standard material specifications to show the quantity of direct material necessary for each job. The specifications include the code number, quantity and standard value of each type of material necessary for a particular job, plus a reasonable provision for wastage and scrap.

When production is not standardised arbitary methods must be used to prepare the budget. The direct material budget, which is divided into types and quantities and expressed in monetary values after provision has been made for the estimated quantities and value of opening and closing stocks, reflects the value and quantity of raw materials required by the production department for the budgeted period.

8.6 Labour budget

Before a labour budget can be prepared a job analysis which shows the labour requirements per job, per department and for the whole factory must be done.

The number of units that must be produced serves as a basis for the determination of the estimated number of hours for the budgeted period.

The budgeted number of hours divided by the standard hours per employee gives the standard number of employees required for the period.

When the various labour rates are established all the factors which can affect the rates must be taken into account. Finally, the labour budget is made up of the number of labour hours required of each grade of labour multiplied by the standard labour rate.

In its completed form the labour budget will show:

☐ the type and quantity of employees to perform the various jobs
☐ the expected costs linked to such labour.

The labour budget represents a forecast of the direct and indirect labour required to satisfy the demand of the production budget.

The monetary values associated with indirect labour are, *inter alia*, included in the manufacturing overheads budget and the sales and administration budgets.

Pension fund contributions, sick fund contributions and all other labour-related costs of direct labourers not recovered as a portion of the direct labour costs can also be treated as manufacturing overheads.

8.7 Manufacturing overheads budget

This budget consists of a summary of the various budgets of all the cost items in the production section which do not fall under direct material or direct labour. Because accounting reports and related information form the basis for budget control, the manufacturing overheads budget must be prepared within the framework of the accounting system.

In order to facilitate the preparation of the manufacturing overheads budget all the costs must be classified as either fixed or variable. Further, the enterprise must be divided into production and service cost centres, with a person responsible for each centre.

It is important that the figures in this budget are forecast as accurately as possible, because it serves as a basis for ascertaining the predetermined overheads rate.

In the manufacturing industry most enterprises make use of variable budgets rather than fixed budgets, because fixed costs have an influence on the fixed overheads rate at various operating volumes. When an enterprise uses standard costing along with budget control the fixed overheads rate is usually based on the normal operating volume for the period.

8.8 Production cost budget

Once the production budget and the separate production costs budgets (material, labour and overheads) have been prepared the entire production costs budget is drawn up. It is a summary of the direct material, direct labour and manufacturing overheads budgets of the production plant and is also usually prepared per production department for the period. In order that the cost of goods available to be sold may be determined the budgeted opening stock of finished goods is included. When the budgeted closing stock of finished goods is deducted from this amount the cost of goods manufactured and sold remains.

8.9 Purchases budget

The purchases budget has to do with all purchases of goods and services by the enterprise for the budgeted period.

Various forms of control over the ordering and purchases function are possible and should be taken into consideration in the preparation of the purchases budget (for example, maximum and minimum order levels and the most economic order size). This budget serves as a basis for determining the cash required for purchases during the budget period.

8.10 Marketing cost budget

All the expenses such as advertising, transport, storage, insurance, collection costs and the salaries, bonuses and commissions of the sales staff are reflected in the marketing budget.

For control purposes the fixed and variable costs must be kept separate from each other, as with manufacturing overheads.

The marketing budget analyses all the sales and distribution costs for every product or group of products in respect of each sales agent and area in order to exercise effective control.

☐ **Advertising budget**

It is important that finished goods are sold as quickly as possible. This is possible only with the aid of an effective advertising campaign. Various methods can be used to determine what amount must be spent on advertising per annum, *inter alia:*

☐ percentage of sales
☐ a fixed amount per unit
☐ forecast of expected costs.

The advertising budget is prepared in coordination with all the budgets, especially the sales budget.

8.11 Research and development budget

To stay at the forefront of technological and economic development it is necessary that an enterprise has a regulated orderly research and development budget. Effective control is obtained by dividing the budget according to the different projects to which attention is being given. Expected completion dates must be indicated and progress reports should be presented regularly.

8.12 Administrative budget

This budget does not have a direct connection with the sales and production budget and represents only an estimate of the expenditure with reference to the formulation of the policy, the leadership and the administration of the organisation.

8.13 Capital budget

This budget consists of the planned investment in land, buildings and equipment. The investment in fixed assets is relatively large and must be seen as long-term planning. That is why its evaluation and planning is a function of top management.

The unpredictability of the future makes investment decisions extremely difficult.

The plant utilisation budget will show if the existing equipment is adequate to provide for the needs of the production budget.

The capital budget must be prepared in minute detail and capital additions must be classified as identifiable projects, each with its own project number.

Seeing that most enterprises have limited financial resources at their disposal, projects requiring capital investment decisions must be weighed up against each other. The time value of money plays an important role and modern techniques like the discounted cash flow method should be used in making the decision. This aspect is dealt with more fully in chapter 14.

8.14 Cash budget

Adequate liquidity is necessary for the survival of any enterprise. The cash budget provides an estimate of all receipts and payments and the manner and period in which they will be received or employed. This budget is prepared once all the other budgets are complete.

The cash budget usually shows the monthly cash position of the enterprise, but it can be subdivided into weekly or daily periods.

When the cash budget is prepared attention must be paid to the following aspects:

- [ ] A clear distinction must be made between cash and credit sales
- [ ] The credit policy followed for the collection of cash from credit sales, as well as discounts allowed to encourage prompt payment and provision for any bad debts
- [ ] The policy in respect of the payment of creditors
- [ ] All cash requirements as required by the operating and long-term budgets

---

Example 65: Cash budget

The management of Budgets Ltd decided to prepare a cash budget for May and June 19.1. The following information is available:

	Actual			Budgeted	
	Feb R	March R	April R	May R	June R
Sales					
Cash	250 600	290 500	305 700	300 000	320 000
Credit	410 500	500 500	585 800	580 000	600 000
Purchases	595 400	685 700	700 800	690 000	710 000
Salaries and wages	65 800	65 800	65 800	65 800	65 800
Sundry expenses	18 700	19 400	25 400	20 500	21 500

Further information

1. Cash in respect of credit sales is collected as follows:
   - 50% within 30 days
   - 30% within 60 days
   - 15% within 90 days
   - 5% is uncollectable

2. The following discounts are allowed on sales:
   10% on cash sales
   5% on credit sales if accounts are settled within 30 days
3. All salaries, wages and expenses are paid in cash
4. Sundry expenses include depreciation of R3 000 per month
5. Sixty percent (60%) of all purchases are on credit and are paid during the month following that of the transaction – the rest represent cash purchases
6. On 30 June a dividend of R5 000 was declared
7. The cash in the bank on 30 April 19.1 was R15 500

Required:
Prepare a cash budget for the period 1 May to 30 June 19.1.

Solution
Cash budget for May and June 19.1

		May R	June R
Opening balance		15 500	(4 300)
Estimated receipts:		759 980	814 315
Cash sales after discount		270 000	288 000
Credit sales	(1)	489 980	526 315
Total cash available		775 480	810 015
Estimated expenses:		779 780	782 300
Credit purchases	(2)	420 480	414 000
Cash purchases		276 000	284 000
Salaries and wages		65 800	65 800
Sundry expenses		17 500	18 500
Closing balance		(4 300)	27 715

(1) Calculation of receipts iro credit sales:

			May R	June R
Feb	(R410 500)	(15% of R410 500)	61 575	–
March	(R500 500)		150 150	75 075
April	(R585 800)		278 255	175 740
May	(R580 000)	(50% × 580 000) – 5%	–	275 500
June	(R600 000)		–	–
Total			489 980	526 315

(continued)

(2) Calculation of expenses iro purchases:

	April R	May R	June R
Cash 40%	280 320	276 000	284 000
Credit 60%	420 480	414 000	426 000
Total	700 800	690 000	710 000

8.15 Budgeted income statement

This budget is prepared after the various operating budgets have been drawn up. It includes the sales budget, purchases budget, production budget and expenses budget.

The budgeted income statement shows the projected income (profit) according to the estimates for the planned period.

8.16 Pro-forma balance sheet

This budget exercises control over the accuracy of all the other budgets. It shows the closing balances of all the assets, liabilities and owners' interest as reflected in the budgets prepared by the different departments. Once the budgeted income statement and balance sheet are complete the necessary ratios for analysis and interpretation purposes can be calculated.

8.17 Master budget

The master budget is obtained by coordinating all the budgets into one main budget. The master budget is management's proposed programme of action for the organisation during the budgeted period.

Example 66: Master budget (including the various subsidiary budgets)

The following information from Delta Company is available for 19.6:

Sales forecast:

(units)	January	February	March	April	May
Product Gim	3 000	4 000	5 000	4 000	4 000
Product Mick	6 000	5 000	5 000	5 000	5 000

Selling price of manufactured products

Gim	R50 each
Mick	R65 each

Requirements per unit of finished product:

	Gim	Mick
Material Foe	2 kg	6 kg
Material Fie	4 kg	2 kg
Direct labour	4 hours	6 hours

Material and labour cost information for 19.6:

Material Foe	R1 per kg
Material Fie	R2 per kg
Direct labour	R4 per hour

Expected overheads:

Manufacturing overheads
Variable	R2 per direct labour hour
Fixed	R79 000 per month (1)

Sales and administrative
Variable	5% of sales
Fixed	R40 000 per month (2)

(1) Including depreciation of R10 000
(2) Including depreciation of R5 000

Trial balance as at 31 December 19.5:

	Debit R	Credit R
Cash	180 000	
Debtors	373 000	
Stock on hand		
Material Foe (40 000 kg × R2)	80 000	
Material Fie (20 000 kg × R4)	80 000	
Product Gim (2 000 × R44)	88 000	
Product Mick (4 000 × R52)	208 000	
Land and buildings	500 000	
Machinery and equipment	650 000	
Accumulated depreciation		320 000
Creditors		220 000
Taxation payable		40 000
Capital		1 000 000
Retained income		579 000
	2 159 000	2 159 000

Further information:

(1) The company is aiming to keep its stock levels at the next month's production and sales requirements.

(2) All sales are on credit. About 40% is collected in the month of sale, 50% in the following month and 9% during the second month after the sale. The balance represents bad debts.

(3) The debtors balance on 1 January 19.6 consists of the following:

	R
From November sales	48 500
From December sales	324 500
	373 000

(4) Information in respect of cash payments:

    (a) Material is paid for in the month after it was purchased.

    (b) Direct labour is paid during the month in which it arises.

    (c) Manufacturing, sales and administrative overheads are spread evenly between the month in which they arise and the following month, in other words 50% is payable in each month.

    (d) Income tax for each quarter is supposed to be paid during the month following the end of the quarter.

(5) The creditors as at 1 January 19.6 consist of the following:

	R
Material purchases	120 000
Sundry expenses	100 000
	220 000

(6) The income tax rate is 40%.

(7) The FIFO method of stock valuation is used.
(Take note of the changes in material prices and product costs.)

Required:

Prepare a master budget for the first quarter of 19.6 for Delta Company.

Solution

1 SALES BUDGET

Product	January		February		March	
	Units	R	Units	R	Units	R
Gim	3 000	150 000	4 000	200 000	5 000	250 000
Mick	6 000	390 000	5 000	325 000	5 000	325 000
		540 000		525 000		575 000

2 PRODUCTION BUDGET (Units)

	GIM		
	January	February	March
Sales requirements (see 1 above)	3 000	4 000	5 000
Required closing stock (see (1) of question)	4 000[1]	5 000	4 000
Total requirements	7 000	9 000	9 000
Less: Opening stock	2 000	4 000	5 000
Required production	5 000	5 000	4 000

	MICK		
Sales requirements	6 000	5 000	5 000
Required closing stock	5 000	5 000	5 000
Total requirements	11 000	10 000	10 000
Less: Opening stock	4 000[1]	5 000	5 000
Required production	7 000	5 000	5 000

[1] Given in the trial balance

(continued)

3 MATERIAL PURCHASES BUDGET

	Material Foe		
	January	February	March
Production requirements:			
Gim (2 kg × production) (see 2)	10 000	10 000	8 000
Mick (6 kg × production)	42 000	30 000	30 000
Total (kg)	52 000	40 000	38 000
Add: Required closing stock			
(see (1) in question)	40 000	38 000	38 000
Total requirements (kg)	92 000	78 000	76 000
Less: Opening stock	40 000[1]	40 000	38 000
Purchase quantity (kg)	52 000	38 000	38 000
Unit cost	R1	R1	R1
Rand value	R52 000	R38 000	R38 000

	Material Fie		
Production requirements:			
Gim (4 kg × production)	20 000	20 000	16 000
Mick (2 kg × production)	14 000	10 000	10 000
Total (kg)	34 000	30 000	26 000
Add: Required closing stock	30 000	26 000	26 000
Total requirements (kg)	64 000	56 000	52 000
Less: Opening stock	20 000[1]	30 000	26 000
Purchase quantity	44 000	26 000	26 000
Unit cost	R2	R2	R2
Rand value	R88 000	R52 000	R52 000
Total (Foe and Fie)	R140 000	R90 000	R90 000

[1] Given in trial balance

4 DIRECT LABOUR BUDGET

	January	February	March
Production requirements Gim (4 hours × production) (see 2 above) Mick (6 hours × production)	20 000 42 000	20 000 30 000	16 000 30 000
Direct labour hours needed	62 000	50 000	46 000
Labour cost per hour	R4	R4	R4
Total direct labour cost	R248 000	R200 000	R184 000

5 MANUFACTURING OVERHEADS BUDGET

	January	February	March
Direct labour hours (see 4 above)	62 000	50 000	46 000
	R	R	R
Variable (R2 per labour hour)	124 000	100 000	92 000
Fixed (given)	79 000	79 000	79 000
	203 000	179 000	171 000

Note: 1 Depreciation of R10 000 per month is still included.

      2 Fixed overheads allocation
        [(3 × 79 000) ÷ 158 000] = R1,50 per direct labour hour

(continued)

6 SALES AND ADMINISTRATIVE EXPENSES BUDGET

	January	February	March
	R	R	R
Variable (5% of sales)	27 000	26 250	28 750
Fixed (given)	40 000	40 000	40 000
	67 000	66 250	68 750

Note: Depreciation of R5 000 per month is still included.

Summary

	January	February	March
	R	R	R
Total manufacturing, sales and administrative overheads	270 000	245 250	239 750
Less: Depreciation	15 000	15 000	15 000
Amount payable in cash	255 000	230 250	224 750

7 DEBTORS COLLECTIONS

	Total	January	February	March	Out-standing 31 March	Provi-sion bad debts
	R	R	R	R	R	R
From November	48 500	43 650	–	–	–	4 850
From December	324 500	270 417	48 675	–	–	5 408
From January	540 000	216 000	270 000	48 600	–	5 400
From February	525 000	–	210 000	262 500	52 500	–
From March	575 000	–	–	230 000	345 000	–
	2 013 000	530 067	528 675	541 100	397 500	15 658

(continued)

8 CASH PAYMENTS

	January	February	March
	R	R	R
Material purchases:			
December	120 000		
January		140 000	
February			90 000
Overheads:			
December	100 000		
January	127 500	127 500	
February		115 125	115 125
March			112 375
Labour	248 000	200 000	184 000
Income tax	40 000		
	635 500	582 625	501 500

Creditors: 31 March 19.6	R
Material purchases (March)	90 000
Overheads	112 375
	202 375

9 CASH FLOW PROJECTION

	January	February	March
	R	R	R
Opening balance	180 000	74 567	20 617
Add: Receipts (see 7 above)	530 067	528 675	541 100
	710 067	603 242	561 717
Less: Payments (see 8 above)	635 500	582 625	501 500
Balance	74 567	20 617	60 217

10 PROJECTED INCOME STATEMENT

	R	Reference to sub-budgets
Sales	1 640 000	1
Less: Cost of sales	1 436 000	
Raw materials	390 000	
Opening stock	160 000	
Add: Purchases	320 000	3
	480 000	
Less: Closing stock	90 000	3
Direct labour	632 000	4
Manufacturing overheads	553 000	5
	1 575 000	
Less: Increase in finished goods stock[2]	139 000	
Closing stock	435 000	
Less: Opening stock	296 000	
Gross profit	204 000	
Less: Sundry expenses	217 658	
Sales and administrative	202 000	6
Bad debts	15 658	7
Net loss	13 658	

[2] Finished goods closing stock

	Gim	Mick	
Stock, 31 March (units)	4 000	5 000	2
Units costs	× R40	× R55	
Material Foe	2	6	3
Material Fie	8	4	3
Labour	16	24	4
Overheads [(R2 + R1,50) per hour]	14	21	5
Total value	R160 000	R275 00	

11 PRO-FORMA BALANCE SHEET

	R	Reference to sub-budgets
Shareholders' interest	1 565 342	
Capital	1 000 000	
Add: Retained income		
(R579 000 – R13 658)	565 342	10
Represented by:		
Fixed assets	785 000	
Land and buildings	500 000	
Machinery and equipment	285 000	
Cost price	650 000	
Less: Depreciation		
(R320 000 + R45 000)	365 000	
Net current assets	780 342	
Current assets	982 717	
Cash	60 217	9
Debtors	397 500	7
Raw materials	90 000	3
Finished goods	435 000	10
Less: Current liabilities (creditors)	202 375	8
	1 565 342	

9 Variable budgets

The budgets discussed thus far have had a fixed character because a fixed amount is predetermined for each cost item. In a manufacturing enterprise where the volume of business fluctuates continuously it is important that a **variable budget** is used.

As the name indicates, a variable budget is one which restates the position if there is a variation from the expected volume on which the fixed budget is based. It usually consists of a number of budgets prepared for various volumes of business.

When preparing the variable budget a decision must be made as to which "unit" management has in mind for measuring the volume of business. It can be measured in physical units, labour hours, machine hours, labour costs, and so on. It is important that a direct correlation between the "unit" and manufacturing overheads exists at the different levels of business activity. Once the normal or standard level of business activity has been determined a variable budget can be prepared.

In the preparation of the variable budget for manufacturing overheads it will be found that some overhead items react differently at different levels of business activity as a result of their fixed, variable and semi-variable character. It is essential that the semi-variable items are classified as either fixed or variable with the aid of techniques such as high-low, graphic, or least squared methods (refer to chapter 4 for elucidation).

The variable budget is used to:

☐ set standards for sales quantities, production costs and distribution costs

☐ compare actual results with budgeted figures at the same level of business activity over the same period

☐ calculate predetermined overheads rates in order to apportion manufacturing overheads to production.

The following is an example of a variable overheads budget:

Example 67

Monthly variable overheads budget

	Various levels of business activity			
Machine hours as basis	700	800	900	1 000
Business activity as %	70%	80%	90%	100%
	R	R	R	R
Cost items:				
Variable	10 500	12 000	13 500	15 000
Semi-variable	3 600	3 700	3 800	3 900
Fixed	8 000	8 000	8 000	8 000
Total	22 100	23 700	25 300	26 900
Overheads rate				
Variable	* 16,00	16,00	16,00	16,00
Fixed	** 15,57	13,63	12,11	10,90
Total	31,57	29,63	28,11	26,90

The division of the semi-variable costs into fixed and variable is calculated as follows with the help of the high-low method:

	Machine hours	Value R
Highest	1 000	3 900
Lowest	700	3 600
Difference	300	300

(continued)

Variable overheads rate: $\dfrac{\text{R300}}{300}$

$\qquad\qquad\qquad = \text{R1,00 per hour}$

Fixed overheads: $\quad$ R3 900 $-$ (1 000 $\times$ R1)
$\qquad\qquad\qquad = $ R3 900 $-$ 1 000
$\qquad\qquad\qquad = $ R2 900

* [R10 500 + (700 $\times$ R1)] $\div$ 700 = R16,00
** (R8 000 + R2 900 $\div$ 700 = R15,57

10 Zero-based budgets

This type of budget has been used with success by local authorities, states and federal governments in America.

As the name implies, the zero-based budget is prepared from scratch each year. It has a dynamic character in that historical figures are not relevant and only estimated data which will be of importance in the future is taken into consideration. This means that the method of merely making price adjustments to last years' figures to provide for inflation is eliminated and that each year every situation must be budgeted for and accounted for once again. Because the zero-based budget is prepared from scratch each year it necessitates a document (also called decision packet) which identifies each function or activity in order to enable management to evaluate the necessity of this activity and to determine its position on the priority scale of the budget.

The general opinion of the zero-based budget is that each manager must prepare an "alternative" budget for each activity within his area of responsibility and all of these are integrated into a decision packet. As an example, an alternative method can include the following:

☐ What will happen if an activity is eliminated?

☐ What will happen if the budget is cut by a certain amount?

☐ What will be achieved with the existing budget if more money is provided?

Every alternative effort represents separate decision levels and the rankings thereof takes place with the assistance of a cost-advantage analysis. From the discussion of this topic it can be inferred that zero-based budgets should rather be installed in enterprises without a profit motive. This system will also not be useful to enterprises which make use of standard costing systems.

STANDARD COSTS

The field of application of standard costs

1 Introduction

Today all sectors of industry are characterised by fierce competition, technological innovation and ever-escalating manufacturing and marketing costs.

The cost of manufacturing a product or providing a service can be calculated in two ways, namely before a job is begun (pre-calculated) or after a job is completed (post-calculated). The last-mentioned method, known as the **historical costs method,** has the following limitations:

☐ The use of historical costs is inadequate to measure performance in the enterprise or to bring about any cost savings.

☐ At the time that historical costs are first known it is already too late to take corrective steps to counter inefficiency.

☐ Historical costs do not give an employee any incentive or motivation to improve his productivity.

☐ Historical costs are of little importance to management with regard to planning, control and decision making.

The limitations of historical costing gave rise to the development of "precalculated" methods. Also, the acceptance and use of predetermined recovery tariffs for overheads in the determination of product costs logically gave rise to the development of standards for direct material and direct labour.

Overheads recovery tariffs represent a predetermined rate based on an estimated cost and a normal level of business activity. The use of these rates makes it possible to value production when the actual historical costs are not known.

In contrast with actual rates, normal rates reflect the expected cost at a certain level of business activity and not the actual costs at the level of activity achieved.

Standard costs correspond, in many respects, with predetermined normal overheads recovery tariffs – **they indicate norms of standards of what costs should be. Standard costs** are the costs of the efficient employment of production resources under current business circumstances by a reasonably competent management and **standard costing** is a system whereby a comparison is drawn between:

☐ what should be done at standard costs

☐ what was done at actual costs.

2 Aims

The purpose of a system of standard costing is to furnish relevant information to management in good time by means of cost reports. This information should immediately show which cost centres or departments are functioning inefficiently, thus enabling management to concentrate on those areas where large differences between actual information and established standards arise.

Standard costing improves cost control in the enterprise by:
- [ ] establishing standards for each cost element
- [ ] determining actual costs for each cost element
- [ ] comparing actual costs with standard costs and determining the differences (variances)
- [ ] analysing the variances and facilitating measures to correct them where these are necessary.

3 Characteristics of standard costing

Because standards are often confused with budgets, the characteristics of standard costing are best highlighted when the two systems are compared with each other.

Budget control has to do with the comparison of the actual results with the budgeted results of all the facets of the enterprise for a given period. Standard costing controls only the cost aspect of the production and distribution of products. Budgets establish the maximum permissible costs while the minimum allowable costs are established by standard costing. If a standard costing system is already in use it facilitates the preparation of such budgets, while a budget control system is of great help in controlling costs. One system can function without the other, but it is a fact that one system supplements the other.

4 The uses of standards and standard costs

Standard costing is generally applied in enterprises which manufacture homogeneous products. It can also be used successfully in enterprises which do piecework (jobs).

Briefly, standard costs are used as follows in the manufacturing process:

- [ ] **Cost control**

  Standards enable management to draw periodic comparisons between actual and standard costs in order to measure efficiency.

☐ **Stock valuation**

If stocks are valued at standard costs it is easy to convert them to actual costs for balance sheet purposes.

☐ **Planning for budget purposes**

The standard costing system facilitates the preparation of the production and the cost and sales budget in its entirety.

☐ **The fixing of prices**

In general there is a close connection between the selling price and the unit cost of a product. Standard unit costs enable management to achieve the best combination of prices and volumes for a given period.

☐ **The keeping of records**

Whenever a standard costing system is used together with actual costs the keeping of records in detail can be reduced such as, for example, stock registers which only have to show the quantities.

5 The classification of standards

Before standards can be established it is necessary to decide at which level of business activity the budgets and standards are going to be based. There is no fixed rule as to the level of business activity that management should use in the standard costing system. Also, more than one basis can be used in the establishment of a standard for a single cost element (for example labour hours and machine hours). If standard hours are chosen as a basis it represents the amount of work that should be completed in an hour.

There are **four** different methods for setting the standard level of business activity within an enterprise:

☐ **Expected actual level of business activity**

This is the level of business activity actually expected for the budgeted period based on the prevailing conditions.

☐ **Basic level of business activity**

This is the level of activity that was set in the past and against which the expected and actual performance can be compared. This method is especially important for statistical purposes.

☐ **Ideal or theoretical level of business activity**

As the name indicates, this level of activity is achieved only if all the conditions are ideal. Naturally this method is impractical, since the conditions can never all be ideal.

☐ **Normal level of business activity**

This is the level of business activity that can be achieved with efficient performance under prevailing conditions. It represents an average figure which aims to absorb and erase total costs, taking into account economic and seasonal conditions. This level is especially suited to establishing a standard for manufacturing overheads.

6 Advantages of standard costing

- [ ] Standard costs serve as a yardstick against which actual costs can be measured.
- [ ] The analysis of variations necessitates consistent control over the entire production process. Standard costing might give rise to cost reduction programmes, since it draws attention to aspects which are not being controlled efficiently.
- [ ] The use of standard costs reduces clerical work, since the value and quantities of the cost elements of each completed product that must be manufactured are already available on a standard cost card and production orders need only be recorded on standard forms.
- [ ] The analysis of cost reports by management is simpler and takes less time.
- [ ] With standard costing greater control is exercised over costs. The object is always to improve work performance and have more efficient material usage. It has everything going for it in that the entire enterprise becomes cost conscious.
- [ ] If a standard costing system is introduced it makes the task of valuing raw materials, half-complete products and completed products easier.
- [ ] When standards are first established they may serve as a stimulus to further planning which will lead to greater efficiency.

7 The implementation of a standard costing system

Before a standard costing system is introduced it is necessary to pay attention to the following aspects:

- [ ] The division of production departments into **cost centres** in order to get greater efficiency and responsibility
- [ ] The **classification of accounts** so that they make provision for actual costs, standard costs and variations
- [ ] The **level of business activity** that will be used as a basis for determining standard costs
- [ ] The establishment of **standard quantities, standard times** and **costs** for each cost element

In order to establish costing standards for each cost element there must be a standard cost card for each product manufactured or service provided. This cost card shows the following:

- [ ] Standard quantities and standard prices of each raw material
- [ ] Standard labour rate and standard hours
- [ ] Standard variable manufacturing overheads

☐ Standard fixed manufacturing overheads
☐ Total standard costs allowed, according to the standard, to manufacture a completed product

It is essential that all possible factors which could exercise any influence are taken into consideration when standards are established, since they must be set with the greatest degree of accuracy possible.

As soon as any changes arise as a result of, for example, economic factors, standards must be adapted accordingly, since it is senseless to work with outdated standards. The success of a standard costing system lies in the standards being as accurate and reliable as possible.

In the next four modules the variances of the different elements are discussed in the light of Diagram D55:

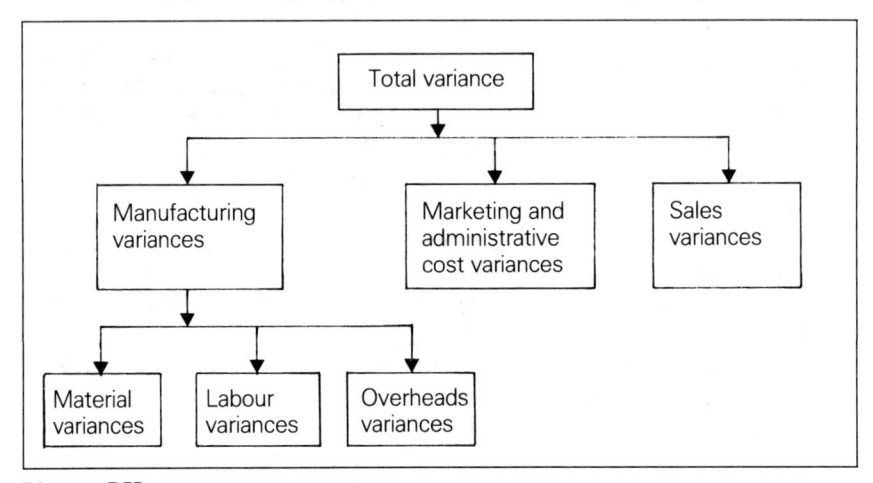

Diagram D55

Module

12.2

Material standards and variances

1 Introduction

Standard specifications must be prepared for the establishment of standard material quantities according to size, mass or any other yardstick. Attention must be given to quantities, prices, rates, quality and grades and provision must be made for normal scrap, losses, wastage and breakages, and so on.

Thus when standards are established there will be a **price** and **quantity standard** for material. The purchasing division establishes the standard prices for material in conjunction with the factory accountant. Market factors, suppliers' quotations and optimum purchase quantities must be taken into consideration. The prices are usually based on historical, current and expected future prices.

The standard material quantity specifications serve as a basis for the determination of the standard quantities required to manufacture one unit of each completed product.

If the actual quantity of material used and the costs incurred differ from the standard quantity and costs allowed this is known as a variance or variation. With regard to material two **main variances** can occur. These relate to the:

☐ **price** of the material
☐ **quantity** of material used.

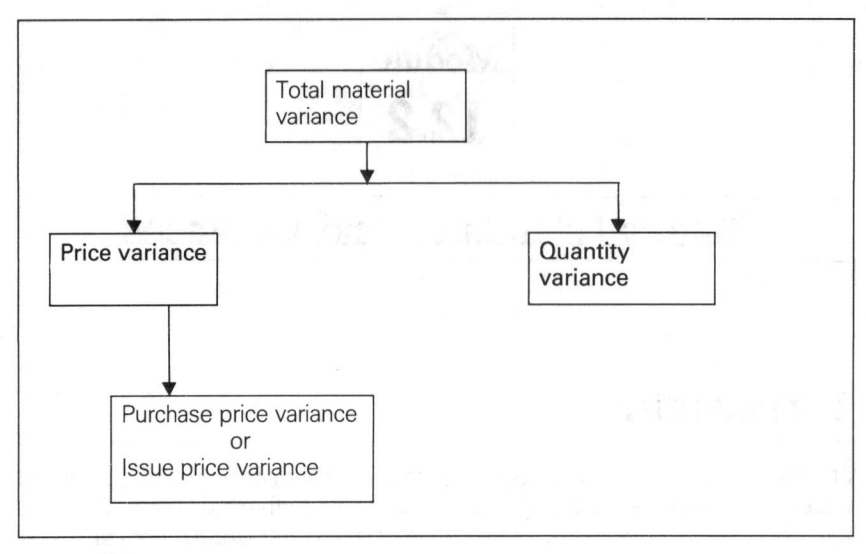

Diagram D56

Diagram D57 provides a clear illustration of the use and determination of the two main variances in respect of material.

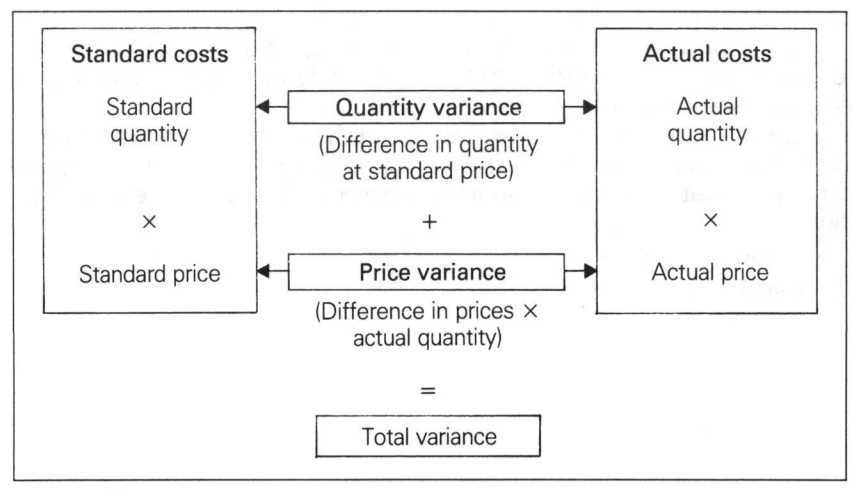

Diagram D57

2 Material price variance

The material price variance can be calculated by means of one of the following two methods:

Purchase price variance, based on the number of units purchased

Issue price variance, based on the number of units issued and used

☐ Purchase price variance

The variance is determined upon receipt of the material and occurs whenever the actual price differs from the standard price. The variance is calculated by taking the difference between the actual cost of the amount purchased and the standard cost (amount purchased × standard price) thereof.

Formula: (AP × AQ) − (SP × AQ), or (AP − SP) AQ

where: AP = actual price
          SP = standard price
          AQ = actual quantity purchased

☐ Issue price variance

This variance is determined when the raw materials are issued. It is the difference between the actual quantity at historical cost and the actual quantity issued at the standard price. The formula is:

Formula: (AP × AQ) − (SP × AQ) or (AP − SP) AQ

where: AQ = actual quantity issued

The purchase price variance is of greater value since it is known at the time that the goods are received. On the other hand price variances, which are calculated at the time of issue, are advantageous in that material stock accounts are kept at actual cost and no adjustment has to be made in respect of stock values at the accounting date.

Material price variances can be attributed to:

☐ faulty standards (mistakes made when establishing the standard prices)
☐ price increases or reductions as a result of unforeseen changes in market prices, good/poor conditions in the purchase department, incorrect calculation of discounts and delivery costs, or bad timing of purchases.

3 Material quantity variance

This variance is also sometimes known as the **usage, efficiency** or **volume variance.** It is calculated by taking the difference between the actual amount of material used at the standard price and the standard quantity of material allowed at the standard price. The concept standard quantity of material allowed means the standard quantity allowed for the actual production and is calculated as follows:

Suppose that 5kg of raw material is the standard set for the manufacture of one unit of a finished product. If 100 units of the finished product are made the standard quantity of material allowed is 500 kg, being 100 units × 5 kg.

The formula for the calculation of the variance is as follows:

Formula: (AQ × SP) − (SQ × SP), or (AQ − SQ) SP

where: AQ = actual quantity of material used
         SQ = standard quantity of material allowed
              for actual production
         SP = standard price

Material quantity variances can be attributed to:

☐ faulty standards (mistakes made when establishing the standard quantity)
☐ good/poor controls over the use of material
☐ better/poorer quality material which results in a better/poorer output
☐ efficient/inefficient working conditions, equipment, supervision, skills of the employees, etc

The total of the material price variance and the material quantity variance is known as the total material variance and can also be calculated as follows:

$$(AQ \times AP) - (SQ \times SP)$$

Variances can be **favourable (F)** or **unfavourable (U)**. If the standard costs are greater than the actual costs the variance is **favourable** because less actual costs were incurred than the standard requires, and if the standard costs are less than the actual costs the variance will be unfavourable because more actual costs were incurred than the standard requires.

Example 68

The standard material costs of finished product X are as follows:
  2 kg raw material Y @ R10 per kg

  Actual information:
    Purchase of raw material Y :   1 000kg @ R9,50 per kg
    Issues of raw material Y :   600 kg
    Units of product X manufactured :   290 units

Required:

Calculate the following variances in respect of material:

  (i)   Purchase price
  (ii) Issue price
  (iii) Quantity
  (iv) Total material variance, if an issue price variance is used

---

Solution

(i) Material purchase price variance : $(AP - SP)\,AQ$
$= (R9{,}50 - R10{,}00)\,1\,000$
$= \underline{R500}$ (F)

(ii) Material issue price variance : $(AP - SP)\,AQ$
$= (R9{,}50 - R10)\,600$
$= \underline{R300}$ (F)

(iii) Material quantity variance :
$= (AQ - SQ)\,SP$
$= (600 - 580^*)\,R10$
$= \underline{R200}$ (U)

     * Standard quantity : $290 \times 2 = 580$ kg

(iv) Total material variance : $(AQ \times AP) - (SQ \times SP)$
$= (600 \times 9{,}50) - (580 \times 10)$
$= 5\,700 - 5\,800$
$= \underline{R100}$ (F)

     Alternatively :   (ii) + (iii)
$= R300$ (F) $+ R200$ (U)
$= \underline{R100}$ (F)

The variances can also be presented diagramatically as follows:

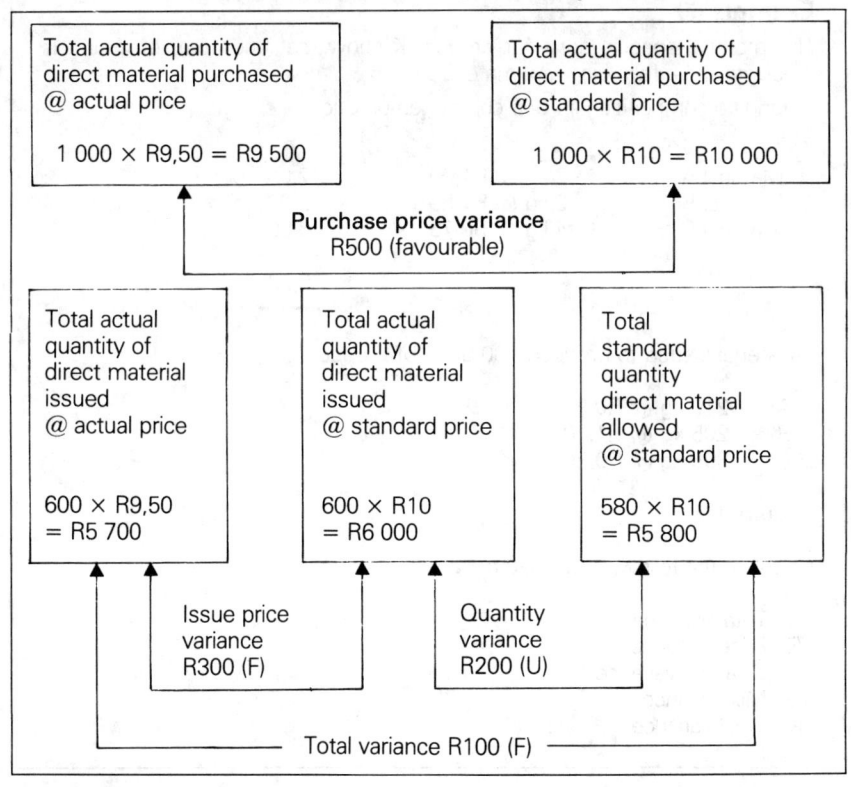

Diagram D58

4 Material sub-variances

When more than one type of material is used in the manufacture of a product and the ratio or composition differs from the standard ratio according to the standard material specifications it is divided into:

☐ a yield variance
☐ a mix or composition variance.

The sum of the two variances is equal to the material quantity variance and can be presented as shown in Diagram D59.

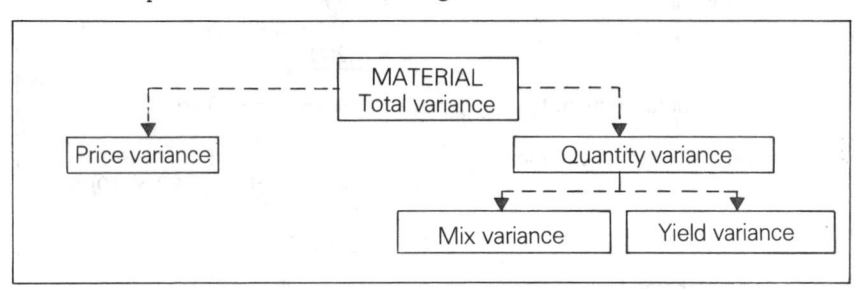

Diagram D59

Example 69

The material specifications for product K show that one completed unit is made from the following raw materials:

Standard composition iro one completed product

			R
Material A	2 kg @ R1,00	=	2,00
Material B	2 kg @ R1,50	=	3,00
Material C	4 kg @ R0,75	=	3,00
			8,00

Material issued to produce 100 units of product K

A	210 kg @ R0,95
B	205 kg @ R1,40
C	395 kg @ R0,80

Required

Calculate the following iro material:

(i) Total variance
(ii) Price variance
(iii) Quantity variance
(iv) Mix variance
(v) Yield variance

Solution

(i) Total material variance   Actual cost – Standard cost

A:	$210 \times 0{,}95$	R199,50
B:	$205 \times 1{,}40$	287,00
C:	$395 \times 0{,}80$	316,00

$$
\begin{aligned}
&= 802{,}50 - (100 \times R8) \\
&= 802{,}50 - 800 \\
&= R2{,}50 \ (U)
\end{aligned}
$$

(ii) Material price variance   (AP – SP) AQ

A	$(0{,}95 - 1{,}00)\ 210$	=	R10,50	(F)
B	$(1{,}40 - 1{,}50)\ 205$	=	20,50	(F)
C	$(0{,}80 - 0{,}75)\ 395$	=	19,75	(U)
			R11,25	(F)

(iii) Material quantity variance   (AQ – SQ) SP

A	$(210 - 200)\ 1{,}00$	=	R10,00	(U)
B	$(205 - 200)\ 1{,}50$	=	7,50	(U)
C	$(395 - 400)\ 0{,}75$	=	3,75	(F)
			R13,75	(U)

(iv) Material mix variance $\left\{ AQ - \left(\dfrac{SQ}{SM} \times AM \right) \right\} SP$

$$
\begin{aligned}
A \quad : \quad & \{210 - (\tfrac{2}{8} \times 810)\}1{,}00 \\
& = (210 - 202{,}50)\ 1{,}00 \\
& = R7{,}50\ (U)
\end{aligned}
$$

$$
\begin{aligned}
B \quad : \quad & \{205 - (\tfrac{2}{8} \times 810)\}\ 1{,}50 \\
& = (205 - 202{,}50)\ 1{,}50 \\
& = R3{,}75\ (U)
\end{aligned}
$$

$$
\begin{aligned}
C \quad : \quad & \{395 - (\tfrac{4}{8} \times 810)\}\ 0{,}75 \\
& = (395 - 405)\ 0{,}75 \\
& = R7{,}50\ (F)
\end{aligned}
$$

Total   = R3,75 (U)

(v) Material yield variance $\left\{ \left(\dfrac{SQ}{SM} \times AM \right) - SQ \right\} SP$

A	$(202{,}50 - 200)\ 1{,}00$	=	R2,50	(U)
B	$(202{,}50 - 200)\ 1{,}50$	=	3,75	(U)
C	$(405 - 400)\ 0{,}75$	=	3,75	(U)
			R10,00	(U)

(Where SM = standard mix and AM = actual mix)

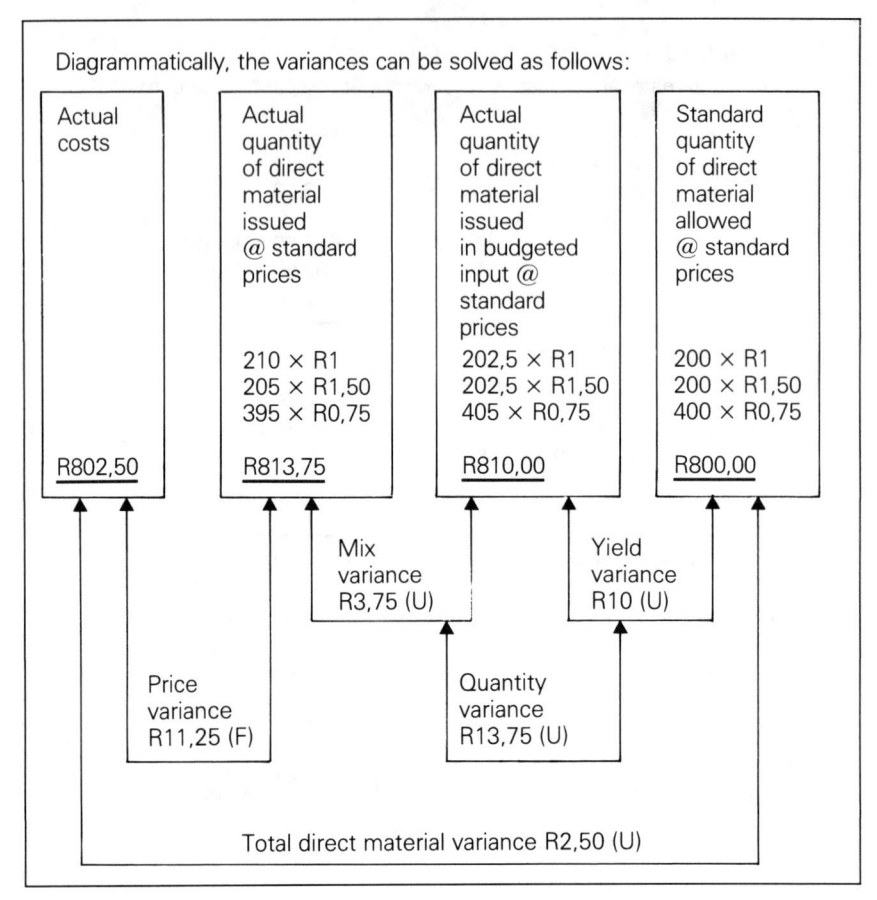

Diagrammatically, the variances can be solved as follows:

Actual costs	Actual quantity of direct material issued @ standard prices	Actual quantity of direct material issued in budgeted input @ standard prices	Standard quantity of direct material allowed @ standard prices
	210 × R1	202,5 × R1	200 × R1
	205 × R1,50	202,5 × R1,50	200 × R1,50
	395 × R0,75	405 × R0,75	400 × R0,75
R802,50	R813,75	R810,00	R800,00

Mix variance R3,75 (U)

Yield variance R10 (U)

Price variance R11,25 (F)

Quantity variance R13,75 (U)

Total direct material variance R2,50 (U)

Diagram D60

The sub-variances have the following uses:

☐ The material mix variance enables management to obtain the optimum composition of material.

☐ The material yield variance shows the over or underusage of raw material. It helps to ensure that the individual raw materials are utilised to the maximum.

5 Recording of material costs

The purchase of material can be recorded in the books by means of the following two methods:

☐ The material is recorded at standard cost and the price variance is recorded on receipt of the material.

☐ The material is recorded at actual cost and the price variance is recorded upon issue.

The first method is recommended, since controls are exercised on receipt of the material.

The recording of material according to the two methods can be illustrated as follows using the information about finished product X in Example 68:

☐ First method: Purchase price variance

The recording of the material purchases at standard cost:

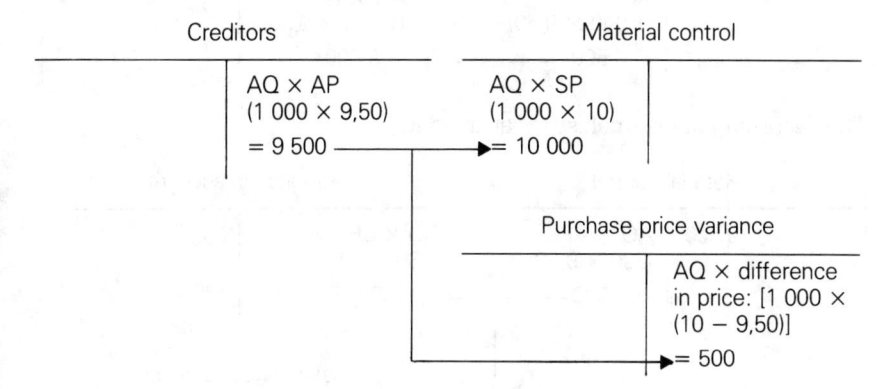

The recording of material issues at standard cost:

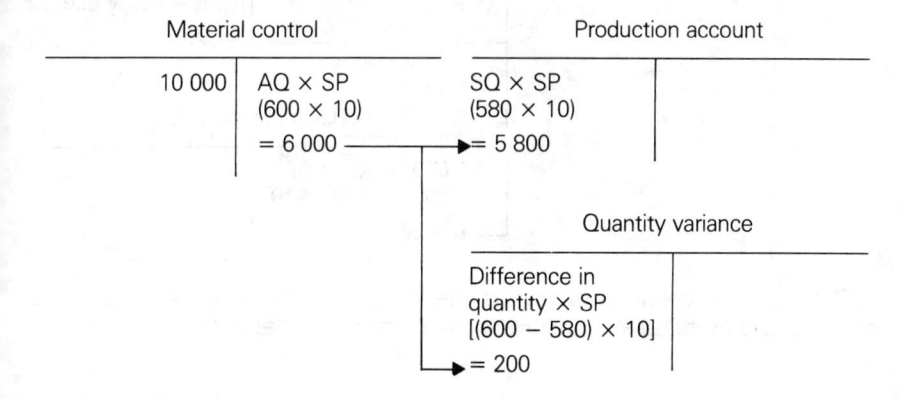

☐ Second method: Issue price variance

The recording of material purchases at actual cost:

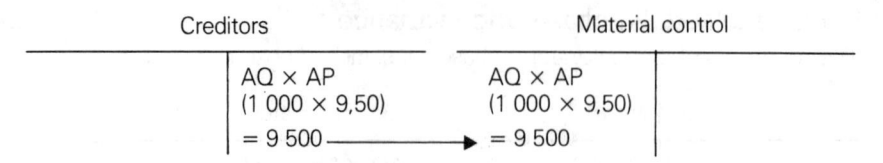

Creditors	Material control
AQ × AP (1 000 × 9,50) = 9 500 ⟶	AQ × AP (1 000 × 9,50) = 9 500

The recording of material issues at standard cost:

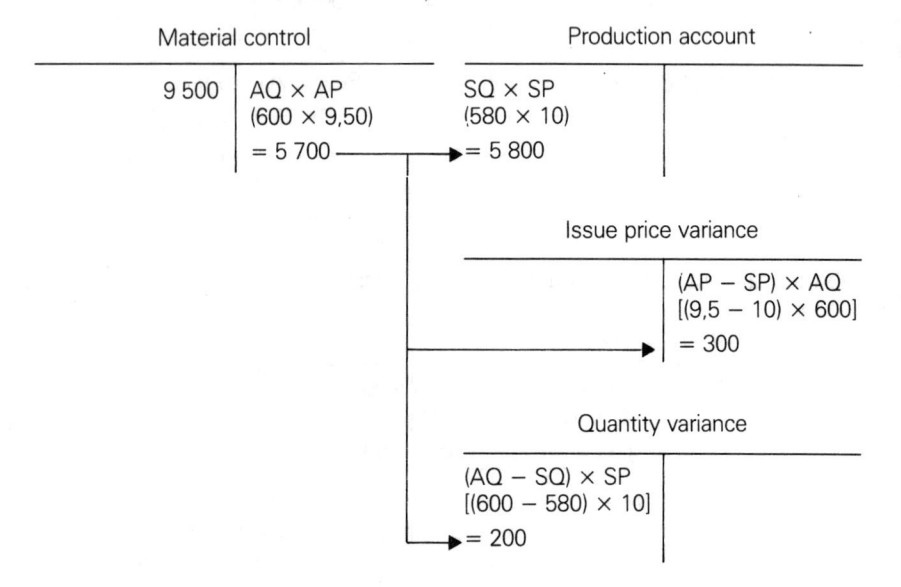

Material control	Production account
9 500 AQ × AP (600 × 9,50) = 5 700 ⟶	SQ × SP (580 × 10) = 5 800

Issue price variance
(AP − SP) × AQ [(9,5 − 10) × 600] = 300

Quantity variance
(AQ − SQ) × SP [(600 − 580) × 10] = 200

True to the accounting principles, the favourable variances in the above accounts are credited and the unfavourable variances debited.

Module

12.3

Labour standards and variances

1 Introduction

As is the case with material, a **price** and a **quantity standard** are established in respect of labour. With regard to labour the word "price" is preferably replaced by **rate** or **tarrif** while the word "quantity" is replaced by **efficiency.**

Rate standards are usually based on the established wage scales paid for the specified type of labour. Time standards for the manufacture of a product are determined with the aid of time and motion studies. When standards are established provision must be made for idle time, which is unavoidable.

The two main variances relating to labour are:

☐ the labour rate variance
☐ the labour efficiency variance.

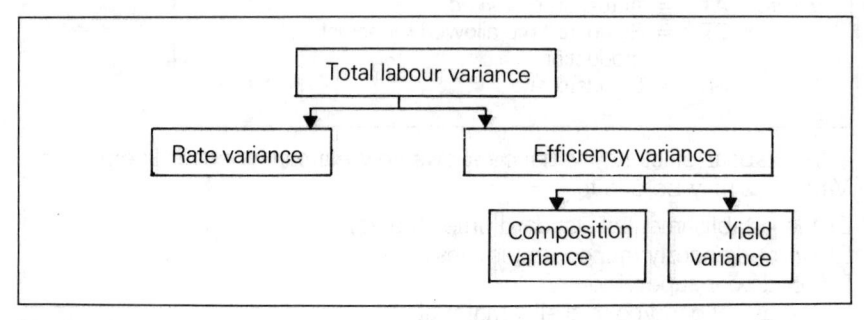

Diagram D61

2 Labour rate variance

This variance is calculated by multiplying the difference between the actual and the standard rate by the actual hours worked. The formula for its calculation is as follows:

(AR − SR) AT or (AR × AT) − (SR × AT)

where   AR   = actual rate paid
         SR   = standard rate
         AT   = actual hours worked

The labour rate variance can be caused by:

- [ ] the establishment of incorrect labour rates
- [ ] changes in wage tariffs
- [ ] poor scheduling of production which gives rise to overtime (overtime is calculated at a higher rate than normal time)
- [ ] the use of better/poorer qualified personnel with higher/lower pay.

3 Labour efficiency variance

The labour efficiency variance is related to the amount of time necessary to manufacture one unit of a product. It is calculated by taking the difference between the actual hours worked at the standard rate and the standard time (hours) allowed for the actual production at the standard rate.

The formula for determining the variance is as follows:

(AT − ST) SR or (AT × SR) − (ST × SR)

where   AT   = Actual time worked
         ST   = Standard time allowed for actual
                production
         SR   = Standard rate

The labour efficiency variance shows how efficiently labour is employed. Variances may be due to:

- [ ] the establishment of standard times (hours)
- [ ] properly/poorly trained employees
- [ ] good/poor supervision
- [ ] the use of good/poor quality material
- [ ] problems with machinery and equipment which result in longer manufacturing hours than budgeted for

Example 70

The following information is available about the labour of the manufacturing department of Proud Labour Limited:

Actual hours worked: 510 @ R4,50 per hour

Units manufactured :
Complete   450 units
Incomplete   200 units (100%
                           complete iro material and 25%
                           complete iro labour and overheads)

Standard labour cost per unit
according to the standard cost card   1 hour @ R4,75 per hour

Required:

Calculate the following:
  (i) Labour rate variance
 (ii) Labour efficiency variance
(iii) Total labour variance

Solution

  (i) Labour rate variance

$$(AR - SR)\ AT$$
$$= (4,50 - 4,75)\ 510$$
$$= R127,50\ (F)$$

 (ii) Labour efficiency variance

$$(AT - ST)\ SR$$
$$= (510 - 500)^*\ 4,75$$
$$= R47,50\ (U)$$

*Standard hours allowed for actual production:

$$= [450 + (25\% \times 200)] \times 1\ \text{hour per unit}$$
$$= [450 + 50] \times 1$$
$$= 500\ \text{hours}$$

(iii) Total labour variance

$$R127,50\ (F) + R47,50\ (U)$$
$$= R80\ (F)$$

Alternatively

$$(AT \times AR) - (ST \times SR)$$
$$= (510 \times 4,50) - (500 \times 4,75)$$
$$= 2\ 295 - 2\ 375$$
$$= R80\ (F)$$

The variances can be shown diagramatically as follows:

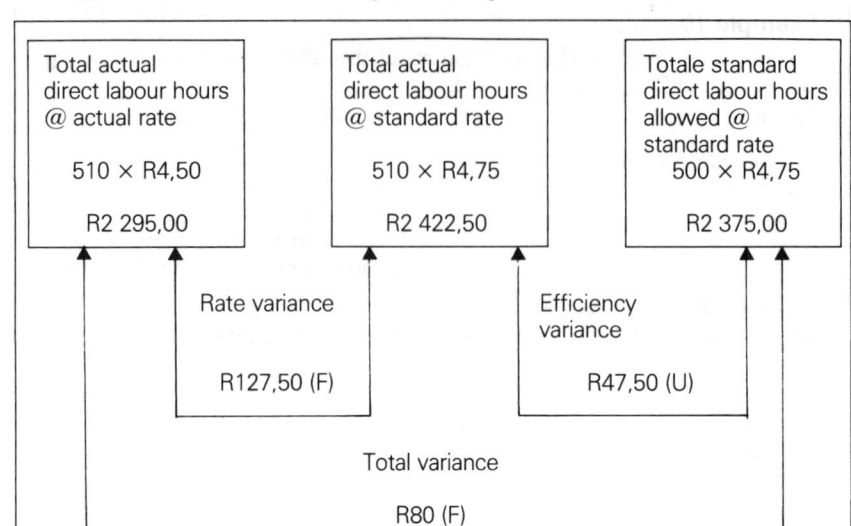

Diagram D62

4 Sub-variances

No matter how accurately standards are established there is still the possibility of idle time due to power failures, raw material shortages, defective machines, etc. This **idle time variance** must be calculated separately and must not be included in the labour efficiency variance, otherwise the employees can be wrongly blamed for inefficiency in respect of problems which are beyond their control.

As is the case with material, the labour efficiency variance can be divided into two sub-variances, namely:

☐ composition variance (mix)
☐ yield variance

If the composition (ratio between the different types of grades of labour) that is used differs from the standard ratio then a **labour composition** or **labour mix variance** exists. The variance is calculated by multiplying the difference between the actual composition and the standard composition of the actual total hours worked and by the standard rates.

The **yield variance** represents the difference between the standard time allowed for the actual production (units manufactured) and the actual time spent multiplied by the standard labour rate.

Example 71

Standard labour costs to manufacture 300 units

		R
100 hours @ R10 per hour	=	1 000
50 hours @ R6 per hour	=	300
		1 300

Deductions

1 150 hours ÷ 300 units = 0,50 hour per unit
2 Standard labour rate per hour of standard mix :
        R1 300 ÷ 150 hours = R8,66 per hour
3 Standard labour cost per unit = R4,33 per hour

Actual labour costs incurred to produce 290 units

		R
80 hours @ R9 per hour	=	720
60 hours @ R5 per hour	=	300
		1 020

Idle time represents 10% of the recorded labour hours.

Deductions

1 Standard time allowed for production:
    290 units × 0,5 hours per unit = 145 hours
2 Standard labour costs allowed for actual production:
    290 units × R4,33 = R1 256

Required:

Calculate the following:

  (i) Labour rate variance
 (ii) Idle time variance
(iii) Labour efficiency variance
(iv) Labour mix variance
 (v) Labour yield variance
(vi) Total labour variance

Solution:

(i) Labour rate variance

= AT × (AR − SR)
= [80 × (9 − 10)] + [60 × (5 − 6)]
= 80 + 60
= R140 (F)

(ii) Idle time variance

= Idle time × SR
= [(10% of 80) × 10] + [(10% of 60) × 6]
= 80 + 36
= R116 (U)

The idle time variance will always be unfavourable because it adversely affects the efficiency of the employees.

(iii) Efficiency variance:

= (Hours worked × SR) − (Hours allowed × Average SR)
= [(80 − 8)* × 10 + (60 − 6)* × 6] − (145 × 8,66)
= 1 044 − 1 256
= R212 (F)

(iv) Labour mix variance

Std mix of AT worked	Actual mix of AT worked	Differ- ence	SR	Variance
			R	R
84	72*	12	10	120 (F)
42	54*	−12	6	72 (U)
126	126			48 (F)

(v) Labour yield variance:

= (Hours allowed − Hours worked) × Average SR
= (145 − 126) × 8,66
= 19 × 8,66
= R164 (F)

Test for correctness of variances:

Efficiency	= Mix + Yield
	= 48 (F) + 164 (F)
	= R212 (F)

(vi) Total labour variance

= Std cost of actual production − actual cost
= R1 256 − R1 020
= R236 (F)

Alternatively the separate variances can be added together, which also serves as a test of the correctness.

*80 hours − 10%; 60 hours − 10%

The variances can be presented diagrammatically as follows:

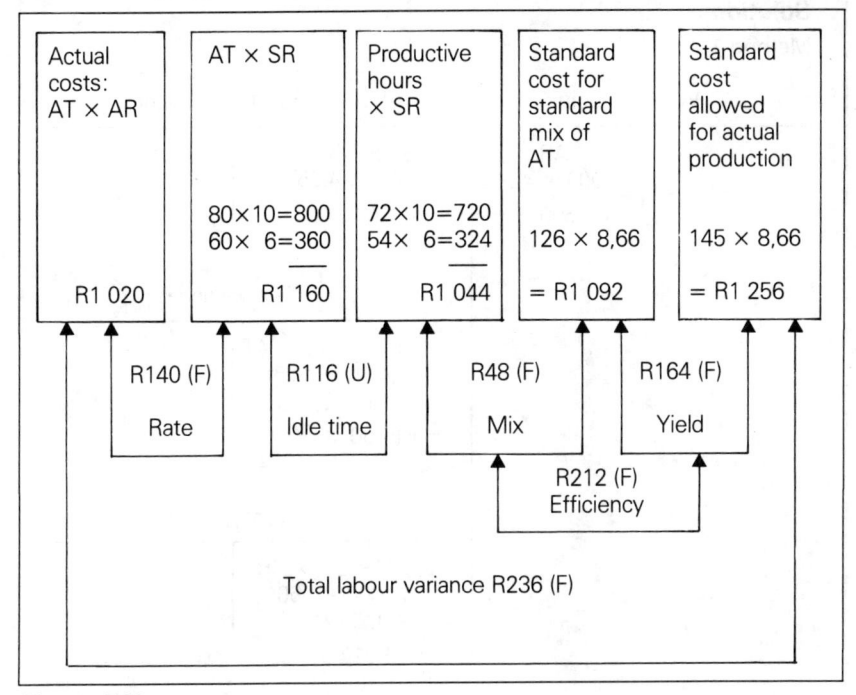

Diagram D63

5 Recording of labour costs

The following example is self-explanatory:

Example 72

Actual time worked	1 000 hours
Actual rate	R4,50 per hour
Standard time allowed for actual production	950 hours
Standard rate	R4,25 per hour

Required:

Show by means of T-accounts how the liability and division of labour is recorded.

Solution
Method 1

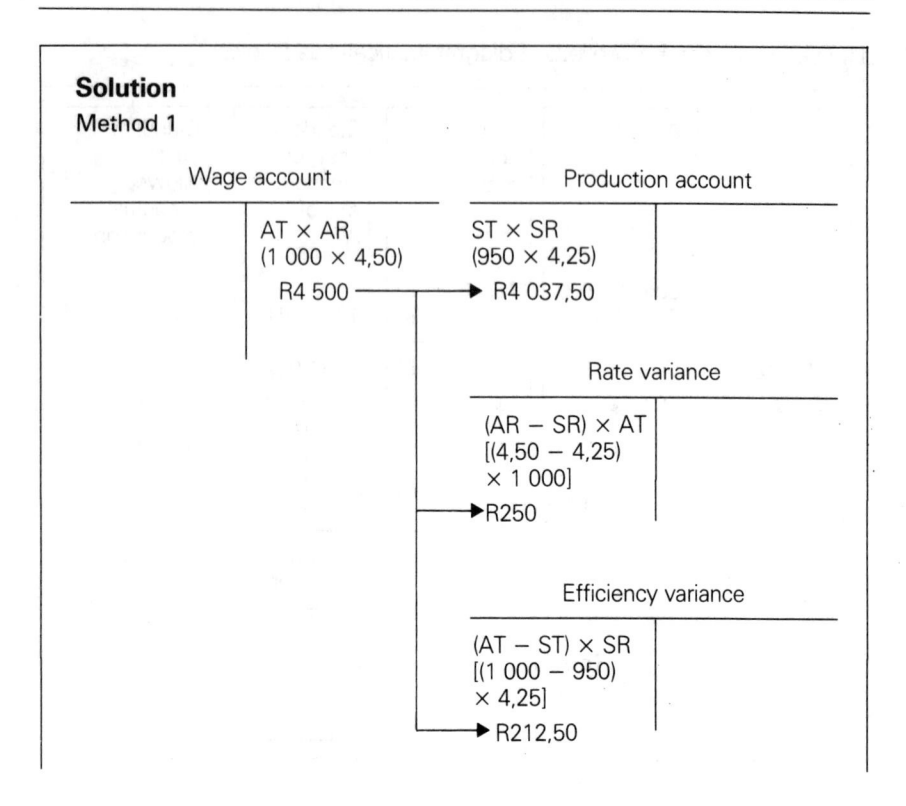

Method 2

The recording of the labour liability:

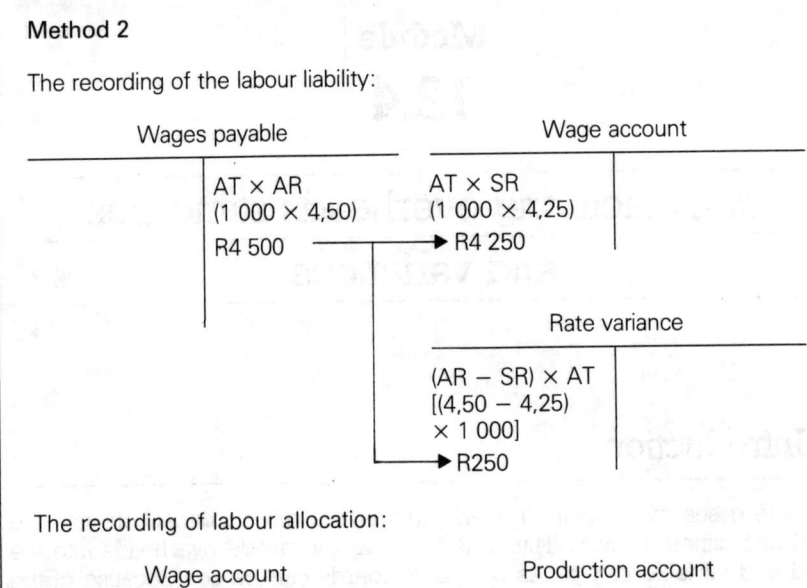

The recording of labour allocation:

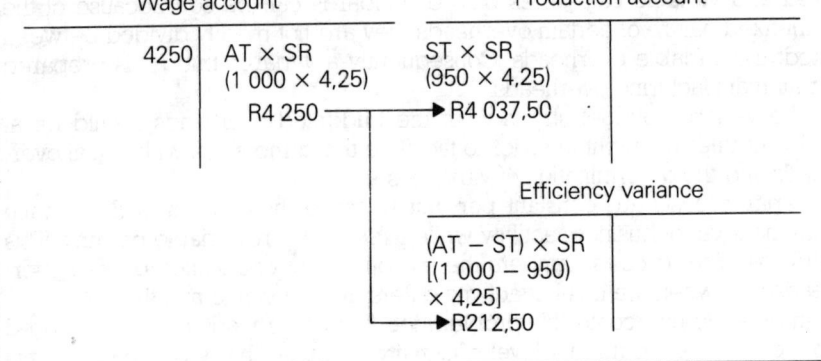

Module

12.4

Manufacturing overheads standards and variances

1 Introduction

In some cases manufacturing overheads have a direct connection with the level of business activity. Thus it is necessary to divide overheads into the **fixed** and **variable** categories before standards can be set. Because of the semi-fixed nature of certain overheads they are not readily divided between fixed and variable overheads. Consequently a variable budget is prepared for all manufacturing overheads.

The variable budget shows what the budgeted overheads should be at different rates of output in order to facilitate the comparison with actual overheads and the determination of variances.

Variable costs are **constant per unit** because they vary in a direct ratio with the level of business activity while fixed costs are **variable per unit.** This attribute of fixed costs hampers the establishment of a standard fixed overheads rate when the level of activity differs from month to month.

In order to overcome this problem the fixed overheads rate is calculated on the basis of the **normal level of activity,** because this is based on normal activity.

Manufacturing overheads variances maybe due to:

☐ the actual level of operations differing from the planned level
☐ the actual overheads differing from the budgeted overheads
☐ the actual hours worked differing from the standard hours.

Different methods can be used to calculate these variances. The method used will depend on the nature of the enterprise and to what extent controls will be exercised.

The individual variances in respect of fixed and variable overheads can be calculated **separately,** or the fixed and variable overheads can be combined and the variances calculated **collectively.** If the fixed and variable overheads are **combined** the variances can be calculated in different ways, of which only the following two will be dealt with:

☐ The two variance method
☐ The three variance method

2 Separate variable and fixed manufacturing overheads variances

2.1 Variable manufacturing overheads variances

Diagram D64 provides a schematic representation of the different variances which fall under variable overheads.

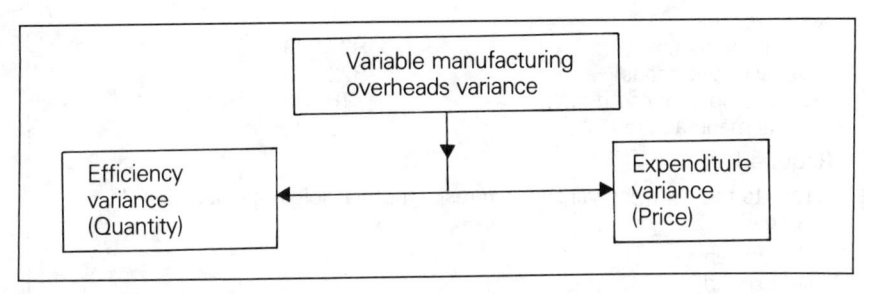

Diagram D64

Overheads tariffs are usually based on direct labour hours or machine hours, or are expressed as a percentage of the direct labour costs. However other bases, as discussed in chapter 4 (manufacturing overheads), can also be used. Unless otherwise stated, labour hours are used as the basis throughout this chapter.

The **efficiency variance** (also called the quantity variance) is calculated by multiplying the difference between the actual hours worked and the standard time allowed by the standard rate for variable overheads. The **expenditure variance** (also called the tariff, rate or price variance) is the difference between the actual and the standard rate for variable overheads multiplied by the actual hours worked.

Example 73 explains variable overheads more fully:

Example 73

The following are the budgeted results at **normal capacity** of Standards Limited, a manufacturing enterprise, for February 19.2 :

Fixed overheads	R27 000	
Variable overheads	R22 500	
Labour hours	15 000	hours

According to the standard, it takes 7,5 hours to manufacture one product.

Actual results:

Fixed overheads	R27 200	
Variable overheads	R22 400	
Labour hours worked	16 000	hours
Units manufactured	2 100	

Required

Calculate the following variances in respect of variable manufacturing overheads:

(i) Efficiency
(ii) Expenditure
(iii) Total variable overheads

Solution

(i) Efficiency variance $(AT - ST)\ SR$ or
$(AT \times SR) - (ST \times SR)$
$= [16\ 000 - (2\ 100 \times 7{,}5)] \times$
$(R22\ 500 \div 15\ 000)$
$= (16\ 000 - 15\ 750)\ 1{,}50$
$= R375\ (U)$

(ii) Expenditure variance $(AR - SR)\ AT$ or
$(AR \times AT) - (SR \times AT)$
$= [(22\ 400 \div 16\ 000) - 1{,}50]\ 16\ 000$
$= R1\ 600\ (F)$

(iii) Total variance   Actual amount −
Standard amount
$= R22\ 400 - (15\ 750 \times 1{,}50)$
$= 22\ 400 - 23\ 625$
$= R1\ 225\ (F)$

where   SR = Variable standard rate (overheads)
AR = Variable actual rate (overheads)

These variances can be presented diagrammatically:

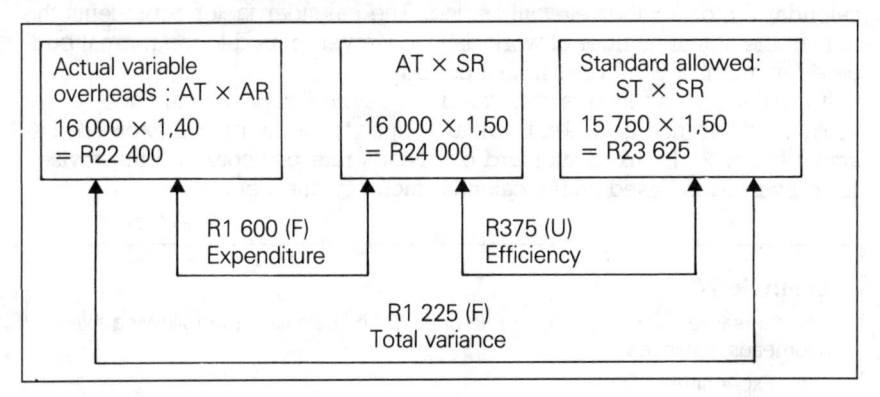

Diagram D65

2.2 Fixed manufacturing overheads variances

The fixed overheads variances (also called the 4 variances method) can be presented schematically as follows:

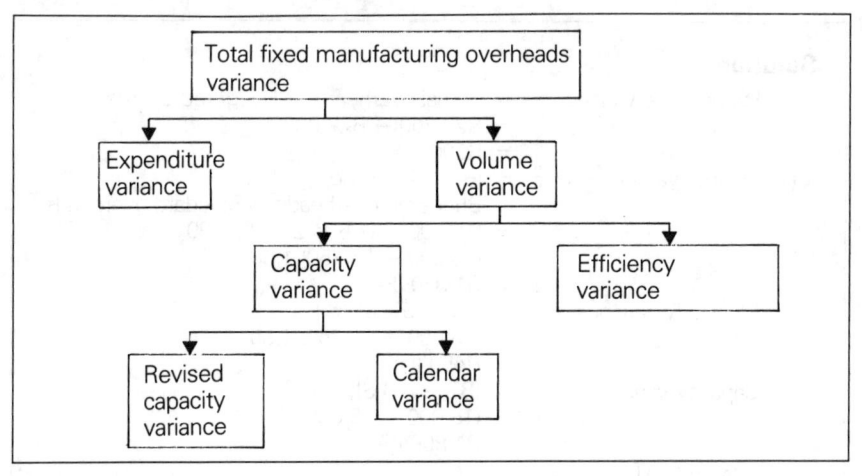

Diagram D66

The two main variances in fixed manufacturing overheads are the **expenditure** and the **volume variances**. The expenditure variance is calculated as the difference between the actual and the budgeted fixed overheads. The volume variance is calculated as the difference between the budgeted and the standard fixed overheads and can be divided into a **capacity** and an **efficiency** variance.

The capacity variance represents the differences between the budgeted time and the actual time valued at the standard fixed recovery rate, while the efficiency variance represents the difference between the actual time and the standard time allowed multiplied by the total standard rate.

In turn, the capacity variance can be subdivided to make provision for a **revised capacity** and a **calendar variance**. The overheads calendar variance represents the difference between the allowable fixed overheads based on the normal capacity and the fixed overheads allowed on the grounds of the **calendar factor** for the relevant period. The calendar factor represents the ratio of the actual number of work days in a given period to the normal budgeted number of work days in that period.

If a calendar variance is calculated the revised capacity variance represents the difference between the actual capacity for the period expressed as **actual hours × the fixed standard overheads rate per hour** and the **revised fixed overheads based on the calendar factor** for the period.

Example 74

Use the same information as in Example 73 and calculate the following fixed overheads variances:

(i) Expenditure
(ii) Volume
(iii) Efficiency
(iv) Capacity
(v) Total variance
(vi) Test the correctness of your variances

Solution

(i) Expenditure variance
= Actual overheads − Budgeted overheads
= R27 200 − R27 000
= R200 (U)

(ii) Volume variance
= (BT − ST) SR or
Budgeted overheads − Standard overheads
= [15 000 − (7,5 × 2 100)] 1,80
= (15 000 − 15 750) 1,80
= R1 350 (F)

(iii) Efficiency variance
= (AT − ST) SR
= (16 000 − 15 750) 1,80
= R450 (U)

(iv) Capacity variance
= (BT − AT) SR
= (15 000 − 16 000) R1,80
= R1 800 (F)

where BT = Budgeted time
AT = Actual time
ST = Standard time for actual production
SR = Standard fixed overheads rate

(v) Total variance
= Actual overheads − Standard overheads
= 27 200 − (15 750 × 1,80)
= 27 200 − 28 350
= R1 150 (F)

(vi) Test :
Total variance
= Expenditure variance + Volume variance
= R200 (U) + R1 350 (F)
= R1 150 (F)

Volume variance
= Capacity variance + Efficiency variance
= 1 800 (F) + 450 (U)
= R1 350 (F)

The status of the variances in respect of fixed manufacturing overheads is determined as discussed under material variances, namely a favourable variance exists when standard costs exceed the actual costs and vice versa. The outcome of the capacity variance as determined above raises problems, since it is favourable despite the fact that the actual hours (16 000) worked are more than the budgeted hours (15 000). The reason for this can be explained as follows. Fixed overheads in total are fixed, but vary per unit. If more hours than budgeted are actually worked without any increase in fixed costs, a greater number of products is manufactured. Consequently the fixed cost per unit will decrease. Fixed costs which are fixed in total, will now be absorbed by a larger production and will be spread over the larger number of products. This will result in a decline in the fixed costs per unit – thus the favourable variance.

When the standard days for a month are based on 30 and a month like February has only 28 days, then there is a **calendar variance.** If a year is taken in its entirety a calendar variance is sometimes self-eliminating and can exist in only some accounting periods during the year.

If the use of time is normally within management's control but the capacity variance is not so easily controllable, it is important that the capacity variance is divided into a calendar and a revised capacity variance.

Example 75

Information for February 19.2 :

	Actual	Budgeted
	R	R
Fixed overheads	27 200	27 000
Number of days worked	22	20
Production (units)	2 100	2 000
Hours worked	16 000	15 000

Required:

Calculate the following :
  (i) Calendar variance
  (ii) Revised capacity variance
  (iii) Capacity variance

Solution

(i) Calendar variance

$$= \frac{R27\,000}{20} \times \frac{(22 - 20)}{1}$$
$$= 1\,350 \times 2$$
$$= R2\,700\ (F)$$

(ii) Revised capacity variance

$$= (BT^* - AT)\ SR$$
$$= \frac{(16\,500 - 16\,000)}{1} \times \frac{27\,000}{15\,000}$$
$$= 500 \times 1{,}80$$
$$= R900\ (U)$$

* Budgeted time revised

$$= \frac{15\,000}{20} \times \frac{22}{1}$$
$$= 16\,500\ hours$$

(iii) Capacity variance

$$= (BT - AT)\ SR$$
$$= (15\,000 - 16\,000)\ 1{,}80$$
$$= R1\,800\ (F)$$

Alternative solution

(i) Calendar factor

$$= \frac{22 - 20}{20} \times \frac{100}{1} = 10\%\ (F)$$

(ii) Calendar variance

$$= 10\% \times Budget$$
$$= 10\% \times R27\,000$$
$$= R2\,700\ (F)$$

(iii) Revised capacity variance

$$= (AT \times SR) - (Factor \times Budget)$$
$$= (16\,000 \times R1{,}80) - (110\%^* \times R27\,000)$$
$$= R28\,800 - R29\,700$$
$$= R900\ (U)$$

* (100% + 10%)

A diagrammatic representation of a consolidation of the variable and fixed manufacturing overheads variances which are calculated separately is:

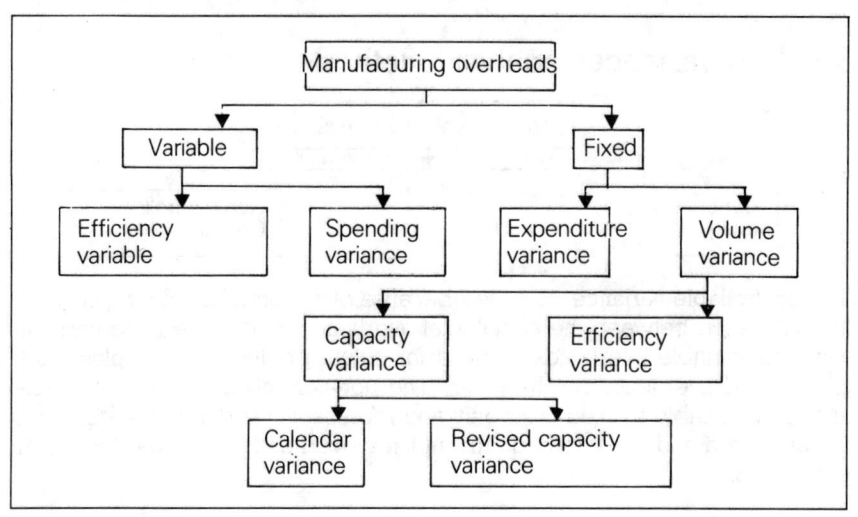

Diagram D67

☐ Causes of manufacturing overheads variances

(a) Expenditure variances (fixed overheads)
   - The equipment stands idle due to power failures, defective machinery, raw material shortages, etc
   - Labour problems as a result of absenteeism
   - Ineffective planning – incorrect scheduling of work or instructions
   - Material problems as a result of defective material
   - Fluctuations in demand

(b) Efficiency variances (fixed and variable overheads)
   The causes of these variances are mainly the same as those of the labour efficiency variance.
   - The degree of efficiency of employees as a result of selection, supervision, training, skills, etc
   - Working conditions – these cause dissatisfaction
   - The re-designing of products
   - Efficient/inefficient planning and control of production

3 Combined variable and fixed manufacturing overheads variances

With this combined method no distinction is made between fixed and variable manufacturing overheads. It is important to note that there is a fundamental difference between this method and the method in which the separate fixed and variable overhead variances are consolidated.

The following is a schematic representation of the two methods found under combined variances:

3.1 Two variances analysis method

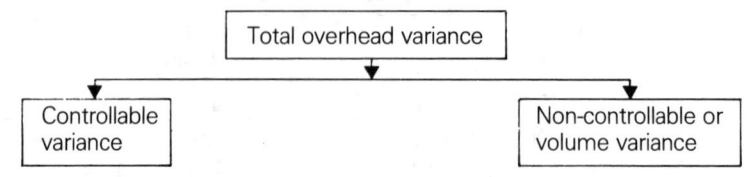

The **controllable variance,** so called because of its controllability, represents the difference between the actual total overheads on the one hand and the standard variable overheads allowed for actual production time **plus** budgeted fixed overheads on the other. The **non-controllable** or volume variance is applicable to fixed costs only and represents the difference between the budgeted and the standard amount fixed overheads is allowed for actual production.

3.2 Three variances analysis method

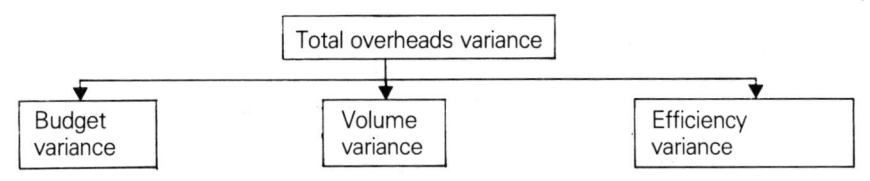

In the three variance method the **budget variance** represents the difference between the actual total overheads and the variable budget, the **volume variance** is the difference between the budgeted and actual fixed overheads, and the **efficiency variance** is the difference between the actual time and the standard time allowed for the actual production multiplied by the standard total overhead rate.

In this method the volume variance can also be devided into a calendar and revised capacity variance.

The above variances are best illustrated by means of a practical problem:

Example 76

Using the information given in Example 73, calculate the following:

(i)   The two variance analysis
(ii) The three variance analysis
(iii) Total overheads variance

Solution

(i) Two variance method

Controllable variance = Actual amount −
[(ST × SRv) + Fixed budgeted overheads]

= (27 200 + 22 400) − [(15 750 × 1,50) + 27 000]
= 49 600 − 50 625
= R1 025 (F)

Volume variance = (BT − ST) SRf

= (15 000 − 15 750) 1,80
= R1 350 (F)

Diagrammatically:

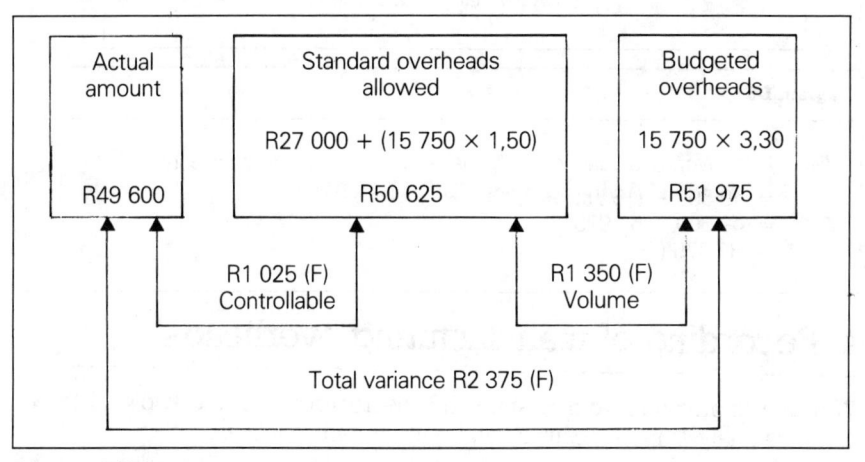

Total variance R2 375 (F)

Diagram D68

(ii) Three variance method:

Budgeted variance $\quad$ = Actual amount − [(AT × SRv) +
Budgeted fixed overheads]

= 49 600 − [(16 000 × 1,50) + 27 000]
= 49 600 − 51 000
= R1 400 (F)

Volume variance (only fixed) = (BT − AT) SRf

= (15 000 − 16 000) 1,80
= R1 800 (F)

Efficiency variance $\quad$ = (AT − ST) SRt

= (16 000 − 15 750) 3,30
= R825 (U)

where   v represents variable overheads
      f represents fixed overheads
      t represents total overheads

Diagrammatically :

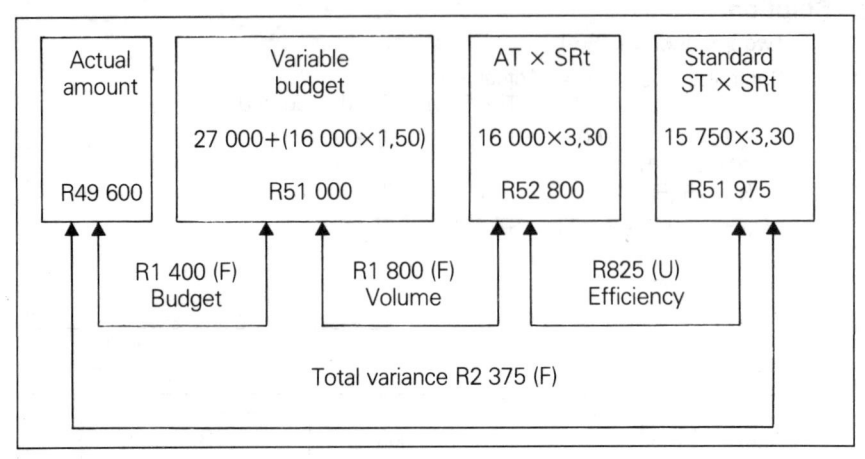

Diagram D69

(iii)   Total overhead variance = Actual amount − Standard amount
=   49 600 − (15 750 × 3,30)
=   49 600 − 51 975
=   R2 375 (F)

4 Recording of manufacturing overheads

With the information from Example 76 the recording of the two and three variance analysis in T-accounts can be illustrated as follows:

Two variance method

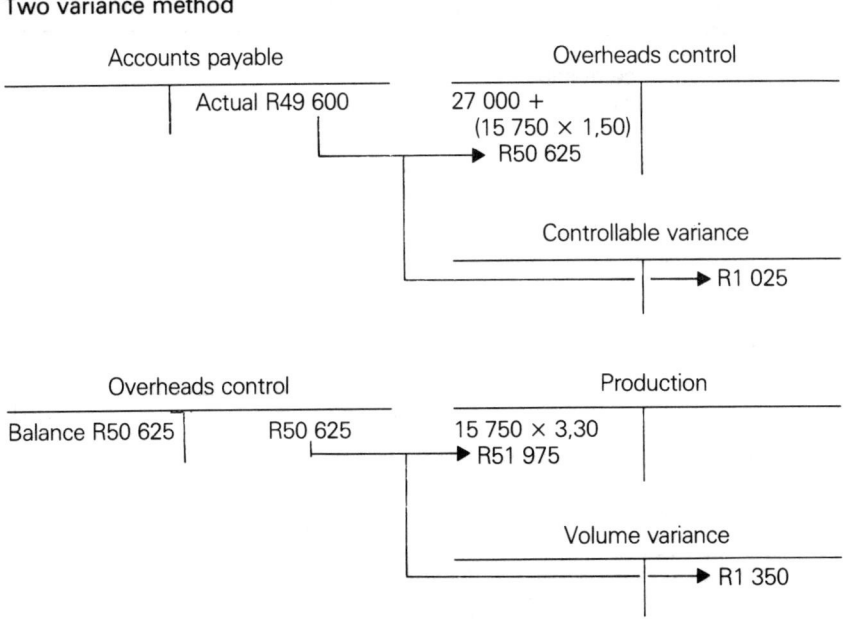

Three variance method

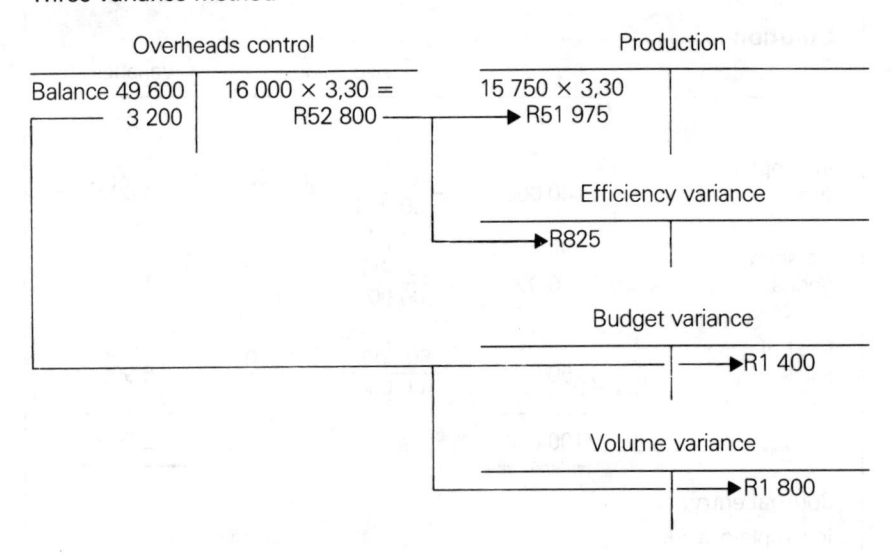

It is advisable to note that if an allocation overheads account is used for allocating overheads to production the balance on this account at the end of the accounting period must be transferred to the overheads control account.

At the end of the accounting period all the variances in respect of the three cost elements which have arisen between the actual and standard costs and which have been recorded must be closed off in one of the following ways:

☐ Transfer the balance on the variance account directly to the cost of sales.

☐ Transfer the balance on the variance account to the cost of sales and the various accounts on which it has a bearing.

If variances are small they are usually transferred to cost of sales. However, if the variances are material the latter method must be used.

Example 77

Supposing the material quantity variance in respect of material A is an unfavourable R12 000 and the following information is supplied:

Material A is found in the following items:

		R
Closing stock incomplete work (Equivalent units)	4 000 × R10	40 000
Closing stock finished goods	1 000 × R10	10 000
Cost of sales	5 000 × R10	50 000
		100 000

Required:

Using the journal entry, close off the unfavourable variance accounts to the various accounts on which they have bearing.

Solution

Account	Amount	Allocation	Variance
	R		R
Incomplete work	40 000	$\dfrac{40\ 000}{100\ 000} \times \dfrac{12\ 000}{1}$	4 800
Finished goods	10 000	$\dfrac{10\ 000}{100\ 000} \times \dfrac{12\ 000}{1}$	1 200
Cost of sales	50 000	$\dfrac{50\ 000}{100\ 000} \times \dfrac{12\ 000}{1}$	6 000
	100 000		12 000

Journal entry:

Incomplete work	R4 800	
Finished goods	1 200	
Cost of sales	6 000	
Material quantity variance		R12 000
Allocation of material quantity variance		

5 Standard costing ratios

From the discussion thus far it is clear that costing standards are an important instrument for evaluating performance and enabling management to control the activities of the enterprise. In order to do further analysis such as "how efficiently are the actual hours worked utilised?, how effectively is the factory's level of activity used," etc, certain ratios can be calculated as shown in Example 78.

Example 78

The budgeted and actual information about a factory for March 19.2 is as follows:

	Budgeted	Actual
Units manufactured	5 000	4 800
Number of hours worked	10 000	10 500

Required

Calculate the following:

   (i) Level of activity or volume ratio
   (ii) Utilisation or capacity ratio
   (iii) Efficiency ratio

Solution

Standard time to manufacture one product $\quad= \dfrac{10\ 000 \text{ hours}}{5\ 000 \text{ units}}$

$$= 2 \text{ hours}$$

(i) Level of activity ratio =

$$\dfrac{\text{Standard time for actual production allowed} \times 100}{\text{Budgeted time}}$$

$$= \dfrac{(4\ 800 \times 2)}{10\ 000} \times \dfrac{100}{1}$$

$$= 96\%$$

(ii) Utilisation ratio = $\dfrac{\text{Actual time}}{\text{Budgeted time}} \times \dfrac{100}{1}$

$$= \dfrac{10\ 500}{10\ 000}$$

$$= 105\%$$

(iii) Efficiency ratio = $\dfrac{\text{Standard time} \times 100}{\text{Actual time}}$

$$= \dfrac{9\ 600}{10\ 500} \times \dfrac{100}{1}$$

$$= 91\%$$

Sales variances

It is important to exercise control over not only manufacturing costs, but also the sales if an enterprise. If only one type of product is manufactured it is usual to calculate only two variances, namely **price**and **quantity.**

Example 79 illustrates the sales variances more fully:

Example 79

Sales:

Actual	1 000 units @ R18 each
Budgeted	1 200 units
Standard cost per unit	R10
Standard selling price per unit	R17,75

Required

Calculate the following:

(i) Sales price variance
(ii) Sales quantity variance

Solution

(i) Sales price variance

$$= (AP - SP)\ AQ$$
$$= (18 - 17,75)\ 1\ 000$$
$$= R250\ (F)$$

(ii) Sales quantity variance

$$= (AQ - SQ)\ SP$$
$$= (1\ 000 - 1\ 200)\ 17,75$$
$$= R3\ 550\ (U)$$

where: AP = actual selling price
SP = standard selling price
AQ = actual quantity sold
SQ = standard (budgeted) sales

Sales variances are the opposite of production variances, because they represent income and not costs. However, sales variances are usually not used on their own, but are linked with **cost of sales variances** because the latter variances have as important an influence on the budgeted gross profit as the sales variances. Therefore the sales and cost of sales variances are often referred to as the gross profit or sales margin variances.

Diagram D70 illustrates the sales and cost of sales variances.

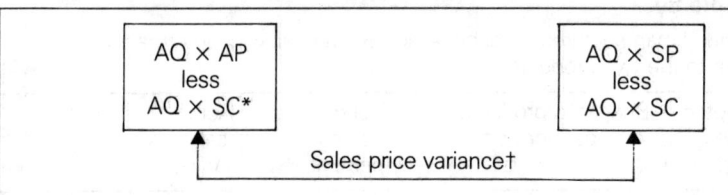

* SC refers to the standard cost of sales
† Seeing that in both cases the cost of sales is calculated at standard, it can be omitted in the calculation of the price variances, which leaves the following formula:

Sales price variance = (AP− SP) AQ

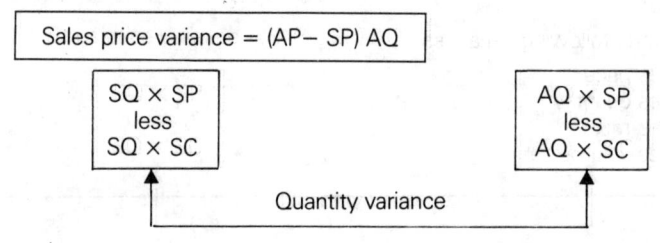

Formula:

Quantity variance = [(SQ − AQ) SP] − [(SQ − AQ) SC]

Alternatively:
Standard gross profit − (AQ × standard gross profit per unit)

The cost price variance is calculated as follows:

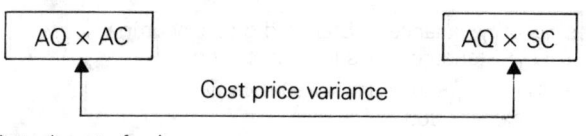

* AC = Actual cost of sales

Diagram D70

The question is what will happen if more than one type of product is manufactured and sold. In such a situation there is also a **mix** or **composition variance** in sales. The following simple example is used to explain its calculation:

Example 80

XY Limited manufactures products A and B. The following information is relevant to the two products:

Budgeted sales (units)	Budgeted production cost per unit	Standard sales price per unit	Actual sales (units)	Sales
	R	R		R
A: 600	10	20	550	9 900
B: 400	5	10	360	3 960
1 000			910	13 860

Required:

Calculate the following variances:

(i) Sales price
(ii) Sales quantity
(iii) Sales mix
(iv) Sales volume

Solution

(i) Sales price variance: Standard sales − Actual sales

A: (550 × R20) − 9 900	= 1 100	(U)
B: (360 × R10) − 3 960	= 360	(F)
	R740	(U)

(ii) Sales quantity variance = Standard gross income − (AQ × Standard gross income per unit)

$$= 8\ 000 - [(550 \times 10) + (360 \times 5)]$$
$$= 8\ 000 - 7\ 300$$
$$= R700\ (U)$$

Standard gross income:

A: 600 × (R20 − 10)	= R6 000
B: 400 × (R10 − 5)	= 2 000
	R8 000

Average standard gross income per unit

$$= \frac{R8\ 000}{1\ 000}$$
$$= R8$$

(iii) Sales mix variance = (AQ × Average standard gross
income per unit) − (AQ × Standard gross income per
unit)
= (910 × R8) − [(550 × 10) + (360 × 5)]
= 7 280 − 7 300
= R20 (F)

(iv) Sales volume variance = Standard gross income
− (AQ × Average standard gross income per unit)
= 8 000 − (910 × 8)
= 8 000 − 7 280
= R720 (U)

Alternatively the sales and cost of sales variances can be calculated separately and then consolidated so that the total gross profit variance can be obtained. Example 81 illustrates such an analysis:

Example 81

	Actual	Budget	Difference
	R	R	R
Sales	12 000	9 000	3 000
Cost of sales	8 000	6 300	1 700
Gross profit	4 000	2 700	1 300
Selling price per unit	1,20	1,00	
Cost price per unit	0,80	0,70	

Required

Calculate the following:

(i)   Sales price variance
(ii) Sales quantity variance
(iii) Cost price variance
(iv) Cost quantity variance
(v)   Total gross profit variance

Solution

    (i) Selling price variance
$$\begin{aligned} &= (AP - SP) \times AQ \\ &= (1{,}20 - 1{,}00) \times 10\,000 \\ &= R2\,000\ (F) \end{aligned}$$

   (ii) Sales quantity variance
$$\begin{aligned} &= (AQ - SQ) \times SP \\ &= (10\,000 - 9\,000) \times R1 \\ &= R1\,000\ (F) \end{aligned}$$

  (iii) Cost price variance
$$\begin{aligned} &= (AC - SC) \times AQ \\ &= (0{,}80 - 0{,}70) \times 10\,000 \\ &= R1\,000\ (U) \end{aligned}$$

  (iv) Cost quantity variance
$$\begin{aligned} &= (AQ - SQ) \times SR \\ &= (10\,000 - 9\,000) \times 0{,}70 \\ &= R700\ (U) \end{aligned}$$

   (v) Total gross profit variance
$$\begin{aligned} &= \text{Total of individual variances} \\ &= R2\,000\ (F) + R1\,000\ (F) + R1\,000\ (U) + \\ &\quad R700\ (U) \\ &= R1\,300\ (F) \end{aligned}$$

☐ Analysis of variances

In order to control the manufacturing performance of an enterprise the actual costs must be compared with the standard costs. Thus the variances which exist are the starting point for further analysis and investigation. This information must be presented to management in an acceptable way in the form of a report which contains only the essential information and management must study and analyse it thoroughly.

People in the manufacturing process to whom management has delegated authority can be held directly responsible for certain variances and after the explanations and feedback have been obtained the necessary corrective steps can then be taken.

Obviously management will devote more attention to variances caused by controllable costs than to those caused by uncontrollable costs. Favourable as well as unfavourable variances must be investigated. Usually unfavourable variances which occur because of high prices, poor raw materials and inefficiencies will be more thoroughly investigated, because they cause losses.

Favourable variances may sometimes give rise to unfavourable variances. For example, if cheaper raw materials which are inferior are purchased the result might give rise to greater usage. It is senseless and time consuming for management to devote attention to all the variances. The principle of management by exception, whereby attention is given only to the variances that are material can be used.

Problems in application

1 Introduction

It goes without saying that standard costs can be used in almost every sphere of management and in conjunction with all the different costing systems. Example 82 illustrates the application of standard costs in conjunction with direct and absorption costs.

Example 82

The following information was obtained from the books of A Limited for Year 1 and Year 2:

Standard cost per unit	R
Direct material	1,00
Direct labour	1,50
Variable overheads	0,50
Variable sales costs	0,25

Standard production per annum   200 000 units
Budgeted overheads (fixed) per annum   R160 000
Selling price per unit   R8

Operating statistics

	Year 1	Year 2
Units sold	160 000	200 000
Units produced	210 000	190 000
Actual overheads (fixed)	R161 000	R162 000
Administrative costs	R 50 000	R 50 000
Selling costs	R 60 000	R 60 000
Variances from standard costs	R 20 000(U)	R 5 000(F)

Required:

Prepare income statements according to:

  (i) the direct costing method
 (ii) the absorption costing methods

Solution   Income statement – direct costs

	Year 1	Year 2
	R	R
Sales 160 000 × R8	1 280 000	
200 000 × R8		1 600 000
Less: Standard variable cost		
of sales 160 000 × 3	480 000	
200 000 × 3		600 000
	800 000	1 000 000
Less: Variable sales and		
administrative costs		
160 000 × 0,25	40 000	
200 000 × 0,25		50 000
	760 000	950 000
Variances from standard costs	(20 000)	5 000
Marginal income	740 000	955 000
Less: Fixed costs	271 000	272 000
Overheads	161 000	162 000
Administrative costs	50 000	50 000
Sales costs	60 000	60 000
Net income	R469 000	R683 000

Income statement – absorption costs

	Year 1	Year 2
	R	R
Sales 160 000 × 8	1 280 000	
200 000 × 8		1 600 000
Less: Standard cost of sales	608 000	760 000
160 000 × R3,00	480 000	
160 000 × R0,80	128 000	
200 000 × R3,80		760 000
Standard gross profit	672 000	840 000
Variances from standard costs	(20 000)	5 000
Gross profit at normal	652 000	845 000
* Overheads over/underapplied	7 000	(10 000)
	659 000	835 000
Less: Sales and administrative costs	150 000	160 000
Variable 160 000 × R0,25	40 000	
200 000 × R0,25		50 000
Fixed: Administrative costs	50 000	50 000
Sales costs	60 000	60 000
	509 000	675 000

(continued)

Determination of overheads rate:

$$\frac{R160\ 000}{200\ 000} = R0,80\ \text{per unit}$$

	R	R
* Actual overheads	161 000	162 000
Applied		
210 000 × R0,80	168 000	
190 000 × R0,80		152 000
Over/underapplied	7 000	(10 000)

Reconciliation of net income according to the two methods:

	Year 1	Year 2
	R	R
Net income per the direct costing method	469 000	683 000
Add: Fixed costs in stock figure		
50 000 × R0,80	40 000	(40 000)
40 000 × R0,80		32 000
Net income per the absorption costing method	509 000	675 000

2 Reconciliation of actual costs with standard costs

As has already been mentioned, a variance exists when the actual situation differs from the standard or budgeted projection. Thus it is clear that the total of all the variances must be equal to the net difference between the standard that was set and what is actually achieved. The reconciliation is illustrated in Example 83.

Example 83

The following information was taken from the books of Stabiel Ltd, which manufactures only one type of product.

	Budgeted	Actual
Opening stock	Nil	Nil
Closing stock	Nil	Nil
Units manufactured	5 600	5 000
Material used (kg)	28 000	26 000
Labour hours	56 000	55 000
	R	R
Material purchased	140 000	133 000
Wages	168 000	170 500
Variable manufacturing overheads	28 000	26 000
Sales	672 000	605 000
Fixed manufacturing overheads	84 000	94 000

(continued)

Required

(i) Calculate the budgeted and the actual net income.
(ii) Calculate the necessary variances to reconcile the budgeted and actual net income.
(iii) Reconcile the net income as calculated in (i) above.

Solution

Because there is no opening and closing stock all the products manufactured are sold. Further, the material usage is equivalent to the material purchases.

(i) **Income statement**

	Budgeted R	Actual R
Sales	672 000	605 000
Production costs	420 000	423 500
Material	140 000	133 000
Labour	168 000	170 500
Overheads – variable	28 000	26 000
– fixed	84 000	94 000
Net income	252 000	181 500

(ii) **Workings**

Standard quantities/hours per finished product:

Material 28 000 kg ÷ 5 600
          = 5 kg

Hours   56 000 ÷ 5 600
            = 10 hours

Material: Standard price   = R140 000 ÷ 28 000
                           = R5

Labour: Standard rate   = R168 000 ÷ 56 000
                           = R3

Overheads: Variable rate   = R28 000 ÷ 56 000
                           = R0,50

          Fixed rate   = R84 000 ÷ 56 000
                           = R1,50

Standard cost per finished product:

			R
Direct material	5 kg × R5	=	25
Direct labour	10 hours × R3	=	30
Overheads	10 hours × R2	=	20
			75

Standard income per finished product:

			R
Sales	672 000 ÷ 5 600	=	120
Costs		=	75
Income			45

(continued)

Variances	F	U
	R	R
Material		
Price (AP × AQ) − (SP × AQ)		
133 000 − (R5 × 26 000)		3 000
Quantity (AQ × SP) − (SQ × SP)		
(26 000 × R5) − (5 000 × 5 × R5)		5 000
Labour		
Rate (AR × AT) − (SR × AT)		
R170 500 − (R3 × 55 000)		5 500
Efficiency (AT × SR) − (ST × SR)		
(55 000 × R3) − (5 000 × 10 × R3)		15 000
Overheads		
Variable:		
Rate (AR × AT) − (SR × AT)		
26 000 − (R0,50 × 55 000)	1 500	
Efficiency (AT × SR) − (ST × SR)		
(55 000 × 0,50) − (5 000 × 10 × 0,50)		2 500
Fixed:		
Expenditure AA − BA		
94 000 − 84 000		10 000
Volume (BT − SR) − (ST × SR)		
84 000 − (5 000 × 10 × R1,50)		9 000
Sales		
Price (AP × AQ) − (SP × AQ)		
605 000 − (R120 × 5 000)	5 000	
Volume (5 000 × R45) − (5 600 × R45)		27 000
	6 500	77 000

(iii) **Reconciliation**

	R
Income (budgeted)	252 000
Net variances	70 500
Favourable	6 500
Unfavourable	77 000
Income (actual)	181 500

where:
- AA = actual amount
- BA = budgeted amount
- BT = budgeted time
- ST = standard time
- AT = actual time
- AP = actual price
- SP = standard price
- SR = standard rate

13

SHORT-TERM DECISIONS

1 Introduction

Cost-volume-profit analysis not only enables management to determine the profitability of the enterprise, but is applicable to virtually all areas in which policy decisions must be made in the short term.

It also illustrates various cost concepts and the manner in which these can be used in a variety of short-term decisions.

It is desirable to work with total costs rather than units costs when making decisions, since the fixed element of the total cost by itself can lead to a misleading unit cost.

2 Cost concepts for decision making

The purpose for which a specific cost is used plays an important role in the business world. Cost information which is suitable for decision making, for example, may not necessarily be used in the preparation of financial statements. Historical costs are used for preparing financial statements, while expected future costs are used for decision making.

Short-term decision making rests on the basic principle that the most economical choice between alternative unique short-term actions must be taken.

The following cost items play an important role in short-term decisions:

☐ Differential costs

Differential costs are the additional costs that arise from a temporary (short-term) increase in the operating volume and are usually aimed at employing unutilised production capacity more fully.

They are used to establish how the total profit of an enterprise will be influenced as a result of a change in production and sales volumes or product mix. Further, differential costs not only deal with the analysis of additional units, but also have a bearing on the following:
- Should a part be made or purchased?
- The closing of a factory or department
- The expansion of the plant
- The taking of pricing decisions, etc

☐ Opportunity costs

Opportunity costs represent the measurable advantage that is sacrificed by the employment of production resources for alternative purposes.

For example, an entrepreneur has the choice of renting a portion of his factory at R2 000 or using it for the manufacture of an additional product. If he decides to manufacture the additional product, the rental income which would have been received is sacrificed and is considered an **opportunity cost** which must be added to the manufacturing costs of the additional product.

Suppose that the additional product that can be manufactured is a spare part which is currently purchased by the enterprise. If the spare part is manufactured the total manufacturing costs will amount to R60 000 against a cost of R61 000 if it is purchased. Diagram D71 illustrates the influence that opportunity costs exercise on the final decision.

	If manufactured	If purchased
	R	R
Total manufacturing costs	60 000	
Total cost of purchasing		61 000
Opportunity cost (rental of a portion of factory)	2 000	
Comparable cost	62 000	61 000

Diagram D71

☐ Relevant costs

Relevant costs are estimated future costs which change when a particular decision is made. Non-relevant costs are not changed by such a decision.

Example 84

An existing machine which will function effectively for another five years can be replaced now with a new machine which will cut labour by half and give the same output. It also has an economic life of five years.

Only some of the cost items applicable to the two machines are given below:

	Old machine	New machine	Difference
	R	R	R
Direct material			
1 000 kg × R3	3 000	3 000	
Direct labour			
500 hours × R5	2 500		
250 hours × R5		1 250	1 250

In the above example direct labour is the relevant cost because it is influenced by the decision and material is a non-relevant cost.

☐ Imputed costs

Imputed costs do not entail actual monetary expenditure and therefore are not reflected in the accounting records. Examples of such costs are interest on capital, the salary of an owner/entrepreneur, etc. When comparative studies are carried out and whenever a decision must be reached such costs must be taken into consideration.

☐ Sunk costs

These are costs that have already been incurred and cannot be changed or cancelled by any decisions now or in the future. An example of such costs is the money used in the past to purchase a fixed asset.

3 Forms of short-term decisions

☐ Price determination

In the business world, costs, competitors, demand and supply are price determining factors. Cost-volume-profit analysis can be used with great success to set prices in the short term.

Example 85

The level of activity of a manufacturing enterprise is currently 50% and at this capacity the manufacture and sales of the product are as follows:

Sales 10 000 units @ R200 each
Variable costs 10 000 units @ R100 each
Total fixed costs for the period R500 000

A survey has revealed that because of strong competition the enterprise must reduce its selling prices drastically in the future if it is to remain competitive in the market. It is estimated that the level of activity can be increased to 75% without any change in fixed costs. Calculate the new selling price per unit if the level of activity is 75% and the enterprise wants to achieve a 10% increase in net profit.

Solution

Income statement at a 50% level of activity

	R	%
Sales (10 000 × R200)	2 000 000	100
Variable costs (10 000 × R100)	1 000 000	50
Marginal income	1 000 000	50
Fixed costs	500 000	——
Net income	500 000	

```
                  Income statement at a 75% level of activity

                                                            R
   Net income (110% × 500 000)                           550 000
   Fixed costs                                            500 000

   Marginal income                                      1 050 000
   Variable costs (15 000* × R100)                      1 500 000

   Sales                                                2 550 000
```

$$\text{Selling price per unit} \quad \frac{R2\ 550\ 000}{15\ 000}$$

$$= R170$$

$$\text{*Level of activity} \quad \frac{75}{50} \times \frac{10\ 000}{1}$$

$$= 15\ 000 \text{ units}$$

☐ Acceptance of a special order

Whenever a special order is accepted at a price below cost the unenlightened are sceptical of the whole affair. When this type of decision must be made the following are prerequisites:
- ☐ The full production capacity must not be in use.
- ☐ Fixed costs must remain unchanged.
- ☐ Current selling prices per unit must not be affected.

Example 86

Trapvas Limited manufactures men's shoes and its level of activity is currently 60 %. The enterprise obtains an order from a neighbouring state several thousand kilometres away to supply 1 000 pairs of shoes, size X, within 30 days of R15 f.o.r. (free on rail). Some of the enterprise's directors are sceptical of the offer, since this size is sold locally at R25 per pair. The variable costs per pair to manufacture and sell this size of shoe are as follows:

	R
Direct material	3
Direct labour	6
Manufacturing overheads	3
Administration costs	1
Selling costs	1
	14

Fixed costs in total for the period are:

Manufacturing overheads	R100 000
Selling and administrative costs	R50 000

If this order is accepted, it can easily be executed with the existing capacity.

Required:
Analyse the proposal and submit it to management for consideration.

Solution

Abridged income statement in respect of 1 000 pairs of shoes

	R
Sales 1 000 × R15	15 000
Variable costs	13 000
Material	3 000
Labour	6 000
Manufacturing overheads	3 000
Administrative overheads	1 000
Marginal income	2 000

Recommendation: Seeing that the factory is not functioning at full capacity the order can be accepted successfully, since the marginal income of R2 000 can be used to recover a portion of the fixed costs and the net income will increase by R2 000.

☐ The elimination of non-profitable products

Marginal costing is an aid which enables management to take decisions with regard to the elimination of non-profitable products and the addition of new products to the product mix of an enterprise.

Example 87

The sales budget of Eddie Limited for the coming period is as follows:

Product	Sales	Variable	Marginal income/(loss)	Committed* fixed costs	Net income
	R	R	R	R	R
A	400 000	200 000	200 000	60 000	140 000
B	500 000	300 000	200 000	75 000	125 000
C	600 000	420 000	180 000	90 000	90 000
D	300 000	270 000	30 000	45 000	(15 000)
E	200 000	210 000	(10 000)	30 000	(40 000)

Management intends to stop the production of products D and E since both will give rise to losses. The sales of the remaining products cannot be increased because the market is already saturated.

Required:

Advise management whether it will be advisable to go ahead with the decision.

* Committed fixed costs represent fixed costs which will not decrease if production is reduced.

Solution

	A	B	C	Total
	R	R	R	R
Sales	400 000	500 000	600 000	1 500 000
Variable costs	200 000	300 000	420 000	920 000
Marginal income	200 000	200 000	180 000	580 000
Fixed costs				300 000
Net income				280 000

	A	B	C	D	Total
	R	R	R	R	R
Sales	400 000	500 000	600 000	300 000	1 800 000
Variable costs	200 000	300 000	420 000	270 000	1 190 000
Marginal income	200 000	200 000	180 000	30 000	610 000
Fixed costs					300 000
Net income					310 000

Recommendation: The greatest benefit is achieved when the production of product E only is stopped. The marginal income that Product D yields (R30 000), can be used to cover a portion of the fixed costs. It is worthwhile to produce any product in the sales mix which yields a marginal income.

The production or sales mix of products is influenced mainly by factors such as the availability of material or labour, etc. The purpose of any enterprise is the maximisation of total profits and this is possible only if the greatest contribution per unit from the limiting factor is achieved.
Example 88 helps to explain the topic more fully.

Example 88

	Products		
	A	B	C
	R	R	R
(Per unit)			
Sales	10	12	15
Variable costs	6	5	10
Marginal income	4	7	5
Marginal income ratio	40%	58%	33,3%

From the above example it appears that Product B is the most profitable, with a marginal income of R7 per unit.

If the example is expanded further to include the number of machine hours required to manufacture the products, the position changes as follows:

	Products		
	A	B	C
Marginal income per unit	R4	R7	R5
Machine hours required to manufacture one unit	1	3	2
Marginal income per machine hour	R4	R2,3	R2,5

Product A is now the most profitable because it gives the largest contribution per machine hour, which is the limiting factor.

Where one or two limiting factors are present the problem can still be solved with the aid of marginal costing. If there are more than two limiting factors the problem can be solved only by means of mathematical equations. This will be discussed in detail in a later chapter on linear programming.

☐ The purchase or manufacture of a part

It is important to devote attention to the following two aspects before any decisions are taken with regard to this topic.

Capacity

A decision is complicated if the capacity of an enterprise is being fully utilised, since the production of the part must occur at the expense of the 'main product'. Alternatively, additional labour, equipment and space must be obtained for this purpose.

Specialisation

Some parts are manufactured on a large scale at reasonable prices by firms which specialise therein, for example globes, batteries and tyres.

The following analysis serves as an illustration:

Example 89

Details of part XOX (10 000 units)	Cost of manufacturing the part	Cost of purchasing the part	Difference
	R	R	R
Direct material	20 000	–	20 000
Direct labour	50 000	–	50 000
Variable overheads	25 000	–	25 000
Fixed overheads	10 000	10 000	–
Purchase of parts	–	110 000	(110 000)
Rental per annum from unutilised portion of factory		(5 000)	5 000
	105 000	115 000	(10 000)

From the above analysis it can be seen that there is a saving of R10 000 if Product XOX is manufactured. Fixed costs have no influence on the decision (non-relevant cost) and can just as well be left out. If the manufacture of the part cannot be accommodated within the existing capacity, additional equipment must be purchased and the decision becomes a capital investment decision.

☐ Joint products

Time and again manufacturing enterprises which produce joint products must make the decision whether to sell the products at the split-off point or process them further.

Example 90

Joint Products Limited manufactures four types of products at a total joint cost of R100 000. The products can be sold at the split-off point or processed further and then sold, as shown in the following table:

Product	Sell at split-off point	Sell after further processing	Costs after split-off point
	R	R	R
A	60 000	150 000	100 000
B	70 000	180 000	90 000
C	40 000	80 000	30 000
D	10 000	15 000	8 000

Required:

Calculate the maximum profit that the enterprise can achieve if the correct decision is made.

Solution

	Products			
	A	B	C	D
	R	R	R	R
Sales – after split-off	150 000	180 000	80 000	15 000
– at split-off	60 000	70 000	40 000	10 000
Additional income	90 000	110 000	40 000	5 000
Costs after split-off	100 000	90 000	30 000	8 000
Income/(Loss)	(10 000)	20 000	10 000	(3 000)

From the above it is obvious that products A and D must be sold at the split-off point and products B and C must be processed further.

(continued)

	Total	A	Products B	C	D
	R	R	R	R	R
Sales	330 000	60 000	180 000	80 000	10 000
Costs after split-off point	120 000	–	90 000	30 000	–
	210 000	60 000	90 000	50 000	10 000
Joint costs	100 000				
Profit	110 000				

☐ Closing down a factory or continuing with production

The viewpoint that a factory must be closed down temporarily whenever there are losses from month to month in the short-term is not always valid, as illustrated in Example 91:

Example 91

The level of operations of Struggle Limited is currently 40% and at this capacity the operating results are as follows:

Abridged income statement for the year ended 30 June 19.1				
			R	%
Sales	40 000 units @	R10	400 000	100
Variable costs	40 000 units @	R8	320 000	80
Marginal income		R2	80 000	20
Fixed costs			160 000	
Net loss			(80 000)	

Management expects that, because of intensifying competition and rising costs, the sales volume will fall further but the selling price per unit will remain constant. Management intends to reorganise the production layout so as to bring a cheaper product onto the market. This will take 12 months to complete. The question is whether the enterprise should cease its activities immediately, which will result in a 10% saving in fixed costs, or continue with production in the short-term until the reorganisation is complete.

Solution

		R
Total fixed costs		160 000
Less: Savings if stop immediately (10%)		16 000
Total loss if production is stopped		144 000

Calculation of lowest sales volume:

$$= \frac{\text{Saving if activities ceased}}{\text{Marginal income per unit}}$$

$$= \frac{R16\ 000}{R2}$$

$$= 8\ 000 \text{ units}$$

Abridged income statement		
		R
Sales	8 000 × R10	80 000
Variable costs	8 000 × R8	64 000
Marginal income		16 000
Fixed costs		160 000
Net loss		(144 000)

From the above calculations it is clear that it is profitable for management to continue with production in the short term until the sales volume reaches the 8 000 notch. At this level the net loss is equal to the total fixed costs less the 10% saving. If the sales volume falls below the 8 000 notch the activities must stop immediately.

☐ Capital investment decisions

Capital investment decisions normally involve long-term planning but comparative costs analyses can make a contribution in this regard, as follows:

Example 92

The management of a manufacturing enterprise is considering replacing an old machine which is still productive with a new one which is cost efficient. The following information about the two machines is available:

	Old machine	New machine
Machine hours per annum	1 500	1 500
Unit production per hour	50	60
Economic life (years)	10	10
	R	R
Purchase price	22 000	30 000
Production costs:		
Variable overheads per annum	3 000	1 200
Material costs per unit	0,10	0,10
Labour cost per machine hour	2,00	2,50
Selling price per unit	0,30	0,30
Current residual value	2 000	–

If the enterprise invests its funds it can earn 15% per annum and the interest rate on long-term loans is 20% per annum.

Required:

Prepare a comparative statement which shows whether the new machine should be purchased, assuming that the full production can be sold and that depreciation is written off according to fixed instalment method.

Solution

	Old machine	New machine
Production:		
1 500 × 50	75 000	
1 500 × 60		90 000
	R	R
Sales:		
75 000 units × R0,30	22 500	
90 000 units × R0,30		27 000
Less: Marginal costs	13 500	13 950
Overheads	3 000	1 200
Material	7 500	9 000
Labour:		
1 500 × R2	3 000	
1 500 × R2,50		3 750
	9 000	13 050

The saving of R4 050 per annum (R13 050 – R9 000) is adequate to finance the purchase of the new machine within seven years:

$$\frac{(30\ 000 - 2\ 000)}{4\ 050}$$

= Approximately 7 years

Alternative solution

	Old machine	New machine
	R	R
Marginal costs	13 500	13 950
Depreciation:		
(R22 000 ÷ 10)	2 200	
[(R30 000 – 2 000) ÷ 10]		2 800
Interest		
$\frac{20 - 15}{100} \times \frac{30\ 000 - 2\ 000}{1}$		1 400
	15 700	18 150
	R	R
Cost per unit:		
R15 700 ÷ 75 000	0,209	
R18 150 ÷ 90 000		0,202

According to the above two solutions it is more profitable for management to buy the new machine.

It is important to note that investment decisions which make use of marginal costing are flawed because they ignore the time value of money.

4 Conclusion

The value of cost-volume-profit analysis as an aid for making short-term decisions has been emphasised in the previous discussion. It is used in the analysis of alternative actions in the short term with the aim of maximising profits on the one hand and making the right costing decisions on the other.

LONG-TERM PLANNING

1 Introduction

The capital budget reflects the short and long-term planning for additions, changes and replacements of all fixed assets. This budget is just as important as the sales budget, since any capital investment is usually relatively large. The uncertainty of the future makes all investment decisions extremely important.

Capital investments involve large risks and obligations of a permanent nature and must be financed from profits, long-term loans, the issuing of shares or working capital. These type of obligations have an influence on the flexibility and the earnings power of the enterprise and may be considered only if management is satisfied that the capital will be employed profitably.

The implementation of a capital budget can be divided into the following three phases:
- [ ] Planning
- [ ] Evaluation
- [ ] Control

☐ Planning

A well-prepared capital budget backed by a thorough research analysis of every alternative possiblity that may exist is absolutely necessary for long-term planning.

The management of a modern business enterprise must think about the profitability of a proposed investment very carefully and if a number of alternative possibilities exist must establish which one will be the most profitable proposition.

☐ Evaluation

A capital budget is evaluated by applying various techniques which will be discussed later in this chapter.

☐ Control

Once a capital project has finally been approved the procedures necessary for controlling its performance until its completion must be established. Any departures from the proposed plan must be reported in good time to higher authorities. Well-planned follow-up action intensifies the planning, evaluation and implementation phases of the capital budget.

The time value of money must be taken into consideration when capital investment decisions are made, since interest rates can be of vital importance.

2 The time value of money

Money has a time value because a certain amount of money has a greater value now than the same amount at some time in the future. This statement is correct as a certain amount which is available immediately can be invested at a certain rate of interest and earn further interest.

The following simple example explains the topic more fully:

Example 93

On 1 January 19.1 A sold B a bicycle for R92. B makes the following proposals with regard to the payment thereof:

> Proposal no 1 : On 1 January 19.1 pay R92
> Proposal no 2 : On 31 December 19.1 pay R100

Required:

Calculate the amount that A must accept, assuming that money can currently be invested at 10% pa.

Solution

In this example there are two amounts which must be compared with each other but which have a bearing on the two different periods. To solve this problem both values must be converted to a common base.

Supposing the future time (31 December 19.1) is taken as a base, then the answer is:

Proposal no 1:
$$R92 \times (1 + i)^n$$
$$= R92 \times (1,1)^1$$
$$= R101,20$$

Proposal no 2: $\quad = R100,00$

(where i = interest rate and n = number of periods)

In practice the present or the current time, in this case 1 January 19.1, is usually taken as the basis for comparing alternative possibilities with each other. The present value (PV) of the two proposals can be compared with each other as follows:

Proposal no 1 : $\qquad\qquad\qquad = R92,00$
Proposal no 2 : $\qquad$ PV* $\qquad\qquad = R90,90$

$$* \text{ where PV} = \frac{\text{Future value}}{(1 + i)^n}$$

$$= \frac{100}{(1 + 0,10)^1}$$

$$= R90,90$$

In the above example the future value (R100) was discounted to the present value (R90,90). In both calculations Proposal no 1 is the most profitable proposition.

Mathematically the present value can be calculated as follows:

110% of the present value $= R100$

$$\frac{110}{100} \times PV = R100$$

$$PV = \frac{100}{110} \times R100$$

$$= R90{,}90$$

For the sake of convenience discount tables have been prepared which eliminate the necessity of using cumbersome formulae for the calculation of the present value. There are two tables, namely **Table A** and **Table B**. (Refer to the tables at the end of the chapter.)

Table A shows the **present value** of **R1** receivable after **n** years at different rates of interest. Table B shows the present value of **R1 receivable annually for n years** at different interest rates. Schematically the two tables can be presented as follows:

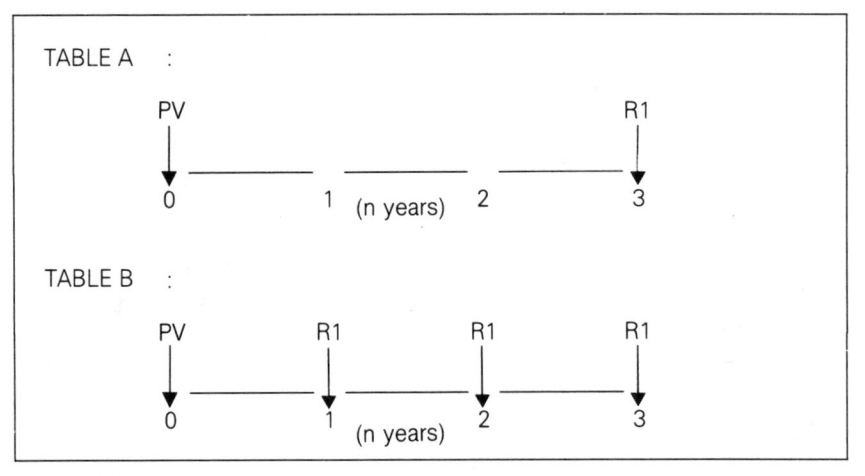

Diagram D72

According to Table A the present value of R1 for one year at an interest rate of 10% pa is R0,909. If R100 is multiplied by 0,909 the discounted amount of R90,90 is obtained. **The conclusion that can be reached is that R90,90 today has the same value as R100 in a year's time.**

It is interesting to note that the figures in Table A show a downward trend to the right for a specific year, since the present values of an amount which is receivable in the future will decrease as the interest rate increases. On the other hand, the "factors" will decrease when going down any interest rate column. The reason for this is the longer the time until the payment the less it is worth.

The conclusion that can be reached is that the longer a person must wait for his money and the higher the interest rate which can be earned the less the amount which is receivable in the future is worth today.

Table B can be used directly and with greater speed than Table A to determine the **present value** of **equal** payments of R1 which is receivable annually for any given **number of years** (n) at a fixed **interest rate** (i). Every figure in Table B can also be obtained by means of accumulation as follows:

		Factor (Table A)	Cumulative (Table B)
Year 1	=	0,909	0,909
Year 2	=	0,826	1,735
Year 3	=	0,751	2,486

When there is a series of equal payments with one or more unequal payments the present value can be calculated as shown in Example 94.

Example 94

Calculate the present value of the following payments if the interest rate is 10% pa:

End of year	Payment
	R
1	1 000
2	1 000
3	1 000
4	1 000
5	1 000
6	900

Solution

Method 1:

			R
Table B :	5 years @ 10%	(3,791 × R1 000)	3 791,00
Table A :	Year 6 @ 10%	(0,564 × R900)	507,60
			4 298,60

Table B is used as the basis because the amounts of the first five payments are the same. The last payment, however, differs and therefore the value factor for the sixth year is taken from Table A.

Method 2:

			R
Table B :	6 years @ 10%	(4,355 × R1 000)	4 355,00
Table A :	Year 6 @ 10%	[0,564 × (1 000 − 900)]	(56,40)
			4 298,60

Table B is used for all six payments, but because the sixth payment is smaller the difference is calculated per Table A and deducted.

Method 3:

			R
Table A :	Year 1 @ 10%	(0,909 × 1 000)	909,00
	2	(0,826 × 1 000)	826,00
	3	(0,751 × 1 000)	751,00
	4	(0,683 × 1 000)	683,00
	5	(0,621 × 1 000)	621,00
	6	(0,564 × 900)	507,60
			4 297,60

In this method only Table A is used to calculate the present value of each payment separately.
(The difference of R1 is due to the fact that the figures were rounded to 3 decimal places.)

From the above it is clear that Method 3 is far too cumbersome and time-consuming, so methods 1 or 2 are recommended.

Discount tables can also be used to **determine the interest rate** that will be earned on a given investment.

Example 95

Determine the discount rate for the following situation:

Value of investment	Annual receipt	Duration of receipts
R	R	Years
3 433	1 000	5

Solution

Calculation of factor : $\dfrac{\text{Value of investment}}{\text{Annual receipts}}$

$= \dfrac{\text{R3 433}}{\text{R1 000}}$

$= 3{,}433$

The exact factor (3,433) appears in Table B opposite the period for 5 years and under the 14% discount rate.

3 Net cash flow

The management of any enterprise will invest funds in a new asset only if the asset can be employed productively in the enterprise and it can ensure a net cash inflow. (Note: net cash inflow = cash inflow minus cash outflow.)

The minimum return (rate of return) that a new investment must earn before an entrepreneur will consider it must be sufficient and more than the interest rate (cost of capital) that must be paid to the suppliers of the borrowed money, or, if it is financed from internal funds, it must be more than the average return for the enterprise. **Cost of capital** represents an equitable anticipated rate of return on the money, which investors require for the risk they take in investing their money in the enterprise.

At this stage it is advisable to point out that the **economic life** of an asset comes to an end as soon as the asset is no longer capable of generating a net cash inflow. The asset might technically still be available for use, but in actual fact it should have a scrap value.

When an asset is replaced the net cash inflow of the new asset must be compared with that of the old asset. Where a new asset is installed from scratch the net cash inflow over the economic life of the asset can be used as a basis.

The following aspects might be decisive in the consideration of a new investment:

- ☐ It is cost efficient and contributes to a decreased cash outflow per unit.
- ☐ It has an increased production volume and the advantages which are associated with it.

An improvement in the net cash inflow is due to either a decrease in the cash outflows or an improvement in the cash inflows, or a combination of the two factors.

4 Evaluation techniques for capital investment projects

Basically these methods can be divided into two categories, namely:

- ☐ methods which ignore the time value of money
- ☐ the discounted cash flow methods which take the time value of money into consideration.

4.1 Techniques which ignore the time value of money

☐ Payback period

This method is based on the principle of calculating the time that elapses before the costs of the project are recovered. This method is easy to apply and understand, but it has the following disadvantages:

- ☐ It does not show the profitability of the project.
- ☐ The life of the investment after the payback period is ignored.
- ☐ It ignores the time value of money.

Example 96

The following details are available in respect of two machines:

	Machines	
	A	B
Cost	R20 000	R20 000
Economic life	5 years	7 years
Average annual net cash inflow during the economic life of the machine	R5 000	R4 000

Required

Calculate the payback period of each machine.

Solution

Payback periods

		A	B
(Cost of machine divided by cash inflow)		$\dfrac{\text{R20 000}}{\text{R5 000}}$	$\dfrac{\text{R20 000}}{\text{R4 000}}$
	=	4 years	5 years

From the above it appears that machine A will be the right one, since it will take only four years to recover the purchase price. If the annual cash inflow after the payback period has expired is taken into consideration the above decision is affected as follows:

Machine B: (7–5 years) = 2 × R4 000 = R8 000
Machine A: (5–4 years) = 1 × R5 000 = R5 000

Machine B produces R8 000 while Machine A produces only R5 000.

☐ Rate of return on average investment (accounting method)

This is the average rate of return that an investment will yield over its expected economic life. Because the value of the investment decreases annually as a result of depreciation, the average value of the investment is used to calculate the rate of return. If the same details as in the previous example are used the average rate of return is the following:

Average rate of return on investment	=	$\dfrac{\text{Average annual income}}{\text{Average book value}}$	
		A	B
		$\dfrac{5\ 000}{20\ 000 \div 2}$	$\dfrac{4\ 000}{20\ 000 \div 2}$
	=	50%	40%

In this method Machine A gives the greater average rate of return on the investment and is thus the best investment.

The greatest critisism against this method is similar to the criticism against the payback period method: it also does not take into account the timing of the cash flow.

4.2 Discounted cash flow methods

☐ Present value method

In this method all the expected future amounts of the cash flow or cash stream are discounted to the present value at the enterprise's minimum required rate of return.

The difference between the present value of the cash stream and the value of the original investment is known as the **net present value.** When the net present value is negative the project is unacceptable because it yields less than that which can be obtained if the money is invested elsewhere at the same interest rate per annum.

Example 97

EDV Limited intends to buy a new machine and has a choice between the following two machines:

| | Machines | |
	X	Y
Cost	R66 000	R56 000
Expected economic life	5 years	5 years
Expected rate of return on investment	10%	10%
Net annual cash inflow	R	R
Year 1	20 000	15 500
Year 2	19 000	15 500
Year 3	18 000	15 500
Year 4	17 000	15 500
Year 5	16 000	15 500

Required

Calculate which machine should be purchased using the present value method.

Solution

Year	Machine X Net inflow	Factor	Present value	Machine Y Net inflow	Factor	Present value
	R		R	R		R
1	20 000	,909	18 180			
2	19 000	,826	15 694			
3	18 000	,751	13 518	15 500 p.j.	3,791	58 761
4	17 000	,683	11 611			
5	16 000	,621	9 936			
			68 939			58 761
Cost of investment			(66 000)			(56 000)
Net present value			2 939			2 761

The net present value of Machine X is greater and therefore it is the right machine to purchase.

☐ Present value index

This method expresses the ratio between the present value of the net cash receipts and the present value of the investment. If the answer is less than 1 the investment is not profitable.

Example 98

Use the same information as in the previous example.

Solution

Formula : $\dfrac{\text{PV of receipts}}{\text{PV of investment}}$

	Machine X	Machine Y
	R68 939	R58 761
	R66 000	R56 000
	= 1,0445	= 1,0493

Machine Y is the better investment when this method is used because it has a larger index value. This valuation method is better than the previous method because it measures the present value in relation to the amount of the original investment.

☐ The discounted rate of return method

With this method the expected interest rate at which the present value of the future cash flows will equal the amount of the original investment is calculated.

Example 99

Use the same information as in the present value method.

Solution

Machine X

Year	Cash inflow	Factor 8%	Factor 10%	Factor 12%	PV 8%	PV 10%	PV 12%
					R	R	R
1	20 000	,926	,909	,893	18 520	18 180	17 860
2	19 000	,857	,826	,797	16 283	15 694	15 143
3	18 000	,794	,751	,712	14 292	13 518	12 816
4	17 000	,735	,683	,636	12 495	11 611	10 812
5	16 000	,681	,621	,567	10 896	9 936	9 072
					72 486	68 939	65 703

Since the amount of the investment is between 10% and 12%, the rate of return can be established only by means of interpolation, as follows:

12% : 65 703 ⎱ Difference 297 ⎱
? % : 66 000 ⎰ ⎰ Difference 3 236
10% : 68 939

$$\frac{297}{3\ 236} \times \frac{(12 - 10)}{1}$$

$$= 0,1836$$

Rate of return $= 12\% - 0,1836$
$= 11,8164\%$

Machine Y

Year	Cash inflow	Factor 8%	Factor 10%	Factor 12%	PV 8%	PV 10%	PV 12%
	R				R	R	R
1 – 5	15 500	3,993	3,791	3,605	61 892	58 761	55 878

12% : 55 878 ⎱ Difference 122 ⎱
? % : 56 000 ⎰ ⎰ Difference 2 883
10% : 58 761

(continued)

$$\frac{122}{2\,883} \times \frac{(12 - 10)}{1}$$

$$= \frac{122}{2\,883} \times \frac{2}{1}$$

$$= 0{,}0846$$

Rate of return $= 12\% - 0{,}0846$

                     $= 11{,}9154\%$

Machine Y gives the greatest return on capital and is the right machine to purchase.

When a percentage which falls outside the interval of the two percentages must be calculated the problem can be solved by means of extrapolation.

Example 100

A future amount which is discounted to its present value gives the following:

At 10%	R500
At 12%	R450

Required

At what percentage must the future amount be discounted to give a present value of R410?

Solution

Using extrapolation:

? %	:	410	
12%	:	450	40
10%	:	500	50

$$\frac{40}{50} \times \frac{2}{1}$$

$$= 1{,}60\%$$

$$\therefore \; 12\% + 1{,}60\%$$

$$= 13{,}60\%$$

5 Income tax, depreciation and scrap value

Income tax plays an important role in capital investment decisions since it has an influence on the amount and thus also on the duration of the cash stream. It is essential that taxation considerations are taken into account when a choice is made between alternative possibilities, because the net cash flow will be affected.

It is also important to bear in mind that depreciation does not represent a cash outflow, but is deductible in the calculation of the taxable income.

Example 101 illustrates the influence of income tax and depreciation on the evaluation technique.

Example 101

The following information is available in respect of a new machine which is being considered as a possible acquisition:

Cost	R60 000
Expected economic life	5 years
Expected rate of return on investment	10%
Net annual cash flow	R18 000
Tax rate	40%

Required

1 Calculate
   (a) the net present value
   (b) the rate of return
2 Calculate the net present value if the machine has a scrap value of R5 000,00 at the end of the fifth year.

Solution

1 (a)

	Tax calculation	Cash inflow
	R	R
Net income (cash inflow)	18 000	18 000
Depreciation (60 000 ÷ 5)	12 000	
Taxable income	6 000	
Taxation (40%)	2 400	2 400
Income after taxation	3 600	
Net cash inflow per year		15 600

Present value factor for 5 years @ 10% = 3,791

Present value of future cash flows:

(15 600 × 3,791)	59 139,60
Cost of investment (60 000 × 1,000)	60 000,00
Net present value (unfavourable)	860,40

(b) Investment = Yield × Discount factor for 5 years

R60 000 = 15 600 × Factor

$$\text{Factor} = \frac{60\ 000}{15\ 600}$$

= 3,846

(continued)

According to Table B, opposite five years the factor falls between 8% and 10%. With the aid of interpolation the following can be calculated since it falls between the interval of the two percentages.

$$
\left.\begin{array}{rll}
8\% & : & 3{,}993 \\
?\,\% & : & 3{,}846 \\
10\% & : & 3{,}791
\end{array}\right\} \; 0{,}147 \; \left.\vphantom{\begin{array}{l}a\\b\\c\end{array}}\right\} \; 0{,}202
$$

$$
\frac{0{,}147}{0{,}202} \times \frac{10 - 8}{1}
$$

$$
= \frac{0{,}147}{0{,}202} \times \frac{2}{1}
$$

$$
= 1{,}455
$$

$$
\begin{aligned}
\text{Rate of return} \quad &= 1{,}455 + 8\% \\
&= 9{,}455\%
\end{aligned}
$$

2		Tax calculation	Cash inflow calculation
		R	R
Net income		18 000	18 000
Depreciation	$\dfrac{60\,000 - 5\,000}{5}$	11 000	
Taxable income		7 000	
Taxation (40%)		2 800	2 800
Income after tax		4 200	
Net cash inflow per annum			15 200
			R
Discounted cash inflow (15 200 × 3,791)			57 623,20
Scrap value (5 000 × 0,621)			3 105,00
			60 728,20
Cost of investment (60 000 × 1,000)			60 000,00
Net present value			728,20

6 Projects having unequal economic lives

There are various ways of solving the problem of projects having unequal economic lives. The **equivalent income method** is the most practical and reliable, since it eliminates the difference in lives to a degree. In this method the net present value of the flow of funds of a project is divided by the present value factor of R1 per period for the life of the project.

Where a choice must be made between projects having different lives the equivalent annual income method is the most practical. This method implies that the net present value of the projects having unequal lives which must be compared must be reduced to a common value. In order that the common value may be determined the net present value of each project must be divided by its present value factor.

$$\text{Formula} = \frac{\text{Net present value}}{\text{Present value factor}}$$

Example 102 illustrates the equivalent income method.

Example 102

The following information is supplied in respect of two machines which are being considered as possible acquisitions:

| | Machines | |
	A	B
Cost	R12 000	R10 000
Expected economic life	5 years	4 years
Residual value		
After 5 years	R2 000	
After 4 years		R1 000
Annual income after depreciation		
and income tax	R3 000	R2 000

The enterprise can invest its money at a rate of 12% per annum which is viewed as an acceptable yield on the investment in the above machines. Depreciation is written off according to the fixed instalment method.

Required

Recommend which machine should be purchased. (Do not take taxation in account.)

Solution

	A	B
	R	R
Annual inflow:		
Net income	3 000	2 000
Depreciation:		
$(12\,000 - 2\,000) \div 5$	2 000	
$(10\,000 - 1\,000) \div 4$		2 250
	5 000	4 250
Present value of inflows:		
Annual income –		
$(5\,000 \times 3{,}605)$	18 025,00	
$(4\,250 \times 3{,}037)$		12 907,25
Residual values –		
$(2\,000 \times 0{,}567)$	1 134,00	
$(1\,000 \times 0{,}636)$		636,00
	19 159,00	13 543,25
Less: Present value		
of outflows		
$(12\,000 \times 1{,}000)$	12 000,00	
$(10\,000 \times 1{,}000)$		10 000,00
Net present value	7 159,00	3 543,25
Equivalent annual income:		
$(7\,159{,}00 \div 3{,}605)$	1 986	
$(3\,543{,}25 \div 3{,}037)$		1 167

Recommendation

According to this method Machine A should be purchased.

7 Conclusion

Capital investment decisions are difficult to evaluate because to a large extent estimated information serves as the basis for deciding about large amounts of money in the long term.

The profitable employment of capital is and remains one of the main responsibilities of management – hence the use of the most sophisticated valuation methods which take the time value of money into consideration as the criteria for decision making. Electronic computers can be used efficiently to analyse and solve this type of management decision.

TABLE A   Present value of R1 after n years

Year	1%	2%	4%	6%	8%	10%	12%	14%	15%	16%	18%	20%	22%	24%	25%	26%	28%	30%	35%	40%	45%	50%
1	0.990	0.980	0.962	0.943	0.926	0.909	0.893	0.877	0.870	0.862	0.847	0.833	0.820	0.806	0.800	0.794	0.781	0.769	0.741	0.714	0.690	0.667
2	0.980	0.961	0.925	0.890	0.857	0.826	0.797	0.769	0.756	0.743	0.718	0.694	0.672	0.650	0.640	0.630	0.610	0.592	0.549	0.510	0.476	0.444
3	0.971	0.942	0.889	0.840	0.794	0.751	0.712	0.675	0.658	0.641	0.609	0.579	0.551	0.524	0.512	0.500	0.477	0.455	0.406	0.364	0.328	0.296
4	0.961	0.924	0.855	0.792	0.735	0.683	0.636	0.592	0.572	0.552	0.516	0.482	0.451	0.423	0.410	0.397	0.373	0.350	0.301	0.260	0.226	0.198
5	0.951	0.906	0.822	0.747	0.681	0.621	0.567	0.519	0.497	0.476	0.437	0.402	0.370	0.341	0.328	0.315	0.291	0.269	0.223	0.186	0.156	0.132
6	0.942	0.888	0.790	0.705	0.630	0.564	0.507	0.456	0.432	0.410	0.370	0.335	0.303	0.275	0.262	0.250	0.227	0.207	0.165	0.133	0.108	0.088
7	0.933	0.871	0.760	0.665	0.583	0.513	0.452	0.400	0.376	0.354	0.314	0.279	0.249	0.222	0.210	0.198	0.178	0.159	0.122	0.095	0.074	0.059
8	0.923	0.853	0.731	0.627	0.540	0.467	0.404	0.351	0.327	0.305	0.266	0.233	0.204	0.179	0.168	0.157	0.139	0.123	0.091	0.068	0.051	0.039
9	0.914	0.837	0.703	0.592	0.500	0.424	0.361	0.308	0.284	0.263	0.225	0.194	0.167	0.144	0.134	0.125	0.108	0.094	0.067	0.048	0.035	0.026
10	0.905	0.820	0.676	0.558	0.463	0.386	0.322	0.270	0.247	0.227	0.191	0.162	0.137	0.116	0.107	0.099	0.085	0.073	0.050	0.035	0.024	0.017
11	0.896	0.804	0.650	0.527	0.429	0.350	0.287	0.237	0.215	0.195	0.162	0.135	0.112	0.094	0.086	0.079	0.066	0.056	0.037	0.025	0.017	0.012
12	0.887	0.788	0.625	0.497	0.397	0.319	0.257	0.208	0.187	0.168	0.137	0.112	0.092	0.076	0.069	0.062	0.052	0.043	0.027	0.018	0.012	0.008
13	0.879	0.773	0.601	0.469	0.368	0.290	0.229	0.182	0.163	0.145	0.116	0.093	0.075	0.061	0.055	0.050	0.040	0.033	0.020	0.013	0.008	0.005
14	0.870	0.758	0.577	0.442	0.340	0.263	0.205	0.160	0.141	0.125	0.099	0.078	0.062	0.049	0.044	0.039	0.032	0.025	0.015	0.009	0.006	0.003
15	0.861	0.743	0.555	0.417	0.315	0.239	0.183	0.140	0.123	0.108	0.084	0.065	0.051	0.040	0.035	0.031	0.025	0.020	0.011	0.006	0.004	0.002
16	0.853	0.728	0.534	0.394	0.292	0.218	0.163	0.123	0.107	0.093	0.071	0.054	0.042	0.032	0.028	0.025	0.019	0.015	0.008	0.005	0.003	0.002
17	0.844	0.714	0.513	0.371	0.270	0.198	0.146	0.108	0.093	0.080	0.060	0.045	0.034	0.026	0.023	0.020	0.015	0.012	0.006	0.003	0.002	0.001
18	0.836	0.700	0.494	0.350	0.250	0.180	0.130	0.095	0.081	0.069	0.051	0.038	0.028	0.021	0.018	0.016	0.012	0.009	0.005	0.002	0.001	0.001
19	0.828	0.686	0.475	0.331	0.232	0.164	0.116	0.083	0.070	0.060	0.043	0.031	0.023	0.017	0.014	0.012	0.009	0.007	0.003	0.002	0.001	
20	0.820	0.673	0.456	0.312	0.215	0.149	0.104	0.073	0.061	0.051	0.037	0.026	0.019	0.014	0.012	0.010	0.007	0.005	0.002	0.001		
21	0.811	0.660	0.439	0.294	0.199	0.135	0.093	0.064	0.053	0.044	0.031	0.022	0.015	0.011	0.009	0.008	0.006	0.004	0.002			
22	0.803	0.647	0.422	0.278	0.184	0.123	0.083	0.056	0.046	0.038	0.026	0.018	0.013	0.009	0.007	0.006	0.004	0.003	0.001			
23	0.795	0.634	0.406	0.262	0.170	0.112	0.074	0.049	0.040	0.033	0.022	0.015	0.010	0.007	0.006	0.005	0.003	0.002	0.001			
24	0.788	0.622	0.390	0.247	0.158	0.102	0.066	0.043	0.035	0.028	0.019	0.013	0.008	0.006	0.005	0.004	0.003	0.002	0.001			
25	0.780	0.610	0.375	0.233	0.146	0.092	0.059	0.038	0.030	0.024	0.016	0.010	0.007	0.005	0.004	0.003	0.002	0.001	0.001			
26	0.772	0.598	0.361	0.220	0.135	0.084	0.053	0.033	0.026	0.021	0.014	0.009	0.006	0.004	0.003	0.002	0.002	0.001				
27	0.764	0.586	0.347	0.207	0.125	0.076	0.047	0.029	0.023	0.018	0.011	0.007	0.005	0.003	0.002	0.002	0.001	0.001				
28	0.757	0.574	0.333	0.196	0.116	0.069	0.042	0.026	0.020	0.016	0.010	0.006	0.004	0.002	0.002	0.002	0.001	0.001				
29	0.749	0.563	0.321	0.185	0.107	0.063	0.037	0.022	0.017	0.014	0.008	0.005	0.003	0.002	0.002	0.001	0.001					
30	0.742	0.552	0.308	0.174	0.099	0.057	0.033	0.020	0.015	0.012	0.007	0.004	0.003	0.002	0.001	0.001	0.001					
40	0.672	0.453	0.208	0.097	0.046	0.022	0.011	0.005	0.004	0.003	0.001	0.001								0.001		
50	0.608	0.372	0.141	0.054	0.021	0.009	0.003	0.001	0.001	0.001										0.001		

TABLE B Present value of R1 received annually for n years

Year	1%	2%	4%	6%	8%	10%	12%	14%	15%	16%	18%	20%	22%	24%	25%	26%	28%	30%	35%	40%	45%	50%
1	0.990	0.980	0.962	0.943	0.926	0.909	0.893	0.877	0.870	0.862	0.847	0.833	0.820	0.806	0.800	0.794	0.781	0.769	0.741	0.714	0.690	0.667
2	1.970	1.942	1.886	1.833	1.783	1.736	1.690	1.647	1.626	1.605	1.566	1.528	1.492	1.457	1.440	1.424	1.392	1.361	1.289	1.224	1.165	1.111
3	2.941	2.884	2.775	2.673	2.577	2.487	2.402	2.322	2.283	2.246	2.174	2.106	2.042	1.981	1.952	1.923	1.868	1.816	1.696	1.589	1.493	1.407
4	3.902	3.808	3.630	3.465	3.312	3.170	3.037	2.914	2.855	2.798	2.690	2.589	2.494	2.404	2.362	2.320	2.241	2.166	1.997	1.849	1.720	1.605
5	4.853	4.713	4.452	4.212	3.993	3.791	3.605	3.433	3.352	3.274	3.127	2.991	2.864	2.745	2.689	2.635	2.532	2.436	2.220	2.035	1.876	1.737
6	5.795	5.601	5.242	4.917	4.623	4.355	4.111	3.889	3.784	3.685	3.498	3.326	3.167	3.020	2.951	2.885	2.759	2.643	2.385	2.168	1.983	1.824
7	6.728	6.472	6.002	5.582	5.206	4.868	4.564	4.288	4.160	4.039	3.812	3.605	3.416	3.242	3.161	3.083	2.937	2.802	2.508	2.263	2.057	1.883
8	7.652	7.325	6.733	6.210	5.747	5.335	4.968	4.639	4.487	4.344	4.078	3.837	3.619	3.421	3.329	3.241	3.076	2.925	2.598	2.331	2.108	1.922
9	8.566	8.162	7.435	6.802	6.247	5.759	5.328	4.946	4.772	4.607	4.303	4.031	3.786	3.566	3.463	3.366	3.184	3.019	2.665	2.379	2.144	1.948
10	9.471	8.983	8.111	7.360	6.710	6.145	5.650	5.216	5.019	4.833	4.494	4.192	3.923	3.682	3.571	3.465	3.269	3.092	2.715	2.414	2.168	1.965
11	10.368	9.787	8.760	7.887	7.139	6.495	5.937	5.453	5.234	5.029	4.656	4.327	4.035	3.776	3.656	3.544	3.335	3.147	2.752	2.438	2.185	1.977
12	11.255	10.575	9.385	8.384	7.536	6.814	6.194	5.660	5.421	5.197	4.793	4.439	4.127	3.851	3.725	3.606	3.387	3.190	2.779	2.456	2.196	1.985
13	12.134	11.343	9.986	8.853	7.904	7.103	6.424	5.842	5.583	5.342	4.910	4.533	4.203	3.912	3.780	3.656	3.427	3.223	2.799	2.468	2.204	1.990
14	13.004	12.106	10.563	9.295	8.244	7.367	6.628	6.002	5.724	5.468	5.008	4.611	4.265	3.962	3.824	3.695	3.459	3.249	2.814	2.477	2.210	1.993
15	13.865	12.849	11.118	9.712	8.559	7.606	6.811	6.142	5.847	5.575	5.092	4.675	4.315	4.001	3.859	3.726	3.483	3.268	2.825	2.484	2.214	1.995
16	14.718	13.578	11.652	10.106	8.851	7.824	6.974	6.265	5.954	5.669	5.162	4.730	4.357	4.033	3.887	3.751	3.503	3.283	2.834	2.489	2.216	1.997
17	15.562	14.292	12.166	10.477	9.122	8.022	7.120	6.373	6.047	5.749	5.222	4.775	4.391	4.059	3.910	3.771	3.518	3.295	2.840	2.492	2.218	1.998
18	16.398	14.992	12.659	10.828	9.372	8.201	7.250	6.467	6.128	5.818	5.273	4.812	4.419	4.080	3.928	3.786	3.529	3.304	2.844	2.494	2.219	1.999
19	17.226	15.678	13.134	11.158	9.604	8.365	7.366	6.550	6.198	5.877	5.316	4.844	4.442	4.097	3.942	3.799	3.539	3.311	2.848	2.496	2.220	1.999
20	18.046	16.351	13.590	11.470	9.818	8.514	7.469	6.623	6.259	5.929	5.353	4.870	4.460	4.110	3.954	3.808	3.546	3.316	2.850	2.497	2.221	1.999
21	18.857	17.011	14.029	11.764	10.017	8.649	7.562	6.687	6.312	5.973	5.384	4.891	4.476	4.121	3.963	3.816	3.551	3.320	2.852	2.498	2.221	2.000
22	19.660	17.658	14.451	12.042	10.201	8.772	7.645	6.743	6.359	6.011	5.410	4.909	4.488	4.130	3.970	3.822	3.556	3.323	2.853	2.498	2.222	2.000
23	20.456	18.292	14.857	12.303	10.371	8.883	7.718	6.792	6.399	6.044	5.432	4.925	4.499	4.137	3.976	3.827	3.559	3.325	2.854	2.499	2.222	2.000
24	21.243	18.914	15.247	12.550	10.529	8.985	7.784	6.835	6.434	6.073	5.451	4.937	4.507	4.143	3.981	3.831	3.562	3.327	2.855	2.499	2.222	2.000
25	22.023	19.523	15.622	12.783	10.675	9.077	7.843	6.873	6.464	6.097	5.467	4.948	4.514	4.147	3.985	3.834	3.564	3.329	2.856	2.499	2.222	2.000
26	22.795	20.121	15.983	13.003	10.810	9.161	7.896	6.906	6.491	6.118	5.480	4.956	4.520	4.151	3.988	3.837	3.566	3.330	2.856	2.500	2.222	2.000
27	23.560	20.707	16.330	13.211	10.935	9.237	7.943	6.935	6.514	6.136	5.492	4.964	4.524	4.154	3.990	3.839	3.567	3.331	2.856	2.500	2.222	2.000
28	24.316	21.281	16.663	13.406	11.051	9.307	7.984	6.961	6.534	6.152	5.502	4.970	4.528	4.157	3.992	3.840	3.568	3.331	2.857	2.500	2.222	2.000
29	25.066	21.844	16.984	13.591	11.158	9.370	8.022	6.983	6.551	6.166	5.510	4.975	4.531	4.159	3.994	3.841	3.569	3.332	2.857	2.500	2.222	2.000
30	25.808	22.396	17.292	13.765	11.258	9.427	8.055	7.003	6.566	6.177	5.517	4.979	4.534	4.160	3.995	3.842	3.569	3.332	2.857	2.500	2.222	2.000
40	32.835	27.355	19.793	15.046	11.925	9.779	8.244	7.105	6.642	6.234	5.548	4.997	4.544	4.166	3.999	3.846	3.571	3.333	2.857	2.500	2.222	2.000
50	39.196	31.424	21.482	15.762	12.234	9.915	8.304	7.133	6.661	6.246	5.554	4.999	4.545	4.167	4.000	3.846	3.571	3.333	2.857	2.500	2.222	2.000

15

MANAGEMENT TECHNIQUES

The management of any business enterprise is obliged, in the complex modern economic situation in which the private sector now is, to use scientific methods to solve management problems. These scientific methods, also known as **quantitative techniques,** make use of, *inter alia,* sophisticated mathematical techniques to aid management with the decision-making process.

Some of the quantitative techniques have already been dealt with in earlier chapters because of their connection with the topics under discussion. For the sake of convenience the chapter references for the techniques which have already been dealt with are given below:

Technique	Chapter	
Economical order quantity	2	Material
Labour turnover	3	Labour
Regression analysis	4	Overheads

The rest of the more general techniques are dealt with in this chapter, namely:

- ☐ Linear programming
- ☐ Network analysis
- ☐ Probability analysis
- ☐ Learning curves
- ☐ Responsibility accounting and transfer prices

Module

15.1

Linear or rectilinear programming

1 Introduction

It has already been shown that cost-volume-profit analysis is a technique used to make an analysis of the influence that volumes exercise on costs, income and profit. It was also shown that profits are maximised when the product mix of an enterprise is such that it results in the largest contribution per unit. Linear programming is a technique used to determine the most economical product mix for an enterprise.

2 The application of linear programming

In practice there are certain factors which have a limiting effect on an enterprise's production and will also exert an influence on marginal income. Examples of such limiting factors are:

- [ ] the availability of raw materials
- [ ] the availability of skilled labour
- [ ] capacity limitations
- [ ] the limited demand for products.

Linear programming is a mathematical technique used to calculate the most economical combination of resources and consequently to maximise profits.

The application of linear programming is illustrated in the following examples:

Example 103

Linear Limited manufactures two products, A and B, for which the production data is as follows:

	A	B
Marginal income per unit	R8	R6
Machine hours necessary to manufacture one unit	4	2
Demand for each product	200	400
Available capacity : 1 000 machine hours		

Required:

Calculate the most economical product mix.

Arithmetical solution

Because Product B gives the greatest marginal income per machine hour all the available hours will be used for the production of Product B.

$$\text{Product B:} \quad \frac{1\ 000 \text{ machine hours}}{2 \text{ machine hours}}$$

$$= \ 500 \text{ units}$$

The maximum demand for product B is only 400 units.
Machine hours necessary to manufacture B : $400 \times 2 = 800$ hours

Product mix: Product B $= \ 400$ units

$$\text{Product A} \quad \frac{200 \text{ hours*}}{4 \text{ hours}} = \ 50 \text{ units}$$

* (1 000 machine hours − 800 machine hours)

Graphical solution

If all the available machine hours are used to manufacture Product A only, then:

A = 250   (1 000 machine hours ÷ 4 machine hours)
B = 0

If all the machine hours are used to manufacture Product B only, then:

B = 500   (1 000 machine hours ÷ 2 machine hours)
A = 0

The enterprise can produce 250 units of Product A or 500 units of Product B, or any linear combination of A and B in a fixed ratio of $4A = 2B$.

Graphically the problem can be solved as follows:

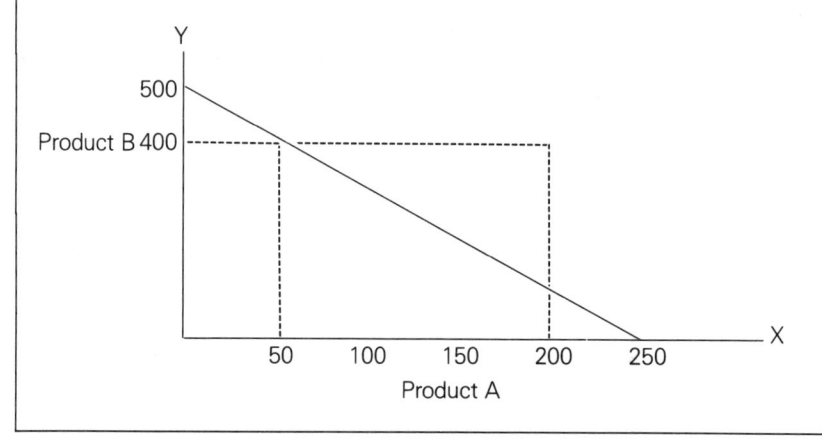

From the graph the solution is the same, namely:

Product A =   50 units (X axis)
Product B = 400 units (Y axis)

The limits in the above example were of such a nature that it could be solved by means of a simple calculation. However, where a number of variants are applicable and the basic method is difficult to apply a computer can be used to solve the linear problem.

The information in the next example is such that it can only be solved algebraically or graphically, because more than one limiting factor is involved.

Example 104

A manufacturing enterprise produces products K and P in two different departments, namely Cutting and Assembling. The following production data is available:

	K	P
	R	R
Selling price per unit	600	1 000
Variable costs per unit	250	400
Marginal income per unit	350	600
Machine hours needed in Department Cutting	2	4
Machine hours needed in Department Assembling	3	2
Total machine hours	5	6

The following machine hours are available during the week:

Department Cutting	80 hours
Department Assembling	60 hours
Total	140 hours

Required:

Calculate the most profitable production mix.

Analysis

A linear programme can be formulated using the above information as follows:

Aim: R350 K + R600 P = the largest marginal income

Limiting factors: $2K + 4P \leqslant 80$
$3K + 2P \leqslant 60$

Because production cannot be negative K is $\geqslant$ nil and P is $\geqslant$ nil

where
K   = the number of units of K that must be manufactured
P   = the number of units of P that must be manufactured
$\leqslant$ = less than or equal to
$\geqslant$ = greater than or equal to

Solution

Algebraic method:

$$2K + 4P = 80 \quad\quad\quad (1)$$
$$3K + 2P = 60 \quad\quad\quad (2)$$

$$2K + 4P = 80 \quad\quad\quad (1)$$
$$6K + 4P = 120 \quad\quad\quad (2) \times 2$$

$$4K \quad\quad = 40$$
$$\therefore K = 10$$

$$2K + 4P = 80 \quad\quad\quad (1)$$
$$(2 \times 10) + 4P = 80$$
$$4P = 80 - 20$$
$$\therefore P = 15$$

Graphical method:

$$2K + 4P = 80 \quad\quad\quad (1)$$
$$3K + 2P = 60 \quad\quad\quad (2)$$

Equation (1):

Assume $P = 0$, then $K = 40$ $(2K = 80)$
Assume $K = 0$, then $P = 20$ $(4P = 80)$

Equation (2):

Assume $P = 0$, then $K = 20$ $(3K = 60)$
Assume $K = 0$, then $P = 30$ $(2P = 60)$

The most profitable product mix can be established graphically with the aid of the two limits as follows:

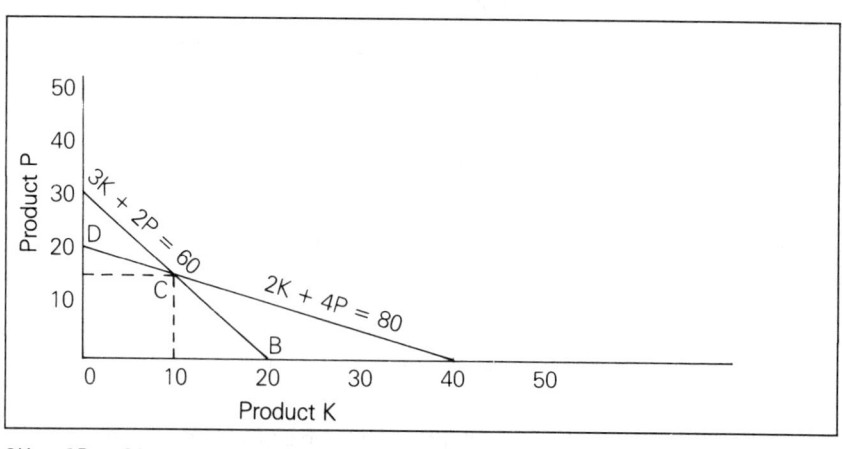

$$3K + 2P = 60 \quad\quad 2K + 4P = 80 \quad\quad D \quad C \quad B$$

The polygon 0BCD presents possible solutions since it shows the various combinations in which the two products can be manufactured. The marginal income of all the corners in the above area can be calculated as follows:

Corner	Combination		Marginal income		Total marginal income
	K	P	K	P	
			R	R	R
0	0	0	0	0	0
B	20	0	7 000	0	7 000
C	10	15	3 500	9 000	12 500
D	0	20	0	12 000	12 000

Corner C denotes the most profitable product mix with the greatest marginal income.

3 Sensitivity analysis

As soon as one or more of the variables changes the product mix also changes. Hence, the product mix that is most profitable under the current circumstances must be determined. Suppose that in the previous example the selling price of K decreased, resulting in a smaller marginal income per unit. It would be more economical to stop the production of K and to increase the production of P to its optimum.

The question is: **When must the production of K be stopped?**

With the help of the following equation it can be established whether, at such a price decrease, only 20 units of P must be produced or whether to continue with 10 units of K and 15 units of P.

$$20 \times (\text{MI of P}) = [15 \times (\text{MI of P})] + [10 \times (\text{MI of K})]$$
$$20 \times 600 = [15 \times 600] + [10 \times (\text{MI of K})]$$
$$12\,000 = 9\,000 + [10 \times (\text{MI of K})]$$
$$10 \times (\text{MI of K}) = 3\,000$$
$$\therefore \text{MI of K} = \text{R}300$$
$$\text{where MI} = \text{marginal income}$$

From the above it is clear that once the marginal income of K falls below R300 the production of K must be stopped and production must be concentrated on P only.

Network analysis

1 Introduction

Network analysis is a technique developed to schedule large projects comprising a variety of jobs (activities) as well as to plan and control the interaction between the tasks and to show the critical parts of the project.

If the duration and the cost of the various activities of a project are of such a nature that they are difficult to analyse, such projects can be processed with the help of a computer.

The two main variants of the technique are:

- [ ] the **critical path method**
- [ ] the **PERT method** (programme evaluation and review technique).

2 Critical path analysis

The **critical path method** involves determining the shortest time in which a project which comprises a variety of jobs (activities) can be completed. The time spent on the activity (or successive activities), that it takes the longest time to complete will thus be the shortest time in which the project as a whole can be completed. The successive activities which it takes the longest time to finish and which thus determine the completion time of the project in total are known as the **critical path.**

This method can be used successfully for the planning and control of the following activities:

- [ ] Construction – the erection of buildings, bridges, etc
- [ ] Maintenance and upkeep of machinery and equipment – the determination of the period when, with the least interruption in the production process, necessary maintenance work can be carried out
- [ ] Developing and planning large projects – for example the Polaris space travel programme in the USA
- [ ] General management – budgets, auditing procedures, etc
- [ ] Transportation – transport network and route planning

A characteristic of the determining of the critical path is that it occurs in the following stages:

- [ ] Planning

☐ Analysis and scheduling
☐ Control

2.1 Planning

The plan of the project, which includes all the activities, is presented graphically by a network of arrow diagrams. Each **activity** in the network is represented by an **arrow** which flows from left to right, while the junction of the various arrows is a **circle** in the framework and represents an **event** or **milestone.**

⓪ ————————> ① ————————> ②
  Activity 0 – 1   Activity 1 – 2

   In the above example ⓪ ① and ② represent the different milestones.

   Each event or milestone is numbered and the number is written in the circle. A milestone which indicates the end of the preceding activity has a higher number than that which it precedes.

   A simple project can be presented diagrammatically as follows:

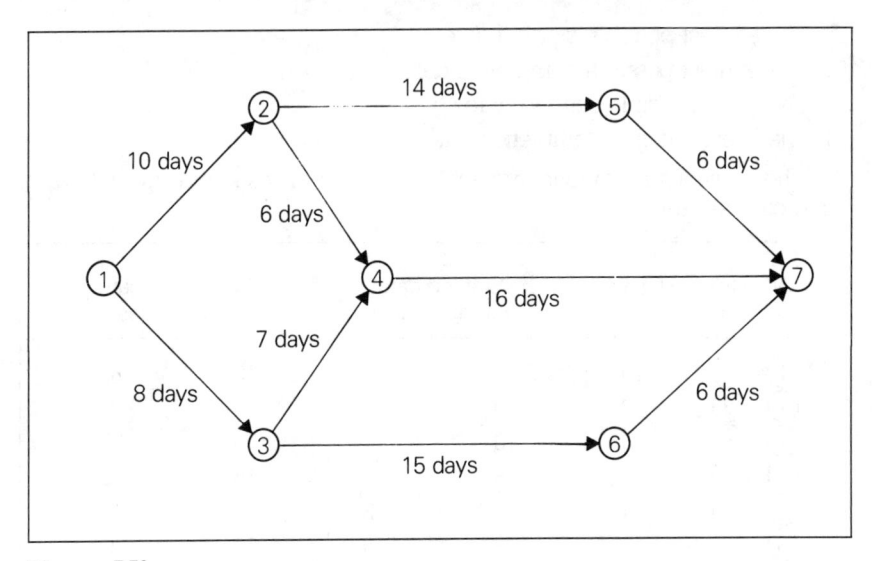

Diagram D73

   The diagram contains the following four paths:

Paths	Duration in days	
①→②→⑤→⑦	10 + 14 + 6	= 30 days
①→②→④→⑦	10 + 6 + 16	= 32 days
①→③→④→⑦	8 + 7 + 16	= 31 days
①→③→⑥→⑦	8 + 15 + 6	= 29 days

Milestones ① and ⑦ are, respectively, the beginning and end of the network. Activities which follow each other, such as ②→④ and ②→⑤ can begin only once activity ①→② is complete. Activities ①→② and ①→③ which take place concurrently, are known as parallel activities. The path which in total it takes the longest time to finish is the **critical path.** In the diagram in question it is ①→②→④→⑦, which takes 32 days to complete. Thus the shortest time in which the project can be completed is 32 days.

Any delay in a job which is not on the critical path has no influence on the total completion time unless the delay is such that a new critical path results.

2.2 Analysis and scheduling

The analysis and scheduling of the critical path involves estimating the duration and calculating the cost of each activity for the entire project. Any variance from the time in which the task must be performed can, if unfavourable, lead to higher costs. Projects whose times and costs are of such a nature that they become too involved for analysis can be analysed by means of a computer.

During the analysis and scheduling stages of the critical path the following concepts come to the fore.

☐ The earliest possible starting date
☐ The earliest possible completion date
☐ The latest possible starting date
☐ The latest possible completion date

If the previous schematic project is taken as an example, the following table can be prepared:

Activity	Duration (days)	Starting date Earliest	Latest	Completion date Earliest	Latest
①→②	10	0	0	10	10
①→③	8	0	1	8	9
②→④	6	10	10	16	16
③→④	7	8	9	15	16
②→⑤	14	10	12	24	26
③→⑥	15	8	10	23	25
④→⑦	16	16	16	32	32
⑤→⑦	6	24	26	30	32
⑥→⑦	6	23	26	29	32

The **earliest starting time** of an activity is determined by taking the longest path from the beginning of the project to the particular milestone. If activity ④→⑦ taken as an example, the longest path leading to milestone ④ will represent the earliest starting date of the activity:

①→②→④ = 10 + 6
         = 16 days

The **latest starting time,** on the other hand, is the latest date on which the activity can possibly begin without delaying the whole project. If activitiy ①→③ is taken as an example, it represents the total project time of the critical path less the longest path in terms of the project time which stretches between milestone ① (start of activity) and ⑦, but which goes via milestone ③.

Latest starting time of activity ①→③:
Critical path – Path ①→③→④→⑦
32 – (8 + 7 + 16) = 1 day

The latest starting time to start with activities following milestone ③ will be the critical path minus the longest path leading from milestone ③ via the activity to the end of the project. For example, the earliest and latest completion dates for activity ③→④ can be determined as follows:

Earliest completion date = Duration + Earliest starting date
                          = 7 + 8
                          = 15 days

Latest completion date = Earliest completion date + Difference
                          between latest and earliest starting date
                        = 15 + (9 – 8)
                        = 16 days
Alternatively: Critical path – Longest route between milestones ④ and ⑦

The difference between the latest and earliest dates of the starting and completion dates is known as the **float.** The float of an activity represents the time by which an activity's duration can be lengthened without lengthening the duration of the entire project, and therefore it is logical that there can be no float on the critical path.

2.3 Control

It is necessary that a project is controlled carefully while it is being carried out. Control includes:

☐ measuring and comparing and reporting results
☐ taking corrective steps where possible.

3 PERT

Like the critical path method, this technique is used to plan projects, to establish completion dates and to control time schedules. It was first used in government research and development projects, where there was a large degree of uncertainty concerning the different completion dates.

In the critical path method every activity is a constant factor, while the PERT analysis makes use of probability factors (as a result of the uncertainty element) to determine the completion date of the project.

First the following three estimates must be made in respect of the duration of each activity:

O = optimistic time or the minimum possible time in which the activity can be completed

W = the probable time necessary to complete the activity

P = pessimistic time or the maximum possible time in which the activity can be completed

With PERT analysis the expected duration of an activity is determined with the aid of the following standard formula which makes provision for the uncertainty factor:

$$\text{Expected time} = \frac{O + 4W + P}{6}$$

Example 105

The following estimates in terms of working days were prepared for a new project:

Activity	Most optimistic time (days)	Most probable time (days)	Most pessimistic time (days)
(1)→(2)	4	6	8
(1)→(3)	3	6	9
(1)→(4)	6	8	16
(2)→(3)	3	4	5
(3)→(4)	2	3	4

Required:
1 Calculate the expected duration in respect of each of the above activities.
2 Prepare a PERT network and show the critical path.

Solution

1 Calculation of expected completion time $= \dfrac{O + 4W + P}{6}$

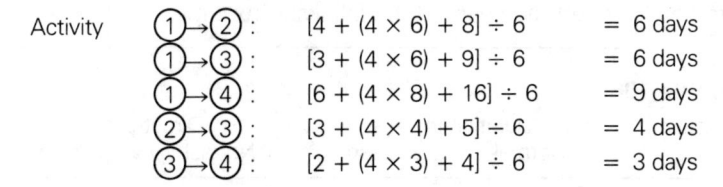

Activity	①→② :	$[4 + (4 \times 6) + 8] \div 6$	= 6 days
	①→③ :	$[3 + (4 \times 6) + 9] \div 6$	= 6 days
	①→④ :	$[6 + (4 \times 8) + 16] \div 6$	= 9 days
	②→③ :	$[3 + (4 \times 4) + 5] \div 6$	= 4 days
	③→④ :	$[2 + (4 \times 3) + 4] \div 6$	= 3 days

2 Network

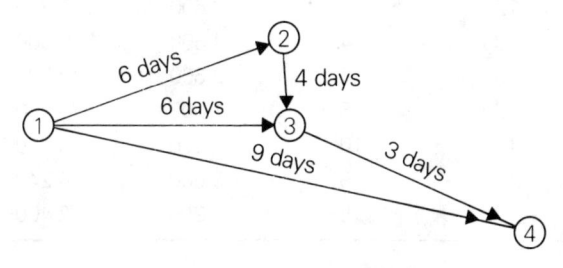

Critical path: ①→②→③→④ = 6 + 4 + 3 = 13 days

Cost values must be included in each activity in the PERT network in order that the cost of a project may be determined and controlled. It is important to establish what influence any changes in the duration of the activity or activities will have on the project cost.

From the outset it is necessary to pay attention to the following terminology:

☐ **Crash time** represents the minimum possible time in which the activity may be completed. It requires the use of additional resources, for example additional employees and machines, to make it possible.

☐ **Crash costs** are the costs of the minimum possible time (crash time) for an activity. Crash costs will always be higher than the normal costs, because they are often coupled with higher wages.

☐ **Normal costs** are the costs associated with the normal time estimate for completing an activity at a level at which the resources are employed efficiently.

☐ The **cost slope** is the average additional cost of shortening an activity by a day or a week or any other time unit. The formula for the calculation of the cost slope is as follows:

$$\text{Cost slope} = \frac{\text{Crash costs} - \text{Normal costs}}{\text{Normal time} - \text{Crash time}}$$

It can be illustrated by means of the following example:

Example 106

Activity	Duration in days		Direct costs	
	Normal	Crash	Normal	Crash
			R	R
①→②	12	10	3 600	3 880
①→④	18	14	4 600	5 000
①→③	9	6	2 600	3 200
②→④	7	6	1 800	1 950
②→⑤	12	10	3 000	3 240
④→⑤	13	9	3 600	4 240
③→⑤	7	5	1 900	2 400

Required:
1 Prepare a network diagram for the project and show the critical path.
2 Calculate the normal costs to complete the project if the fixed costs amount to R100 per day.
3 Calculate the minimum cost of the project if it is to be completed in 25 days.

Solution
1   Network diagram:

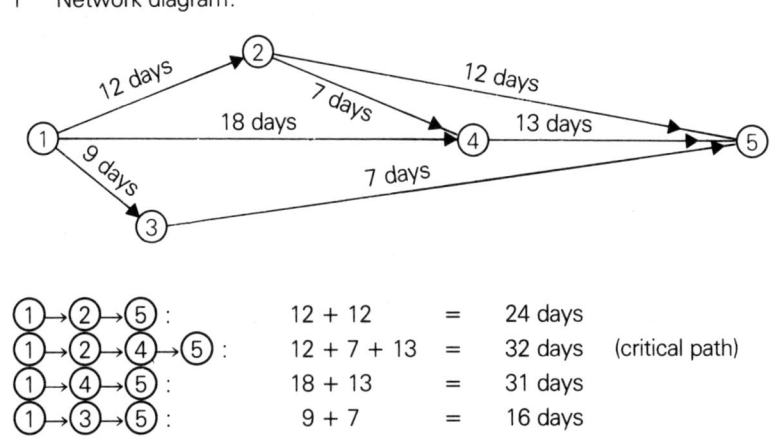

①→②→⑤ :	12 + 12	=	24 days
①→②→④→⑤ :	12 + 7 + 13	=	32 days (critical path)
①→④→⑤ :	18 + 13	=	31 days
①→③→⑤ :	9 + 7	=	16 days

2 Normal costs:
   Direct   = 3 600 + 4 600 + 2 600 + 1 800 + 3 000 + 3 600 + 1 900
             = R21 100

   Fixed   = 32 days × R100
             = R3 200

   Total   = R24 300

3
Activity	Calculation	Cost slope
		R
①→②	(3 880 − 3 600) ÷ (12 − 10)	140
①→④	(5 000 − 4 600) ÷ (18 − 14)	100
①→③	(3 200 − 2 600) ÷ (9 − 6)	200
②→④	(1 950 − 1 800) ÷ (7 − 6)	150
②→⑤	(3 240 − 3 000) ÷ (12 − 10)	120
④→⑤	(4 240 − 3 600) ÷ (13 − 9)	160
③→⑤	(2 400 − 1 900) ÷ (7 − 5)	250

The four routes can be shortened as follows:

Path	Normal time	Crash time
①→②→⑤	24	(10 + 10) = 20
①→②→④→⑤	32	(10 + 6 + 9) = 25
①→④→⑤	31	(14 + 9) = 23
①→③→⑤	16	(6 + 5) = 11

Path ①→③→⑤ falls within the duration of the critical path and none of the activities form part of it. Therefore it is not necessary to shorten this path.

The most economical network for 25 days can be compiled as follows:

Path	Time
①→②→⑤	10 + 12 = 22
①→②→④→⑤	10 + 6 + 9 = 25
①→④→⑤	16 + 9 = 25
①→③→⑤	9 + 7 = 16

There are now two critical paths of 25 days each. Path ①→④ with a low cost slope, cannot be shortened further because this will delay activity ④→⑤, which is on the critical path.

The additional costs of the new path are as follows:

Activity	Cost slope	Reduction	Additional variable costs
			R
(1)→(2)	140	2	280
(1)→(4)	100	2	200
(2)→(4)	150	1	150
(4)→(5)	160	4	640
		9	1 270

Minimum cost :	R
Normal cost	24 300
Less: Saving in fixed costs (7 × R100)	700
	23 600
Add: Additional variable costs	1 270
	24 870

Module

15.3

Decisions and uncertainty

1 Probability

Linear programming is a technique which is so developed that it enables a decision maker to make the right decision between alternative choices with certainty. Probability theory, on the other hand, is applied where the decision maker does not know what is going to happen in the future, such as the uncertain demand in the future for fashionable clothes.

When the probability of an event is based on data from the past and the circumstances can be repeated by means of tests, this is known as **objective probability** and can be determined without personal judgement. An example of this is that the probability of throwing a five with a six-sided die is 16,67%. It can be calculated as follows:

All the possible consequences:

$$= \frac{\text{Number of times an event can occur}}{\text{The possible number of results}}$$

$$= \frac{1}{6}$$

$$= 0,1667 \text{ or } 16,67\%$$

Probability is expressed as a decimal figure between 0 and 1.
The following two basic rules are valid for probability:

☐ If it is certain that a specific event will occur the probability is equal to 1, and if it is impossible the probability is 0. In such a case the decision can be made with certainty.

☐ If the probability that a specific event might occur is between 0 and 1 (not exactly 0 or 1) then the decision maker is not sure whether the event is going to occur and a decision is based on **uncertainty**.

Example 107

A vegetable trader can purchase avocado pears in quantities of 50, 100 and 200 from the local vegetable market daily. The following table shows the estimated daily demand for the product:

Quantity	Probability
50	0,12
100	0,28
150	0,40
200	0,20

Required

Calculate the average expected daily demand for avocado pears.

Solution

Quantity	Probability	Average daily demand
50	0,12	6*
100	0,28	28
150	0,40	60
200	0,20	40
	1,00	134

* 50 × 0,12

There is an element of risk attached to all decisions, since the actual result of a given event may deviate from the expected result. With decisions based on **risk** a probability is allocated to each possible outcome of the given event.

Example 108

An enterprise manufactures and sells a perishable product. The maximum daily production is 500 units. The following information is available:

	R
Selling price per unit	20
Variable costs	10

Products which are not sold during the day must be removed at a cost of R0,10 per unit.

(continued)

A survey of sales during the previous 150 days shows the following:

Demand	Number of days	Probability
100	10	0,07
200	30	0,20
300	50	0,33
400	40	0,27
500	20	0,13
	150	1,00

Required:

Calculate the number of units that must be manufactured daily to yield the maximum profit for the enterprise.

Solution

Demand (units)	Probabi-lity	Alternative contributions per production volume				
		100	200	300	400	500
		R	R	R	R	R
100	0,07	70	$(1)^1$	(71)	(142)	(213)
200	0,20	200	400	198	(4)	(206)
300	0,33	330^3	660	990^2	657	323
400	0,27	270	540	810	1 080	807
500	0,13	130	260	390	520	650
	1,00	1 000	1 859	2 317	2 111	1 361

[1] If 200 units are manufactured and only 100 units are sold, then
100 units × R20 − [(200 × R10) + (100 × 0,10)]
= − R10 × 0,07
= R0,70 loss on the day's transactions (rounded to R1)

[2] $[(300 \times R20) - (300 \times R10)] \times 0,33 = R990$

[3] $\dfrac{100}{300} \times 990 = 330$

From the solution it is clear that 300 units is the optimum stock with a profit of R2 317.

This problem can be solved by a shorter method, as follows:

Formula : Cumulative probability $\geqslant \dfrac{c_1}{c_1 + c_2}$

where c_1 = profit on each perishable product
and c_2 = cost of each perishable product

Quantity	Frequency probability	Cumulative probability
100	0,07	0,07
200	0,20	0,27
300	0,33	0,60
400	0,27	0,87
500	0,13	1,00

$$\text{Cumulative probability} \geq \frac{c_1}{c_1 + c_2}$$

$$\geq \frac{10}{10 + 10}$$

$$\geq 0,50$$

The first daily demand where the cumulative probability is greater than or equal to 0,50 is 300 units (between 0,27 and 0,60).

The optimum quantity to be purchased daily is thus 300 units.

2 Decision trees

Thus far our discussion has dealt with situations where a single decision had to be taken. Decision tables can be used effectively to help the decision maker when a series of decisions must be taken at different stages and one decision gives rise to the next.

A decision table, better known as a decision tree, is actually a diagram showing the following:

☐ – a point when a choice must be made between alternatives

◯ – a point when different events may occur

Example 109

Venture Limited, which in the past maintained a level of activity of 80%, is currently using only 60% of its factory potential which results in an utilisation loss of R100 000 per annum.

In order to recover the loss to some extent the enterprise is planning the manufacture and marketing of either Product M or Product N. This effort will not result in any further fixed costs.

The planning provided the following information:

	Number of units	Probability
Marketing of product M:	100 000	0,4
	40 000	0,4
	5 000	0,2
		1,0

(continued)

Marketing of product N:	80 000	0,5
	30 000	0,4
	10 000	0,1
		1,0

	Product M	Product N
	R	R
Selling price per unit	10	6
Production cost per unit (variable)	4	2

Required:

Draw a decision tree and determine the expected values.

Solution

Decision tree

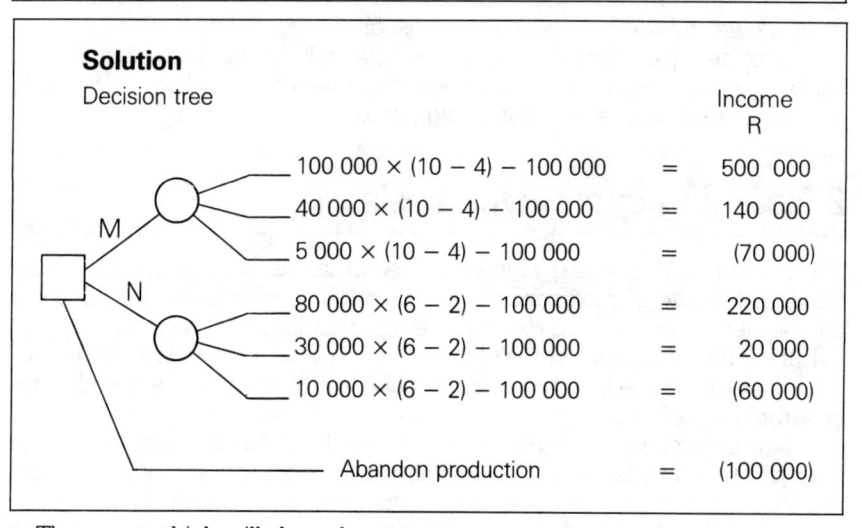

		Income R
100 000 × (10 − 4) − 100 000	=	500 000
40 000 × (10 − 4) − 100 000	=	140 000
5 000 × (10 − 4) − 100 000	=	(70 000)
80 000 × (6 − 2) − 100 000	=	220 000
30 000 × (6 − 2) − 100 000	=	20 000
10 000 × (6 − 2) − 100 000	=	(60 000)
Abandon production	=	(100 000)

The event which will show the greatest expected value is the choice.

Test

			R
Product M	R500 000 × 0,4	=	200 000
	R140 000 × 0,4	=	56 000
	(70 000) × 0,2	=	(14 000)
			242 000
Product N	R220 000 × 0,5	=	110 000
	20 000 × 0,4	=	8 000
	(60 000) × 0,1	=	(6 000)
			112 000

From the above it is obvious that product M will be the right product.

Module

15.4

Learning curves

1 Introduction

As a worker becomes more proficient at his work through repetition he makes fewer mistakes and completes his job faster.

The tendency of a person to master a **new task that he is learning** until he achieves his optimum speed takes on a fixed pattern. This has given rise to the concept **learning effect** or **learning curve**.

2 Learning curve hypothesis

The learning curve was designed to predict labour hours fairly accurately because the **rate of proficiency** of each worker increases and labour hours tend to decrease in a fixed pattern as the performance is repeated.

During the Second World War American experts and advisors in the air-force industry studied the influence of the learning effect on the manufacture of aeroplanes.

A learning curve of, for example, 90% results in the cumulative average time per unit decreasing by 10% when the production quantity is doubled. Suppose it takes an average of 60 hours to manufacture the first unit of a finished product. The cumulative average time of the ensuring units will have a 90% learning effect as follows:

Units	Cumulative production	Cumulative time per unit (hours)	
1	1	60	
1	2	54	(90% × 60)
2	4	48,6	(90% × 54)
4	8	43,74	(90% × 48,6)

Once the learning effect is complete the decrease in the cumulative time per unit will stop.

The following activities are subject to the learning effect:

☐ The execution of new activities or activities which, in future, will be carried out by different production methods

☐ New workers who are not acquainted with the methods
☐ The use of new types of raw materials
☐ Short production runs which immediately precede the following activity

---

Example 110

A manufacturing enterprise receives an order to manufacture 16 units of a special type of product. It is estimated that it will take 100 hours to manufacture the first unit. Management is of the opinion that use can easily be made of an 80% learning curve.

Required:
Calculate the total number of hours to complete the order.

Solution

Cumulative output	Average time per unit		Cumulative hours	
1	100		100	
2	80	(80% × 100)	160	(80 × 2)
4	64	(80% × 80)	256	(64 × 4)
8	51	(80% × 64)	408	(51 × 8)
16	41	(80% × 51)	656	(41 × 16)

The above solution in table form has shortcomings. For example, it does not show the cumulative hours to manufacture five units. In order to bridge this disadvantage the example can be solved graphically as follows:

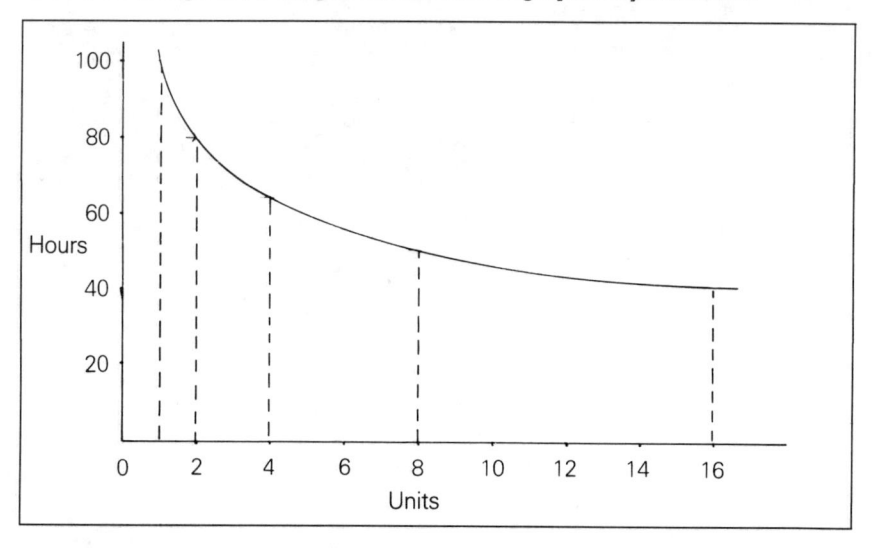

The above curve tends to have a large slope initially and gradually flattens until it is almost a straight line when the learning effect on the individuals is complete.

3 Conclusion

Learning curves provide management with an important planning instrument in that they help with

☐ the calculation of quotations
☐ the establishment of labour standards
☐ the preparation of production budgets.

They also serve as a control instrument in so far as they help with the evaluation of performances in the factory by comparing the actual production hours with those of the learning curve.

Module

15.5

Responsibility accounting

1 Introduction

Responsibility accounting is an internal communications system which supplies accounting information for management and control purposes to each responsibility centre or section in the enterprise. In order that this may be achieved authority must be delegated from the highest level to the different supervisors. The system must be reasonable; it must motivate the employees to achieve the goals of the enterprise and, at the same time, furnish adequate information to top management so that each responsible person's performance may be evaluated.

2 Responsibility centres

The implementation of responsibility accounting necessitates the division of the enterprise into responsibility centres where performance can be controlled and evaluated effectively. These centres are:

- ☐ cost centres
- ☐ profit centres
- ☐ investment centres.

☐ Cost centres

A cost centre represents a section or segment of sections where managers are responsible for the costs which originate there. (Cost centres have already been discussed in the chapter dealing with overheads.) All costs which originate directly from the cost centre are identified with the foreman or manager responsible for control over such cost centres. These costs are known as controllable costs and must be kept separate from non-controllable costs, which are allocated from other sections.

☐ Profit centres

These are centres where managers are held responsible for the control of costs and income. A profit centre can consist of different cost centres, each of which is controlled by its own foreman who is responsible to the manager of such a profit centre.

Where a section markets its production mainly to another section in the enterprise such selling prices are known as transfer prices. Net income serves as a measure for evaluating the performance of a manager in a specific profit centre. It also includes ratios such as net income to turnover, gross profit to turnover and the stock turnover ratio.

☐ Investment centres

In these centres it is the responsibility of the manager to control not only the income and costs, but also all investments. Returns on amounts invested are the usual measures for effective control.

3 Responsibility budgets

As the period which has been budgeted for progresses it is the duty of the managers of the responsibility centres to compare the actual information with the budgeted information. Differences must be analysed and, if they are caused by controllable factors, corrective steps must be taken.

The aim of the budget process is to ensure that the enterprise as a whole earns a satisfactory return on capital. In order to achieve this an effective system of planning and control is necessary for each centre in the enterprise.

Responsibility reports are indispensable for responsibility budgets as they show all the variances between budgeted and actual figures. Favourable as well as unfavourable variances must be analysed further.

The type of item which is analysed will determine how often responsibility reports must be presented.

4 Transfer prices

Transfer prices are used to assign values to goods and services exchanged between different sections.

Transfer prices create problems for the profit and investment centres and must be devised so that they are advantageous to every centre in terms of performance evaluation and decision making. Divisions which act independently must always guard against unnecessarily high transfer prices, since it is sometimes cheaper for a particular section to purchase on the open market instead. The determination of transfer prices must be in the best interests of the various sections and the enterprise as a whole.

The following methods can be used to determine transfer prices:

☐ Market price

If there is an existing market with an established price for the given product the market price is an ideal basis for determining the transfer price. If the market price includes marketing costs it is logical that the transfer price will be equivalent to the market price less marketing costs. The disadvantage of this method is that a suitable market price is not always available.

☐ Negotiated price

Where a suitable market price for a particular product is not available a price is established by negotiation between the section that is buying and the section that is selling. The disadvantage of this method is that the managers want only their own sections to benefit.

☐ Total cost price

The use of total costs is probably the oldest method of price determination due to its simplicity and the ease with which it can be implemented. This method is not suitable for enterprises with a decentralised structure because it is necessary for these enterprises to measure the profitability of the different sections exactly.

☐ Marginal cost price

As a basis for the determination of transfer prices marginal costs do not eliminate all the faults of total costs, but they are acceptable in the short term. The greatest disadvantage of this system is that the manager of one section makes a profit at the expense of the manager of another section. Normally sections are not willing to market their products at marginal costs, therefore this system is not generally used unless a particular profit centre has some unutilised capacity.

Whichever method is used to measure the performance of a section it always remains advisable to use at least the differential costs of the goods transferred from one section to another for decision making purposes.

5 Rate of return

With responsibility accounting the determination of a rate of return is a special problem for investment centres since the manager is responsible for not only the profit, but also the investment required to give that return. The most general method of determining the rate of return is the following:

$$
\text{Formula} = \frac{\text{Income}}{\text{Assets}}
$$

The problem that sometimes occurs is whether to make use of total or net assets. As an alternative the rate of return can be determined with the aid of the following two formulae:

Profit margin on sales: $\dfrac{\text{Profit}}{\text{Sales}} \times \dfrac{100}{1} = \%$

Asset turnover: $\dfrac{\text{Sales}}{\text{Capital employed}} = \text{times}$

Example 111

	R
Sales	20 000
Profit	2 000
Capital employed	10 000

Solution

Profit margin on sales: $\dfrac{\text{R2 000}}{\text{R20 000}} \times \dfrac{100}{1}$

$= 10\%$

Asset turnover $\dfrac{\text{R20 000}}{\text{R10 000}}$

$= 2 \text{ times}$

A combination of the above two answers gives the required rate of return as follows:

$$10\% \times 2 = 20\%$$

5.1 Residual income

This technique is a method for determining the income of a section over and above the minimum planned rate of return of the enterprise. The following illustration serves as an example if the residual income is used as a criterion for measuring the performance of a section.

Planned rate of return:	10%		12%	
	Section A	Section B	Section C	Section D
	R	R	R	R
Investment	50 000	31 000	50 000	31 000
Income	6 000	4 000	6 000	4 000
Less: Expected rate of return 10%	5 000	3 100		
Expected rate of return 12%			6 000	3 720
Residual income	1 000	900	Nil	280

The net income, or residual income, after the minimum return has been taken into account, is the "profit" of that particular section. As is clearly illustrated in the above example, the amount invested and the rate of return are important factors.

16

PROBLEMS

Chapter 1

1.1

Briefly discuss the most important differences between financial and management accounting.

1.2

Discuss briefly what you understand by the following concepts:
(a) Relevant information
(b) Costs
(c) Expired and unexpired costs
(d) Commercial costs
(e) Period costs
(f) Conversion costs
(g) Primary costs

Chapter 2

2.1

Distinguish the following concepts by discussing the characteristics of each concept briefly, emphasising the differences between the concepts:
(a) Buffer stock and safety stock
(b) Economic stock and technical stock
(c) Direct and indirect material
(d) Economic order quantity (EOQ) and re-order point.

2.2

The following information applies to the finished product stock of Alpha Manufacturing Limited:

19.6	Production		Sales		Selling and administra- tive costs
	Units	Unit price	Units	Selling price	
		R		R	R
First quarter	800	31,40	750	60,50	15 150
Second quarter	1 000	30,60	900	58,30	16 250
Third quarter	1 400	30,20	1 500	56,20	25 200
Fourth quarter	1 000	30,90	1 100	58,10	21 500

On 1 January 19.6 the opening stock consisted of 200 units with a cost price of R30,00 each.

Required:

Using the FIFO method of stock valuation calculate the following:

(a) The value of closing stock as at 31 December 19.6
(b) The cost of sales
(c) The net profit for 19.6

Please note: For additional practice you can repeat the calculations using the weighted average method of stock valuation.

2.3

(a) A company marketing a single product on a continuous basis requests you to help it to determine the most economic order quantity, the average and safety stock and the re-order point of the product. The following information is available:

Normal delivery time	2 weeks
Maximum delivery time	4 weeks
Normal annual usage (units)	57 200
Purchase price per unit	R15
Average annual storage cost per unit	R0,75
Cost of placing an order	R150
Prime interest rate	15%
Production weeks per year	52

The stock is financed by means of an overdraft

(b) Will it be more advantageous for the company if a quantity discount of 2½% on an order of 2 500 plus units can be negotiated?

(c) What will the most economic order quantity be if the company changes its stock financing policy and makes use of supplier's credit, in terms of which payment is due only 42 days after delivery of the products?

Chapter 3

3.1

Describe briefly what you understand by the following concepts:
(a) Productivity
(b) Labour turnover
(c) Time card
(d) Job card
(e) Piece wage
(f) Halsey bonus scheme
(g) Direct and indirect labour.

3.2

The time sheet of employee Jones shows that he has worked 44 hours during a 40-hour working week. On both Monday and Saturday he worked two hours overtime. The normal overtime compensation ($1^1/_2$ × normal wage) is paid.

His normal wage is R6 per hour.

Medical and pension contributions (6% and 10% of normal wage respectively) are paid on a 50:50 basis by employer and employee. PAYE (12% of taxable income) is the only other deduction made.

Required:
(a) Calculate Jones' net earnings for the week.
(b) Assume that Jones is the company's only employee and show how his wage for the week will be recorded.
(c) Calculate the labour tariff per hour for Jones assuming that a year comprises 52 working weeks, that he is entitled to three weeks annual vacation leave and that the company is closed for eight public holidays per year. Normal idle time is estimated at $7^1/_2\%$ and a leave bonus equal to three weeks' wage is paid.

3.3

Ten persons work as a group in a factory. When weekly production of the group exceeds the standard production of 200 units per hour, each man is paid a bonus for the additional production above standard. The bonus is calculated as follows: Calculate the percentage by which the groups' production exceeds the standard. Divide the percentage by 2 and multiply the answer by a basic wage of R10,50 per hour in order to determine an hourly bonus. The production record for the first week of March shows that 100 000 units were manufactured in 420 hours.

Required:
Calculate the following:
(a) The bonus rate and the amount of the bonus for the week.
(b) The total wages of Jan Publiek who worked 41 hours at a rate of R8,00 per hour.

Chapter 4

4.1

Briefly discuss the following concepts:
(a) Budgeted overheads
(b) Applied overheads
(c) Actual overheads
(d) Overapplied overheads
(e) Underapplied overheads

4.2

The Trans-Karoo Company purchased a vehicle for R20 000 on 1 September 19.4. Depreciation is written off at 20% pa according to the reducing balance method. The company's financial year end is 28 February.

Required:

(a) Calculate the book value of the vehicle on 28 February 19.7.
(b) Calculate the book value of the vehicle at 28 February 19.7 if depreciation is to be written off according to the straight-line method of depreciation.

4.3

A company carrying out a single manufacturing process encounters problems with control over its manufacturing overheads, especially at varying capacity levels.

Therefore it has been decided to divide the total manufacturing overheads into its fixed and variable elements, in the hope of simplifying control over total overheads.

The following information is available:

Month	Units manufactured	Total overheads
		R
January	4 000	70 000
February	4 300	75 000
March	4 500	76 000
April	4 800	82 000
May	4 700	81 000
June	5 000	85 500
July	5 300	89 500
August	5 200	88 900
September	4 900	84 000
October	4 800	81 500
November	4 600	79 500
December	4 300	74 600

Required:

(a) Calculate the fixed monthly portion of the manufacturing overheads using the 'high-low' technique.
(b) Calculate the variable portion of the manufacturing overheads on a unit base using a scatter graph.
(c) Calculate the monthly variances of the expected allowance for total overheads from the actual results obtained for the following four months of the year:

Month	Total overheads	Units manufactured
	R	
January	72 000	4 100
February	72 500	4 200
March	74 300	4 400
April	85 000	5 000

The calculation can also be made (as an exercise) using the least squares method.

4.4

Dealers Limited collected the following statistics in order to allocate their overheads among the various departments:

	Production department A	Production department B	Service department
Number of employees	36	24	20
Value of equipment	R15 000	R9 000	R6 000
Floor space utilised	400 m²	300 m²	200 m²
Material used	R40 000	R30 000	R5 000
Direct labour hours	1 300	700	905
Machine hours	450	305	195

The following amounts represent the expected overheads for 19.7:

	R
Rent of factory buildings	2 250
Depreciation on equipment	900
Electricity	900
Protective clothing	800
Cafeteria	720
Insurance: Buildings	450
Equipment	750

Overheads allocation rates are based on labour hours, while the secondary apportionment of the service department takes place according to machine hours.

Required:

Determine the overheads allocation rates of each of the two production departments for 19.7 using the stepped method of allocation.

4.5

The following information applies to the activities of the Alpha Manufacturing company for 19.6:

	Production departments		
	A	B	C
Direct labour hours	14 100	23 500	16 200
Direct labour costs	R160 400	R241 600	R158 600
Manufacturing overheads	R274 000	R193 420	R101 700

The following estimated percentages of service department contributions to other departments have been developed:

Work performed for:	Service departments		
	Personnel	Administration	Engineers
	%	%	%
Personnel	0	5	0
Administration	10	0	8
Engineering department	8	11	0
Department A	17	21	38
Department B	41	35	34
Department C	24	28	20
	100	100	100
Costs of service departments	R16 500	R48 600	R29 200

Required:

(a) Allocate the cost of the service departments and calculate the total overheads rate per labour hour for each production department. (Start with the service department performing the most work for the other service departments.)

(b) The following information applies to a certain product manufactured by the company:

    Direct material used R96
    Direct labour: Dept A .... 1 hour
                     Dept B .... 2 hours
                     Dept C .... 2 hours

Calculate the **total** manufacturing costs of the product.

4.6

Manufacturers Limited manufactures a single product which goes through three manufacturing departments. Service department Z serves all three of these departments. A flexible overhead budget for the coming year has been compiled for each of the departments as follows:

Department A: 50% per direct labour cost
B: R3,60 per direct labour hour
C: R4,20 per direct labour hour
Z: R1,20 per direct labour hour
of each of the producing departments.
The following budgeted information is also available:

Department	Fixed overheads	Direct labour cost	Direct labour hours
	R	R	
A	18 000	60 000	6 000
B	9 600	44 000	4 000
C	11 600	26 000	2 000
Z	9 000		

The cost of the service department is allocated to the production departments on the basis of direct labour cost. The actual information for the year is as follows:

	A	B	C	Z
Direct labour hours	6 500	4 200	2 100	
	R	R	R	R
Direct labour cost	59 000	41 000	30 000	–
Total manufacturing overheads	50 000	27 000	17 000	26 000

Required:
(a) Calculate the predetermined overhead rates for each of the production departments.
(b) Calculate the over- or under applied overhead for each of the departments.
(c) Journal entries in respect of:
   (i) closing the manufacturing overhead control account
   (ii) distributing service department costs
   (iii) applying manufacturing overhead costs to production
   (iv) closing over or under applied manufacturing overhead costs.

Chapter 5

5.1

The Electrical Company manufactures and markets three types of products. The marketing and distribution costs for the past year were as follows:

	R
Salaries of sales personnel	39 000
Bonuses of sales personnel	3 500
Commission of sales personnel	21 000
Sales office costs	8 000
Advertising costs: Direct regarding product	50 000
General	14 000
Transportation costs	15 000
Storage costs	6 000
Packaging	8 000
Credit and recovery costs	3 200

The following information is to be used in the allocation of costs:

Details	Product A	Product B	Product C
Number of sales personnel			
(all receiving the same salary)	5	6	2
Number of orders	600	700	300
Direct advertising costs	40%	35%	25%
Storage space utilised per m^3			
per R100 sales	4	5	10
Sales	R250 000	R300 000	R150 000
Average price per order	R410	R450	R510
Number of units sold	25 000	15 000	5 000

Required:

Use the information given above to allocate the costs to each product, and also show what the cost of each product per R100 of sales is.

5.2

The following information applies to an enterprise which manufactures and markets two products, product A and product B:

	R
Sales	12 000 000
Cost of sales	6 000 000
Sales office costs	1 000 000
Advertising costs	170 000
Storage costs	108 000
Transportation costs	144 000
Packaging costs	54 000

Additional information:

(a) The selling prices are as follows:
        Product A   R2 per unit
        Product B   R4 per unit

(b) The ratio of sales of product A to B with regard to sales value is 2 : 1.

(c) Advertising costs: Direct   Product A   R50 000
                                 Product B   R60 000
                  General   (In total)   R60 000

(d) The cost of sales for product A amounts to 80c per unit.
(e) Number of orders executed:
   Product A   400 000
   Product B   100 000
(f) Storage space utilised (m^3 per R100 sales):
   Product A   2
   Product B   5

Required:
Prepare an income statement showing the net income per product.

Chapter 6

6.1

The following information was obtained from the records of Beta Ltd:

	May	June
Units manufactured	30 000	35 000
Units sold	27 000	36 000
	R	R
Costs incurred:		
Direct material	75 000	91 000
Direct labour	60 000	70 000
Manufacturing overheads:		
Variable	15 000	17 500
Fixed	45 000	45 000
Selling and administrative costs:		
Variable	45 000	52 500
Fixed	20 000	20 000
Selling price per unit	20	20

There was no opening stock.
The FIFO method of stock valuation is used.

Required:
(a) Calculate net profit for each month separately using:
   (i) the absorption costing method
   (ii) the direct costing method
(b) Reconcile the net profit obtained, using the two methods.

6.2

The following information was obtained from the books of Alpha Ltd:

	R
Manufacturing costs per unit:	
Fixed	3,50
Variable	5,50
Selling and administrative costs per unit:	
Fixed	0,50
Variable	1,50
Selling price per unit	12,00
Normal capacity (per month)	8 000 units

During January 19.7 the company manufactured 7 500 units and sold 7 000 units. During the following month 8 500 units were manufactured and 9 000 units sold.

Required:
(a) Compile a separate income statement for each month according to:
    (i) the absorption costing method, where closing stock is valued at standard.
    (ii) the direct costing method.
(b) Reconcile the net profit obtained, using the two methods.

6.3

The following data was derived from the records of A Ltd for Year 1 and Year 2:

Standard cost per unit:

	R
Direct material	1,00
Direct labour	1,50
Variable overheads	,50
Variable selling costs	,25

Standard production per year	200 000 units
Budgeted overheads fixed per year	R160 000
Selling price per unit	R8,00

Operating data:

	Year 1	Year 2
Units sold	160 000	200 000
Units produced	210 000	190 000
	R	R
Actual overheads (fixed)	161 000	162 000
Admin costs	50 000	50 000
Selling costs	60 000	60 000
Variations from standard	20 000 (U)	5 000 (F)

Required:
Income statements using:
(a) direct and
(b) absorption costing methods.

Chapter 7

7.1

Delta Limited, with a normal capacity of 2 000 labour hours per month and a budgeted monthly manufacturing overhead of R70 000, uses a job costing system.

During May 19.6 an order to manufacture 100 units of a certain product was received (Job 101). The scheduling section compiled the following cost estimate for the execution of the job:

Material per unit	R12,50
Labour per unit	3 hours @ R7 per hour

During May 19.6 all the material for Job 101 was issued, but only 80 units were manufactured and completed.

Required:
(a) Calculate the value of the uncompleted Job 101 on 31 May 19.6.
(b) Calculate the over or underapplied manufacturing overheads with regard to Job 101 for May 19.6 if the actual overheads for the month amounted to R75 000. (No material or labour variances have been noted for the month.)

7.2

The following information with regard to a specific contract stretching over three years is available:

		R
Contract price		2 000 000
Incomplete work at cost price:	R	
Year 1	300 000	
Year 2	800 000	
Year 3	1 700 000	

Estimate additional costs which will have to be incurred in order to complete the contract:

	R
Year 1	1 300 000
Year 2	850 000

Required:
(a) Calculate the profit which has to be brought into the financial statements annually if the percentage of completion method is used and the percentage is applied as follows:
  (i) Percentage completion applied to the total contract price
  (ii) Percentage completion applied to the estimated profit.

(b) Calculate the profit which should be disclosed annually where the more conservative method of cash received is applied if the following amounts were received annually as part of the contract price:

Year 1	R270 000
Year 2	R450 000
Year 3	R1 180 000

7.3

The following information applies to Prospect Limited which manufactures and markets product X :

Manufacturing:

Material: opening stock	40 000 kg
Value	R100 000
Purchased during the year 180 000 @	R2,70 per kg
Material: closing stock	20 000 kg

Direct labour:

Hours worked during the year	80 000
Rate per hour	R10,00

Manufacturing overhead: applied on direct labour hours at a rate of R6,00 per hour

Work in process:

Opening stock	R100 000
Closing stock	R80 000

Finished goods (units):

Manufactured	20 000
Sold	18 400
Opening stock	4 000
Selling price per unit	R250

The following information is also available:

1	Actual manufacturing overhead	R464 000
2	Prospect Limited uses FIFO in costing all its inventories.	
3	Manufacturing overhead over- or under-applied must be charged to cost of sales.	
4	Actual cost of opening inventory of finished goods	R95 per unit
5	Administrative and marketing cost	R1 120 000

Required:

(a) Statement of cost of goods manufactured and sold for the year ended 28 February 19.1.

(b) Income statement for the year ended 28 February 19.1.

Chapter 8

8.1

Kudu Manufacturers manufactures a single product in two consecutive processes and uses a process costing system to control the costs. Raw material is added at the beginning of each process, while conversion costs are incurred uniformly throughout the process.

The following information is available for the month May 19.7:

	Process 1	Process 2
	Units	Units
Opening stock incomplete units	5 000	Nil
(50% complete with regard to conversion costs)		
Units placed into the process during the month	20 000	–
Units completed:		
Transferred to the next process	15 000	–
Transferred to finished goods		12 000
Closing stock incomplete units	10 000	3 000
(60% complete with regard to conversion costs)		

Required:

Calculate the equivalent completed units for the month (as for the FIFO method of stock valuation).

8.2

Impala Manufacturers manufactures a single product in three consecutive processes. Material is added at the beginning of each process while conversion costs are incurred uniformly. The losses arising in each process are normally equal to 5% of the units placed into process during the month and arise when 50% of the conversion costs have been added.

The following information for May 19.6 is applicable to process 2:

	Units
Opening stock incomplete units	4 000
Received from Process 1 during the month	30 000
Spoilt units	2 000
Transferred to Process 3 during the month	27 000

	R
Opening stock incomplete units:	
Cost of previous process	20 400
Material	23 800
Conversion costs (40% complete)	13 440
Input during the month:	
Cost of previous process	152 475
Material	175 275
Conversion costs	250 690

The closing stock of incomplete work was 70% completed with regard to conversion costs.

Required:

(a) Draft a process cost report for May 19.6 using the FIFO method of stock valuation.

(b) Show how the information contained in the process cost report can be shown in a combined quantity and cost statement.

(c) Draft a process cost report for May 19.6 using the weighted average method of stock valuation.

8.3

Process Manufacturers manufactures a single product in three consecutive processes. Material is issued only to department 1 while conversion costs are incurred uniformly in each department.

The production statistics and production costs for the week were as follows:

	Dept 1	Dept 2	Dept 3
Opening stock incomplete goods	25 000	30 000	20 000
Stage of completion:			
Material	80%	–	–
Labour & overheads	40%	50%	60%
Units started in production	50 000	–	–
Units completed and transferred	55 000	70 000	82 000
Closing stock incomplete goods	20 000	15 000	8 000
Stage of completion:			
Material	50%	–	–
Labour & overheads	60%	60%	75%
Production costs for the week:	R	R	R
Opening stock incomplete goods			
Cost in preceding dept	–	70 500	86 700
Cost in current dept:			
Material	26 000	–	–
Labour	10 000	20 000	24 000
Overheads	4 000	10 000	12 000
Costs during the week:			
Material	78 750	–	–
Labour	31 350	76 800	114 000
Overheads	25 650	57 600	83 600

Required:

Combined production report and cost statement. The FIFO method was used in costing the initial work-in-process inventories.

8.4

Olifant Manufacturers manufactures a single product in two consecutive processes and uses a process costing system. The spoilage arising in the second process takes place at the **end** of the process.

The following information for May 19.9 applies to the first process:

	Units
Work in process (opening)	6 000
(100% complete with regard to material and 75% with regard to conversion)	
Units received during the month from the previous process	30 000
Increase in units due to material added	10 000
Units completed during the month and transferred to finished products	40 000
Rejected units (normal spoilage equal to 5% of units completed)	2 500

Closing stock work in process was 50% complete with regard to material and 25% with regard to conversion.

All stock must be valued according to the weighted average method.

The following costs were noted for May 19.9:

	R
Opening stock work in process	204 000
Cost of previous process	90 000
Material	60 000
Conversion costs	54 000
Costs incurred during the period	1 479 975
Costs of previous process	609 200
Material	386 925
Conversion	483 850

Required:

Draft a cost allocation statement reflecting the allocation of the above costs.

8.5

Zebra Manufacturers obtains a by-product (shavings) from the manufacturing of two main products, namely wooden benches and wooden tables. The manufacturing of the two main products is inseparable due to the fact that the wood left over after the requirements for a table have been cut out of a beam can be used for the manufacturing of benches without wastage.

It is the firm's policy that none of the joint manufacturing costs should be allocated to the by-products, but merely to the main products according to physical measure. It has been found that one table contains the same quantity of material and entails the same conversion work as $1\frac{1}{2}$ benches.

Furthermore, the company follows the policy of not attaching any value to the closing stock of the by-product and writing off the total costs after split-off as a period cost against the income of the by-product. The net income generated by the by-product is shown as "other income" in the income statement.

The following information is available for the previous financial year:

Units completed during the year:

Benches	850
Tables	500

Units sold during the year:

Benches	700
Tables	475
Shavings	1 800 kg

Incomplete units (closing)*

Benches	50
Tables	100
Shavings collected during the year	2 000 kg

Selling prices:

Benches	R60 per unit
Tables	R80 per unit
Shavings	R110 per 50 kg

	R
Costs incurred:	
Costs before split-off point	
Material	30 000
Conversion	20 400
Costs after split-off point:	
Conversion	
Benches	8 000
Tables	7 500
Shavings	3 000

* 100% complete in respect of material and 50% complete in respect of conversion. No costs have been added after split-off.

Required:

Draft a cost and income statement reflecting the financial results of each product.

8.6

Sharp Manufacturing Company uses a process costing system. Out of the primary manufacturing process of the two main products a by-product is obtained. The contribution generated by the by-product is set off against the cost of sales of the main products. Stocks are valued according to the weighted average method.

The following information for December 19.1 is available:

	R
Stock 1 December 19.1	12 839

Material	7 415
Conversion costs	5 424

Production costs during the month:

Material	65 114
Conversion costs	50 444

Production for the month (equivalent completed units):

Main product A	6 900 units
Main product B	5 800 units
By-product	1 100 units

Sales during the month:

Main product A	6 200 units @ R14 per unit
Main product B	4 700 units @ R15 per unit
By-product	1 050 units @ R4 per unit

The primary manufacturing costs (costs before separation) are split between the main products according to the physical measuring method. When an order for the by-product is received it is packed according to a special method and delivered at a cost of R2 per unit.

Required:
Draw up a combined cost and income statement for December 19.1 which will show the profit/loss for each product separately.

Chapter 9

9.1

Anzac Limited operates an integrated accounting system. The following trial balance was extracted from the integrated general ledger on 30 April 19.7:

	Dr R	Cr R
Raw material stock	69 000	
Incomplete work	17 000	
Completed goods stock	31 000	
Debtors	100 000	
Creditors (material)		70 000
Creditors (expenses)		29 000
Accrued wages		5 000
Bank	20 000	
Land and buildings	180 000	
Machinery and equipment at cost price	120 000	
Accumulated depreciation:		
Machinery and equipment		30 000
Issued share capital		300 000
Unemployed profits		103 000
	537 000	537 000

The following is a summary of transactions which took place during May 19.7:

Transaction reference	R
1 Sales on credit	160 000
2 Purchases of raw material on credit	46 000
3 Raw materials returned to supplier	2 000
4 Production overheads incurred on credit	44 000
5 Selling and distribution costs incurred on credit	21 000
6 Administrative costs incurred on credit	18 500
7 Direct wages incurred and charged against production costs	21 000
8 Raw materials issued to production	40 000
9 Raw materials issued to production maintenance departments	5 000
10 Raw materials returned to stores from production	1 000
11 Cost of completed goods sold	105 000
12 Payments received for credit sales	165 000
13 Payments made for material purchases	50 500
14 Payments made to expense creditors	70 000
15 Direct wages paid	17 000

Additional information:

(a) Depreciation on machinery and equipment has to be provided for at a rate of 10% per annum on the cost price (16).
(b) Production overheads are absorbed on the basis of 250% of direct wages incurred (17).
(c) Selling and distribution costs and administrative costs incurred during May 19.7 are redeemed in total against income in the same month.
(d) Incomplete work on 31 May 19.7 is valued at R20 000 (18).

Required:

Open and enter the applicable accounts for May 19.7 from the given information and draft a trial balance as at 31 May 19.7.

9.2

Kay Engineers Ltd operates separate financial and cost accounting systems. The following balances appeared in the costing ledger on 1 July 19.4:

	R
Raw material control account	30 000
Production control account	45 000
Completed goods control account	15 000
Costing ledger control account	90 000

The following is a summary of the transactions of the company for the year ended 30 June 19.5:

Transaction reference	R	R
1 Purchases raw material		150 000
2 Direct labour	90 000	
3 Indirect production labour	40 000	130 000
4 Production overheads incurred		72 000
5 Production overheads absorbed		110 000
6 Administrative expenses incurred		19 000
7 Administrative expenses absorbed		18 500
8 Selling expenses incurred		14 000
9 Selling expenses absorbed		14 200
10 Raw materials issued to production		130 000
11 Sales		290 000
12 Incomplete work 30 June 19.5		150 000
13 Completed goods at cost price 30 June 19.5		9 000

Required:

Show the necessary accounts in the costing ledger for the year ended 30 June 19.5

9.3

Naxy Ltd operates a non-integrated accounting system. The financial accountant compiled the following income statement at the end of April 19.8. Based on this income statement and information supplied to the cost accountant, the reconciliation statement (also presented below) was compiled.

NAXY LIMITED Income statement for the month ended 30 April 19.8	
	R
Sales	2 000 000
Less: Cost of goods sold	1 200 000
Material used	631 000
Opening stock	121 000
Purchases	640 000
	761 000
Closing stock	130 000
Direct labour	250 000
Production overheads	320 000
Incomplete work	3 000
Opening stock	73 400
Closing stock	70 400
Cost of goods manufactured	1 204 000
Opening stock (completed goods)	91 200
	1 295 200
Closing stock (completed goods)	95 200
Gross profit	800 000
Add: Discount received	60 000
	860 000
Less: Other operating expenses	660 000
Administrative expenses	220 000
Selling expenses	300 000
Discount allowed	100 000
Interest on debentures	40 000
NET INCOME	R200 000

Reconciliation statement between profit per financial accounts and profit per cost accounts	
	R
Net income per financial accounts	200 000
Differences in stock valuation:	3 700
Add: Raw materials (closing stock)	1 500
Incomplete work (opening stock)	1 800
Completed goods (opening stock)	2 600
Completed goods (closing stock)	1 000
	6 900
	3 200
Less: Raw materials (opening stock)	2 200
Incompleted goods (closing stock)	1 000
Other items:	80 000
Add: Discount allowed	100 000
Interest on debentures	40 000
	140 000
Less: Discount received	60 000
	283 700
Less: Production overheads overabsorbed	4 000
Profit per cost accounts	R279 700

Required:

Draw up the following accounts as they would appear in the general ledger:
(a) Raw material control account
(b) Work in process control account
(c) Completed goods control account
(d) Cost profit and loss account.

9.4

Beta Limited operates separate financial and cost systems. The following income statements are compiled:

In the costing ledger:
Income statement for the year ended 28 February 19.2

	R
Sales	500 000
Less: Cost of sales	280 000
Material	110 000
Labour (direct)	80 000
Overheads applied	90 000
Gross profit	220 000
Less: Net income (15% of sales)	75 000
Expenses	145 000

In the financial ledger:
Income statement for the year ended 28 February 19.2

	R
Sales	500 000
Less: Cost of sales	264 300
Opening stock	60 000
Add: Purchases	120 000
	180 000
Less: Closing stock	65 700
	114 300
Factory wages	100 000
Factory costs	50 000
Gross profit	235 700
Less: Marketing cost	150 000
Administrative cost	100 000
Selling and distribution	50 000
Net income	85 700

Additional information:

		1 March 19.1	28 February 19.2
1	Inventory records	R	R
	Material	20 000	20 500
	Incompleted goods:		
	Material	30 000	30 200
	Labour	10 000	15 000
2	Factory wages:	R	
	Direct labour	80 000	
	Indirect labour	20 000	

3   Included in the purchases of materials is R5 000 for indirect materials used during the year.

Required:

Reconcile the net profit in the financial books with that in the cost books.

Chapter 10

10.1

Determine and complete the missing figures in each of the situations given below:

	Situation									
	1	2	3	4	5	6	7	8	9	10
Sales	R8 360	R500	–	–	R28 000	R342 000	–	–	R500	R200
Variable costs	–	R250	–	–	–	–	–	–	–	–
Fixed costs	R2 520	–	R160	–	–	–	R280	–	–	–
Total costs	–	–	–	–	–	–	–	–	–	–
Net income	–	–	R80	–	R4 200	–	–	R20	R90	–
Marginal income	–	–	–	R1 500	–	–	–	–	–	–
Marginal income ratio	40%	–	–	25%	–	30%	40%	50%	–	40%
Break-even value	–	–	R400	R4 000	–	–	–	–	R320	–
Margin of safety	–	–	–	–	–	R142 000	–	–	–	–
Margin of safety ratio	–	16%	–	–	37,5%	–	30%	40%	–	25%

10.2

A company projects the following profit plan:

	Per year
Planned volume	500 000 units
	R
Sales	1 250 000
Production costs:	
Direct material	400 000
Direct labour	300 000
Variable overheads	300 000
Fixed overheads	200 000
Net income	50 000

Required:
(a) Assuming no increase in fixed costs, what would be the effect on profit of making and selling an additional 20 000 units per year?
(b) How would profits change if selling price was increased by 10% and the volume of units sold decreased by 10%?
(c) If selling price is reduced by 10% how much additional sales are required to produce the planned net income of R50 000?
(d) If a 10% wage increase goes into effect with how much will sales price per unit have to be increased to keep the marginal income ratio at 20%? Assume the volume of sales remains 500 000 units.

10.3

The Duncan Company is presently operating at 60% capacity and at this capacity the financial results are as follows:

		R
Sales		1 260 000
Manufacturing costs:	Material	105 000
	Labour	140 100
	Fixed overheads	400 000
	Variable overheads	30 000
Selling and administrative costs:		
	Fixed	200 000
	Variable	228 900

Management is of the opinion that in the future the undertaking will work at 70% capacity without any change in selling price and fixed costs.

Required:
(a) Income statement at a capacity of 70%.
(b) Determine the value of the new break-even sales.
(c) Determine the safety ratio at a capacity of 70%.
(d) Graphically represent the value of the new break-even sales at a capacity of 70%.
(e) If in future the company is to work at 70% capacity and it is assumed that there is to be an increase in selling price and fixed costs which will

increase the marginal income ratio to 65% and the safety ratio to 45%, determine the following:
(i) By what amount would sales have increased?
(ii) What is the value of the new break-even sales?
(iii) What is the new net income?
(iv) By what amount would fixed costs have increased?

10.4

The management of an enterprise provides you with the following information:

	Year 1	Year 2
Sales (units)	10 000	12 000
	R	R
Material costs	25 000	30 000
Labour costs	20 000	24 000
Manufacturing overheads	32 000	35 000
Selling and administrative costs	10 000	12 000
Selling price per unit	10	10

Required:
(a) Using a graph, determine:
 (i) the fixed costs of the enterprise
 (ii) the break-even quantity.
(b) Calculate the sales volume (in monetary value) if the enterprise wants to obtain a profit of R18 000 after company tax of 40% has been deducted.

10.5

The following information relates to an undertaking which manufactures a single type of product:

	Fixed	Variable	R
Sales 80 000 units @ R10			800 000
Less: Cost of sales:			
	R	R	
Direct materials		120 000	
Direct labour		160 000	
Manufacturing overheads	200 000	80 000	
	200 000	360 000	560 000
Gross income			240 000
Less: Selling and administrative costs	60 000	40 000	100 000
Net income			140 000

Required:
(a) Determine the break-even point graphically.
(b) By calculation verify your answer as determined in (a).
(c) Calculate the margin of safety ratio.

(d) Calculate the effect on the break-even sales value when each of the following variations are made (separately) to the above figures:
    (i) a rise in sales price of 10%
    (ii) a rise in sales volume of 10%
    (iii) a rise in variable costs of 10%
    (iv) a rise in fixed costs of 10%

10.6

EDV Limited is presently operating at 80% capacity, at which the company manufactures 8 000 units which are sold at R50 each.

The following statement shows the operating results at various capacity levels:

DETAILS	LEVEL OF ACTIVITY			
	60%	70%	80%	90%
	R	R	R	R
Direct material	60 000	70 000	80 000	90 000
Direct labour	45 000	52 500	60 000	67 500
Overheads	105 000	112 500	120 000	127 500
Selling and administrative costs:				
Fixed	20 000	20 000	20 000	20 000
Variable: 10% of sales				

It has been decided to operate at 65% capacity in future.

Required:
(a) Calculate the following at a capacity of 65%:
    (i) The value of break-even sales
    (ii) The margin of safety ratio.
(b) By what amount must the selling price per unit increase in order to keep the marginal income ratio at 40% if a 3% increase in material is implemented? Assume that the volume of sales remains constant at a capacity of 65% and that the variable selling and administrative costs are R32 500 in total.

10.7

The management of a manufacturing enterprise contemplates adding a new type of product to its present manufacturing activities.

The following information is available after a proper market research has been made:

Estimated annual sales	50 000 units
Estimated costs:	R
Direct material	75 000
Direct labour	50 000
Variable manufacturing overheads	25 000
Fixed manufacturing overheads	50 000
Selling and administrative costs	10% of sales

Required:

(a) Calculate the selling price per unit if the undertaking wants to earn a net income of R1,40 on each product.
(b) Calculate the break-even sales in value and quantity with the assumption that the selling and administrative costs are fixed.
(c) Calculate the margin of safety ratio.
(d) Calculate the sales volume in money if the undertaking wants to realize a net income of R30 000 after a company taxation of 40% is deducted. Assume that all selling and administrative costs are fixed.

10.8

Roos Limited manufactures product A. In comparison with previous years the demand for the product declined tremendously during the past year. The undertaking is investigating the possibility of rather in future manufacturing product B, with an unlimited demand, and selling it at R2,00 per unit. The existing plant may be converted at a cost of R14 800 to produce 50 000 units of product B. The following information refers to the previous year in respect of product A.

Units manufactured and sold represented by a capacity level of 10 000 machine hours:	100 000 units @ R1,00 each
Net income:	R30 000
Margin of safety ratio:	60%
Opening and closing stocks:	Nil

Required:
Calculate the following:
(a) The fixed cost in total if product A only is manufactured.
(b) The break-even value and the margin of safety if 50 000 units are sold and the net income in total amounts to R25 000.
(c) The change-over point in terms of machine hours beyond which it will be more profitable to produce product B rather than product A. Assume the capacity level can be increased to 15 000 machine hours without a further increase in fixed costs.

Chapter 11

11.1

Bee Gee Limited made the following forecasts for the financial year ending 30 June 19.2:

Estimated sales			Stock in hand	
Finished Product	Units	Unit price	Opening stock	Closing stock
		R		
OM	22 000	150	8 000	11 000
DOM	40 000	160	10 000	12 000
KROM	30 000	220	9 000	8 000

RAW MATERIALS

	Stock on hand			Composition of finished products		
	Unit price	Opening stock	Closing stock	OM	DOM	KROM
	R	Units	Units	Units	Units	Units
X	10	6 000	5 000	1	–	4
Y	8	15 000	12 000	3	2	5
Z	11	8 000	13 000	6	8	1

DIRECT LABOUR

Finished products	Number of hours	Labour rate
		R
OM	3	8,00
DOM	6	4,50
KROM	8	9,50

Additional information:

1 Budgeted manufacturing overheads amount to R2 362 800 in total.
2 Overheads are allocated to production on the basis of direct labour costs.

Required:

Draft the following for the year ended 30 June 19.2:
(a) Sales budget
(b) Production budget (units)
(c) Direct material purchases budget
(d) Direct labour budget
(e) Manufacturing overheads budget
(f) Completed goods budget
(g) Cost of sales budget.

11.2

The following is an abridged balance sheet of Manufacturers Limited on 31 December 19.2:

BALANCE SHEET ON 31 DECEMBER 19.1	
	R
Ordinary shares of R1 each	210 000
Retained income	47 000
	257 000
Fixed assets	130 000
Land and buildings	80 000
Machinery	50 000
Net current assets	127 000
Current assets	174 000
Stock on hand	80 000
Debtors	80 000
Bank	14 000
Less: Current liabilities	47 000
Creditors	32 000
Provision for dividends	15 000
	257 000

Additional information:

1 An analysis of costs reveals the following:

	R
Direct material	192 000
Direct labour	96 000
Variable overheads	48 000
Fixed overheads	104 000

2 Gross income amounted to R40 000.
3 Budgeted sales for 19.2:

	First quarter	Second quarter	Third quarter	Fourth quarter
	R	R	R	R
Sales	100 000	110 000	120 000	125 000

4 It is estimated that, as in the past, fixed costs will remain the same while variable costs will vary in the same ratio to sales.
5 Fixed costs include depreciation of 10% on machinery. The original cost price of the machinery is R80 000.
6 The dividend will be paid during June 19.2.
7 The company plans extentions to the factory to the value of R30 000. The contractor will be paid an amount of R10 000 monthly until the work is completed on 31 December 19.2. No depreciation will be written off on the new extension until the work has been completed.

8   Experience has shown the amount due to creditors is usually equal to two months purchases of direct materials whilst stock and debtors should remain equal to the value of two months sales.

Required:

Draft the following:

(a) Budgeted income statement for each quarter of 19.2 in columnar form.

(b) Budgeted balance sheet on 31 December 19.2

11.3

The abridged balance sheet of a manufacturing company on 31 December 19.1 was as follows:

BALANCE SHEET ON 31 DECEMBER 19.1					
	R		Cost	Depreciation	Balance
Share capital	320 000				
Retained income	26 000		R	R	R
Creditors	6 000	Land and buildings	200 000	–	200 000
Provision for taxation	20 000	Machinery	100 000	40 000	60 000
		Furniture	20 000	8 000	12 000
		Vehicles	50 000	10 000	40 000
			370 000	58 000	312 000
		Stock:			23 000
		Raw material A			5 000
		Raw material B			2 000
		Completed goods			16 000
		Debtors			30 000
		Bank			7 000
	372 000				372 000

The following details are planned for 19.2:

Only a single product is manufactured and the composition thereof according to standard is as follows:

				R
Material A	2 kg @ R2,50	=	5,00
B	4 ℓ @ R0,50	=	2,00
Labour	2 hours @ R3,00	=	6,00
Overheads	2 hours @ R1,50	=	3,00
Total			16,00

	R
Estimated sales 11 000 items @ R20 each	
Desired closing stock: Raw material A	6 000
Raw material B	3 000
Work-in-process	–
Completed goods	25 600
Selling costs	4 400
Administration costs	10 000

Provision for depreciation is calculated as follows:
  Machinery 10% on cost
  Furniture   5% on cost
  Vehicles   10% on cost

Company tax 50%

The credit period granted by suppliers and the delay in payment of debtors can be taken as one month.

Required:
(a) Sales budget
(b) Production budget (units)
(c) Purchases budget
(d) Cost of sales budget
(e) Completed goods budget
(f) Budgeted income statement
(g) Cash flow budget
(h) Budgeted balance sheet.

11.4

The following items were extracted from the trial balance of Quickthink Limited on 30 November 19.1:

	R
Bank (favourable)	2 000
Debtors	40 000
Stock on hand	24 000
Creditors	18 000

The following analysis is available:

	Sales	Selling and Administrative costs	Salaries and wages
	R	R	R
October 19.1 (actual)	30 000	9 000	5 000
November 19.1 (actual)	40 000	10 000	6 000
December 19.1 (estimated)	50 000	11 000	7 000
January 19.2 (estimated)	30 000	9 000	5 500
February 19.2 (estimated)	35 000	9 500	4 500

The enterprise encourages debtors to pay invoices within two weeks of sales by granting a cash discount of 4%. Debtors are expected to settle their accounts as follows:

60% within the period in which discount is granted
20% within 30 days after the goods have been sold
15% within 60 days after the goods have been sold
5% irrecoverable.

Creditors are paid as follows for purchases:
50% on delivery
The balance 30 days after invoice.

Closing stock is calculated as follows:
600 units plus 40% of the sales estimated for the following month (units).

Salaries and wages and selling and administration costs are paid in the month incurred. Fixed selling and administration costs, including depreciation amounting to R2 000 per month, amount to R6 000 per month. The remainder varies directly in relation to sales. Stock is purchased at R15 per unit and sold at a profit of 33⅓% on cost.

Required:
Draft a cash budget for December 19.1 and January 19.2.

11.5

Cashflow Limited decided to draft a cash budget for three months, namely March, April and May 19.2. The following information is available:
1 Favourable bank balance on 1 March 19.2 – R10 000.
2 Sales before taking any discounts in respect of credit sales into account:

		TOTAL	CASH	CREDIT
		R	R	R
December 19.1	(actual)	20 000	12 000	8 000
January 19.2	(actual)	22 000	13 000	9 000
February 19.2	(actual)	26 000	14 000	12 000
March 19.2	(budgeted)	27 000	15 000	12 000
April 19.2	(budgeted)	24 000	14 000	10 000
May 19.2	(budgeted)	23 000	12 000	11 000

3 In order to encourage prospective buyers, the following discounts on sales are granted:
10% on cash sales
5% on credit sales if accounts are settled within 30 days.
4 Debtors are expected to settle their accounts as follows:
65% within 30 days after the goods have been sold
25% within 60 days after the goods have been sold
8% within 90 days after the goods have been sold
2% irrecoverable.
5 Creditors are paid as follows for purchases:
60% on delivery
40% 30 days after date of invoice.
6 Delays in payment of overhead costs and selling and administration costs average one month.
7 Because wages are paid on specific days, you can assume that only ¾ of one month's budgeted wages are paid in that month and the remainder in the following month.

8   On 31 March 19.2 furniture was sold for R200, resulting in a loss of R50. A post-dated cheque was received on 31 May.
9   The production records in respect of finished goods reveal the following:

	Actual	Budgeted		
	February	March	April	May
	R	R	R	R
Opening stock	7 000	10 000	9 000	8 000
Production: Material	10 000	8 000	7 000	7 500
Labour	8 000	6 000	5 000	4 000
Overheads	4 000	3 000	2 500	2 000
	29 000	27 000	23 500	21 500
Less: Closing stock	10 000	9 000	8 000	7 000
Cost of sales	19 000	18 000	15 500	14 500

Required:
(a) Draft a cash budget for March, April and May 19.2.
(b) Calculate the amount of outstanding debtors on 31 May 19.2 before bad debts have been written off.

11.6

The management of Planning Limited supply you with the following information:
1   Actual and budgeted sales:

	R
July 19.1	160 000
August 19.1	180 000
September 19.1	200 000
October 19.1	210 000
November 19.1	190 000
December 19.1	180 000

2   Abridged balance sheet on 30 September 19.1

	R	
Shareholders' equity	322 500	
Fixed assets	100 000	
Net current assets	222 500	
Current assets		342 500
Stock		120 000
Debtors		220 500
Bank		2 000
Less: Current liabilities		120 000
Creditors		120 000
Capital employed	322 500	

3   Rent and insurance amounts to R120 000 pa, payable monthly.
4   Variable selling and administration expenses are estimated at 20% of sales. It is payable in the month of sale.
5   The gross profit percentage is 40% on sales.
6   Depreciation on fixed assets amounts to R14 400 pa.
7   Cash sales are estimated at 10% of total sales. Debtors are expected to settle their accounts as follows:
75% within the first month of sale
25% within two months of sale.
8   The purchases for each month are based on the sales of the following month, whereas creditors are paid in the month after sales.

Required:

Draft the following:

(a) A monthly cash budget for October, November and December 19.1 in column form.

(b) A budgeted income statement for the three months ending on 31 December 19.1.

(c) A pro-forma balance sheet on 31 December 19.1

11.7

The following represents an abridged balance sheet of Sak and As Limited on December 19.1:

	R
Share capital – ordinary shares	229 000
Retained income	35 000
Creditors	12 000
Provision for taxation	10 000
	286 000
Land and buildings	150 000
Machinery:	60 000
At cost	100 000
Accumulated depreciation	40 000
Furniture and fittings:	14 000
At cost	30 000
Accumulated depreciation	16 000
Stock:	42 575
Raw materials: O	9 900
P	7 200
Finished products: As	13 400
Sak	12 075
Debtors	11 000
Bank	8 425
	286 000

The following details are planned for 19.2:

1 Two types of product, namely product AS and product SAK , are to be manufactured, the standard composition being as follows:

Finished product AS		R
Raw material O	5 units @	2,20 each
P	4 units @	3,60 each
Direct labour	12 hours @	5,05 per hour
Manufacturing overheads	12 hours @	4,00 per hour

Finished product SAK		R
Raw material O	11 units @	2,20 each
P	6 units @	3,60 each
Direct labour	14 hours @	5,05 per hour
Manufacturing overheads	14 hours @	4,00 per hour

2 Expected sales:

Product AS	8 000 units @	R150 each
SAK	2 000 units @	R210 each

3 Stock on hand:

	Opening stock	Expected closing stock
Product AS	100	110
SAK	70	80
Raw material O	4 500	5 000
P	2 000	3 000

4 The budgeted manufacturing overheads, after being classified as fixed and variable, are as follows:

Fixed	150 000
Variable	347 040
Total	497 040

5 The following cash flow items are budgeted for for the year:

	R
Sales	1 619 000
Goods purchased	310 000
Sundry costs	430 000
Wages and salaries	677 000
Selling and administration expenses	150 000
Receiver of Revenue	10 000

6 Provision for depreciation as in the past:

Machinery	10% on cost price
Furniture and fittings	5% on cost price

7 Company tax: 45%

Required:

Draft the following budgets for 19.2:
(a) Sales budget
(b) Production budget (units)
(c) Direct material usage budget
(d) Direct material purchases budget

(e) Direct labour budget
(f) Closing stock budget
(g) Cost of sales budget
(h) Budgeted income statement
(i) Cash budget
(j) Pro-forma balance sheet.

11.8

The SA Company uses the following information to compile the annual budget:

1 Statement of financial position at 30 June 19.1

	R
Cash	72 000
Debtors	225 000
Net fixed assets	240 000
Stock:	
Direct material	287 640
Work in process	145 000
Finished goods	441 000
Share capital	600 000
Retained earnings	648 640
Creditors	162 000

2 Basis for compiling the budget: *Units*

(a) Quarterly sales forecasts:

3rd Quarter 19.1	15 000
4th Quarter 19.1	12 000
1st Quarter 19.2	12 000

(b) Selling price per unit — R125,00

(c) Stockholding policy:
Finished goods – 30% of the following quarter's requirements should be on hand at the end of each quarter.
Direct material – 40% of the following quarter's requirements should be on hand at the end of each quarter.

(d) Manufacturing costs (per unit)

	R
Direct material	51
2 kg material A	36
1 kg material B	15
Direct labour (2 hours)	24
Overheads	23
Variable (based on direct labour hours)	16
Fixed (based on normal monthly activity of 5 000 units)	7

(e) Administrative and marketing costs:
Advertising   R12 000 per quarter
Commission   R6,25 per unit
Administrative   R90 000 per quarter

(f) Cash payment policy:
All direct materials are purchased on credit. 65% of these purchases are paid for during the quarter of acquisition and the remainder is paid for in the following quarter. All other payments are made when the obligation is incurred.

(g) History of debt collection:
25% of sales are for cash and the remainder on credit. 50% of all credit sales are paid for during the month of sale and the remainder during the month following the month of sale. (Assume that the monthly sales within each quarter are equal.)

(h) Additional information:
(i) Prices, costs and the production process remain the same.
(ii) Income tax rate: 50%
(iii) Depreciation is provided for at 20% per annum according to the reducing balance method and is included in the fixed manufacturing overheads.
(iv) The company plans to buy and install new equipment to the amount of R10 000 at the end of September 19.1.
(v) The amount of work in process remains the same throughout the year.
(vi) Variences in production cost are written off against the cost of sales, whilst stocks are always valued at standard cost.

Required:
(a) Draw up the following budgets:
(i) Sales budget (3rd and 4th quarter)
(ii) Production budget in units (3rd and 4th quarter)
(iii) Material purchase budget (3rd quarter)
(iv) Cash budget (3rd quarter)
(b) Draw up (i) a projected income statement for the third quarter and (ii) a pro-forma balance sheet as at 30 September 19.1

Chapter 12

12.1

Denver Limited manufactures a single product in standard lots of 200 each. The standard cost statement for the production of 200 units is as follows:

	R
Material: 30ℓ of A @ R3,00	90
20ℓ of B @ R1,00	20
Labour 30 hours @ R2,50	75
Overheads 25 machine hours@ R2,00	50
Standard cost for 200 units	235

The standard overheads rate is determined as follows:

Fixed: $\dfrac{R5\ 100}{3\ 400} = R1,50$

Variable: $\dfrac{R1\ 700}{3\ 400} = R0,50$

Transactions during the six months were as follows:

(a) Material purchased on credit:

Material A	1 000ℓ @ R2,90
	2 000ℓ @ R3,10
	1 500ℓ @ R3,25
Material B	2 000ℓ @ R0,90
	1 500ℓ @ R0,95

(b) Direct labour costs:

	1 000 hours @ R2,45
	1 500 hours @ R2,55
	1 750 hours @ R2,60

(c) Actual manufacturing overheads: R6 750

(d) Material used for production on a FIFO basis:

Material A	4 400ℓ
Material B	3 250ℓ

(e) It takes 3 500 machine hours to manufacture 30 000 units.

(f) There was no incomplete work at the beginning or end of the period.

Required:

Calculate the following variances:

(a) Material: purchase price, issue price, quantity, mix and yield
(b) Labour: rate and efficiency
(c) Overheads: two and three variances analysis.

12.2

A cabinet-maker uses a standard costing system in the manufacturing of a certain piece of furniture.

The standard cost per unit of the product is as follows:

Wood 30 metres @ R150 per 100 metres
Direct labour 4 hours @ R3 per hour
Manufacturing overheads: Variable: 4 hours @ R0,50 per hour
                                  Fixed: 4 hours @ R1,50 per hour

Units budgeted for the period   480

500 pieces of furniture were manufactured during the period, resulting in the following costs:

Wood used	15 500 metres @ R151 per 100 metre
Hours worked	1 950 @ R3,10 per hour
	(days worked – 22, while 20 days were budgeted for)

Actual manufacturing overheads: Variable   R900
                                        Fixed   R3 100

Required:

Calculate the following:

(a) Material variances
(b) Labour variances
(c) Variable overhead-variances

(d) Fixed overheads variances (the calender variance forms part of the fixed overheads variance).

12.3

Voorwaarts Limited manufactures a single type of product and uses a standard costing system in the calculation of the cost price. The standard cost per unit of the product is compiled as follows:

	R
50 kg Material @ R20	1 000
20 hours direct labour @ R5	100
Overheads: 30 machine hours @ R1,50	45
	1 145

The following variable budget was used to calculate the overheads rate:

ACTIVITY LEVEL			
	80%	90%	100%
Machine hours	24 000	27 000	30 000
Overheads:	R	R	R
Variable	24 000	27 000	30 000
Fixed	15 000	15 000	15 000

Additional information:

Material purchased and issued:	52 000 kg @ R20,10 per kg
Direct labour cost:	19 900 hours @ R5,10 per hour
Finished products completed:	1 000
Actual manufacturing overheads:	R45 500

Stock on hand:

	Opening stock (units)	Closing stock (units)
Incomplete work (in respect of which all the required material has been issued and 50% is completed in respect of labour and overheads)	20	80

Required:

Calculate the necessary variances in respect of :
(a) Material
(b) Labour
(c) Manufacturing overheads (only the two variances method).

12.4

The X Company uses a standard costing system for recording transactions in respect of the manufacturing of Product Y. The standard cost of Product Y is compiled as follows:

	R
Direct material 100 kg @ R1,50	= 150
Direct labour 50 hours @ R3,00	= 150
Manufacturing overheads 50 hours @ R2,00	= 100
	400

There was no incomplete work at the beginning of the month.
The operating results for the month were as follows:

1   Material purchased on credit 250 000 kg @ R1,48 per kg
2   Material issued 198 000 kg
3   Direct labour 91 000 hours @ R3,05 per hour
4   Actual factory overheads R182 598 (budgeted R50 000 fixed, R150 000 variable)
5   Units manufactured:
    Transferred to completed goods: 1 700 units of Product Y.
    In process: 200 units (100% complete in respect of material and 50% complete in respect of labour and overheads).
6   Credit sales – 1 500 units @ R600 each
7   Selling and administration costs paid per cheque R80 000.

Required:

(a) Calculate the necessary variances for the three cost elements. Only the three variances analysis is required in respect of overheads.
(b) Entries in the general ledger accounts in respect of the above transactions.

12.5

Standard Limited uses a standard costing system and manufactures a single type of product. The standard cost per unit is compiled as follows:
50 kg material @ R2 per kg
20 Labour hours @ R1,80 per hour
Overheads:
  Fixed – 25 machine hours @ R2,00 per machine hour
  Variable – 25 machine hours @ R1,00 per machine hour

Actual costs during the year were:

	R
Direct material	25 200
Direct labour	16 200
Manufacturing overheads	20 400

The budgeted overheads amounted to:	Fixed	R14 000
	Variable	R7 000

During the year the following variances arose:

		R	
Material:	Price	1 200	unfavourable
	Quantity	1 000	favourable
Labour:	Rate	260	favourable
	Efficiency	360	unfavourable
Overheads:	Budget	750	favourable
	Volume	300	favourable
	Efficiency	2 700	unfavourable

Required:

Calculate the following:
(a) units manufactured during the year
(b) unit price of material issued
(c) the actual labour hours worked
(d) the actual labour rate
(e) the actual machine hours worked
(f) the budgeted units for the year
(g) the standard machine hours allowed for actual production.

12.6

Protea Limited uses a standard costing system in the manufacturing of a single type of product. The standard cost per unit of the product is compiled as follows:

Direct material: 10 kg × R4,50 per kg
Direct labour: 10 hours × R2,40 per hour
Variable overheads: 5 machine hours × R3,00 per hour

The following is a report on the first month's activities:

	Actual costs	Standard costs	Variance analysis		
			Total	Price or rate	Usage or efficiency
	R	R	R	R	R
Direct material used	382 800	405 000	22 200	13 200 (F)	9 000 (F)
Direct labour	183 600	168 000	15 600	10 800 (U)	4 800 (U)
Variable manufac- turing overheads	100 800	105 000	4 200	7 200 (F)	3 000 (U)

Incomplete work at the end of the month amounts to 3 000 units, for which all the material required has been issued, and one third is complete in respect of labour and overheads.

Required:

Calculate the following:
(a) Units manufactured during the month
(b) Material actually used in kg
(c) The actual labour hours worked
(d) The actual labour rate

(e) The standard machine hours allowed for production
(f) The actual machine hours worked.

12.7

Lowveld Limited manufactures a product which has the following standard material composition in respect of 25 200 completed products:

Raw material	Quantity	Standard price/kg
		R
K	50 kg	2
L	200 kg	3
M	150 kg	5

To manufacture 25 200 units, the following raw materials are used:

Raw material	Quantity	Unit price
		R
K	55 kg	2,10
L	230 kg	3,50
M	155 kg	4,75

The following information refers to manufacturing overheads:

Budgeted information:

Total fixed overheads	R150 000
Variable overheads per direct labour hour	80c
Estimated production represented	125 000 labour hours

According to standard it takes 5 hours to manufacture one item:

Actual information:

Units manufactured		25 200
Labour hours		126 710
Manufacturing overheads:	Fixed	R150 000
	Variable	R103 200

Required:

Calculate the following:
(a) Total material variance
(b) Material price variance
(c) Material quantity variance
(d) Material mix variance
(e) Material yield variance
(f) Standard overheads per item
(g) Overheads applied to production
(h) Overhead variances according to two and three variances analysis
(i) Enter the manufacturing overhead according to the three variances analysis in the necessary T-accounts of the enterprise.

12.8

The Duineveld Manufacturing Company manufactures one product by continuous process and uses a standard cost system for its cost accounting.

Stock of material, work in process and finished goods are carried in the accounts at standard cost.

The normal capacity of the company's factory has been set at 192 000 direct labour hours per year and the company's standards are based on that level of operations.

	R
Standard cost per unit:	
Direct materials (2 kg @ R2 per kg)	4,00
Direct labour (3 hours @ R3,50 per hour)	10,50
Manufacturing overheads (3 hours @ R1,60 per hour)	4,80
Total standard cost	19,30
Manufacturing overheads budget for the year:	R
Fixed overheads	134 400
Variable overheads	172 800
Total overheads	307 200

The production budget for April was based on 17 160 direct labour hours. April production, in terms of units of output, was as follows:

Units completed during April	5 850
Units in process: 30 April	
(100% complete in respect of material and	
80% complete in respect of conversion costs)	500
	6 350
Units in process: 1 April	
(100% complete in respect of material and	
60% complete in respect of conversion costs)	350
	6 000

Costs incurred during April	R
Direct materials purchased (12 480 kg)	25 584
Direct materials used (12 150 kg)	?
Direct labour (17 284 hours)	64 815
Manufacturing overheads	26 900

Required:
(a) Calculate the standard cost of work in process at 30 April.
(b) A journal entry to record the purchases of material during April.
(c) A work in process ledger account with an opening balance of R4 613 to record all debits and credits for April.
(d) Calculate the following variances for April:

Material	:	quantity
Labour	:	efficiency and rate
Total overheads	:	spending, capacity and efficiency

12.9

Dennekruin uses a standard costing system in the manufacturing of a single type of product.

The following information shows the budgeted and actual figures for January 19.2:

	Budget	Actual
	R	R
Sales 1 250 @ R1 200	1 500 000	
1 180 @ R1 250		1 475 000
Cost of sales (per unit)	1 010	980
Material 2,8 kg @ R150	420	
2,5 kg @ R156		390
Labour 13 hours @ R14,00	182	
12 hours @ R14,50		174
Variable overhead	182	192
Fixed overhead	226	224

Additional information:

1. There was no opening or closing stock.
2. In determining the standards an assumption was made that the company operates at full capacity.

Required:

In respect of January 19.2:
(a) Draft a standard budget.
(b) Calculate all the different variances.
(c) Reconcile the standard income with the actual income .

Chapter 13

13.1

Protea Limited's current activity level is 55%. The operating results for the past accounting period at a capacity of 55% show the following:

	R
Sales 200 000 @ R4,95	990 000
Less: Total costs	994 000
Variable manufacturing costs	450 000
Fixed manufacturing costs	200 000
Selling and distribution costs:	
Variable	80 000
Fixed	110 000
Administration costs:	
Variable	64 000
Fixed	90 000
Net loss	4 000

A mail-order organisation offers to purchase 20 000 units at R3,50 each. If the order is accepted, variable administration costs will increase by only R5 000 and packaging costs by R6 000.

Some members of the board of directors are of the opinion that if the selling price was to be reduced by 5% and R10 000 was spent on advertising, the activity level would increase to 66%. The precarious position of the company would then improve so that it would not be necessary to make use of the mail-order organisation's offer.

Required:
Analyse the matter for consideration by management.

13.2

A manufacturing company manufactures and sells three types of products. The following information is available:

	Product A	Product B	Product C
	R	R	R
Sales:			
25 000 @ R2,00	50 000		
35 000 @ R1,50		52 500	
40 000 @ R1,25			50 000
Variable costs	20 000	26 250	30 000

Required:
Determine, if total fixed costs amount to R30 000:
(a) the value of break-even sales
(b) the value of sales if a profit of R50 000 is made (the sales mix ratio will remain the same)
(c) the profit, if total sales amount to R200 000
(d) the maximum profit if the production volume of the most economical of the three products was increased by 10% without any change in fixed costs.

13.3

A manufacturing enterprise manufactures ball-bearings using a special type of metal as raw material. The following budget was drafted for the coming year:

	Ball-bearings		
	SP4	SP 5	SP 6
	R	R	R
Raw materials	12 000	8 000	15 000
Labour	5 000	3 000	6 000
Variable overheads	1 000	600	1 200
Fixed overheads	2 000	1 200	2 400
Selling value	24 000	16 000	30 000
Units sold	2 000	2 000	2 000

After the budget had been drafted it became obvious that the full demand for raw materials could not be met. Due to the shortage of raw materials only 75% of the raw materials requirements could be supplied. However, despite the shortage, the unit price of raw materials will remain unaltered. The value of the opening and closing stocks of raw materials, and incompleted work may be ignored.

Required:

Calculate the product mix which as a result of the shortage of raw materials will result in the maximum profit for the enterprise.

The value of raw material and work-in-process opening and closing stock can be ignored.

13.4

Meenee Limited manufactures three joint products in the same production process. All three products can be sold either at or after the split-off point. If the products were to be processed further, no additional fixed costs would result. The following information has been collected for the budget for the coming financial period:

Products	Units	At split-off point		After split-off point	
		Joint costs	Sales value	Cost	Sales value
		R	R	R	R
Z1	1 000	?	40 000	10 000	50 000
Z2	2 500	?	80 000	25 000	115 000
Z3	1 500	?	50 000	15 000	60 000
		100 000	170 000	50 000	225 000

Required:

Submit a statement to management which indicates the most profitable plan of action.

13.5

Taffie Limited used components TA and AF, which are purchased from suppliers, in the manufacturing of product TAF. Because the enterprise does not function at full capacity and has 15 000 unutilised machine hours available during the year, the possibility of manufacturing components TA and AF is investigated. An investigation of costs revealed the following:

	TA	AF
	R	R
Production costs: Variable	16	5
Fixed	2	1
Total per unit	18	6
Units required during the period	3 000	5 000
Machine hours per unit	3	2
Cost if components are purchased	R20	R6

Machine hours are used as basis for the application of overheads to production. The purchase of components does not influence fixed overheads.

Required:

Advise management whether it would be worthwhile to use the unutilised capacity for the intended purpose or whether the components should rather be purchased. Motivate your answer by means of calculations.

13.6

A manufacturing enterprise is presently operating at 50% capacity, at which level the company is manufacturing 60 000 units at R3 each. The operating results for the past year were as follows:

	R
Sales 60 000 @ R3	180 000
Less: Cost of sales	190 000
Variable	120 000
Fixed	70 000
Net loss	(10 000)

Due to competition it is expected that the volume will decrease even further and that the selling price per unit will have to be decreased to resist the competition. Management intends to reorganise production over a period of 12 months in order to manufacture at a lower production cost per unit after the reorganisation. Before the reorganisation project can be implemented, it must be determined whether to continue working at a loss or to close down completely until the commencement of the new activities? If manufacturing was to be ceased immediately certain fixed costs would be reduced by R15 000.

Required:

Furnish management with a statement indicating whether it would be desirable to continue production or to cease production completely for 12 months.

13.7

An enterprise is considering the replacement of an existing machine with a new machine. The following information is available in respect of the two machines:

	Old machine	New machine
Purchase price	R3 000	R12 000
Machine hours per year	2 400	2 400
Labour costs per machine hour	R2	R3
Unit production per hour	10	15
Repairs and maintenance	R160	R200
Indirect material	R300	R360
Power	R400	R350

The old machine's economic life is estimated at ten years with no salvage value. Depreciation, written off for a period of five years, currently amounts to R1 500. The cost of the new machine must also be written off over ten years. An offer of a R500 trade-in allowance has been made on the old machine.

Required:
A comparative statement in which you recommend whether or not the new machine should be purchased.

Chapter 14

14.1

Montana Limited evaluates two machines for investment purposes.
    The following information is available:

	Machine A	Machine B
	R	R
Cost price	70 000	75 000
Salvage value at end of life	10 000	15 000
Annual net cash inflow before taxation:		
Year 1	30 000	50 000
Year 2	30 000	40 000
Year 3	30 000	30 000
Year 4	30 000	20 000
Estimated life span	4 years	4 years
Tax rate	40%	40%
Cost of capital	15%	15%

Depreciation is written off on the fixed instalment method.

Required:
Determine which one of the two machines is the most profitable by using each of the following methods:
(a) Payback period
(b) Rate of return on average investment
(c) Present value method.

14.2

The management of Omega Limited is considering replacing one of its existing machines with a new machine which will increase production. The following information is available in respect of the two new machines from which the choice will have to be made:

	Machine A	Machine B
Cost price	R16 000	R20 000
Expected economic life	5 years	6 years
Company taxation rate	40%	40%
Expected average annual income		
before deducting taxation	R7 000	R7 500
Expected salvage value	R1 000	R2 000

Required:
Using the following evaluation techniques, recommend which one of the machines should be purchased:
(a) the pay-back period
(b) the rate of return on the average investment
(c) the net present value if the expected rate of return on capital is 15%.

14.3

Decisionmakers Limited is considering replacing an existing machine, currently in use for three years, with a new one. The following information in respect of the two machines is given:

	Old machine	New machine
Cost price	R250 000	R400 000
Salvage value at end of period		R 50 000
Market value	R100 000	
Income:		
Year 1 ⎫	R120 000	–
Year 2 ⎬ Actual	R120 000	–
Year 3 ⎭	R120 000	–
Year 4 ⎫	R120 000	R150 000
Year 5 ⎪	R120 000	R150 000
Year 6 ⎬ Expected	R120 000	R160 000
Year 7 ⎪	R120 000	R170 000
Year 8 ⎭	R120 000	R150 000
Estimated economic life in years	8	5

The cost of capital is currently 15% and the taxation rate is 40%. Depreciation is written off on the fixed instalment method. Any profit or loss on the sale of the machine can be ignored for taxation purposes.

Required:
(a) Advise management as to whether the existing machine should be replaced with the new machine. Substantiate your answer with the necessary calculations.
(b) Calculate the pay-back period in respect of the two machines.

14.4

Computer Services Limited is confronted with the question whether an additional computer should be purchased or rented. The annual income which can be derived from an additional computer is estimated as follows:

	R
Year 1	600 000
2	650 000
3	700 000
4	750 000

The computer can be purchased for R1 400 000 or rented for an annual amount of R400 000 plus 10% of the income earned by the computer. In both instances installation costs will amount to R50 000. Due to new developments the computer will have to be replaced after four years, at which point it will have no re-sale value.

The annual operation costs are as follows:

	Years			
	1	2	3	4
	R	R	R	R
If purchased (excluding depreciation)	120 000	120 000	130 000	140 000
If rented (excluding rent)	100 000	100 000	110 000	121 000

An annual rate of return of 16% is required.

Required:

Calculate whether the company should purchase or rent the computer. (Show all your calculations.)

14.5

The West Coast Company is considering the manufacturing and marketing of a new product. A special machine costing R60 000 will be required for this purpose. The expected useful life of the machine is 4 years with no salvage value at the end of its life span.

The following information is available:

Estimated net income:	R
Year 1	10 000
2	8 000
3	7 000
4	6 000

The tax rate is 40% and the cost of capital is 15%. The undertaking will make use of loan capital due to shortage in funds which is at present available at 18% per annum.

Required:

Advise whether the machine should be purchased, by using the present value method as criterion.

Chapter 15

15.1

Project Limited identified the following activities necessary for the completion of a certain contract:

Activity	Previous activity	Normal time	Normal cost	Crash time	Accelerated or speed cost
			R		R
A	–	13	20 000	12	25 000
B	A	13	15 000	10	18 000
C	A	12	10 000	12	10 000
D	A, C	8	12 000	8	12 000
E	A	10	8 000	8	11 000
F	A, B	5	6 000	5	6 000
G	A, C	7	4 000	5	5 000
H	D, F	6	5 000	5	6 500
I	G	9	8 000	8	11 000
J	H, I	7	10 000	7	10 000

Required:
(a) Draft a network diagram for the project.
(b) Identify the different paths and indicate which is the critical path.
(c) Calculate the normal cost of the project.
(d) Calculate the earliest starting time of the event which preceeds activity H.
(e) Calculate the latest starting time of the event which preceeds activity G.
(f) Calculate the total cost if the project has to be completed in 45 days.
(g) Calculate the optimistic time of activity G if the following estimates were applicable for the calculation of the normal time:
   (i) pessimistic time – 12 days
   (ii) most likely time – 6 days

15.2

An analysis of the activities of project "PERT" revealed the following:

Activity	Previous activity	Duration (days)
a	–	6
b	–	7
c	b	5
d	a	8
e	a	16
f	c + d	12

The completion time for the project is of the utmost importance in view of the fact that the company functions in a highly competitive market. Each day by which the completion time is lessened has the effect of increasing income by an additional R400.

The possible lessening of the completion time of the project and the consequences thereof are estimated as follows:

Activity	Lessened by	Additional cost per day for each day lessened
		R
a	2 days	160
b	3 days	200
c	2 days	90
d	2 days	80
e	4 days	300
f	3 days	150

Required:
(a) Draw up a network diagram for the project and identify the critical path.
(b) Calculate the most profitable completion time for the project and the benefit derived.
(c) Draw up a network diagram for the project according to the most profitable completion time.
(d) At present one machine is used to perform activity e. The production capacity of this machine, which is fully utilised, is 20 units per half hour. In order to reduce the time of completion, management is considering replacing the machine with two smaller, newly developed ones, each with a production capacity of 30 units per hour. A normal working day is 9 hours.
Advise management if taking this decision is worth while.

15.3

Blits Limited manufactures two products. The following information is available:

	Products	
	K	P
	R	R
Selling price per unit	24	28
Variable costs per unit	10	16
Material ONE (R2 per kg)	4	6
Material TWO (R4 per kg)	2	4
Other costs	4	6
Demand for product per month (units)	20 000	12 000

Additional information:
1   Raw material available per month: ONE   60 000 kg
                                      TWO   18 000 kg
2   Total fixed costs per month is R25 000.

3 Production time: Unlimited machine hours available.
4 No stocks of raw material or finished goods are carried forward from one month to the next.

Required:
(a) Calculate the marginal income per limiting factor.
(b) Calculate the product mix to be manufactured and sold per month in order to realize the maximum profit.
(c) Calculate the maximum profits which can be generated if it is possible to sell all products manufactured.

15.4

Progression Limited manufactures heavy duty machinery. The enterprise normally experiences a cumulative learning curve on all new models. The following information is applicable to a new type of machine which the enterprise plans to manufacture and which it expects to have a specific learning effect on labour.

Labour time for the first unit	900 hours
Labour rate	R15 per hour
Variable overhead costs (based on direct labour)	50%
Direct materials used	R5 000 per machine

Required:
(a) Calculate the expected total cost of manufacturing the first 32 machines of the new model if a learning effect of :
  (i) 80%
  (ii) 90% is expected.
(b) Calculate the selling price per machine if a 20% profit on the selling price is applicable and a learning effect of 80% is expected.
(c) Assume that the following information is applicable when the machine is manufactured:

Number of machines	Total time in hours
1	900
2	1 260
4	1 764

Calculate the percentage of the learning curve which is applicable.

15.5

An enterprise plans to expand the activities in its existing factory. A choice has to be made based on the following information:

	Products		
	A	B	C
ng price	R20	R30	R40
iable costs	R10	R16	R21
les prognosis	20 000 (20%)	10 000 (10%)	5 000 (20%)
based on empirical	30 000 (30%)	15 000 (30%)	15 000 (35%)
probabilities)	40 000 (40%)	20 000 (40%)	20 000 (30%)
	50 000 (10%)	30 000 (20%)	30 000 (15%)

Required:
Which product should the enterprise add to its existing activities if the capacity is of such a nature that only one product can be accommodated?

15.6

A manufacturing enterprise plans to manufacture a new product and to market it at R10 per unit.
    The marketing manager estimates the probable sales as follows:
        100 000 units (40%)
        50 000 units (60%)

The management accountant estimates the manufacturing costs as follows:

Variable costs per unit:	R5	(30%)
	R8	(70%)
Fixed costs in total:	R150 000	(60%)
	R200 000	(40%)

Required:
Use a decision tree to calculate the estimated net income.

Index

A

abnormal wastage 184
absorption costing 100
accounting entries 23
activity 359
actual manufacturing overheads 54, 59
administrative budget 253
advertising budget 253
allocation 65
allocation rate 55, 56
applied overheads 55,58
appropriate market value 176
asset 6
average stock 15
avoidable cost 6

B

balance sheet 9–10
basic level of business activity 272
bin card 21
bonus points 39
bonus system 38
break-even analysis 225
break-even graph 232
break-even point 226
break-even value 226
break-even quantity 226
budget control 244
budget factor 248
budgeted income statement 256
budgeted overheads 56
budgeted period 247
budget personnel 248
budgeted variances 302-303
budgets 244
buffer stock 15
by-products 171, 172

C

calendar factor 298
capacity 326
capacity ratio 306
capital 84
capital budget 253
capital investment decisions 329
cash budget 254
cash flow 341
certified work 124
changeover point 228
clock card 32
codification 20
common cost 172

controllable variance 302
construction contracts 122
conversion cost 11, 12
cost 6
cost carrier 62
cost centre 62, 375
cost elements 14
cost flow 90
cost ledger 108
cost ledger contra account 207
cost of capital 339
cost price variance 309-311
cost slope 364
cost structure 240
cost quantity variance 311-312
cost-volume-profit analysis 223
cost-volume-profit ratio 228
crash cost 364
crash time 364
critical path 358-366
cumulative probability 370

D

decision trees 370, 371
departmentalisation of manufacturing overheads 62
depreciation 59
differential cost 320
differential piecework system 38
direct cost 100
direct labour 10, 40
direct material 10
discounted rate of return 343
discounted tables 349, 350

E

economically obsolete 60
economic life 60, 339
economic order quantity 18, 19
economic stock 15
effect of interest 19
efficiency variance 306-307
Emerson efficiency scheme 39
employment procedures 29
equation method 229
equivalent completed units 148
equivalent income method 346
expected actual level of business activity 272
expected return 228
evaluation techniques 339
evaporation 183